Art therapy:
a handbook

Open University Press
Psychotherapy Handbooks Series
Series editor: Windy Dryden

TITLES IN THE SERIES

Published titles:

Individual Therapy: A Handbook
Windy Dryden (ed.)

Integrative and Eclectic Therapy: A Handbook
Windy Dryden (ed.)

Hypnotherapy: A Handbook
Michael Heap and Windy Dryden (eds)

Couple Therapy: A Handbook
Douglas Hooper and Windy Dryden (eds)

Child and Adolescent Therapy: A Handbook
David A. Lane and Andrew Miller (eds)

Art Therapy: A Handbook
Diane Waller and Andrea Gilroy (eds)

Art therapy: a handbook

Edited by
DIANE WALLER
and
ANDREA GILROY

Open University Press
Buckingham · Philadelphia

Open University Press
Celtic Court
22 Ballmoor
Buckingham
MK18 1XW

and
1900 Frost Road, Suite 101
Bristol, PA 19007, USA

First Published 1992
Reprinted 1994

A catalogue record of this book is available from
the British Library

Library of Congress Cataloging-in-Publication Data

Waller, Diane Elizabeth, 1943–
        Art therapy: a handbook/Diane Elizabeth Waller, Andrea Jane Gilroy.
            p.   cm. — (Psychotherapy handbook series)
        Includes bibliographical references and index.
        ISBN 0-335-09886-X. — ISBN 0-335-09885-1 (pbk.)
            1. Art therapy.   I. Gilroy, Andrea, 1949-   II. Title.
        III. Series.
        RC489.A7W35   1992
        616.89'1656—dc20   91-28641
                                                                                                          CIP

Typeset by Colset Private Limited, Singapore
Printed in Great Britain by Biddles Limited, Guildford and Kings Lynn

Contents

The editors and contributors   vii

Introduction   xi
ANDREA GILROY AND DIANE WALLER

Part I   Theoretical, political and institutional issues   1
1   Art therapy: a theoretical perspective   3
    DIANE WALLER AND TESSA DALLEY
2   Art therapy: new problems, new solutions?   25
    JOAN WODDIS
3   The organizational context of art therapy   49
    JACKY MAHONY

Part II   The practice of art therapy   71
4   Using art therapy with 'chronic' long-term psychiatric patients   73
    CHRISTINE WOOD
5   Art therapy with elderly people in statutory care   90
    ROGER WILKS AND ANGELA BYERS
6   Art therapy with people who have severe learning difficulties   105
    ROBIN TIPPLE
7   Art therapy with families   125
    MICHAEL DONNELLY
8   Art therapy with children and adolescents   140
    ROGER ARGUILE
9   Art therapy in the treatment of women with eating disorders   155
    MARY-JAYNE RUST
10 Art therapy in the treatment of alcohol and drug abuse   173
    JACKY MAHONY AND DIANE WALLER
11 Brief art therapy in acute states: a process-oriented approach   189
    SHEILA MCCLELLAND

Part III   Training and research   209

12   The training of art therapists: past, present and future issues   211
      DIANE WALLER
13   Research in art therapy   229
      ANDREA GILROY

Name index   248
Subject index   251

The editors and contributors

ROGER ARGUILE studied at Loughborough and Exeter Universities before completing his Master of Fine Art Degree at the University of Reading in 1978. In 1985 he gained a Diploma in Art Therapy at Goldsmiths' College, University of London, and now practices as Senior Art Therapist at St Mary's School for Children with Special Needs in Bexhill-on-Sea, East Sussex. He is also a part-time tutor at the Art Psychotherapy Unit, Goldsmiths' College. Roger lectures in Britain and abroad, and is a practising artist.

ANGELA BYERS worked from 1982 to 1984 in a large psychiatric hospital and it was during this time that she became aware of the many back wards where elderly mentally ill people live. This greatly influenced her studies when she trained in Art Therapy at Goldsmiths' College, University of London, where as part of the course programme she worked with elderly residents of Netherne Hospital in Surrey. From 1985 to 1990, Angela worked for Sutton Social Services in five residential homes for elderly people. She now works at Spingfield Hospital in South London where she has some involvement with the elderly inpatients as an art therapist.

TESSA DALLEY is an experienced art therapist who has worked both clinically and in teaching for many years. Currently she works part-time at a consultation and therapeutic centre for children and adults in London, as a supervisor for practicing art therapists and in private practice. Working with colleagues, she has published several books on art therapy.

MICHAEL DONNELLY trained as an artist and practiced as an art therapist in the NHS from 1972 to 1989. He is now a General Manager working for the Mental Health Services and is an honorary member of BAAT. His main research interests concern the use of storytelling as a therapeutic medium and the use of art therapy in engaging children in family work.

ANDREA GILROY teaches at the Art Psychotherapy Unit of Goldsmiths' College, University of London. She has completed a DPhil on 'Art therapists and their art' and actively promotes research within the profession of art therapy. She edited *Pictures at an Exhibition: Selected Essays on Art and Art Therapy* (Routledge, 1989) with Tessa Dalley.

SHEILA McCLELLAND is senior art therapist at the Princess Royal Hospital, Haywards Heath, and is a part-time tutor in the Art Psychotherapy Unit of Goldsmiths' College, University of London. She is engaged on research into the process oriented psychology model of art therapy.

JACKY MAHONY has worked full-time for the past eight years at the Henderson Hospital Therapeutic Community and is now Deputy Manager of a Day Centre in Kent. She is researching the use of art therapy in connection with drug and alcohol problems.

MARY-JAYNE RUST trained as an art therapist at Goldsmiths' College and has since worked in a variety of settings including a men's prison and the Women's Therapy Centre, London. She specializes in working with women with eating disorders and currently runs a small private practice in conjunction with giving lectures and running workshops and groups.

ROBIN TIPPLE works at Harperbury Hospital and Harper House Children's Service. He is interested in the application of psychoanalytic and psychodynamic theories to mental handicap. His work with children and adults has prompted him to study the relationship between cognitive processes and the awareness and expression of the emotions.

DIANE WALLER is an art therapist and group psychotherapist. She is Head of the Art Psychotherapy Unit at Goldsmiths' College, University of London, and President of the British Association of Art Therapists. Her research interests lie in the field of the history and sociology of professions, art therapy in particular, and in cross-cultural issues in psychotherapy training and practice. Her other major interest is in the ethnography of the Balkans, where she has lived and worked over many years.

ROGER WILKS trained in art therapy at Goldsmiths' College, University of London, from 1986 to 1987. Prior to this, he worked in adult psychiatry, an area he has continued to be involved with at Netherne Hospital in Surrey. He is now Senior Art Therapist at the Henderson Hospital, Surrey. Working with the psychotic patient as well as taking an active interest in the elderly are two areas of specialization in his broader hospital and community-based work.

JOAN WODDIS trained as an art therapist in 1979 after working for many years as an art teacher in special education. She has since combined lecturing at the Art Psychotherapy Unit at Goldsmiths' College, University of London, with training and subsequent practice in group psychotherapy. She was Chair of the British

Association of Art Therapists from 1985 to 1989 and is a member of both its Council and Registration Board.

CHRISTINE WOOD is an art therapist who has been working in the public sector since 1978. She has worked with adolescent and adult clients and is currently employed by Sheffield Health Authority to work with the clients of an inner city psychiatric service. She was for a number of years the editor of *Inscape*, the Journal of the British Association of Art Therapists. In 1984 she initiated the development of the Art Therapy training course at Sheffield University, a course on which she still teaches. Since 1989 she has been involved with Joanna Weller in research work into a project using art therapy with elderly people. This project is supported by the Gulbenkian Foundation.

Introduction

When we began our task, in 1989, the aim was to produce a book which gave a broad outline of the current theory and practice of the profession of art therapy in Britain today. Our audience was to be the general reader, one who might be familiar with either art or with psychiatry but who knew little of art therapy *per se*. We therefore asked our contributors to review the pre-existing art therapy literature and describe, in general terms, art therapy practice in their area and to follow this with description of their particular approach, illustrated with a case-study.

When the first drafts arrived we began to realize that something differing from other books oriented towards the general reader was in the making. In reviewing the literature authors had commented on the variety of art therapy theories and clinical approaches in their field (for example, Robin Tipple, Michael Donnelly) and described their practice as based in existing theory but modified by the realities of their own clinical work. Some were critical of the art therapy literature and a few pointed out an apparent, or perhaps potential, Anglo-American divide (Jacky Mahony and Diane Waller, Andrea Gilroy). It seemed to us that authors were alluding to much in their observations that was new and so we encouraged them to emphasize personal points of view and to develop and present new ideas.

That the book and its chapters have changed so much during the period of writing and editing is indicative of the current period of considerable change that the profession is going through. The contextual chapters on professional issues, training and research (by Joan Woddis, Diane Waller and Andrea Gilroy respectively) had to be re-written and up-dated several times in order to keep abreast of events. Since this book began Art Therapists have applied to, and been accepted by, the Council for the Professions Supplementary to Medicine (CPSM) for state registration; the National Joint Council has recognized the post-graduate Art Therapy Diploma as an approved qualification; the British Association of Art Therapists (BAAT) has now approved, and the training institutions are now planning, two-year post-graduate courses; and there have been two Arts Therapies Research conferences. These are important developments for art therapy as a whole, as work in the community becomes harsh reality and the pressure to evaluate and audit effective clinical practice grows. The possibility of professionals working in the different European Community member states also offers a major challenge to art therapists in the UK, as art therapy has developed from more 'medical' roots elsewhere in Europe yet is a regulated profession only in Britain and Holland. What is interesting, and is demonstrated concretely in this book, is that practitioners' thinking about their work is evolving in parallel with, and as rapidly as, developments in the wider political arena.

Art therapy has often drawn on theoretical concepts from allied professions to inform its own practice (see Diane Waller and Tessa Dalley for further examination of this issue). The first art therapists were artists who, without training in the mental health field of the time, undertook to provide art sessions for patients in a variety of settings (Waller 1991). In more recent times art therapists have created theoretical frameworks informed by developmental psychology, psychoanalysis and psychotherapy (for example, Naumberg 1966, Wadeson 1980, Schaverien 1991). It seems to us that art therapy has now demonstrably absorbed what is relevant and useful, although some art therapists might say that the profession is not so much informed by psychodynamic models as dominated by them, at the cost of losing (what are in our view assumed) inherent therapeutic properties of art-making.

The chapters in this book seem to us to represent a growing maturity in art therapy theory and practice; clinicians are describing a synthesis of psychodynamic theory and practice, and the fundamental premiss of the whole activity, art, can be seen to be gaining a new emphasis. This is not to say that 'art as healing' for the maker is in the ascendant, but rather that these art therapists seem to be increasingly drawing on their fundamental training and practice as artists to enrich their understanding of imagery produced within the therapeutic alliance.

Robin Tipple, for example, speaks of the importance of art history and an experiential knowledge of painterly processes in reaching an understanding of his profoundly handicapped client; Christine Wood describes the importance of the physical environment where the art activity takes place and the influence and atmosphere of several art therapy rooms; Roger Wilks and Angela Byers show how effective and moving the making of imagery becomes without a verbal, consciously insight-oriented exchange between client and art therapist; Andrea Gilroy outlines the similarities between artistic and therapeutic processes, and research. Sheila McClelland's dramatic account of process-oriented psychology and art therapy provides a radical new framework in which art-making moves away from the quiet, slow and contemplative (as desribed by Christine Wood), to an energetic, challenging and action-oriented art therapy and art-making practice.

Hence this book represents new ideas in art therapy theory and practice, some of which are quite radical. It incorporates what has become 'established' art therapy, draws upon it and in some cases, moves away. It may no longer represent the working practices of the profession as a whole but presents the 'vanguard' of art therapy and, we hope, points the way to further developments in the 1990s.

The book falls into three sections. It begins with outlines of the theoretical frameworks of art therapy, and of the political and institutional contexts in which art therapists work. The middle section comprises the clinically based chapters which describe art therapy in practice with a variety of patient groups. The book concludes with consideration of art therapy education and the possibilities for future development through research.

References

Naumberg, M. (1966) *Dynamically Oriented Art Therapy: Its Principles and Practice*, NY: Grune and Stratton.
Schaverien, J. (1991) *The Revealing Image*, London: Routledge.
Wadeson, H. (1980) *Art Psychotherapy*, NY: Wiley.
Waller, D.E. (1991) *Becoming a Profession: The History of Art Therapy in Britain*, London: Routledge.

PART I

Theoretical, political and institutional issues

—

Art therapy: a theoretical perspective

DIANE WALLER AND TESSA DALLEY

The way that we come to some understanding about mental illness or handicap is mediated by the social context in which we, as art therapists, live and work. In presenting an overview of some of the main theoretical positions that have informed the practice of art therapy from its beginnings to the present, we have taken into consideration two aspects: paradigms of understanding – that is, the way in which practitioners or theorists have developed their definition of art therapy; and paradigms of intervention or treatment – that is, the way that it works in practice. The second derives from the first but is always mediated by the dimension of social policy on professions in the health and social services, and especially on those concerned with the care and treatment of the mentally ill or mentally handicapped.

We suggest that art therapy is a term which has been used to describe a collection of diverse practices, held together fundamentally by their practitioners' belief in the healing value of image-making. It has meant and still means very different things to different people, including to art therapists themselves. Sometimes doctors, nurses, occupational therapists, art students and volunteers believe they are 'doing art therapy' when they offer art materials to patients, encourage them to paint murals, try to analyse their drawings, set art and craft exercises, encourage the making of Christmas cards and decoration of wards, or send patients to art therapy departments to 'learn how to paint'.

We have to bear in mind that art therapy is one of the newest occupational groups in the NHS and social services and that other, longer standing professions feel equally misunderstood. Occupational therapists, for example, are still struggling to get rid of their image as 'basket makers' and to be recognized as skilled professionals who make an essential contribution to health care. It is doubtful whether many people could make an accurate definition of the role of psychologist, psychiatrist or psychotherapist, let alone describe the work of an orthoptist.

Our aim in this chapter, then, is to describe the theory and practice of art therapy in Britain by reference to both past and present models, and to arrive at a clearer definition of what it means today. We shall explore the various ways in which practitioners have described what they do, and the theoretical positions which appear to have informed their practice, to see if and how this has changed over the years.

The current 'official' definition of an art therapist

The current public definition of an art therapist in use by the Department of Health is as follows:

> A person who is responsible for organising appropriate programmes of art activities of a therapeutic application with patients, individually or in groups, and possesses a degree in art and design or a qualification considered equivalent for entry to an accepted post-graduate training course, and also a qualification in art therapy following the completion of an accepted course at a recognised institution of further or higher education.
>
> (DHSS: Personnel Memorandum 6.3.81)

There is, however, no definition of art therapy in any document of the Department of Health. The most current public definition agreed by the British Association of Art Therapists (BAAT), and used in a document entitled 'Artists and arts therapists: a brief discussion of their roles within hospitals, clinics, special schools and in the community' (1989:5), is as follows:

> The focus of art therapy is the image, and the process involves a transaction between the creator (the patient), the artefact and the therapist. As in all therapy, bringing unconscious feelings to a conscious level and thereafter exploring them holds true for Art Therapy, but here the richness of artistic symbol and metaphor illuminates the process.
>
> Art Therapists have a considerable understanding of art processes, are proficient in the area of non-verbal and symbolic communication, and aim to provide an environment in which patients feel safe enough to express strong emotions.
>
> Aesthetic standards are of little importance in the context of Art Therapy – rather the expression and condensation of unconscious feelings that art-making engenders are at the heart of the therapeutic transaction.

This document was prepared for circulation to all health and social services departments and to teachers of children with special needs and advisers. We can see that there is a difference between the two statements, in that the first focuses on seemingly practical 'activities' and the second on processes involving the unconscious. The first definition does not reflect the move which has been made over the past ten years towards a psychotherapeutic model of treatment. It rather reflects the association with occupational therapy that the Department of Health insisted upon when art therapists were assimilated on to the Whitley Council in 1982.

A definition of art therapy by art therapists as opposed to other professionals or administrators has been offered by BAAT in its recent application for State

Registration for art therapists under the Council for Professions Supplementary to Medicine. The definition is as follows:

> Art therapy is a form of therapy in which the making of visual images (paintings, drawings, models etc.) in the presence of a qualified art therapist contributes towards externalisation of thoughts and feelings which may otherwise remain unexpressed. The images may have a diagnostic as well as a therapeutic function, in that they provide the patient and the therapist with a visible record of the session, and give indicators for further treatment. Art therapists may work with the transference – that is, the feelings from the past which are projected on to the therapist in the session. Such feelings are usually contained by the art work, and this enables resolution to take place indirectly if necessary.

Transference in art therapy

The question of the transference and the way in which it manifests itself in the art therapy session needs some brief explanation here and will be discussed again later in the chapter when referring to models of art therapy deriving from the object-relations school. Transference is generally understood by psychotherapists to mean the bringing of feelings and emotions by the patient from the past into the here and now of the therapy session. It is as if the therapist becomes the patient's mother, father and so on. Once such feelings become part of the session, they can be explored by patient and therapist together. In art therapy, the transference may be visually and metaphorically represented in an image. It is concrete and able to be shared – verbally or non-verbally: to give a very simple and perhaps rather obvious case example:

> a patient, after several individual art therapy sessions, immediately after entering the room, draws his cat. The cat looks very angry and is about to claw a mouse. The patient says nothing, smiles and is friendly. He puts the picture aside and spends the rest of the session talking about a work problem. He ended the session with a painting of a pleasant landscape, his usual style of painting. The therapist is tempted to say something about the pictures but holds off. She feels powerless to intervene at that point. In subsequent sessions it emerges that the patient saw his relationship with the therapist in this way, he being the mouse. He felt like this with all women and wanted to be like the cat. It was only several sessions later that he owned these feelings, when looking back at his cat drawing. The therapist had felt uncomfortable in the sessions (as if she was being trapped and clawed), but waited till he was ready to get in touch himself. He was then able to express the distress and anger he had felt as a small boy, feeling himself at the mercy of his mother. The rage had been repressed so effectively that he had become severely depressed and impotent. He had very strong defences and used his facility with words to hide his feelings.

The issue of the transference in art therapy was taken up by Schaverien (1982). She says that in art therapy the transference is often involved with the person of the therapist (as in the example above) even though the communication may be centred on the picture. She also makes an interesting link between transference and power, pointing out that because art therapists are artists (feeling themselves not engaged in hierarchical relationships), they may be reluctant to admit or realize the power of their role as therapists. The art therapist, as the person concerned and prepared to listen, does frequently become the object of transference. Schaverien reminds us, too, that counter-transference also occurs (1982: 10).

The issue of transference is particularly subtle in an open art studio (as opposed to a private art psychotherapy space, for example) where there is lack of privacy and several patients may be working individually on art work. It would be easy, Schaverien suggests, to ignore or not to notice transference and counter-transference in such conditions. Failure to be aware of this essential element of the therapeutic relationship (perhaps because the dominant model of the institution is the 'scientific medical model') would be to deny the full potency of the art therapy process.

Dalley (1984) takes up the issue of transference again:

> As with any therapeutic endeavour, the relationship between the therapist and client is of central importance. Art is used as a medium through which this relationship develops. Although the art production becomes the focus of the relationship, the strong feelings that develop between patient and therapist are usually concerned with transference.
>
> (1984: xxii)

Dalley goes on to point out that the dynamics of transference and counter-transference are complex. Sometimes psychoanalysts consider that focusing on an art production detracts from the 'real work' between therapist and patient. Dalley suggests that, whereas transference is the main tool of a psychotherapist, art is the central therapeutic agent for an art therapist, even though transference develops and is a powerful phenomenon within an art therapy relationship.

Historical perspectives

The dynamic, or 'non-directive', approach, which is very different from an 'activity-based' treatment, has its roots in psychoanalysis and child-centred art education. The latter originates from the late nineteenth-century Viennese art educator, Professor Franz Cizek, whose friends and colleagues were prominent members of the Vienna Secession Movement, a group of young intellectuals and artists who revolted against traditional 'academic' art. This movement was carried forward in Britain during the 1930s and 1940s by R. Tomlinson (1934), Wilhelm Viola (1942), Marion Richardson (1948) and some of Cizek's pupils who settled in London. These authors were well known as practitioners and advocates for the child-centred approach, and had a considerable influence on art teacher training in Britain. A similar phenomenon occurred in the USA, with the art teacher Florence Cane whose sister, Margaret Naumburg, is considered to have been one of the founders, if not *the* founder of art therapy in the USA and a major influence on many British art therapists. A psychologist by background, she later become a psychoanalyst. She was also a keen amateur artist.

Margaret Naumburg and Edith Kramer

In her first published monograph (1947) Naumburg draws on case histories compiled between 1943 and 1945, referring to 'free art expression' rather than art therapy, and seeming to view the art activity and art objects as concrete versions of a dream. Later, in 1958, Naumburg offered the following definition of art therapy:

> The process of art therapy is based on the recognition that man's most fundamental thoughts and feelings, derived from the unconscious, reach expression in images rather than in words.
>
> (1958: 511)

and

> The techniques of art therapy are based on the knowledge that every individual, whether trained or untrained in art, has a latent capacity to project his inner conflicts into visual form. As patients picture such inner experiences, it frequently happens that they become more verbally articulate.
>
> (ibid.)

The emphasis, then, is on the images which arise from the patient's unconscious and which contain conflicts. The assumption is that once these conflicts are made concrete, they can be more easily understood (by patient and therapist), which in turn would assist in their resolution. Image-making, because it taps pre-verbal feelings, is more able to produce this resolution than words.

In her later books, Naumburg developed the 'dynamic' model of art therapy, referred to in BAAT definitions earlier, which made use of the transference relationship between patient and therapist, suggesting that art or spontaneous image-making was a means to furthering therapeutic communication (Naumburg 1966).

Ulman (1983), in writing an obituary for Naumburg in the *American Journal of Art Therapy*, mentions that her views eventually departed from those of her sister, so that by 1958, she was convinced that her work had its roots in the transference relationship between patient and therapist. She also believed that if an art therapist were well versed in psychotherapy, then art therapy could function as an independent treatment method, or an alternative to verbal psychoanalysis.

Naumburg stressed the importance to the patient of allowing 'spontaneous' image-making to take place, and in encouraging the patient to develop free associations to their pictures in the same way as a Freudian analyst obtains free associations to a patient's dreams. She felt that the art therapist's role differed from that of a Freudian psychoanalyst, because he or she could not remain as 'passive' or as 'blank screen' as the analyst. Naumburg was critical of the way those few Freudian analysts who accepted the spontaneous art works of their patients received them. Usually they would interpret them in the same way as the symbolism of dreams or fantasies without encouraging their patients' free association to the meaning of their pictures. She saw the art therapist's position as more akin to that of psychoanalysts like Sullivan, Horney, Fromm and others, who emphasized the active interpersonal relation between analyst and analysand. In addition, the activity of a patient in a dynamically oriented art therapy did not only consist of expression through spontaneous pictures but also included much verbal communication with the art therapist, centring around the patient's conflicts and problems. When art therapy and its techniques were introduced to a patient it would depend on the patient as to how this was done and the techniques might vary considerably. In other words, it was not a question of giving the patient 'exercises' or insisting that they use particular techniques without reference to the patient's needs.[1]

To bring Naumburg's unease about the relationship between Freudian analysis and art therapy into the present, David Maclagan, an art therapist who has worked for several years in the National Health Service as well as in art therapy education, has been concerned to consider the relationship of verbal psychotherapy theory to the practice of art therapy. In a recent article (1989), he asks: 'Does this reliance on ideas about word-based therapy marginalise the "language of art" in our work?' He felt that the therapeutic models adopted by some art therapists (according to recent literature) were, by implication or effect, at odds with the inherent nature of the pictorial imagery they dealt with. He feels there is a danger of polarization:

> . . . the art gets concentrated in the process of creating the pictorial image, while 'therapy', when it is not assumed to be inherent in this process, takes place in a different frame of mind, signalled by a shift from the implicit and non-verbal mode of picture making to the more or less explicit mode of verbal 'interpretation'.
>
> (Maclagan 1989: 10)

Thus the pictorial image might lose its special status as a result of this process; the image might be introduced in the same way as a dream account or a memory image – as the raw material which the therapy is going to digest:

> As a result its 'artistic' aspect – what Freud called the 'aesthetic gloss' – is treated with suspicion, as an alibi to be seen through instead of having any psychological quality of its own. If there is an 'art' in this analytic work, then it is all too often a devious, detective art, concerned with un-doing what the pictorial image is composed of and weaving into it a web of its own devising.
>
> (1989: 10)

Maclagan maintains that whatever psychic events may be presumed to lie behind the pictorial image, they cannot be simply identified with it; they have had to work themselves out into a manifest and externalized form which is accessible to more than one person. The picture is in between patient and therapist, and can be used as a vehicle through which many things can be said, by either party. So whether or not the picture itself expresses transference feelings, it can be the object of transference phenomena.

Maclagan makes an important point when he says that the 'art' in art therapy (or art psychotherapy) invokes a particular way of working with images in general and not just pictorial images: one in which non-rational processes are given a positive value and collaborated with in much the same way as in art:

> The way in which we talk about pictures in this psychotherapeutic context should be essentially faithful to the nature of imaginative imagery, and there should be a close correspondence between the aesthetic qualities of the picture and the associative or metaphoric discourse with which we feel around it.
>
> (1989: 11)

Looking at images in this way fundamentally affects the way in which art therapists work. The image is no longer valued for its 'diagnostic' perspective, searching for biological causes behind events (as, say, the psychiatrists who engaged artists to help in their research on the effects of leucotomy on perception, or in the hope that study of the patients' art products would lead to more effective diagnosis of psychiatric disorder – see Waller 1991: 97–105). Rather, Maclagan feels, we are looking for exactly those qualities which get left out of case-studies, but because art therapists have, in large part, worked in psychiatric hospitals where there is a prevailing 'medical model', they have tended to get caught up in this reductive method of working and ignored the

> complex realm where metaphoric translation between word and image takes place in both directions, where the 'aesthetics' has to do with a fine tuning sense of their imagistic appropriateness to each other.
>
> (1989: 11)

The importance of art activity as a healing process in itself was stressed by another American founder art therapist, Edith Kramer, a contemporary of Naumburg's and an art teacher by background. Kramer considered that engaging in the art-making process gave an opportunity to externalize, re-experience and resolve conflicting feelings (Kramer 1958). Unlike Naumburg, Kramer did not work with the transference, but preferred to focus on the art object as a 'container of emotions' and she related to patients through their art. She herself was influenced by Freudian psychoanalysis, believing that art could be a means of sublimating feelings, but she felt this to be positive, in that, for example, out of destructive and aggressive feelings could emerge an object (drawing, painting, model and so on) which would symbolize these feelings and thus prevent them being acted out.

Kramer felt that the spontaneous production of images was invaluable in gaining access to the patient's inner life and therefore a legitimate part of art therapy, but by no means the whole of it, for art therapy was also concerned with the task of integration. She was keen that the concept of 'spontaneity' in art therapy should be properly understood and not confused with 'undisciplined, aimless manipulation of the art materials':

> Untrammeled scribbling and messing are as unlike spontaneous, expressive use of art materials (and as unlikely to lead to it) as aimless chatter is unlike free association in psychoanalytic treatment.
>
> (1980: 9)

Important developments in the United Kingdom

Several British art therapists or writers about art therapy were, like Naumburg and Kramer, in part influenced by Freud, although many found his attitude towards art somewhat limited. For example, Ralph Pickford, Professor of Psychology at Glasgow University, was ready to acknowledge that his approach to art therapy was strongly influenced by his own analysis, although he does not focus exclusively on a Freudian model in his book *Studies in Psychiatric Art* (1967). He defined art therapy as

> a mode of expression by which the patient may be said to communicate his problems and conflicts to himself . . . a constructive link between the unconscious and the conscious . . . a form of communication between the patient and other people.
>
> (1967: 24)

Pickford believed that the art productions of both patients and non-patients could help them to express and utilize unconscious aggression and sexuality and to sublimate them. The art objects could enable a patient to integrate previously fragmented aspects of their personality, which could lead to restoration of 'unity and harmony within the artist's ego' (ibid.: 25)

An art therapist who was closely associated with Pickford through their joint founding of the Scottish Society for Art and Psychopathology was Joyce Laing. While art therapist at the Ross Clinic, Aberdeen, Laing compared the paintings of patients suffering from tuberculosis (TB) with those of Expressionist artists, suggesting that by externalizing inner conflicts through art, patients with a predisposition towards certain physical diseases might be prevented from fully developing the disease (Laing and Main 1963). She noted that Adrian Hill's work with TB patients was carried out after they had developed TB and whilst they were recuperating. Hill firmly believed that drawing and painting not only helped to ease the tedium of long periods of convalescence but helped to speed recovery (Hill 1951). Laing suggests that art therapy might be used as a form of 'preventative medicine' as well as in 'rehabilitation'. (This notion has received more attention in recent years – *Inscape*, Spring 1988, for example – but is still not well developed.)

A British art educator who had much in common with Kramer and was influential on the development of art therapy was Marie Petrie. In a similar way to Hill, Petrie saw art as contributing to the 'regeneration' of Britain after the Second World War. Like Kramer, she focused on the 'healing' and 'integrative' aspects of art. She left Britain for the USA shortly after her book *Art as Regeneration* was published (1946) and is best known there as an art educator with a strong interest in art therapy.

Some aspects of Naumburg, Kramer and Petrie's approach also impressed Irene Champernowne, Jungian analyst and director of the Withymead Centre for Psychotherapy through the Arts from 1942 to 1967. Withymead has had a considerable influence on the development of some aspects of art therapy in Britain, in that it provided the first informal training courses in the subject during the 1950s and 1960s and was a source of personal learning for several founder members of the profession. It was the first community on record where psychotherapy was combined with the arts (for a detailed account of Champernowne's role see Waller 1991: 109–25).

Jung has provided an attractive theoretical model for many art therapists, because of the importance he gave to his patients' art work and the fact that he drew, painted and wrote poetry himself. Unlike Freud, he saw the art object as having integrative potential and not as sublimation or displacement. *Man and His Symbols* (1964) is probably one of Jung's most popular books among art students and intending art therapists. This is an attempt to explain his theory of the significance of symbolism in dreams and art. The appeal to art therapists is understandable, given the richness of the illustrations and the associations which Jung and his fellow authors have made to myths, legends, films, paintings, poetry, fairy tales and so on: the world of the imagination is indeed valued.

Many art therapists have been influenced by Jung's work, particularly because of his view of creative work as 'integrative'. The late E.M. Lyddiatt, for example, in the forward to her book *Spontaneous Painting and Modelling: A Practical Approach in Therapy*, states that her work is based on the principles and teaching of Jung. She notes:

> . . . that his views on the value of spontaneous painting and modelling are not more frequently acted upon may be due to the fact that they are not well known or understood.
>
> (1971: 2)

Lyddiatt confirms Kramer's point (although she does not mention Kramer's work in her book but does cite Naumburg) about the 'seriousness' of spontaneous painting by describing it as 'a technique which although not always precise can be learnt'. She goes on to say that it is an 'introverted' activity, a way of linking the conscious and the unconscious so that a new attitude can come into being: 'It is a deliberate effort to let a mood speak without seeking to control it, and without being overwhelmed by it' (1971: 3).

The influence of Jung on Lyddiatt's practice is subtle but revealed in her emphasis on the 'integrative' possibilities of the art work. This attitude is developed by the late Patricia Nowell Hall who in *Art Therapy: A Way of Healing the Split* (1987) tells us that her ideas and feelings about art therapy had crystallized around the ideas and techniques of Jung 'who places the arts firmly at the centre of his mode of therapy'. She notes:

> Jungian principles and techniques give a sense of direction and meaning as an explanatory model, and offer ways of mobilizing inner psychic resources through the transcendent function of symbol-making towards greater integration and individuation. Jung believed that creativity is a basic instinct and that the releasing of creativity and creative energy is essential for mental health.
>
> (1987: 160–1)

She goes on to describe Jung's two basic approaches which could help to bring about balance and greater integration of unconscious and conscious, ego and self – these he called the 'way of creative formulation' – that is, fantasy, dreams, active imagination, symbols and art; and the way of understanding – that is, intellectual concepts, verbal formulations, conscious awareness and abstractions, claiming that one tendency seems to be the regulating principle of the other and both are bound together in a compensatory relationship (1970: CW 14, para. 706).

Michael Edwards, who spent several years as an art therapist at the Withymead Centre, and more recently trained as a Jungian analyst, gives a concise description of the Jungian model of art therapy in a book edited by Rubin (1987). In a chapter entitled 'Art, Therapy and Romanticism' (1989) Edwards draws attention to the work of both Jung and Freud within the context of Romanticism:

> . . . Freud and Jung were well read in German Romantic philosophy and greatly influenced by it . . . Freud's theories brought earlier concepts of the unconscious into a new and more structured synthesis. Jung, without substantially contradicting Freud, elaborated differently emphasized views of the unconscious and 'subjective reality'.
>
> (1989: 82)

Edwards goes on to suggest that neither Jung nor Freud would probably have approved of being described as Romantic, but in allowing phantasy to have a central role in healing through spontaneous image-making or other forms of active imagination, they gave subjectivity its due place.

As with all influential theoretical models, their validity has to be considered in the context of contemporary society. There is now much evidence about the way that ethnic groups in Britain and elsewhere have been disadvantaged by the 'eurocentric' nature of much psychological, psychoanalytic and psychiatric theory and treatment (Gould 1981, Rack 1982, Littlewood and Lipsedge 1984, Dalal 1988). Dalal's work in particular has brought to light the frank racism inherent in Jung's work. Even though we have to take into account that he was reflecting his historical and class position, we cannot ignore the very serious charges which Dalal has made – that Jung's perception of black people is racist and that these same views permeate the entire fabric of Jung's psychological theory. Furthermore, Dalal contends that these are woven into the theoretical foundations of two major Jungian concepts, the collective unconscious and individuation (see also Gould 1981: 114–16) and that in Jung's recourse to history, he shows no consciousness of any other than European and a remarkable ignorance of the debt owed by European civilization to non-Western cultures.[2]

The point of raising this issue here is to stress the need for a constant critical review of theoretical positions. Art therapists in Britain (and elsewhere) are coming from a multitude of ethnic backgrounds and working with people from different races, cultures and social positions. Concepts that inform our work are increasingly being examined from the point of view of race, gender and class. For example, the summer 1990 issue of *Inscape* was the first to be devoted to 'Transcultural issues in Art Therapy' following the establishment of a working group within BAAT who set out to examine issues of race and transculture in the profession.

The ability to be able to work cross-culturally in art therapy is vitally important in current practice. Waller (1989) explored the subject in some detail, pointing out a whole range of differences from the subtlety and nuances of the American under-standing of practice to the gulf between cultural and social foundations of such countries as Bulgaria, Japan and Greece. She comments that she once heard a psychoanalyst declare that he could work in Hampstead or in Japan and still use the same approach to his patients. 'That remark stuck in my mind'. (Waller 1989: 179). She goes on to explore work with many client groups with different cultural roots and attitudes towards art and therapy which were quite different from those of 'western' Europe.

It is these kind of issues that are central to thinking about race and ethnic origins. The question arises whether it is preferable that the therapist is of the same ethnic or racial group as that of the client. It is arguable that this maximizes potential understanding of the cultural issues and therefore strengthens the therapeutic alliance and indeed that difference of colour, race or cultural origin impedes work in therapy. The counter argument to this is that difference can enhance and bring problem areas into the therapeutic arena more quickly and therefore they can be worked with more effectively.

Part of the thinking behind this debate can be seen in terms of understanding psychoanalytic processes and where we choose to place the emphasis of the work. Some would consider external factors of race, environmental and social issues to be of central importance to both therapist and patient in treatment. But others might consider that it is internal processes that are most important within the therapeutic alliance and that therapeutic work should only revolve around trans-ference and counter-transference relationships in the session itself. The influence of the transference model (referred to already on pp. 5–6), which in its simplest form sees all the clients feelings towards the therapist as stemming from past rela-tionships, puts emphasis on the importance of the inner world which is free from external factors and influences.

The child in art therapy

This model of transference was central to the work of Melanie Klein, who pioneered psychoanalysis of children in the early 1920s. In what later became known as the object relations theory, she introduced the notion of the 'internal world' and identified two positions between which the infant moves in the first year of life. This departed from the Freudian concept of stages through which the child develops. The two positions are concerned with the relationship between the infant and its mother, and the first 'object' to which the infant initially relates is that of mother's breast (Klein 1957).

At first the infant experiences intense love and hate towards this first object and it is the resolution of this ambivalence that forms the basis of ego devel-opment. The infant deals with the ambivalence towards the breast in the first stage – the paranoid-schizoid position – by splitting it into two separate part objects (good and bad). The depressive position is reached when the infant is able to accept ambivalence and the good and bad become aspects of the same object-mother. This leaves the infant in a state of loss as he feels that it is his own destructive feelings that have destroyed the good breast. The infant experiences guilt which leads to a desire to restore and re-create the lost loved object.

It is this theoretical viewpoint that has shaped the Kleinian view of art: that is, that the wish to re-create or restore provides the motivation to create and paint. Hannah Segal (1991), in her discussion of art and the inner world, felt that the artist is working through the infantile depressive position every time a new piece of work is started. The artist's aim is to re-create a new reality and it is this capacity that is the essence of art. An artist is therefore able to re-create the phantasy and to give it life in the external world. This process mirrors the small child's acknowledgment that mother has an independent life of her own. The basis of the urge to paint, in Klein's view, lies in this desire to make reparation for the destructive infantile feelings to mother. Segal explains that for true reparation to take place there must be admission of the original destruction or there will only be denial. She felt that a certain 'incompleteness' is essential in a work of art, in that it combines the destroyed and the made whole, the good and the bad.

Klein's theories emphasize the child's powerful innate 'instincts' more than the environment and little significance is attached to actual mothering and the external environment of the child. It is clear to see how this relates to the transference model of therapy where less consideration is given to the external factors of the patient, and indeed how this model can be appropriate in some art therapy practice (for example, Weir 1987).

Later object relations theorists were to give the external environment more importance, including the mother and the care of her baby as an important first environment (Winnicott 1971, Milner 1990). Post-Kleinians have varied in their development and interpretation of these theoretical viewpoints. Bion (1962), Bick (1968) and Meltzer (1975) have given some important insight into the way that early infantile experience can be used to understand patients in analysis. Harris (1979) describes how observation of mother–child interaction has contributed to analytic training. She points out that the essential intimacy and nakedness of the analyst–patient relationship is more analogous to the mother–baby relationship than any other.[3]

Klein pioneered her theory in the face of fierce resistance by the male-dominated, medically oriented psychoanalytic profession at that time. Although based on Freudian principles, her theories caused a significant number of analysts to reconsider the necessity for analysts to be medically trained and to accept lay people and women into the developing analytical movement. Joined by Anna Freud, the child analysts came into the forefront of analytic thinking. It was Klein's basic discovery that all child's play had symbolic significance that led to the development of her play technique. The main task is to understand and interpret the child's phantasies, feelings, anxieties and experiences expressed by play, or if play activities are inhibited, then the causes of such inhibition.

Klein came to understand that the whole range of a child's play – the toys that he or she chose to play with and the drawings that were made, for example – within the session was a series of enactments of phantasy life and was the child's own way of relating their worst fears and anxieties. Klein emphasized that one of the most important aspects of her play technique was the analysis of the transference (1955: 16). Her ideas differed from Freud's in her emphasis not on the reconstruction of a past relationship which is transferred on to the therapist, but rather on the development of the relationship within the therapeutic setting:

> The transference is therefore understood as an expression of unconscious phantasy in the here and now of the session and is moulded upon the infantile mechanisms with which the patient managed his early experiences. The patient is bound to deal with his conflicts and anxieties reexperienced towards the analyst by the same methods he used in the past. That is to say, he turns away from the analyst as he attempted to turn away from his primal objects.
>
> (1952: 55)

These ideas have been important for art therapists working with children, although there tends to be greater emphasis placed on the making, or not making, of an art object rather than the verbal analysis of it:

> The process of making an image, for example, can act as a therapeutic agent for expression in itself. This tends to make the sessions less verbal, with less interpretation, as much of the work is done through the art process. The third object made within the therapy creates another dimension within the transference and counter-transference process and tends to hold the significance of what is being communicated by the child.
>
> (Dalley 1990: 171)

The importance of the image in work with children is that often it is an external expression of some unconscious internal state which has yet to emerge into consciousness. Inevitably there will be differences in approach according to the child in therapy (see, for example, Case and Dalley (1990) and Arguile, Chapter 8 of this volume).

Art therapists are mostly working with communication of inner experience which might not be possible to describe in words until it is more fully formulated in the child's mind and outer experience. This can be understood in terms of the symbolic relationship that the child has towards the artwork which both corresponds to and is mirrored by the way the child relates to his or her environment.

The origins of symbolic expression are clearly described by Klein in the early stages of infantile development, and its relation to art therapy is central to our consideration. Weir (1987), using Kleinian theory as the basis of her work in art therapy, gives a useful definition of a symbol as:

> . . . that which involves a mode of indirect and figurative representations of an unconscious idea, conflict or wish. In other words, the projected and repressed impulses of the psyche, detached from the original 'object' are instead transferred to another. In this sense psychoanalysis holds any substitute formation to be symbolic.
>
> (1987: 110)

The use of symbolic behaviour is a necessary development of the ego as a defence against separation. Weir describes how the infant, having internalized an image of mother, needs to be able to maintain this image in her absence. This image becomes projected on to external objects in order for the child to be able to re-create the mother–child relationship in the outside world, thus enabling him or her to become gradually more independent of her. This describes Winnicott's idea of a transitional object whereby the child's toy symbolizes the mother, but having been created by the child, it is in phantasy under his or her omnipotent control.

Returning to cross-cultural issues for a moment, it seems possible that symbolic expression can transcend cultural experience, and remarkable similarities in images made by clients from many different cultural origins can be seen. A recent case-study illustrates this clearly, and when language cannot be used as the main means of communication, understanding is generated through the symbolic expression of the imagery (Goldberg 1991).

In operating within a model of art therapy which stresses the importance of the art object to the child's psychic development, the onus is on the art therapist to keep the child's images safe within the therapy room, to maintain confidentiality and to hold interpretation at bay until there is understanding from the child's own experience and a sense of what he or she is trying to communicate in the images. In this respect, Winnicott's sensitive work on interpretation has helped the prac-tising art therapist in stressing the importance of letting patients make their own interpretations. He says:

> Magical interpretations pre-empt the patient's separateness; he is robbed of a mind of his own. The mother does not give the infant a feed, the infant gives the mother the opportunity of feeding him. The clues provided by the patient facilitate the analyst's capacity to interpret. It is not so much a question of giving the baby satisfaction as of letting the baby come to terms with the object.
>
> (1965: 59–60)

It was Winnicott's extensive understanding of early mother–child relationships that lead him to his description of an intermediate area of 'experiencing' between inner and outer realities and to the concept of the 'transitional object' which has importance for art therapists. By stressing the environment that the mother created for her infant, and the importance of this for the infant's healthy growth, he used the term 'good enough' mothering which provided the baby's ego with a supportive environment in which to develop. It is mother's capacity to adapt to the baby's stages of independence and separation which allows objects to become separate and real. This helps the infant to develop the capacity to experience a relationship to external reality. It is this 'intermediate area' of experience through which the infant can separate from mother through the use of 'transitional objects and transitional phenomenon', which Winnicott related to the capacity to play. He describes how the transitional objects to which the baby becomes lovingly attached are significant in terms of early stages of symbol formation. They allow the infant to feel able to exist within the 'potential space' – not inside nor outside a person but the 'place' between them. This 'safe place' between mother and baby is where the baby's symbolic functioning will develop and flourish and in which he or she can *play*. The 'potential space', designated as the lay area between mother and child, becomes and develops as the 'location of cultural experience'.

Winnicott emphasized the importance of play for both children and adults. Play facilitates growth; it is universal and leads to group relationships. In Winnicott's view, psychoanalysis was a highly specialized form of play and if a person could not play, it was the work of the therapist to help him or her to do so. This concept, together with the value Winnicott put on play within the 'intermediate area', has contributed greatly to art therapists' ability to work with the child's inner and outer realities. His theory of 'potential space' can be seen to have an important influence on the understanding of artistic expression.

Marion Milner, who has played a central role in the enquiry into art and its relationship to psychoanalysis, has added to Winnicott's notion of transitional phenomena and location of cultural experience. Milner, like Winnicott, saw the need for experience of a non-purposive state, a ticking over of the unintegrated personality, an experience of formlessness. The reflecting back of this state is carried out by the mother to the infant and by the therapist to the patient. Milner adds a further dimension in the use of play and art:

> In play there is something half-way between day dreaming and purposeful instinctive or expedient action. As soon as a child has moved a toy in response to some wish or phantasy, then the scene created by play is different, and a new situation sets off a new set of possibilities; just as in free imaginative drawings the sight of a mark made on paper provokes new associations, the line, as it were, answers back and functions as a very primitive type of external object.
>
> (1955: 2)

Much of Milner's understanding comes from her own experience of being a painter. Rather than thinking about creativity as above all 'to preserve and re-create the lost object', Milner felt the primary function of art was in creating 'what has never been seen' by means of a newly acquired power of perception through the interaction of conscious and unconscious modes of thinking typified in the creative process. This raises the question of whether one is merely remaking what one has previously had but lost, or whether one can create new attitudes and relationships on the basis of new powers of insight into the inner world. This leads into the even more fundamental question that concerns psychoanalysis, art and art therapy – whether change is possible and whether something new and original can be made? Milner's writing certainly forces us to consider these important questions and they have been highly influential in subsequent writings by Winnicott, and by Stokes (1963) and Fuller (1980).

Art therapy and group work

So far we have tended to discuss theories which have related to individual work in art therapy. Yet the two disciplines of art therapy and group analysis both emerged around the same time in Britain, that is during the post-Second World War rehabilitation movements. Waller (1991) has described the work of some of the pioneers of art therapy (Hill, Simon, Adamson) which certainly involved group work, usually in open studio settings, with an informal structure rather like that found in an art school studio. The reasons for adopting this model are

suggested later in the book (see Waller's Chapter 12 on training). The art therapists were reliant on their own experience of studio groups. In the hospital groups,
patients would come and go and paint and draw in their own time and space when
the studio was open and the therapist present. This studio arrangement meant
that the patients were often subtly influenced by each others' style, colours, and
art medium in this shared space. The space became like the art work itself –
private and personal but at the same time public and shared, and could be entered
at the discretion of the artist/student. The interaction between the tutor/therapist
and the patient(s) in the room dramatically changed the dynamics. Contact was
usually on a one-to-one basis, with possibly an intimate personal discussion about
the content of the work, which led to the exclusion of the others in the room. The
experience of being excluded was, of course, shared.

The early art therapy groups (as opposed to studio sessions) evolved out of an
understanding and growing awareness of the effect of the movement of the tutor/
therapist on the individuals in the shared space. More formalized sessions developed in which time boundaries were established and the therapist still interacted
with each individual in the group, but more attention was given to strong feelings,
such as envy and jealousy, that were stirred up by this process, thus affecting the
whole group as well as individuals. Such feelings could be expressed by the group
members either verbally or through the images, which could also have a 'voice of
their own'. The powerful effect of the therapist in this situation led to an increased
curiosity about group dynamics and exploration by some art therapists of the
effects of running art therapy groups based on psychodynamic principles, in
which they observed clear boundaries of time and space, and worked with transference. They found that unconscious themes of the group were often reflected in
the images made by group members, allowing a powerful group consciousness to
develop.

Only recently, however, has the relationship between group analytic psychotherapy and art therapy been formally considered, which is surprising given that,
as previously mentioned, group analysis began its life in Britain around the same
time as art therapy. When art therapy groups took place in therapeutic communities they were, on the whole, 'at the edge' of the treatment programme and art
therapists had to struggle to make them an integral part. (Maclagan 1985,
Schaverien 1985).

The problem of if and how art therapy could be integrated into a group analytic
framework was grappled with by Waller during group training at the London
Centre for Psychotherapy between 1977 and 1981, thanks to the open-mindedness
of a training group supervisor, Robin Davis. The effects on a group of having art
materials available, having the expectation that they could be used but there being
no instruction as to how and when they should be used, was a departure both from
the verbal model of group analysis and from art therapy groups where individuals
produced their own work, but the dynamics of the group and the relationship of
the art work to these dynamics had not usually been systematically investigated.
McNeilly (1983, 1984, 1987, 1990) has written eloquently about this process,
which he describes as 'group analytic art therapy' and which he too began to
formulate whilst undergoing group training at the Institute for Group Analysis.
McNeilly writes:

The approach is psychodynamic allowing for the totality of the group experience. The image making is but a part of the process. As with Gestalt principles, the art production shifts from fore to background.

(1987: 8)

There is an important issue here in McNeilly's suggestion that the art production shifts to the 'background'. He describes a typical meeting of between four and ten people in a small group or over twelve in a large group, meeting for one-and-a-half to two hours. No rules exist that members should produce an image, but if they do not this is explored in the verbal section. Within the group structure, no rigid time limit is given to the painting and so on, but McNeilly structures the group to give about half the time to painting and half to talking. Everything is open for discussion. Such a structure, together with the notion of the images being in the 'background', suggests a separation between the processes of image-making and group dynamics, rather than a 'synthesis' of the models. As Maclagan pointed out (see pp. 8–9) the image may lose its special status as a result.

Skaife (1990) has drawn attention to the issue of structuring time in a group which involves both making and talking. She discusses two approaches to her groups, one in which she structures time for painting and so on and time for talking, and the other where this was decided by the group rather than the conductor. (The conductor does not join in the image-making.) The result could be that the group decides to spend all its time in one or other mode: i.e. one week they paint but do not talk, but in the next two weeks they discuss the work. The art therapist may draw attention to this process as with any other.

In a limited-life dynamically oriented group, such as a series of workshops over a week or over an academic year, we have noticed that issues of birth, childhood, adolescence, adult sexuality and death often emerge most strongly through the images and through the interaction between the images and the group members and conductor.

Another approach to art therapy groups was presented by Liebmann (1986), based on her experiences in mental health day services. This approach appears more 'informal', with some emphasis on social interaction, and is exemplified by Swainson (1990: 162) who describes a typical group in which members 'drift in during the setting up period' and spend varied amounts of time painting, sitting, chatting or watching others at work. Neither the dynamics of the group nor its matrix appear to be made use of. It is 'leader centred' with most interaction appearing to be between the leader and the individual members. There is emphasis on the 'safety' of the group and its supportive nature, but it is not clear where aggressive or 'difficult' feelings between group members or about the conductor can be expressed (perhaps within the art work itself?). Other art therapists introduce 'themes' at the beginning of the group, usually after spending several minutes in discussion to see if an appropriate theme suggests itself.

McNeilly started a fierce debate within the profession in his article 'Directive and non-directive approaches in art therapy' (1984) in which he criticized the 'theme-centred' approach to art therapy groups. He felt that by suggesting themes therapists met their own need for control, and although they may see it as an aid to allow the unconscious entry to the group, it was more than likely that it was about the therapist's need to avoid transference and counter-transference:

> The therapist plays safe when he suggests a theme. He avoids the adventure of finding direction in the initial chaos. The direction that one hopes the group will take is the road to the unconscious, trusting that it will find its own way.
>
> (1984: 9)

Letters in response to McNeilly, published in the following *Inscape* (1985) came from Thornton (pp. 23–4) and seven members of the Bristol Art Therapy group, including Liebmann (p. 25). They took issue with the notion that therapists who used themes did so for their own security and felt that he had focused upon the work of inexperienced therapists who may have used inappropriate themes. Thornton drew attention to an alternative model, that of Systems/Family therapy in which a hypothesis was made from what was already known, with potential goals held in reserve. A related theme or range of themes is held in mind, but this could be amended following a 'round' in which people were asked to share something of their current experience. Thornton sees the therapist in this context as a 'servant of the group', clarifying its aims and asking the group if the theme was relevant, always leaving freedom of choice. Thornton, however, concurs with McNeilly that it is possible for a therapist to 'stand in the way of one's own availability for transference and impose one's personality by using technique defensively' (p. 22).

The debate continues, with polarization appearing to have lessened in favour of considered discussion of the role that the image-making process can play within group psychotherapy. In September 1990, a special section of the journal *Group Analysis* was devoted to the relationship between group analysis and the arts therapies. It became clear that the approach of 'group analytic art therapy' (or 'group interactive art therapy' – Waller 1989) was being modified to suit a wide range of client groups from long-stay mentally handicapped people (Strand), women with eating disorders (Levens), day centre clients (McNeilly) and psychotic patients (Greenwood and Layton 1987).

Conclusion: art therapy in the 1990s – the current position

Changes in the structure of the NHS and in the care and treatment of the long-term mentally ill in the so-called 'community' have necessitated changes in the way that art therapists organize their practice. Long-stay patients are likely to be discharged and to become day-hospital attenders, having access to art therapy only for brief periods of time. In addition, patients admitted to acute psychiatric wards are liable to be severely distressed, but will be discharged at the earliest possibility. Rather than adapting models from long-term therapy to brief work, it is possible to devise a new approach, using as positive the fact that only a few sessions may be available. This approach is equally applicable to groups as to individuals (see, for example, Yalom 1983, Gustafson 1986).

A model combining art therapy with the process model of psychotherapy has been developed by Sheila McClelland as a result of her lengthy experience of work in acute psychiatry and is included in this book as probably the only published formulation of the model to date. Unlike the models discussed above which tend to emphasize the 'non-directive' or 'non-active' role of the therapist, the 'process' model requires that the therapist be very active but in a way which enhances rather than controls the patient's ability to participate in his or her own healing. Extreme sensitivity and much experience of personal therapy is required of the therapist in this approach because of its active use of counter-transference.

This brings us to the issue of extended training in art therapy (discussed in Chapter 12) to take into account the challenges of integrating the art therapy service into a wide range of health care options, and to the importance of having a clear theoretical framework on which to base practice. Ideally this should take into account both the image-making process, the importance of different materials to that process, the relationship between patient and therapist, and above all the needs of a particular patient, be they in a psychiatric day centre or an out-patient clinic of a general hospital, in a mainstream school or a school for autistic children, in a centre for substance abusers or an Aids clinic. Art therapists work in all these areas and others too. They have the possibility of re-examining some of the theories which have informed their colleagues in the past, and of using their skills as artists *and* therapists to arrive at new formulations which can be tested through careful practice and research.[4]

Notes

1   Because Naumburg and many of her contemporaries were influenced by Freud's work, it may be useful to point out, very briefly, that Freud considered that the 'neurotic's' phantasy life is and remains individual but the artist – who might become neurotic because he (or she) has withdrawn from an unsatisfying reality into the world of imagination – can, through sublimation, turn his phantasies into some social use by creating art. Through this process the artist is able to objectify and make available to others his mental life. So through a process of transformation, the artist turns his personal phantasies and day-dreams into works of art which contain both manifest and latent content. The manifest content is but a device for concealing the real meaning and source of power of the work, which is the latent content. The latter relates to those instinctual needs and drives which are often repressed in a 'civilized' society (for example, rage, greed, Oedipal wishes). The creation of a work of art, in Freud's terms, would also involve the reconciliation of the pleasure principle with the reality principle. (See Freud's *Introductory Lectures on Psychoanalysis* (Vol. 16), pp. 375 7.)

2   In responding to Dalal's paper, Charles Rycroft welcomes it but reminds readers just how universal Jung's enthnocentric arrogant attitude towards 'savages' and 'primitives' was among European intellectuals of his generation (but Jung wrote *Man and his Symbols* in 1961, we should note). Rycroft says that this bogus Darwinism is also found in Freud, Ernest Jones and Wilhelm Reich, and has been discarded by modern anthropologists. He also points out that Jung's anti-semitism needs to be examined.

3   Infant observation which involves close weekly observation, detailed recording and discussion of the experience enables the observer to participate in a more unconscious way and learn from counter-transference responses. The observer must allow herself to feel but to think about these feelings in order to restrain herself from acting on them. By learning this receptivity, the analytic student will be able to receive increasingly the

projection of the more primitive infantile part of the patient's personality. Analysts can experience first hand the intensity of the infantile urges and responses of mother which Winnicott describes as the 'white hot' experience of the therapy room and as such forms the origins of transference and counter-transference relationships.

4 In this theoretical overview of art therapy, we have outlined those models which it appears are used by the majority of qualified and practising art therapists, and which have been formulated in the literature, particularly in Britain. There are a few art therapists in Britain who acknowledge the influence of psychological theories and philosophical systems such as, for example, 'Client-centred Therapy' (Carl Rogers), 'Gestalt Therapy' (Fritz Perls), 'Steinerien Art Therapy' (Rudolf Steiner) in their practice. As yet we have been unable to discover any published theoretical framework for their practice.

References

Bick, E. (1968) The experience of the skin in early object relations, *The International Journal of Psychoanalysis* 49, 484–6.

Bion, W. (1962) *Learning from Experience*, London: William Heinemann Medical Books Ltd.

British Association of Art Therapists (1989) Artists and art therapists: a brief discussion of their roles within hospitals, clinics, special schools and in the community. Standing Committee of Arts Therapists, c/o BAAT, 11a Richmond Road, Brighton BN2 3RL.

Cane, F. (1951) *The Artist in Each of Us*, Vermont: Art Therapy Publications.

Case, C. and Dalley, T. (eds) (1990) *Working with Children in Art Therapy*, London: Routledge.

Dalal, F. (1988) Jung: a racist, *British Journal of Psychotherapy* 4(3): 263–79.

Dalley, T. (ed.) (1984) *Art as Therapy*, London: Tavistock.

—— (1990) Images and integration, in C. Case and T. Dalley (eds) *Working with Children in Art Therapy*, London: Routledge.

—— *et al.* (1987) *Images of Art Therapy*, London: Routledge.

Edwards, M. (1989) Art, therapy and romanticism, in A. Gilroy and T. Dalley (eds) *Pictures at an Exhibition*, London: Routledge.

Fuller, P. (1980) *Art and Psychoanalysis*, London: Writers and Readers.

Goldberg, D. (1991) From monsters to moons: universal and culturally-specific symbols in psychotherapy, *Inscape*, Summer: 5–11.

Gould, S.J. (1981) *The Mismeasure of Man*, London: Pelican.

Greenwood, H. and Layton, G. (1987) An out-patient art therapy group, *Inscape*, Summer: 12–19.

Gustafson, J.P. (1986) *The Complex Secret of Brief Psychotherapy*, London: W.W. Norton.

Harris, M. (1979) Paper on The Contribution of Observation of Mother–Infant Interaction and Development to the Equipment of a Psychoanalyst or Psychoanalytic Psychotherapist. London: Tavistock Clinic.

Hill, A. (1945) *Art Versus Illness*, London: George Allen and Unwin.

—— (1951) *Painting Out Illness*, London: Williams and Norgate.

Jung, C.G. (1953) *The Collected Works of C.G. Jung*. Edited by H. Read *et al.*, Princetown and London: Bollingen Series XX.

Jung, C.G. (1964) *Man and His Symbols*, Aldus/Jupiter.

Jung, C.G. (1970) *Mysterium Coniunctionis*, vol. 14 of *The Collected Works*, London: Routledge and Kegan Paul.

Klein, M. (1952) The Origins of Transference in *The Writings of Melanie Klein*, London: Hogarth Press, pp. 48–56.

—— (1955) The psychoanalytic play technique: its history and significance, in M. Klein, P.

Heimann and R.E. Money-Kyrle (eds) *New Directions in Psychoanalysis*, London: Tavistock.

—— (1957) Envy and gratitude, in *The Writings of Melanie Klein*, London: Hogarth Press and Institute of Psychoanalysis.

Kramer, E. (1958) *Art Therapy in a Children's Community*, Illinois: Thomas.

—— (1980) Symposium: Integration of divergent points of view in art therapy, in E. Ulman and C. Levy (eds) *Art Therapy Viewpoints*, NY: Schocken Books, pp. 8–9.

Laing, J. and Main, A. (1963) *Expressionism through Illness*, Aberdeen: The Aberdeen Collection. Royal Cornhill and Associated Hospitals.

Liebmann, M. (1986) *Art Therapy for Groups*, London: Croom Helm (now Routledge).

Levens, M. (1990) Borderline aspects in eating disorders: art therapy's contribution, *Group Analysis* 23(3): 277–84.

Littlewood, R. and Lipsedge, M. (1984) *Aliens and Alienists*, London: Penguin.

Lyddiatt, E.M. (1971) *Spontaneous Painting and Modelling*, London: Constable.

Maclagan, D. (1985) Art therapy in a therapeutic community, *Inscape*, Autumn: 7–16.

—— (1989) The aesthetic dimension of art therapy: luxury or necessity? *Inscape*, Spring: 10–13.

McNeilly, G. (1983) Directive and non-directive approaches in art therapy, *The Arts in Psychotherapy* 10(4): 211–19. Reprinted (1984) *Inscape*, December.

—— (1987) Further contributions to group analytic art therapy, *Inscape*, Autumn: 8–11.

—— (1990) Group analysis and art therapy: a personal perspective, *Group Analysis* 23(3): 215–24.

Meltzer, D. (1975) Adhesive identification, *Contemporary Psychoanalysis* 11(3): 289–303.

Milner, M. (1950) *On Not Being Able to Paint*, London: Heinemann.

—— (1955) The role of illusion in symbol formation, in M. Klein (ed.) (1977) *New Directions in Psychoanalysis*, London: Maresfield Reprints.

—— (1990) *The Suppressed Madness of Sane Men*, London: Routledge.

Mindell, A. (1982) *Dreambody: The Body's Role in Revealing the Self*, Santa Monica: Sigo Press; London: Routledge.

—— (1988) *City Shadows: Psychological Interventions in Psychiatry*, London: Routledge.

Naumburg, M. (1947) Studies of the free art expression of behaviour disturbed children as a means of diagnosis and therapy, *Nervous and Mental Diseases Monographs*, NY: Cooleridge Foundation.

—— (1958) Art therapy: its scope and function, in E.F. Hammer (ed.) *Clinical Applications of Projective Drawings*, Illinois: Thomas.

—— (1966) *Dynamically Oriented Art Therapy: Its Principles and Practices*, NY: Grune and Stratton.

Nowell Hall, P. (1987) Art therapy: a way of healing the split, in T. Dalley *et al.* (ed.) *Images of Art Therapy*, London: Routledge.

Petrie, M. (1946) *Age and Regeneration*, Elek.

Pickford, R. (1967) *Studies in Psychiatric Art*, Illinois: Thomas.

Rack, P. (1982) *Race, Culture and Mental Disorder*, London: Tavistock.

Richardson, M. (1948) *Art and the Child*, London: University of London Press.

Rubin, J.A. (ed.) (1987) *Approaches to Art Therapy*, NY: Bruner/Mazel.

Schaverien, J. (1982) Transference as an aspect of art therapy, *Inscape*, Winter: 10–16.

—— (1985) Creativity and the institution, *Inscape*, Autumn: 3–6.

Segal, H. (1991) *Dream, Phantasy and Art*, London: The New Library of Psychoanalysis, Tavistock/Routledge in association with the Institute of Psychoanalysis.

Skaife, S. (1990) Self-determination in group analytic art therapy, *Group Analysis* 23(3): 237–44.

Stokes, A. (1963) *Painting and the Inner World*, London: Tavistock.

Strand, S. (1990) Counteracting isolation: group art therapy for people with learning difficulties, *Group Analysis* 23(3): 255–63.

Swainson, C. (1990) Art therapy and homeless people, in M. Liebmann (ed.) *Art Therapy in Practice*, London: Jessica Kingsley Publications.

Tomlinson, R. (1934) Catalogue for Exhibition of Children's Drawings and Paintings at County Hall, London.

Ulman, E. (1983) Obituary of Margaret Naumburg, *American Journal of Art Therapy* 22(4).

Viola, W. (1942) *Child Art*, London: University of London Press.

Waller, D.E. (1989) Musing cross culturally, in A. Gilroy and T. Dalley (eds) *Pictures at an Exhibition*, London: Routledge.

—— (ed.) (1990) Group analysis and the arts therapies, *Group Analysis* 23(3): 211–84.

—— (1991) *Becoming a Profession: Art Therapy 1940–1982*, London: Routledge.

Weir, F. (1987) The role of symbolic expression in its relation to art therapy: a Kleinian approach, in T. Dalley *et al.* (ed.) *Images of Art Therapy*, London: Routledge.

Winnicott, D.W. (1965) *The Maturational Process and the Facilitating Environment*, London: Hogarth Press.

—— (1971) *Playing and Reality*, London: Tavistock.

Yalom, I. (1983) *In-patient Group Psychotherapy*, NY: Basic Books.

2

Art therapy: new problems, new solutions?

JOAN WODDIS

Introduction

In July 1990, art therapists heard the news that the National Joint Council for Local Authorities had approved a Local Government Board recommendation that the professional qualifications of art therapists should be included within the Council's scheme of conditions of service. There was great rejoicing at this news which meant, in effect, that art therapists working in the Social and Community Services would be recognized as qualified professionals and the door to the establishment of a career structure and an infrastructure of practice in that area was at last open. What the good news also contained was another message: that art therapists must re-examine their practice in the light of the new situations, client groups, staff teams and management structures in which it would have to take hold and survive. Will the approaches that have evolved over the years for the treatment of patients in largely closed psychiatric institutions be appropriate to the needs of the wide range of clients with whom art therapists may well work in the future? In this chapter I hope to find some answers to this question.

It is now 25 years since the foundation of the British Association of Art Therapists and it is interesting to note how many of the issues confronting the profession remain constant, changing perhaps in detail but not in essence. However, the quality of practice and how it relates both to fellow professionals and to the climate of the times, and the changes, not only in the client populations art therapists seek to engage with but also in the wider communities to which they belong, indicate that the profession must develop and further evolve. I shall refer to these changes in more detail in my examination of art therapy in the Social and Community Services and art therapy in Education.

Since the assimilation of art therapy by the Whitley Council, the approval of its training by the Department of Health and Social Security and the consequent establishment of a structure for clinical practice (DHSS PM 82 6/2 86 1), the profession, through its association, has sought to improve the training, working conditions and standards of practice of its members. The detailed history of how art therapy moved from an occupation group to a profession is described in Waller (1991). Here I would point to the formulation of *The Principles of Professional Practice* (1986) (see Appendix B) and the *Professional Responsibilities of Art Therapists* (1989) (see Appendix C) to indicate the refinement and professional advance that agreed practice has undergone in the last decade.

Both documents seek to clarify working issues that have exercised art therapists for some years, but that have assumed great importance since the establishment of a career structure in the health services. The establishment of an effective referral system by which clients are selected for treatment, the precise definitions of 'confidentiality' and 'accountable agent', and the profession's agreed position on the exhibition of clients' work are among the matters addressed in detail. These important propositions, together with the establishment of a *National Register of Art Therapists in 1986*, see art therapy today as growing larger and more organized as a profession, though still, historically, a recent one.

It was in the light of these professional developments, and a steadily increasing number of Registered Art Therapists (to date more than 600) that the 1990 Annual General meeting of the British Association of Art Therapists (BAAT) proposed without dissent that the profession move towards state registration. The application to become a state-registered profession by an extension of the Professions Supplementary to Medicine Act of 1960 began its progress in September 1990, when a detailed submission was made to the Council for such professions, the Council for the Professions Supplementary to Medicine (CPSM). The submission, written by BAAT's President, Dr Diane Waller, was a lengthy and comprehensive document. Its brief was to address the issue of professional status, based on a structure of seven given principles – for example, the existence of a systematic body of knowledge, a recognized period of training and an agreed code of conduct. In December, the application was considered by a specially convened working party of the CPSM. It attracted much support, and it was agreed that it should pass to the full Council for approval. At the time of writing, the structure of a new Board of the CPSM is not finalized; it will certainly include art therapists and music therapists, whose applications ran in tandem, and at some date in the future drama therapists will make a similar application for inclusion.

It is in the light of these important professional developments, and the public interest and general awareness of art therapy and the work of its practitioners, that this chapter is written. Here I intend to examine the ways in which the structures of engagement, the involvement with client groups and also the expectations placed on art therapists are changing and how art therapy practice keeps pace with this process.

The shift of psychiatric care from its traditional hospital base to the community into a network of small community homes, day centres and 'drop-in' facilities, provides the opportunity for art therapists to work formally with a wide range of clients. The recent emergence of Art Therapy in Education as an effective adjunct to the school-based provision for children with special needs, again suggests that modes of practice based on in-patient psychiatric care will be re-assessed and modified.

Art therapists are already being appraised within the NHS, as 'medical audit' is one of the key measures within the recent White Paper (1989), and they are being asked to define precisely what they do and what they hope to achieve. As the debate between the ideology of the movement known as 'Healing Arts' (which sees the arts as therapy in themselves) and the psychodynamic 'art psychotherapy' position intensifies, I shall survey the Hospital Arts movements.

The use of art therapy as a diagnostic element is gaining acceptance in the treatment of child abuse cases, and here again I shall explore how practice might benefit from further definition, and the aims of treatment be clarified. These I believe to be some of the most telling issues facing the profession today, some crucial to development, others milestones along the road of our professional history.

The story so far: art therapy practice in the Health Service

From its earliest beginnings the profession of art therapy and its development as a career has grown in an atmosphere of challenge and opposition, as Waller's account of its history demonstrates (Waller 1991). Since the establishment of a career structure within the NHS in 1981, the status, conditions and salaries of art therapists have steadily improved and their emergence from under the well-intentioned but largely constraining wing of occupational therapy to whom they were 'linked' by the Department of Health, is generally accepted.

New management structures have necessitated some adjustment in the construct of an 'autonomous art therapist'; the profession's stated goal for many years. Historically art therapists were often seen as being part of the occupational therapy service, not only in terms of management and finance, but also clinical practice, and the need to be a free-standing component in the overall treatment of patients was a vital issue for the profession. Waller (1987b), has explored this question in detail and concludes: 'There is no reason why art therapists and occupational therapists, both having clearly acknowledged their own professional identity, should not work together for good clinical practice (indeed they often do).' (197–200) Currently, in common with other NHS professionals including medical staff, art therapists now take their place in a structure of 'line management' in which the administrational superior of any given practitioner may not necessarily be a member of that profession, and consequently complete autonomy is not really possible.

In practice the immediate manager of an art therapist may well be an occupational therapist or a clinical psychologist, albeit a senior member of staff. Art therapists are adamant that such managerial responsibility should not be confused with clinical seniority, and they continue to see themselves responsible to the head of the clinical team, the so-called 'referring agent', who will generally be the consultant psychiatrist. This relationship has been successfully argued and attained in many institutions but the process continues and remains a major working issue for many in the field.

The growth of the profession within the stringent economic climate of the last two decades has produced increasing demands on art therapists and other professions to evaluate their service, project its future place within a given health authority and assess its usefulness. In an internal document for the attention of

BAAT members ('Norms of practice'), Donnelly (1986), then ex-officio chair of
BAAT, observed that there are no national norms for the establishment of art
therapy posts, and it is important for the profession that it devise a system for
assessing how many art therapists might be required to provide a comprehensive
service.

It appears that the present system is an arbitrary one, where local conditions
prevail, often as a matter of tradition rather than any analysis of patient need.
There exist clinical teams where the work of the art therapist depends on the
patronage of the consultant, art therapy referrals being seen within his or her
'gift'. In other situations the art therapist is perceived as providing a service in a
marginalized position, so that their practice becomes an extra benefit rather than
an integral part of treatment. Norms of practice, argued Donnelly, need to be
elucidated if the parameters of an effective art therapy service are to be
recognized. He suggests a number of alternative approaches to the quantification
of art therapy posts, observing that they may be seen in ratio to several factors –
for example, the number of patient attendances per week, the number of psychiatrists, the number of beds or places, the total population or as a response to special
needs. The relationship between the demand for, and the supply of, any professional group's services is not straightforward, much depending on how the
demand is calculated.

The occupational therapy (OT) profession, whilst being much larger than art
therapy, presents some interesting parallels. There has been no agreed national
policy on the growth of this profession, but it has increased from 3,359 registered
practitioners in 1971 to 9,306 in 1987, an increase of 177 per cent. This growth
reflects the pressures exerted on employing authorities, for example population
ageing, changed perceptions and treatment of mental illness and also of rehabilitation. In the absence of any government norms for the number of OT posts which
should be established it seems that the number actually in existence will roughly
suggest the demand. This conclusion is very misleading, not only for OT, but
even more so for art therapy. Thus, for instance, the *Survey of Conditions of Service for
Registered Art Therapists* (Teasdale *et al.* 1990, revealed that 17.8 per cent of art
therapists were employed in Social and Non-statutory Service Day Centres. In all
but one case these therapists worked in inner-city boroughs, mostly in Greater
London. If the 'supply and demand' argument is applied here it would seem that
no art therapy service is required in these institutions within the County Councils
of the UK.

There is a concentration of art therapy provision in the South-East (perhaps
another parallel with OT, a reflection on the proximity of two of the training
institutions) and it seems that little rational thought is being given by the concerned government departments to the overall requirements of the population for
an art therapy service. It is striking that even in the hostile climate of the cuts in
Health Service provision, new art therapy posts continue to be established, but
Donnelly's document was not widely circulated or officially published so it is not
surprising that his suggestions have not been examined by NHS-based art therapists in any organized way, although there have been informal discussions at
local level. In the event of a clear method being designed to indicate the number of
art therapists required to serve a particular population, the profession's continued

argument for an increase in the numbers of art therapists employed would be justified. Unlike occupational therapists, art therapists are not obliged to collect 'minimum data records' (the so-called 'Korner statistics'), and the most realistic reflection of their current working practice is to be found in the BAAT meetings, and in their own records.

There is a need for a suitable structure for the analysis of practice, in terms of appropriate methods of data collection that would combat art therapists' resistance to the classification of their practice so often perceived through the framework and constructs of other disciplines. So the need to quantify and assess practice, at one time something that art therapists tended to avoid, is becoming a necessity, not simply in order to survive in a demanding working environment but also as a way of improving practice itself as exercises of comparison and evaluation inevitably precede the refinement of ideas. NHS art therapists will increasingly be asked to address the issue of 'outcomes', the process by which the relative success of treatment is measured after a patient's discharge from the institution. The gauging of success or failure in therapeutic practice is a complex endeavour and one that surely would entail the assistance of the client.

The incidence of re-admittance seems to be the chosen, if somewhat simplistic, method of evaluation extant at present. There is a good case for well-structured research projects in this area, but individual art therapists might begin by closely monitoring a small group of patients for a given period after discharge in consultation with whatever after-care services prevail. A useful development occurred when, in the face of these inevitable demands on a newly established professional group, the post of Art Therapy Adviser to the Department of Health was created in the Spring of 1989. The office entails informing and advising national management on matters of conditions of service, salary re-grading and the status of art therapists, and BAAT was delighted to nominate Diane Waller, its president, for this role.

It is a new experience for the profession to find an art therapist able to advise the management side of the Whitley Council, for this is what Diane Waller's appointment entails, and it highlights the necessity for more art therapists to take on managerial roles at a local level. Past experience of line managers, who were often occupational therapists, experiencing confusion in disentangling their clinical-supervisory and managerial responsibilities, required negotiations at the level of the institution, and working traditions were often difficult to overturn.

But precedents have been set and management practices modified throughout the UK – a process still in train. Perhaps members of all relatively new professions experience themselves as beleaguered in an uncaring environment, and as such cling to the concept of 'us and them' long after it is appropriate. Many art therapists traditionally see themselves as 'us' and reject the thought of ever being on the 'other side', and there are, perhaps, a number of reasons for this. Art therapists are more likely to see themselves as artists, offering an essential 'alternative' form of treatment, and thus 'outsiders' in a scientific environment. Moreover, many of the first practitioners now prominent in the profession were influenced by the anti-psychiatry movement of the 1960s and saw the medical establishment as essentially dehumanizing. However, there are obvious advantages to be gained from working with a manager who has a clear understanding of one's practice, and those art therapists who have developed management skills are of enormous value to the profession.

The White Paper, 'Working for Patients' (HMSO 1989) outlines the government proposals following their review of the NHS in January 1989. The document contains several key measures which are proving to be of concern to members of BAAT, and a recent article 'Comments on the White Paper' (BAAT, August 1989) states, 'The main concern of the White Paper seems to be to contain and reduce the level of public expenditure for the Health Service and does not address (its) continued under-funding.'

The proposed move to delegate greater responsibility for the services to the local level means that individual hospitals will be given more control over the running of their own affairs. The BAAT document reflects the criticisms already widely voiced that the White Paper introduces a market-based competitive philosophy to the NHS and is mindful that the 'quality and sensitivity of our work will suffer under the financial pressure to stay within adequate budget limits' (BAAT 1989: 5). The fear that therapeutic practice will be seen as less cost-effective than some other forms of treatment exists among art therapists working in clinical settings, as does the suspicion that the proposed system will encourage a two-tier health service in which the private sector will feed off the public. By tradition, art therapists and their professional body are committed to comprehensive treatment which is free at the point of consumption, unfettered by market fluctuation and financed from general taxation. The White Paper does not refer specifically to art therapy, and practitioners will look in vain for any demonstration of an understanding of their work, and are likely to remain for the most part unconvinced by the arguments.

It is likely that a tighter and more formally structured form of practice will be necessary in this highly competitive climate and that some of the systems that art therapists have set up in the past will no longer prove viable. The 'open door' arrangement which has prevailed in many hospitals since the 1940s in which the art therapy room is seen as a haven in a hostile environment, where music might be playing and tea may well be served and where all are welcome for as long or as short a time as they can tolerate the atmosphere, will not be seen as a serious form of treatment, bur rather as a diversionary activity, and consequently more difficult to justify. (Liebmann describes an art therapist making coffee for a group of patients on an acute admissions ward to 'help the atmosphere to be informal and social' (1986: 67–8). I fear it is likely that the committed practitioners that Liebmann describes many undermine the continuance of their own work by such attitudes.)

There are now many practitioners in the field who are developing structures of practice within the psychodynamic mode of art therapy, where the client-centred approach is informed by the disciplines of group analysis (McNeilly *et al.* 1990; 211–45), analytic (Schaverien 1987: 74–109, Weir 1987: 109–28) or brief psychotherapy (see McClelland, Chapter 11 of this volume). It follows that such practice contains clear elements of boundary-setting and a more focused view of the suitability of different clients to different forms of therapeutic encounter. A carefully developed referral system and a clear understanding of the parameters of the diagnostic interview will be a necessity in this approach, as will be the ability, on reflection, to direct referred clients to another form of treatment.

Art therapy is not a homogenized service, where the same experience is offered to all presenting patients, but rather a constellation of different treatments. A flexible approach, where clearly differentiated models of practice exist, suggests that art therapy can be available and useful to a very wide range of clients.

First-admission acute patients may benefit from clearly defined individual sessions with a continuation after discharge at prescribed intervals as in brief psychotherapy or cognitive analytic psychotherapy, whereas regularly returning short-stay patients might be part of an art therapy group in the 'slow–open' mode, both as in- and then as out-patients. In these instances the psychodynamic interplay between therapist, client and imagery is the centre-piece of the action, whereas the need for long-stay institutionalized patients now facing life in the community is perhaps a closed regular group in which art-making itself may appear to contain the process, whilst being part of the therapeutic relationship. This is accurately described by Miller (1984) who tells how a patient suffering from acute physical pain was able to externalize her feelings through an image. Miller (1984: 133) writes, 'The visual arts are (also) able to express abstract qualities and feelings with great precision.' This credo surely unites differing models of practice.

I have described just a few examples, and practising art therapists will doubtless have others, but it remains certain that a more quantifiable service, capable of analysis both in terms of client need and institutional audit, will be needed in the near future.

The transfer of psychiatric care into the community

The proposed changes in health-care provision have particular significance within psychiatry, for it is this sector that employs the majority of art therapists. The principle of the transfer to the community of long-stay patients, a generally accepted move, was greeted with guarded approval by the profession in the early 1980s, and indeed this support had been there since the policy was first put forward officially in 1962. It was believed that such a transfer must be seen to be more than changing the label on the out-patients door to 'Community Care', and art therapists wanted assurances that they would be able to continue to work with their patients in day centres, community homes and hostels. They argued for the establishment of a network of community art therapists, appointed in addition to hospital-based colleagues, who would still be required for those patients remaining in the institution for a short or indefinite period.

In November 1986, 70 hospital-based art therapists were asked to find out what plans existed for the transfer of their service to the community. At that time less than ten community posts had been created and even fewer centres with a strong therapy input were being planned. Some time later, as reported in the *Survey of Conditions of Work of Registered Art Therapists 1988* (Teasdale *et al.* 1990), nearly 150 NHS-employed art therapists responded to questions on the transfer of National Health Services to the community (see Appendix A). Although half of these practitioners said they regarded at least part of their working week as being devoted to providing community health facilities, the majority said this involvement was less than seven hours a week. Only eight members reported that their contract of employment was a more or less full-time community commitment.

The notion of day units, possibly conducted on therapeutic community lines for the use of both acute and long-stay patients, remains largely a matter of precept not practice. To borrow a concept from the *Warnock Report on Special Education* (Warnock *et al*. 1978) the notion of care and provision being a fluctuating need rather than a geographical location seems yet to be accepted, and the issue of differences in approach between practice in community and hospital settings remains a crucial factor.

The publication in 1988 of the Griffiths Report, *Community Care: Agenda for Action* (Griffiths *et al*. 1988) did little to clarify the situation, for whilst stressing the need for community health services to remain within the NHS and for their quality and extent to improve, it also sought to establish that primary responsibility for future community care should be with the local authorities. Let us turn our attention, then, to the art therapy practice which already exists within the public sector.

Art therapy in the social and community services

Apart from the NHS, more art therapists work within social services than any other area, and it was in June 1987 that BAAT, mindful of the increasing numbers of its members working in the social and community services (and therefore joining the Trades Union NALGO) set up the Community Services Sub-committee. Its brief was to consider issues arising from the need to establish career structures outside the NHS, principally in the social services, but also in non-statutory work, child care, the Home Office, agency work and education. (This latter task was soon to be transferred to a specialist pressure group of Art Therapists in Education.)

It was acknowledged that the creation of a recognized career structure was a massive task, particularly in times of acute financial stringency, but individual art therapists were already gaining recognition in social work settings, their qualification being tied to an appropriate notch on the social work salary scales, thus setting useful precedents for future negotiations. However, it seemed that the majority were seen as 'unqualified', and their practice and training largely unacknowledged or not understood. The Committee made an early decision to concentrate its efforts on local authority employment (both in the social and non-statutory services) and lost no time in beginning the task of collecting data on the working conditions of art therapists, later to be published as a report – *Conditions of Service of Registered Art Therapists in Great Britain* (BAAT/MSF 1989).

The publication in March 1988 of the Griffiths Report (Griffiths *et al*. 1988) pointed to the need for improvement in both quality and scope of provision of these services. The financial implications were not, unfortunately, clearly addressed, but the point was not lost on the art therapy profession that the transfer of provision from the NHS to local authorities would be significant for art therapists who had no structure within this field of employment. Griffiths proposed three options:

1 seconded services from the NHS;
2 locally agreed transfers to local authority employment;
3 redundancy from the NHS linked to redeployment.

The government's proposals for the decentralization of negotiation of pay and conditions emphasized the need for art therapists working in the social services to press their case with their own local authority. The Community Services Subcommittee saw as part of its role the support and advising of art therapists in this position and counselled the development (with their employers) of individual job descriptions and contracts of employment. This was seen as clarifying and protecting future posts, and became one of the major recommendations of the Committee's strategy report published in early 1989.

The decision was also taken to concentrate the profession's efforts in persuading the National Joint Council's (NJC) National Committee for Vocational Qualifications to recognize the postgraduate Diploma in Art Therapy with salary scales and conditions of service pinned to a point on the NJC scales at least comparable to those offered to art therapists through the terms of the Whitley Council agreements with the professions allied to medicine. It seems likely at the time of writing that at least a quarter of BAAT's registered art therapists are employed by social services and the Conditions of Service Report confirmed that most of them belong to NALGO. The necessity for mounting a campaign through that Trades Union seems clear. However, the report made an important recommendation in its first point of strategy, that whilst conceding that many art therapists working in social services took on a variety of roles as part of a multi-disciplinary team, the priority must still be to work towards the recognition of their postgraduate training and experience together with their practice, by the employing local authorities.

There was obviously great satisfaction when, in early July 1990, the National Joint Council for Local Authorities accepted the applications of the BAAT and APMT (Association of Professional Music Therapists) for inclusion of their professional qualifications under Appendix A of the Council's scheme of Conditions of Service and further recognized such professionals as validated for local authority employment. Accordingly, and in line with the proposals of the Griffiths Report, the lobbying of local authorities was suggested with a view to them increasing their capacity to employ art therapists, and it was proposed that a campaign to encourage the setting up of Community Art Therapy teams should begin, and this exercise is already in train.

BAAT had long since devised salary guidelines for art therapists who work sessionally, outside the NHS, but their remains a need for a close look at the working conditions of these practitioners. As in other fields – education and custodial work, for example – there exists scope for the re-examination of practice in terms of new demands of employment, and how the variety of tasks and working responsibilities undertaken by art therapists outside strictly clinical settings actually modifies the norms of their professional practice. But this raises the question, which forms of professional practice? The art therapy profession has its

roots deep in psychiatric care and residential institutions. It has sought to counter-
act the medical model of mental illness but has, until recently, largely existed in
settings where this was the prevailing ideology. The multi-disciplinary team
allowed for the existence (sometimes grudgingly) of an art therapist within its
ranks, and the adherence to defined boundaries of practice was a necessity for the
profession's survival.

As art therapy moves outside the Health Service, however, and into custodial
care, drug rehabilitation programmes, the probationary service, womens' refuges
and support centres for the homeless, practitioners will be asking what changes of
procedure will occur and what modifications of conduct and technique will follow.
It seems likely that there will be less narrow specialization and a more eclectic
approach wherein all workers in a given setting have both a responsibility to the
enterprise in general and an area of specialized practice in particular, which will,
perhaps, be wider than the 'treatment team' approach of the hospital concerned
with in-patient care. Many art therapists will find themselves in the role of 'key
worker' addressing practical problems, and in such a relationship with their
client, a classic psychoanalytic stance (the approach of, an increasing number,
albeit a minority, of art therapists) will not be appropriate. The danger could be
that when the familiar boundaries of practice shift, they may disappear entirely if
new systems are not created. The perception of the art room as a defined and
unique territory within the hospital has long underpinned the practice of art
therapy in clinical settings; if the space no longer clearly exists, or is shared and
less defined, will practice itself be similarly eroded?

It seems logical that those art therapists who seek work within the parameters of
psychotherapy will find this impossible if they also assume a practical, advisory
relationship with their clients. It will therefore be important for them to persuade
their colleagues that their roles of key worker and therapist must not conflict and
that these connections must be with different individuals. But perhaps other
models should be explored.

The techniques of brief psychotherapy, a series of focused aims and objectives
based on growing self-awareness, would not be inappropriate to practise within
these settings, and the power of the image to condense and encapsulate feelings,
which lies at the heart of art therapy, could surely be part of that process. I am not
arguing for a dilution of practice, but recommending that the needs of a particular
client group will suggest what type of approach is the most fitting both for their
welfare and that of the service that addresses their needs, and art therapists should
lose no time in devising models that both fulfil these demands and draw on their
unique practice. The notion of a mix of skills will be useful here, I believe. Social
workers, for example, may also work 'dynamically' with some clients, be
'advisers' to others, and art therapists are increasingly working alongside this
professional group. It would be disastrous if, just at the moment when art therapy
is at last being recognized within these varying structures, it is also seen as too
exclusive or expensive to be part of them.

I suspect that answers will have to be found and solutions contrived to some of
these difficult questions before we can hope for the establishment of a career
structure, notwithstanding the increasing need for client care in both the social
and non-statutory services. The recognition and establishment of art therapy in

these fields is long overdue and is probably still the most important task facing the profession.

Art therapy in education

Within the education system the current existence of different modes of art therapy practice confirms the role that it might play were there a defined structure for it. There is as yet no establishment for art therapists within schools and it is interesting to note that although the 1981 Education Act seeks to make provision for those pupils with special needs as identified in the Warnock Report (Warnock *et al.* 1978), which recommended the integration of the majority of the special-school population into mainstream education, as yet the contribution that art therapy can make is largely unacknowledged.

In the generally accepted sense the praxis of art therapy and art teaching has important differences and addresses complementary constellations of needs, so is it possible to design a model of practice that might exist within our mainstream primary and secondary schools? I believe that it is, and I derive my thinking from the conclusions of the aforementioned Warnock Report (1978) which stated that specialized intervention in the face of identified special need should not be seen as a constant, but a variable provision, and as such might operate for some students throughout their school-days, but for others for briefer periods of crisis or difficulty.

Briefly, it is seen that as many as 40 per cent of pupils will, at some point in their education, need additional support in order to cope with their learning difficulties. These may arise from educational, physical, behavioural or emotional causes. This figure covers not only those pupils transferred from special schools, but also many already within mainstream establishments.

The major coping strategy set up as a result of the Education Act (1981) is the practice of 'statementing'. This aims to identify the child's special needs and delineates the necessary educational provision to meet them. However, the subsequent Education Act of 1988, which centred on the introduction of the National Curriculum, required standardized learning targets for all schools, and therefore a resultant intensification of assessment procedures by teachers. It is easy to see how this development may exacerbate the problems experienced by many of their pupils.

Art therapists do not perceive all difficulties undergone by children as being of an educational origin although they may well be acted out in school. An increasing number of art teachers some years into their careers are training as art therapists and it is by this means that art therapy is gaining hold for its practice in the education service. As the law stands any professional working with pupils within the school environment who does not occupy an accepted career role must be a qualified teacher.

An increasing number of head teachers are recommending the appointment of art teachers who are art therapists to their staff in order to, in some part, address the difficulties experienced by establishments that attempt to practise the ideas of child-centred education, in an unfavourable climate. It is felt that the integration of art therapy into these schools creates a new structure to address the special needs of statemented children and ultimately improve their performance both in learning and social skills. In this model of practice, art therapists work as specialist practitioners and a future career structure might well have parallels with that of speech therapists, who see children regularly within the school on a withdrawal basis, both individually and in small groups, whereupon the necessity for art therapists to be teachers would disappear. There is already a small number of art therapists who, although they are not qualified teachers, work in independent schools, and it is here that their training and practice is recognized and their role most clearly defined. (Arguile, in Chapter 8 of this volume, and also in Arguile [1990], describes this arrangement in some detail.)

The most suitable model for practice in school would probably be one where transactions between therapist and child are conducted in individual sessions or small psychodynamically based groups. The essential requirement would be that the therapist would not be involved in any other activities with his or her clients, and that attendance at the sessions would be unimpeded by the demands of the school curriculum. This mode, probably most appropriate to special schools, or special needs departments within mainstream schools, will necessitate some rethinking by head teachers and their staffs – for the effectiveness of the enterprise will really hinge on the understanding of the importance of boundary issues and a clear definition of therapy sessions as opposed to timetable needs. It is only in such an environment that the development and understanding of transference phenomena can occur. In this example, art therapy would constitute an area of clinical expertise in an educational setting and as such would certainly be preferable to the current practice of referring children to weekly sessions at the Child or Adolescent Psychiatry Department at their local hospital. (It has been argued by Waller [1984: 11] that an awareness of the elements of therapy practice can inform the performance of art teachers who, following their art therapy training, seek to return to the classroom and work therapeutically.)

It is entirely valid to suppose that a knowledge of boundary-setting, the recognition of projections (both from teachers and pupils) and the ability to understand classroom transactions in terms of group dynamics would greatly enrich the performance of teachers who are faced with mounting difficulties. If an art teacher trains as an art therapist, he or she may still concentrate on the artwork of the children rather than on their unconscious feelings, but she or he would also be aware of the processes occurring between teacher and pupils on an individual or intergroup basis. This is clearly the case for the number of art therapists who commit themselves to the teacher/therapist role, and their effect is generally felt throughout their schools, not simply in their own classrooms or studios.

Even in the face of the development of agreed national curricula and the obligation to involve all students in the General Certificate of Secondary Education examination procedures, it may be possible for the art teacher/therapist to modify his or her techniques of instruction to include a high level of personal choice for their students and to evolve a less directive and non-judgemental approach.

A successful therapeutic encounter is, on a personal level, an informative experience. It involves both learning and unlearning and could be said to facilitate education in itself. Teacher/therapists in the past often felt that if they were not able to set up the psychodynamic model described earlier, the only recourse was to fall in with the general trend of art teaching within their schools. Whilst it is not reasonable to suppose that the teacher/therapist should work with transference issues, many of the skills of counselling, listening, feeding back and discussion of realistic goals will be useful. This would surely be no more than a return to the 'child centred' approach now in danger of being lost in the market economy of quantifiable results.

It is a way of working that I believe could exist effectively in a mainstream setting, given goodwill and respect from colleagues, a relationship that would have to be earned, rather than expected as a right. Accordingly one might propose art therapists working in mainstream schools, though not necessarily with students defined as being in special need, either on an individual basis (as would probably be the case in primary education) or in large secondary establishments as part of the team that addresses educational and behavioural problems. In providing a therapy service within a given school, practitioners might well offer short-term individual sessions in terms of crisis intervention and follow-up longer term involvements, possibly in art therapy groups, and special support initiatives.

These last might be for newly arrived students, for those facing GCSE examinations or option choices, or perhaps thematic groups concerned with racism or sexual identity. They would certainly include staff support groups. There will be many other examples, naturally, but my point is that such a service would extend and enrich the over-stretched educational psychology resources, would neither compete or be confused with the art teaching programme, and, given the opportunity, could prove itself invaluable to both students and teachers in mainstream schools.

Art therapy and child abuse

Art therapists have become increasingly concerned about the apparent increase in child abuse. Unlike social workers, art therapists do not have any statutory involvement with their clients and so their relationship and its transactions are freely entered into, and at the time of writing drawings and paintings are not admissible evidence in British courts. However, art therapists may find themselves caught in the conflict between upholding the interest of the child in terms of the therapeutic alliance and their relationship to the team that holds statutory responsibility for the families in their care. DHSS guidelines state: 'The safety of the child must at all times be of paramount importance and must override all other considerations' (DHSS 1986: 1–2).

Art therapists will undoubtedly find themselves working with many more confirmed or suspected abuse cases, as fellow professionals begin to acknowledge that the process is of benefit to such children. It is therefore important to clarify at the point of referral whether there is suspicion of abuse or whether it has been proved. In the latter case the work of the therapist will be focused on the re-establishment of trust and the hoped-for recovery from disastrous events – in short, the regaining of the ability to form relationships, and here the art therapists's feet are on firm ground.

It is when suspicion and the resultant need to build up a body of evidence become the motivating forces, that the diagnostic role of the art therapist is at its most _ate. The moment at which the therapist shares her suspicions with those of ner colleagues who must act upon them is therefore a critical one. The DHSS guidelines further state: '. . . the sharing of information is on a "need to know" basis, and is for those directly concerned with the family and who have the duty legitimately to perform a service on its behalf . . .' (p. 6).

As potential diagnosticians, British art therapists do not in the main see the encoding of images as part of their work, neither do they perceive that repeated configurations necessarily indicate a particular symptom or event. They will generally only interpret a client's imagery in the light of the therapeutic relationship, transference issues and the client's needs. Images are of course seen as making manifest the history, memories and wishes of the client, but in the contextual sense, never as absolute equivalents. This point was clearly made in 'Art therapy and the law: sexual abuse' (BAAT, November 1988), a document compiled from the afternoon conference of the same name organized by BAAT in March 1988.

It is interesting to note that American art therapists vary in their practice from their British counterparts on this issue, and a search for an agreed symbolic language of 'indicators' of child abuse seems to be in progress (Burgess *et al.* 1981: 50–8). Happily British art therapists seem to have resisted this temptation, although they remain under some pressure from concerned colleagues to make evaluations which confirm the original suspicion, particularly where the child concerned is thought to be at great risk. It is inescapable that therapists may sometimes perceive 'the safety' of their client in a different light to that of their colleagues – this matter will always need to be explored, as a strong suspicion of abuse cannot remain within the boundaries of the session.

There is a growing number of instances where art therapists are being requested to attend court as witnesses for the prosecution. The hazards to the subtle balance of the therapeutic alliance are great in such a situation, and the possibility of paintings being produced in evidence, with attendant demands for interpretation, is one that most art therapists in this field rightly dread. There is a danger of 'shrinking' practice in order to fit the needs of other professionals, and by the agency of tightly organized and defined interpretation encouraging a mythology of secret messages. I do not dispute the condensation of history and emotion that the images of such clients may contain, but observe that the need for an 'outcome' by colleagues with responsibility for action will inevitably pressurize art therapists if they are not acutely aware of the risks involved.

The imagery produced in these sessions, whilst undoubtedly being a response to a tragic sequence of events, cannot be viewed as 'proof'. It must take its place among available evidence as an adjunct, not an exhibit; it is surely not part of an art therapist's duty to appear in court or to build up a case. On reflection, probably the safest and most cautious role for the practitioner in this situation is the classic psychoanalytic stance, where the client leads the therapist and the process itself gradually engenders trust. How art therapists themselves deal with the consequences of their own disclosures to their colleagues or to the police is not a straightforward matter, for what can happen to the therapeutic alliance when the therapist 'tells'? Regular supervision by a fellow professional is obviously a requirement in such practice, but the overall need must be to build a therapeutic relationship that is sensitive and supporting without ever seeking to dramatize or sensationalize.

Hospital arts and art therapy

Over the years a certain belief, in some respects a mythology, has arisen concerning the intrinsic healing properties of the art-making process (Moss 1987: 7, 8, 24). This postulates that the act of artistic creation is, of itself, healing, and this effect does not necessarily involve the intervention or even the presence of another. Art therapists remain divided about this but it is necessary to readdress some of the assumptions of such a credo. Its history, in terms of the profession, dates back to the late 1940s when artists began to be employed in British psychiatric hospitals; these practitioners sought to work therapeutically and those psychiatrists and psychoanalysts, for example Marion Milner and Irene Champernowne, who had already found the production of drawings and paintings to be an invaluable element in the therapeutic process were a source of support (Waller 1991: 73–9). The principle that art therapists were first and foremost artists was established during those early years and this understanding continues today, as is demonstrated in the context of training and the parameters of the career structure.

Over recent years a new discipline has sought to establish itself within the Health Service, that of 'health-care arts', and a new group of professionals, 'hospital artists', is emerging. This process was accelerated in 1985 when the Attenborough Report, *Arts and Disabled People*, was published. An increasing number of 'artists in residence' were appointed to hospital staffs, generally for periods of not more than a year, and training programmes, research initiatives and a proposal for a national centre quickly followed. It became important for art therapists to elucidate the comparative roles of art therapists and hospital-based artists. Generally speaking, art therapists were clear on their position but rejected the basic division between 'artists' and art therapists. They argued that art therapists *were* artists who had sought to draw on their background, education and skills in their practice as therapists, and their identity as artists was intrinsic to that practice. They supported any endeavour that would improve the environment of hospitals and treatment centres, and endorsed the desirability of increased access to the arts for people obliged to spend long periods of time in those institutions.

However, the idea that involvement in the process of that improvement – for instance, painting a mural or providing exhibitions of paintings for waiting rooms – would of necessity be advantageous to such patients was not accepted. Diane Waller wrote in 'Standing Committee of Arts Therapies Professions Report' (Waller 1987a: 13), '. . . the notion that the arts are, per se, 'healing' has yet to be proved, despite many elaborate claims to this effect'. The Standing Committee reaffirmed that the process of art therapy was not simply providing the means for clients to paint, in the belief that this would somehow make them feel better, but a psychodynamic process, based on a relationship explored within defined boundaries, the 'therapeutic alliance', where the elements of transference, projection and fantasy are manifested in imagery as well as behaviour and discourse.

However, the question that the art therapists asked was: Why, if one is satisfied with one's identity as an artist, seek to be an art therapist at all? Why adapt the artist's unique relationship with his or her work to the constraints of therapeutic practice? It seems that the awareness lies within the parameters of professional practice itself and the triangular relationship between therapist, client and imagery which so attracts those artists who go on to train as art therapists. Their deeper motivation for this course of action usually becomes apparent during training where such issues are explored and the experience of training art therapists is similar to their contemporaries in psychotherapy or psychoanalysis, that is that their apparent altruism and fascination may be underpinned by deeply personal need, as described in Andrea Gilroy's doctoral research (Gilroy 1992). Their training alerts them to this system, and they continue to work with it, probably throughout their professional lives. It is thus possible to avoid the danger of patronizing their clients or assuming a role where the art process is seen only as a generalized amelioration of their plight, not as a serious treatment. Where therapeutically disposed but essentially untrained artists work with patients, this hazard may not be recognized. It is possible for hospital-based artists and art therapists to work felicitously together – this does in fact happen in some institutions, but it requires a clear declaration of intent from both parties.

It appears that where artists address the needs of the environment not only to decorate, but also to assist in its design as a 'machine for living in', they have an effective role to play. But it is vital that this task should remain free of patient participation. It follows that the art therapist colleagues of such artists must be equally clear of *their* role, perhaps following some of the models suggested earlier in this chapter. With a clear understanding of the demarcation of tasks and a disposal of myth-making in terms of the healing properties of working under the direction of a trained artist, it is possible for successful co-operation to develop, and for management to be accordingly educated.

It would seem that the existence of the hospital arts movement has provided art therapists with a significant challenge and the opportunity to clarify both what they hope to do and what they in reality achieve. If that is the case, then what was sometimes seen as a threat could be the basis of a useful advance in professional practice.

Conclusion

When the British Association of Art Therapists celebrated the 25th anniversary of its foundation in 1988 its members rightly congratulated themselves on the increased influence of the discipline and the widening horizons of its practice. The profession is better organized within and more widely recognized outside its boundaries today, but the necessity for development that I have described here contains elements of potential hazard, where the historic criticisms of art therapy again break the surface. The issue of the apparent brevity of professional training (which is addressed elsewhere) is one which is being confronted but not entirely solved and this will surely have implications in the future 'harmonization' exercises within the European Community. British art therapists will surely argue that their profession is the most organized and sophisticated in terms of its training procedures and its practice and that, along with only Holland in Europe, it has a career structure within the state medical service.

Many of our colleagues in Europe who currently practise art therapy do so in conjunction with another discipline: psychiatry, psychotherapy, family therapy or psychoanalysis, and art therapists in this country, who have engaged in the prolonged fight for recognition of the profession as discrete treatment, may well fear a dilution of their skills if their practice is seen as an adjunct to another enterprise.

The pressing need for research and the devising of new models appropriate to art therapy is a task that will not disappear as the increasing demands for appraisal and measurement of practice occur. This is not merely, I believe, in the interests of cost effectiveness, but a genuine need to resource effectively patient care. Art therapists will ultimately have nothing to lose in attempting to assess their practice and make judgements on its usefulness. It is vital that they themselves be involved in this process, which is clearly now inevitable, and do not see it as a hostile or destructive prescription. It is for art therapists themselves to explore and delineate the modifications necessary for their practice to continue to be effective professionally; it is no longer sufficient to believe in its power as an act of faith.

It is arguable that over the years of growth of the profession, some of its members, bedevilled by isolation and covert criticism, developed a 'siege mentality' which set themselves apart from their colleagues, in an attitude of necessary (or so it seemed) self-protection. There is now a pressing need for co-operation with colleagues of other disciplines, for dialogue and discourse as well as argument and for the exploration of new methods of practice in the light of new demands.

The traditional attitudes of the art therapist, the intuitive skills of empathy, insight and creativity are every bit as valuable as scientific method, but our work must be presented and analysed in an organized and understandable way if we are to survive at an institutional level. Assertions that are based only on feelings of wish fulfilment and beliefs that are naively expected to be shared without any real evidence will no longer be a fitting stance for the profession of art therapy in the 1990s. It will not be productive to collude with the legend of the artist as being set apart from the demands and constraints of life and it will certainly be short sighted to perpetuate the falsehood that artists are somehow 'visual' and therefore non-verbal!

I have referred to the debate between 'art as healing' and 'art psychotherapy' which is continuing within the BAAT as I write, and it is to be hoped that in time it will be clear that art psychotherapists are not eschewing their roots, foundations and history, but see their practice as part of an evolving discipline, committed to improvement in the lives of their clients and the services which care for them.

There seems to be, at present, a growing awareness of the importance of inner feelings and the inheritance of the individual and common history – ideas that, until very recently, seemed to exist only within the confines of psychoanalysis. It is a striking paradox that this apparent need to understand our lives more fully coexists within our culture with feelings of powerlessness and frustration in the face of the world's anguish. How we use this increasing awareness will continue to be a matter of concern and debate, and clearly not solely for art therapists, but the great existential questions will surely continue to lie at the heart of their practice.

Appendix A

9. Transferral of National Health Services to the community

In concluding the questionnaire we used the opportunity to ask all National Health Service Art Therapists about service development in their area. This seems a particularly pertinent question at present in the light of the recommendations made to the Government by the Griffiths Report on future responsibilities for 'Community Care' (1987).

9.1. (55.2%) of Health Service respondents said that they regarded at least part of their working week as being devoted to providing community health facilities.

However, from those who responded the majority (51.3%) said that their community work was for less than 7 hours per week.

At the other end of the Health Service Art Therapy spectrum only 8 members (5.9%) said their contract of employment was a more or less full-time community service commitment.

9.2. When asked about their community care caseload, it was clear from the responses from Art Therapists that the number of out-patients using Art Therapy was low. (16.4%) said they saw between 6–10 patients each week as a community service, and (11.9%) said they saw between 11–20. Referral of these patients was made from a variety of sources.

9.3 Whilst the majority of community Art Therapy services were wholly National Health Service funded, 14.8% of services were joint funded mainly with Social Services.

9.4 We finally asked Health Service Art Therapists whether they were aware of plans to transfer services within their institution to the community, to which 47.8% said yes. 90.6% – the vast majority of these practitioners – reported that they had been consulted and were involved in the transfer and planning of services.

(Source: Teasdale *et al.* (1990) *Survey of Conditions of Service for Registered Art Therapists*, London: MSF.)

Appendix B

Principles of professional practice for art therapists

Confidentiality

Transactions between the Art Therapist and the client should be confidential and kept within the framework of the therapeutic team.

Record keeping

A record of attendance should be kept and all art-work should be named, dated and stored during the therapeutic relationship. For very long-term clients problems of storage may mean that the position needs to be reviewed. It is advisable that art therapy case notes and art work should be kept for a minimum of three years.

Exhibitions

The Art Therapist should obtain permission from the client for the use of any information, verbal, recorded, written, or pictorial, acquired within the therapeutic relationship for the purposes of publication or education or exhibition, after fully disclosing to the client the nature of the use of such materials.

This principle may be waived three years after the close of treatment. In all cases anonymity should be respected.

Art Therapists should never be involved in the sale of work produced in the therapeutic setting.

The referral system

A written referral should be sought from an accountable agent. In the case of self-referrals a written referral would follow after the initial contact where possible.

Art Therapists should retain the right not to treat certain clients, following an agreed assessment procedure.

Caseload

Art Therapists should have adequate time to attend ward rounds, staff meetings, case conferences etc., and should negotiate one half day per week (or pro rata) for the administration of the art therapy department.

Art Therapists whilst liaising with other disciplines should ultimately specify their own case loads to suit their own preferred method of working, i.e. individual and/or group sessions. It is recommended that a 'closed' group should not exceed 8–10 people and an 'open' session should not exceed 12–15 people. There should be adequate time between sessions for preparation and record-keeping, and some record should be kept of all sessions.

Professional support/supervision

It is in the interests of Art Therapists to seek regular clinical supervision, ideally within the workplace.

This may take the form of individual or group sessions conducted preferably by an experienced Art Therapist.

Art Therapists should also seek support from other institutions, regional groups of BAAT, or related professionals.

Training

It is desirable that Art Therapists should have both study leave and financial support from their employment in order to attend in-service training programmes, lectures, workshops, and professional conferences. Art Therapists contributing to training programmes for colleagues or students should receive payment from their employers.

Minimum conditions

Art Therapists should have adequate facilities within which to practise. At the absolute minimum this would include: a self-contained room large enough for group work, a sink and running water, storage space and an administration area and telephone. Naturally this facility should comply with the standards set by the 'Health and Safety Act'.

Management

Art Therapists should have control over a financial allocation for materials and equipment and see maintenance of equipment levels as their responsibility.

Art Therapy should be directly represented on institutional management structures.

Self-employed art therapists

Art Therapists should adhere to professional rather than commercial standards in making known the availability of their service.

Art Therapists should communicate the availability of their service to related professions and referring agencies.

Art Therapists in private practice should ensure they receive adequate clinical supervision.

Art Therapists who work privately are advised to carry suitable insurance.

(Source: British Association of Art Therapists (1986) Principles of professional practice, BAAT.)

Appendix C

Professional responsibilities of art therapists

General position

The general position with regard to professional responsibilities held by art therapists.

An art therapist has a professional responsibility to provide to any National Health Service client the best available care and treatment within their competence and experience; to act in the interests of the client and to observe confidentiality of information.

The Principles of Professional Practice for art therapists issued by the British Association of Art Therapists merely states that, '. . . transactions between the art therapist and the client should be confidential and kept within the framework of the therapeutic team'. However, within multi-disciplinary teamwork, complete confidentiality cannot be observed, and the sharing of some client information is therefore a requisite of such teamwork.

In these circumstances guidelines on confidentiality may usually indicate that information shared should not pass beyond the team members. It is, of course, essential and the responsibility of the person providing the confidential information to ensure that those persons receiving it are discrete, reliable and responsible.

Further, it is vital that consent be obtained from patients or, in the case of children or adolescents, from parents or guardians to share information about them in this manner. Should consent not be obtained this must be accepted and will inevitably limit team collaboration.

The general legal position

The legal responsibilities of medical practitioners are enshrined in the National Health Act, 1946.

The additional responsibilities of consultant psychiatrists are contained in the Mental Health Act, 1983, and have recently been reaffirmed by the Royal College of Psychiatrists.

It is to be noted that the Royal College have distinguished carefully between 'Medical' and 'Clinical' responsibilities.

All health professionals have a 'duty of care' towards their clients which requires them to take reasonable care in all circumstances. The Tort of Negligence also requires professionals to recognise and observe the limits of their professional training and competence and to satisfy themselves that those to whom they refer their clients are appropriately qualified and or competent.

Some legal decisions may result in an apportionment of responsibilities. This, however, is a complication rather than a contradiction of the principle of individual 'duty of care'.

The Nodder Report – paragraph 6.17, D.H.S.S. 1980 – a major Department of Health and Social Security document, is clear on this point. . . .

There is, as we understand it, no basis in law for the commonly expressed idea that a consultant may be held responsible for the negligence on the part of others simply because he is the 'responsible medical officer'; or that, though personally blameless, he may be held accountable after the style of a military commander. A multi-disciplinary team has no 'commander' in this sense.

It follows that no professional can be held responsible for another professional's actions, unless he has full managerial authority over that person.

Medical versus clinical responsibilities

Medical responsibilities arise from formal training, qualifications and experience in medicine. The term 'clinical' has come to cover a variety of skills, professions and settings, and is too general to identify clear areas of professional responsibility.

By convention some medical practitioners also assume a responsibility for 'co-ordinating' the input of other professionals. The need for co-ordination in health care should not be confused with issues of leadership and 'ultimate' responsibility. Co-ordinating responsibility should normally coincide with prime responsibility.

Further, it is not possible to find a satisfactory nor generally accepted definition of the terms 'overall responsibility' nor 'ultimate responsibility'. These terms, arising from and often vigorously asserted in interprofessional disputes, are of little value because;

a they are too vague, and
b they are incompatible with the principle of individual professional responsibility arising from the Tort of Negligence.

For these reasons, and following the lead of the Clinical Psychologists, the Association has abandoned the use of these terms.

Prime responsibilities and primacy

The term 'prime responsibility' refers to the co-ordinating authority in casework, both in networks and in more formal terms.

The term suggests that prime responsibility includes the authority to:

a make personal assessment of the general needs of the case at the time of the assumption of prime responsibility;
b undertake personally any action needed, or to initiate such action through other staff;
c refer, when and as necessary, to colleagues and other independent agencies for collaboration in further assessment or action, or for action in parallel;
d keep continuous awareness of the progress of the case and take further initiatives as necessary;
e decide when to relinquish extended collaboration with colleagues or when to terminate all further action on the case.

The term 'Primacy' refers to the 'automatic' assumption of prime responsibility by a particular team member; that is to say, where primacy operates, the client is referred to and is under the continuing care of the person with the primacy, and not to the team.

A 'Key Worker' in a case may or may not hold primacy or prime responsibility for the case. The key worker is the front line contact for the client or family.

It is conceivable that the key worker would be a different person both from the professional taking prime responsibility in a particular case, and from the person assuming primacy in the team generally. Likewise, it is possible for one person to take all three roles in a particular case.

Clearly, to ensure clarity and efficiency of service for the client, it is important that the responsibilities of different professionals are explicitly agreed, both in the general functioning of the team and in the particular casework.

Authority and accountability

It is important to distinguish what people 'feel responsible for' from what they are actually responsible for, i.e. their 'formal accountability'. The test of accountability is that if . . .

... a person did not do something, did it poorly, or deviated from an established policy or procedure, the person could be considered negligent or to have breached their contract, and sanctions could be applied as a result – an extreme sanction being that they could be sacked. Accountability cannot be delegated.

(Ovretveit, 1984)

Accountability is not a binary concept

It is not the case that a person is accountable for all the actions of certain staff, or is not accountable in anyway even for keeping informed about their actions. Thus although an art therapist may not be held accountable for the clinical decisions of another art therapist, he/or she may be held accountable for recognising divergencies from the accepted standards of professional practice and other limits, and for taking what action he/or she can.

Authority, like accountability, is a social rather than a personal matter. Just as accountability needs to be distinguished from a person's feelings of responsibility, so the social facts of authority should be distinguished from the personal power of an individual, which may be based on experience, expertise, or personal charisma. Authority is the socially-established right to exercise sanctions over others, to initiate tasks, and to deploy resources. Authority can be delegated, but personal power cannot.

Authority is linked to accountability by a simple principle; the accountability of a role must match the authority of a role. This, therefore, means, an individual cannot reasonably be held accountable for matters over which he/or she has no authority.

The authority of leadership roles should be clearly defined and understood so as to prevent problems arising and to give a complete sense of professional expectations.

Four distinct leadership roles may be identified as follows:

Monitoring: authority to inquire, to persuade and to report, but not to instruct;
Co-ordinating and monitoring: additional authority to bring together relevant people and to report unresolved issues to a higher authority.
Policy setting: co-ordinating and monitoring authority plus additional authority to formulate policy, to keep specified staff within policy limits and to take disciplinary action where these limits are not observed, but not to override clinical decisions.
Full management: full authority and accountability for all aspects of the work of designated staff, including a veto on staff appointments, selection, delegation of work, staff appraisal, disciplinary action and evaluation of clinical work.

It is clear from the above terms that no one member of a multi-disciplinary team has any formal authority over other disciplines. It is usually informal authority which is exerted in such situations. However such authority problems may be resolved by the use of such mechanisms as illustrated below. ...

... often only certain aspects of authority of a leadership role are clearly specified ... other aspects ... are usually clarified and established as situations arise ... in effect a higher authority gradually clarifies the authority of the post ... as disputed cases arise. However, there are important areas of authority which need to be defined when the post is created. This is necessary to prevent too many issues being referred to a higher authority ... and to make clear to the powers they are assigned to carry out their work.

Ovretveit (1984).

Dual accountability

Professionals working in multi-disciplinary teams may experience divided loyalties, but strictly speaking have not usually had 'dual accountability' i.e. formal accountability to two different individuals for different aspects of their role.

With general management in the National Health Service, dual accountability may become much more prominent. For example, an art therapist may work in a team whose members are 'managerially accountable' to the 'Unit General Manager' but the art therapist is also 'professionally accountable' to a District Manager.

Obviously phrases such as 'professional accountability' are too vague. It is crucial to clarify or negotiate as far as possible which team members are responsible to whom for what.

Autonomy

Sometimes clinical 'autonomy' is asserted as a defence against imposed or assumed 'authority'.

In team conflicts both concepts are often used unclearly or inappropriately. Ovretveit (1984) distinguishes 'clinical autonomy' from 'practice autonomy'.

Clinical autonomy as far as art therapists are concerned is . . .

> . . . the freedom to exercise discretion in art therapy casework with individual clients, within reasonable available resources and other limits, and without that discretion being overridden or scrutinised by a higher authority, unless negligence or infringement of limits is suspected.

Clearly, therefore, where there is an apparent conflict of interest between the therapeutic role on the one hand, and other roles, the art therapist can insist that the integrity of the therapeutic role is maintained and is paramount, within available resources and other limits.

Practice autonomy is,

> . . . the freedom to exercise discretion in the immediate management and running of a practice, department or speciality, within defined limits and available resources and without that discretion being overridden or scrutinised by a higher authority unless negligence or infringement of limits is suspected.

(Ovretveit, op cit)

No autonomy is infinite. Clinical autonomy is exercised with the policies and priority constraints set by a manager (or policy setter).

Practice autonomy operates within resource and policy constraints of a manager, management team or health authority.

(Source: British Association of Art Therapists (1989a) Professional responsibilities of art therapists, BAAT.)

References

Arguile, R. (1990) 'I show you?: Children in art therapy, in C. Case and T. Dalley (eds) *Working with Children in Art Therapy*, London: Tavistock/Routledge, pp. 192–216.

The Attenborough Report (1985) *The Arts and Disabled People*, London: Carnegie UK Trust.

British Association of Art Therapists (1986) Principles of professional practice (see Appendix B).

—— (1988) Art therapy and the law: child abuse.

—— (1989a) Professional responsibilities of art therapists.

—— (1989b) Comments on the White Paper *Working for Patients*.

Burgess, A.W. and McCausland, M.P. (1981) Children's drawings as indications of sexual trauma, *Psychiatric Care* **19**: 50–8.

DHSS (1986) *Working Together for the Protection of Children: Guidelines for the Treatment of Child Abuse*, London: HMSO, pp. 1–2.

Donnelly, M. (1986) Norms of art therapy practice, unpublished.

Gilroy, A. (1992) Art therapists and their art. Unpublished DPhil. thesis, University of Sussex.

Griffiths, R. *et al.* (1988) *Community Care: Agenda for Action*, London: HMSO.

Liebmann, M. (1986) *Art Therapy for Groups*, London: Croom Helm.

Miller, B. (1984) Art therapy with the elderly and the terminally ill, in T. Dalley (ed.) *Art as Therapy*, London: Tavistock, p. 133.

McNeilly, G. Skaife, S. and Waller, D. (1990) Group analysis and arts therapies, *Group Analysis* **23**(3): 211–45.

Moss, L. (1987) *Art for Health's Sake*, London: Carnegie UK Trust, pp. 7, 8, 24.

Schaverien, J. (1987) The scapegoat and the talisman: transference in art therapy, in T. Dalley *et al.* (eds) *Images of Art Therapy*, London: Tavistock, pp. 74–109.

Teasdale, C. (1988) Community Care – A Report, *BAAT Newsletter*.

—— *et al.* (1990) *Survey of Conditions of Service for Registered Art Therapists*, London: Manufacturing Science Finance.

Waller, D. (1984) Similarities and differences between art teaching and art therapy in T. Dalley. (ed.) *Art as Therapy*, London: Tavistock, p. 11.

—— (1987a) Report on the arts therapies professions, in *BAAT Annual Report*.

—— (1987b) Art Therapy in adolescence, in T. Dalley *et al.* (eds) *Images of Art Therapy*, London: Tavistock, pp. 197–200.

—— (1991) *Becoming a Profession – A History of Art Therapy from 1940-1982*, London: Routledge.

Warnock, M. *et al.* (1978) *Warnock Report on Special Education*, London: HMSO.

Weir, F. (1987) The role of symbolic expression in its relation to art therapy: a Kleinian approach, in T. Dalley *et al.* (eds) *Images of Art Therapy*, London: Tavistock, pp. 109–28.

White Paper (1989) *Working for Patients*, London: HMSO.

3

The organizational context of art therapy

JACKY MAHONY

Introduction

Art therapy cannot be practised in a vacuum. Approaches are diverse and how they are applied will depend on the personal orientation of the art therapist concerned, the client group and the setting or organization in question. All these aspects need to be carefully considered in order to provide an integrated service. However, of all the many contributing factors that will affect the practice of art therapy, a major influence upon its functioning is likely to be that of the organization itself.

Integrating art therapy into an existing organization or setting can be difficult (see Cole 1975, Waller 1983, 1989, Waller and Boyadzhiev 1983, Molloy 1984, Maclagan 1985, Schaverien 1985, Edwards 1986 and 1989, Waller and Gheorghieva 1990). Indeed the introduction of a different discipline or modality, or even a new worker with a different methodology, into an established institution holds the potential for unanticipated problems (see Hamer 1989), friction and conflicts with other members of staff or disciplines, or the kind of far-reaching effects as written about, for instance, by Stanton and Schwartz (1954), Menzies (1970) and Baron (1987).

I shall be writing this chapter from the position of art therapist at the Henderson Hospital Therapeutic Community and will be examining the conditions that apply to art therapy at the Henderson as a specific example of the development of a different modality in an existing system. I will be discussing a problem that I have encountered in my work and, although it may perhaps be specific to the Henderson where particular conditions obtain, there will nevertheless be a more general application to other organizations and settings. My focus is on the resistance to art and art therapy at the Henderson in favour of 'work'/production-oriented groups and verbal psychotherapy groups. This resistance seems to involve a conflict of ideologies and value systems. I will look at the Henderson as a case-study in order to illuminate theoretical issues, attempting to take the position of 'participant-observer' when illustrating how the resistance affects the practice of art therapy. A therapeutic community is, of course, a very particular type of institution, but being a small, near autonomous system and one that is self-examining, the example of the Henderson may serve to highlight problems of introducing art therapy into any organization. This is not to suggest it is inevitable that there will be a clash of ideologies when art therapy is introduced into a therapeutic community. At another community the situation may be completely different. My aim is rather to show in this chapter how the culture of the organization is shaped by its history and how this will influence subsequent practice. Examining the history and cultural 'roots' of an institution can provide vital insight into its dynamics.

When there is a problem of integrating a new or different discipline, it has to be recognized and acknowledged by the worker or workers concerned. It will be manifested in a variety of ways according to the organization – for example, lateness of arrival to meetings on the part of staff and clients; non-attendance by clients or staff to groups and meetings; relegation of the worker(s) to the smallest/ most unsuitable facilities; institutionalized and systematic undermining (covert and unacknowledged); reduction of status; lack of official recognition (in brochures and so on); idealization. Given the recognition of an unsatisfactory situation, the next task is to understand the nature of the problem, its dynamics and their cause with a view to achieving, where possible, a more constructive and effective way of working. There will be reasons for what is happening, and hopefully change can be brought about or limitations acknowledged.

Theoretical considerations

All organizations are in a state of constant flux and change – dynamics constantly alter. As living systems, the components that go to make up the system – human beings – mutually interact in a highly complex way. Seemingly small events, when analysed, can be seen significantly to affect apparently unrelated parts, and eventually the organization as a whole (Stanton and Schwartz 1954). The endurance of a system depends on it remaining in equilibrium despite changes – it is in balance (James 1983). Given the need to maintain a balance, it is not surprising that the introduction into an organization of a discipline with a different ideology and cultural basis, such as art therapy, will have ramifications.

In his paper 'The institution as metaphor', Henzell (1983) describes how an institution possesses both overt and covert self-definitions – the covert level often being 'of a symbolic nature and sometimes unexaminable in terms of the institution's overt self-definitions' (p. 14). He explains:

> . . . the creation of an institution appeals to the practices, forms and goals of already existing institutions at both real (overt) and symbolic (covert) levels. An institution is metaphorical in the sense that, at its initiation, it will borrow schema and forms from other domains . . .

> (ibid.: 14)

He uses the example of Freudian psychoanalysis borrowing 'terminology from medicine, pathology and 19th century engineering: (the ''psychopathology'' of everyday life, "symptom" formation, "drives", "magnetic attraction", activating "forces", etc)'. He continues: '. . . like metaphors institutions also both enable and restrict certain forms of experience. Some schemata are allowed but others forbidden.' (p. 15) This sets a hidden agenda for the institution and unless perceived may present unaccountable difficulties for those within and unaware of it.

Several papers have been written about art therapy training in Bulgaria (Waller 1983, Waller and Boyadzhiev 1983, Waller and Gheorghieva 1990) which highlight the problems of introducing a new approach that not only had a different philosophy from the prevailing one but involved cross-cultural issues. The project of which Waller and Gheorghieva were co-directors was part of the World Health Organization's mental health programme and came under a priorital area entitled 'Psychosocial factors in primary health care'. Gheorghieva writes:

> . . . we wanted the project to be adaptable, and to be accepted by the system. It was a project through which we could ensure, for the first time in Bulgaria, that a truly regulated psychotherapeutic and psychosocial practice would emerge.
>
> (p. 33)

Psychiatric institutions themselves selected the trainees who thus:

> . . . represented the psychiatric system. It was in a way a test of the system . . . we did not have a truly motivated group. But we had a group consisting of people through which the system was ready to accept the change that we are proposing.
>
> (ibid.: 33)

Eventually an important function of the project became clear which would have been helpful to have understood at the beginning:

> . . . the project tested the level of openness of the psychiatric system towards psychosocial approaches and simultaneously stimulated the system to open a bit more . . .
>
> (ibid.: 35)

A hidden agenda (as described previously by Henzell) for the project.

Edwards has written about art therapists in large, traditional psychiatric institutions in terms of survival (1986, 1989). He considers:

> . . . possibly the most intractable problem facing art therapists concerns integrating their work into the institution in which they are employed. Integration is likely to prove problematic even in those situations where art therapy is clearly understood and recognised as being of worth . . . the problems art therapists face in this area cannot be explained simply in terms of personal issues, philosophical conflicts or confusion about roles. Neither should we place too much faith in the hope that the problem of integration may be finally resolved through even the most open and honest exchange of views, within the framework of a multi-disciplinary team meeting . . .
>
> (1986: 9–10)

He gives a comprehensive account of the difficulties surrounding working in a large institution and sees these as falling into three areas: recognition, integration and validation. He warns that the pressures to validate art therapy in scientific terms in order to become accepted may involve a devaluing of the 'language and concepts available to help us understand the nature of our work' (1989: 175). Orthodox psychiatry draws its ideas and power from science but this, he points out, is only one way of looking at the world. In concluding he emphasizes the importance of supervision and that recognition by the art therapist of their own needs is essential for their survival and that of art therapy itself.

Molloy (1984) looks at the problems of incorporating art therapy into traditional rehabilitation services. He states:

> As well as needing a job, enough to eat and a roof over their heads, people also need to find something in their lives that goes beyond day to day living, something that caters for spiritual and emotional needs.
>
> (ibid.: 2)

He describes how art therapy can contribute to the treatment in a rehabilitation setting, and points out:

> Unless attention is given to the underlying emotional conflicts throughout rehabilitation, they will simply force their way through and render practical progress impossible.
>
> (ibid.: 4)

It is clear from his paper just how fundamental the problems are for an art therapist when such a radically different philosophy is employed. Even the atmosphere can be undermining to the actual practice. Although the art therapist may feel it is impossible to practice in such a climate, Molloy considers:

> . . . more is at stake than a method of treatment. If art therapists do not take up this challenge, mental health services will be deprived of a whole way of thinking; one that focuses attention upon emotional problems in depth, rather than at a superficial level . . .
>
> (ibid.: 10)

Schaverien (1985) compares the psychiatric treatment methods of two hospitals – one a large psychiatric hospital and the other a therapeutic community – and their influence upon the practice of art therapy. She shows how 'the environment can either foster or inhibit creativity' (p. 3). In the large Victorian hospital, although changes had taken place, she appears doubtful as to how effective these could be:

> . . . the problem with traditions is that they tend to live on in the structure of the institution, in the layout of the building and in the terminology used by those who staff them.
>
> (ibid.: 3)

She looks at the roles of inmates and professionals in such an institution and states that by going along with and accepting the system, 'this adjustment which is common among patients and staff is death to creativity on any level' (p. 4). She considers that in this setting, '. . . art therapy is only able to exist within certain boundaries . . . even when given backing . . . can rarely offer a truly creative experience.' (p. 5) By contrast, the empowering of the patients in her account of the development of the therapeutic community and its philosophy, seems potentially fruitful ground for the growth of creativity. Indeed, the art department in the therapeutic community where she worked sounds inviting and she states that art was an 'integrated aspect of such a unit, the whole aim of which was release of creative energy' (p. 6).

Schaverien seems to be implying that there were complementary aims for art therapy and the therapeutic community she describes. Maclagan (1985), on the other hand, refers to the tension that arises between the verbal emphasis in the groups and the non-verbal imagery of art therapy in a community where verbal group psychotherapy was the main form of treatment. He describes the advantages of art therapy in such a setting for getting in touch with such aspects of the unconscious as the chaotic and the aggressive: 'even the unknown, the bottomless, or the inhuman can be "held" by being given form' (ibid.: 8). However, he notes that there is a lack of contact for other staff with the group and that there is a risk of art therapy 'drifting off into a somewhat separatist role, and of its methods coming into conflict with the practice of other groups' (ibid.). Despite these difficulties he emphasized the positive contribution of art therapy to this therapeutic community:

> The mere existence of a group in which irrational material is regularly tapped, and in which feelings, even if profoundly negative ones, are given a formal anchor, must have a considerable, if invisible, effect in preventing unconscious images from being confined within the individual, where they may fester in poisonous privacy.
>
> (ibid.)

Nowell Hall (1987) described her work in a day hospital run on therapeutic community lines, where she saw her approach as complementary to the main orientation of the unit:

> I had a growing conviction about art therapy . . . that its power lay most centrally with the 'art' and the creative process and I began to see that it could have a more powerful role to play in fostering individual growth than merely as an adjunct and catalyst to the verbal group psychotherapy.
>
> (ibid.: 160)

She states that the structure of the activity offered a chance for 'private space – a chance to go inside and reflect while being with others (particularly important in the group and communal culture . . .'(p. 184). The images helped people to verbalize as well as communicate and express 'more "dangerous" things to others (and also themselves) with or without words' (p. 184). In some institutions the existence of an art therapy department may stem from unformulated and unconscious reasons but at the hospital where Nowell Hall practised, the need seems to have been formulated in that patients and staff realized that there was a need to

> redress the balance by finding a complement to the verbal, analytical and more problem-centred approach; a need to help synthesis, to integrate

more effectively intellectual understanding with the feeling and experience.

(ibid.: 162)

Robinson (1984) explores problems raised by introducing art therapy with a Jungian approach into a pre-existing therapeutic framework and rather than focus on a particular setting, he draws on his experience in a therapeutic community for adolescent boys. He compares the emphasis given by a Jungian approach to the internal needs of the individual and the emphasis given by a therapeutic community ideology to the needs of the group and external behaviour. He considers that: 'A therapeutic community makes for very fertile ground given its strong familial, even tribal character and the energy generated by a large group of adolescents.' (ibid.: 83) However, he indicates the possible limitations of a therapeutic community for art therapy with a Jungian approach where the need for a safe, sheltered place and spontaneity are necessary for exploring the inner recesses of the individual unconscious. For Robinson, the emphasis of a therapeutic community on theoretical interpretation, the focus on behaviour and often the exposure and probing of 'deeply concealed psychological hurt' (p. 91) appears very much at variance to his approach. The therapeutic community of Withymead, founded by Gilbert and Irene Champernowne in 1942, offered a very different orientation from other early therapeutic communities. Central to this Jungian community was the use of arts. Stevens (1986) says of their community: 'At Withymead one felt the strength of people's commitment to work in the studios . . . there everybody felt that artistic creation was *real* work.' (pp. 84–5, author's emphasis).

(One might add 'real work rather than diversion' – the hidden message of many institutions being that art is not 'serious'.) Rehabilitation and adaptation to society was not one of the aims of this community in which a central aim was to develop the latent creative possibilities in all patients. Any activity was understood in terms of the symbolic processes at work in the individual, rather than focusing on the dynamics of the group.

At Barlinnie Prison, in Scotland, the Special Unit was developed for difficult and violent prisoners. The Unit was based on Maxwell Joneses model and the community system developed by Dennis Briggs in the American penal system. Stephen (1982) describes the early development:

> When the unit opened . . . it was apparent that traditional work models were not relevant because of the size of the unit, the numbers of prisoners involved and the personalities of the prisoners involved. Again the medical model of occupational therapy was adopted as acceptable, with the daytime activities being seen as therapeutic rather than productive. However, the arrival of art in all its dimensions opened up wider possibilities. Gradually, it was accepted that these (the Arts) should replace traditional work concepts.
>
> (ibid.: 47)

The art therapist at Barlinnie, Joyce Laing, adds:

> Now it has happened, it is difficult to imagine a prison unit of this nature

functioning without the arts. In the Barlinnie Special Unit the creative arts have become an integral part of daily living.

(Laing 1982: 56)

In the literature which I have discussed so far, art therapists have pointed out that the institutional context in which art therapy is practised must be taken into account if one is to understand the often puzzling attitudes of colleagues towards the discipline. There are similarities, for instance, between the evolution of art therapy at Barlinnie and the Henderson, as the following case-study of art therapy within that institution will illustrate.

The Henderson

The Henderson Hospital has a history of gradual development over more than 40 years as a socio-therapeutic model of a therapeutic community that found its particular role in the treatment of personality-disordered patients (see Whiteley 1980). Social analysis is its main tool.

Although modifications have been made, Maxwell Joneses original pattern for a therapeutic community developed in the 1950s remains. The Henderson is 'permissive', 'egalitarian', 'democratic' and 'communalistic' (four ideological themes of the unit identified by Rapoport 1960). It is a small residential unit with the prime function of therapy – facilitating change in the people who are in it. It is an exercise in living which provides opportunities for 'living – learning' situations (Mahony 1979): '. . . the institution's total resources, staff and patients, are self-consciously pooled in furthering treatment' (Jones 1968: 85).

The patients, or 'residents' as they are called, are young adults with emotional and social difficulties and a psychiatric diagnosis of personality disorder. They are of average or above average intelligence and live in the unit on a voluntary basis for up to one year; many have had psychiatric treatment and may also be criminal offenders. Almost all the residents have suffered severe privation or deprivation in one form or another in their early years and their lives have often been characterized by broken relationships and self-destructive behaviour.

The treatment method now is a combination of sociotherapy and group psychotherapy. In the early days Jones (1956) said there was a single therapeutic goal, namely the adjustment of the individual to social and work conditions outside – without any ambitious psychotherapeutic programme, implying that there was a rehabilitation emphasis. Nowadays the main approaches are tolerance of deviant behaviour, with the aim of achieving an understanding of its meaning through social analysis, and reality confrontation, aimed at learning from the experience and experimenting with new behaviour. Each day is highly structured with elaborate procedures that govern all that happens – rules and rituals are important and formal roles exist for implementing the aims of the unit. The 24 hours of each day are divided up into small and large, formal and informal groups. These may have social, administrative, management or psychotherapeutic functions, but all exist primarily for interactions to take place so that they may be examined and hopefully understood. Responsibility is shared between staff and residents in administrative, policy and management decisions as far as is appropriate and realistic, including the management of crises and problems, and decisions about who is admitted or discharged. There is a deliberate blurring of status differences amongst the staff, with for example, consultants joining in the cleaning and everyone going to a Sports Day.

The Henderson Hospital began life as part of the Belmont Hospital, Sutton, Surrey. I see these roots in the mother institution as a significant factor in influencing the growth and orientation of the later Henderson and consequently the development of art therapy at the unit. I shall therefore give a short outline of the history (see the Appendix to this chapter for a fuller history) from which it will be seen that work, industrial training, the protestant work ethic and utility are highly significant features of the institutions that pre-date the Belmont Hospital and hence the Henderson.

For almost the first 50 years (1853–1902) the institution was a Poor Law School for destitute children where an industrial training was given. It then had a brief career as a hospital for fever convalescents which closed and reopened as a home for 'mental deficients'. From 1908 to 1915 it became the Belmont Workhouse for Men. Twelve London parishes reputedly sent their worst characters there (men they were not able to accommodate themselves), and it was famed for its repressive regime. In 1910 there were riots because of the bad conditions. Occupations included wood-chopping, farming and oakum picking. From 1915 to 1922 it was a place of internment for enemy aliens and a hospital for German POWs. In 1922 it again became a workhouse called the 'Belmont Institution', and it was again notorious for terrible conditions. In 1928 it was renamed the 'London Industrial Colony': conditions improved and the occupations available to the inmates increased to include bricklaying and carpentry. In 1930 the Local Government Act of 1929 brought the Board of Guardians to an end and the Colony passed to London County Council. A more humane regime was introduced and renamed 'Sutton Training Centre'. Occupations widened again to include such things as tailoring and boot repairs. This whole period from 1853 to the Second World War was dominated by the effects of a deterrent Poor Law with all its cruelties, suffering and humiliation. Belmont's inmates were those unable to survive in the new industrial society. This characteristic and the sociological link with work, and industrial training, carried on through the next period.

In 1939 Sutton Training Centre closed to become the 'Sutton Emergency Unit' staffed by the Maudsley Hospital, which had been evacuated south to Sutton and north to Mill Hill School. Sutton became associated with the treatment of acute combat neuroses by physical methods, whereas Mill Hill Emergency Hospital was concerned more with a psychological and sociological approach. Maxwell Jones was assigned a 100 bed unit for 'Effort Syndrome' (Cardiac Neurosis) at Mill Hill, and the treatment led to didactic large group meetings which eventually began to include current social problems and the beginning of patient government.

Jones used similar methods in 1945 in a unit near Dartford for the rehabilitation of the most disturbed POWs returning from Europe and the Far East (Jones 1953). Everyone was found work in the local community as part of the treatment, and the success of the venture prompted the Ministries of Health, Labour and

Pensions to open the Industrial Neurosis Unit for 'social misfits' in 1947 at Sutton on an experimental basis (Jones 1968). The name was changed to the Industrial Rehabilitation Unit where the emphasis was on resettlement in work, and later changed again to the Social Rehabilitation Unit. The Unit's function became primarily concerned with the treatment of 'character disorders' and in 1959 became autonomous and renamed the Henderson Hospital. In 1954, Jones was awarded the CBE in connection with his work on rehabilitation and ten years of service on the National Advisory Council of the Ministry of Labour (Whiteley 1980).

To bring us up to the more recent past, Stuart Whiteley, who took over from Jones in 1966, reviewed the Henderson's development in a paper written in 1980 when the hospital was under threat of closure. Referring to the reissue of the book, *Community as Doctor* (Rapoport 1960) in 1967, he notes that there was at this time

> a general movement at Henderson towards a greater observation of the principles enunciated in Rapoport's postulates since we observed that some of the *same issues and problems of the early study still remained.* The new staff were less concerned with the old days and thereby more flexible and open to change. We moved from the rehabilitatory end of the spectrum towards the treatment goal and introduced a more consciously psychodynamic and sociodynamic perspective. In particular the *old workshop instructors were put aside.*
> (Whiteley 1980: 51, emphasis added)

One of the issues he was referring to that is relevant to the context of art therapy at Henderson was the conflict Rapoport pointed out 'between the *psychotherapeutic and treatment aims of the medical staff and the rehabilitatory aims of the lay workshop instructors*' (p. 46). He goes on 'we . . . became more role specific and conscious of the need for specialised training in group work in small, large and activity based groups' (p. 51). The present 'Creative Therapist' post (my own job title) grew out of the original lay 'Workshop Instructor' post.

From the historical background it can be seen that an almost unbroken strand concerning work, work training and production runs through the entire life of the institution that became the Belmont Hospital, and that this was continued by Maxwell Jones with his early emphasis on resettlement in work.

Art and art therapy at the Henderson

In the life of the Henderson, art therapy as a discipline is a relative newcomer. There is only one reference concerning the use of art in the early days in the unit's book of 1953 (Jones), where drawing was experimented with as a technique. Different types of group discussion were being explored as an alternative to individual interviews with 'the doctor'. Pomryn (1953: 91–2) described how a combination of music and drawing was introduced into the group activity and how attempts were made to link the images with their creator's psychiatric condition. It appears the experiments continued for a while with other patients in the unit taking part, but it seems there was soon a return to purely verbal discussion groups.

The marked absence of references to art (other than the one above) in the

Henderson's development seems significant and a description of the structure of the Industrial Neurosis Unit sheds some light on the difficulties there have been in introducing art therapy into the formal programme:

> . . . it is important that the work done in hospital should approximate as far as possible to the working conditions they will find outside. We believe that occupational therapy of the diversional type would be unsuitable for our population; art classes, etc. are encouraged in the patients' spare time, but the routine work day of 10 a.m. to 12. a.m. and 2 p.m. to 4 p.m. must be adhered to.
>
> (Jones 1953: 26)

Thus, at this early formative stage the unit's culture is determined and moulded by the kind of work ethic referred to above where traditional work concepts are of central importance. Art was seen as diversional and outside of the formal programme. When briefly tried out as a technique within the formal programme, it was administered by a doctor (serious) and not by an artist (not-serious).

Cole (1975) describes his experiences as the second art therapist at the Henderson. When he arrived there in 1973 he inherited a group entitled 'Fine Arts Group' – a 'work' group. He saw it as a priority to change the name and it became the 'Art Workshop'. The group was seen as 'slightly odd – much in the same way that the art department seems to be regarded in many secondary schools. . .' (p. 8) and was under pressure to 'produce':

> . . . a group that was expected to be almost totally concerned with the production of candles and pottery for sale to visitors and others, to earn the group money to buy more materials to start off this strange recurring process once more. Therefore, as a practice, it seemed to fall somewhere between social, occupational and industrial therapy. There were some individuals struggling with their own, often very expressive work, which was almost actively discouraged by most of the Community (following staff directives), as being 'skiving' real work, or being too individual. There was no attempt to use the actual work therapeutically, except in its execution.
>
> (ibid.: 9)

Whilst the pressure to 'produce' is less intense now, it still appears at times on covert levels, as I will later describe. Cole writes, '. . . there seemed to be a need expressed amongst the residents for some form of art therapy . . .', but when trying to introduce it, it became apparent that it was 'viewed with caution and suspicion by some staff'. He considers that '. . . it was tolerable to have a "productive" and "social therapy" orientated art group but not to have a psychotherapeutically . . . orientated art group.' (p. 9). He finally managed, after a great deal of work, to introduce two sessions a week that had a psychotherapeutic emphasis into the Art Workshop. He used 'Projective Art' methods where a common theme was decided by the group. In the other sessions the Art Workshop was encouraged to do:

> . . . group projects, such as murals . . . For, it is essential if there is to be continuing staff support for the art psychotherapeutic aspects of the group's

work, that the original function of work groups in Hendersonian terms is also maintained.

(ibid.: 10)

The psychotherapeutic orientation of art therapy still sits with discomfort now at the Henderson, and even though it has been established in the programme for four years, some members of staff have verbalized wanting to go back to the socio-therapeutic orientation of the art 'work' group.

In the introduction to this chapter I proposed that there has been and continues to be resistance to art and art therapy in favour of 'work'/production-oriented groups and verbal psychotherapy groups and that this resistance seems to involve a conflict of ideologies and value systems. In the past the problem has been manifested as follows:

1 Art does not seem to have appeared in the formal programme for 20 years or more. Acting and psychodrama, on the other hand, were mentioned very early on in some of the literature.
2 Since I have been working at Henderson it has taken several years to establish art therapy as a discrete discipline.
3 There seems to have been a resistance to recognizing that art therapy is a psycho-therapeutic method, art being well-established as a so-called 'work' group rather than as an art therapy group. When I arrived the art therapy group was a very peripheral part of the programme.
4 There has been pressure on the art work group to 'produce' objects, as graph-ically described by Cole (1975).
5 Art therapists have been employed but an art therapy group as such either did not exist or was as previously described.
6 There appears to exist an ambivalence towards the use of art – for example, my post is that of 'Creative Therapist' rather than that of 'Art Therapist', despite several art therapists having been previously employed.
7 There was little official recognition of art therapy, or even evidence that it existed at all, other than good art facilities, i.e. no office, no job description and little mention in information leaflets to residents, visitors and other professionals.

As the current art therapist in post I see myself as responsible for providing an art therapy service appropriate to the needs of the Henderson and its residents. However, the post I applied for was entitled 'Creative Therapist' and evolved from that of lay workshop instructor. More recent post-holders have included occupational therapists, art therapists and a social therapist 'with special interest' in art. Previous art therapists have not stayed in post very long (18 months, two years) and other staff have reported that they were isolated in the staff team. Since the workshop instructor post there seem to be continuing difficulties which have yet to be satisfactorily resolved.

The history of the post leads me to several hypotheses. It may, for example, be felt that the person is more important than the profession/service; the title 'Crea-tive Therapist' might indicate an ambivalence towards art therapy and also seems to suggest that the organization has an unformulated need for somebody or something that is not provided by the rest of the structure, perhaps to complement or provide a balance to a predominantly verbal culture. Rapoport (1960) and Whiteley (1980) refer to conflicts surrounding rehabilitatory/treatment dilemmas, and Whiteley remarks there was a conscious move in the unit towards more specialized training. But Cole (1975) pointed out that the art workshop was accused of not making any essential product or performing any practical function.

There still seem to be unacknowledged residues of an ideology from Henderson's history that may no longer be appropriate or may cloud the conceptual thinking about the structure of the unit. Throughout its history, starting with the Poor Law Schools and Workhouse, there was at the Henderson an almost unbroken sociological link with work, industrial training and rehabilitation. The inmates of Belmont were the impoverished, the deprived and the destitute, casualties from the industrial revolution unable to fit into this society. Maxwell Joneses orientation, with his links with the Ministry of Labour, seemed to be one of rehabilitation for work. The roots of the inherited culture of Henderson relate directly back through industrial rehabilitation to the Victorian workhouse with its attendant work ethic.

With work groups, the therapeutic value intrinsic in repairing or replacing broken chairs or windows can be seen to reside not in the creative process of these acts, but in their social value in relation to the community, the social responsibility and taking one's place in the community. Value is obtained not within the creative processes of the individual but rather in the manner and consequences of his or her social interaction with others. Part of the therapeutic effect is the degree to which the individual making the repairs is prepared to subordinate his or her own desires, which might be to take the afternoon off, read quietly or go to the pub, in favour of the collective good. This is one of the areas of tension within a therapeutic community (and indeed in most psychiatric hospitals) between art therapy and work-oriented therapy. It is also the area where there is conflict between two defined roles of a therapeutic community, i.e. the task of facilitating the therapeutic community process and the task of attending to the individual needs of the resident. There is a danger of overcompensating in favour of utility. The community process attends to 'external' behaviour/socio-cultural adjustment/rehabilitation, i.e. sociotherapy, whilst individual needs attend to 'inner' psychic processes/individual personality integration/treatment, i.e. psychotherapy.

The strain towards utility from which, amongst other factors, art therapy has suffered in the past, has had a strong hold. Rapoport (1960) considered that there was continual strain towards making the hospital a miniature version of society outside in order to avoid institutionalization. Resolution of the 'treatment or rehabilitation' dilemma is the central aim of Rapoport's entire book, and in examining the implications of his research, he recommends distinguishing conceptually between activities oriented to *treatment* aims and activities oriented to *rehabilitation* aims. It is in this context that the art work group and the art therapy groups have arisen – one kind of art group with sociotherapeutic aims and the other with psychotherapeutic aims. In the past, art therapy at Henderson was not seen to fall within the area of 'treatment' but instead grew out of the sociotherapeutic side – the work group. That it has become more accepted as a psychotherapeutic method is in line with a trend developed gradually over the years. In this respect, I consider that the change in title of the post lay 'Workshop Instructor' to that of 'Creative Therapist', whilst demonstrating ambivalence towards art therapy, none the less represents an analogous change in direction for the Henderson away from its inherited cultural tradition. It could be seen to signify within the formal structure of the organization that the previous emphasis on rehabilitation and work therapy was been replaced by one that actively fosters creativity by employing a member of staff with that designation.

The awareness on the part of the staff that art therapy can operate at another level where there is less ability to maintain control and rationalize may have affected the development of art therapy in several ways. It seems to be identified by staff and residents on a largely unconscious level with 'feelings'; the art therapy groups are seen as a place to 'express how you are feeling'. For the majority of residents and consequently the organization as a whole, this is a dangerous encounter (as written about by Maclagan (1985)), but an encounter that is at the heart of the therapeutic work that has to be done. Now art therapy is a component of the treatment programme for every resident, in contrast to it being an option. Due to the fire in 1987, it is no longer located in a separate building rooted in Henderson's past, but within the Henderson itself, thereby achieving a more integrated position both physically and structurally within the programme. For the time being a reasonably satisfactory resolution regarding the position of art therapy seems to have been achieved. I will now describe the implementation of a new art therapy programme at the Henderson in some detail, and consider the effects on my practice as an art therapist.

Practice

Until January 1987 art therapy was a voluntary, open group occurring once a week and it was 'in competition' with three other groups. It then changed to become something in which all residents take part throughout their stay, together with a weekly experience of psychodrama. It is a greatly enhanced situation offering a group experience that can grow and develop using two very different approaches. An experience in psychodrama can be worked on two days later in art therapy and followed up in psychodrama the following week and so on. In terms of the community life on a particular day, the art therapy group might be working on one particular aspect and the psychodrama group on a contrasting aspect of a particular dynamic. Prior to January 1987 art therapy and psychodrama had been peripheral groups in the programme. Their position as 'open', voluntary groups that were part of a choice of groups gave certain 'messages' that I felt were detrimental. The fact that there was a choice of groups could have indicated that not everyone could benefit from them or use them. Approximately a third of the residents never attended art therapy, or came once and said they had 'tried' it and they didn't 'get anything out of it'. Art therapy was a choice alongside 'welfare', a group where DHSS matters are discussed and sorted out, and 'visitors', where residents talk to visitors about the unit. New residents were encouraged to go to both these latter two groups, thereby inferring that art therapy might be damaging in certain circumstances. Similarly, psychodrama was a choice with 'leavers' and 'role play', and psychodrama staff felt, at that time, that residents should be in a certain phase of treatment (i.e. the middle) when attending psychodrama – therefore helping to produce the myth that it was a dangerous group.

Because the art therapy and psychodrama groups were open and only occurred once a week, they were probably seen as unimportant and low in status, implying a lack of confidence in their effectiveness. The peripheral position of the groups could be seen to reinforce the importance placed on talking or predominantly verbal modes of expression. It is sometimes said that the treatment *is* talking, but an important part of the treatment is examination of and experimenting with behaviour which includes non-verbal forms of expression and action or doing things.

In its position in the programme, the art therapy group was underused and undervalued. I felt this affected the potential use of the group by its members and the value they placed on their work and participation in it. Although there was a core group of members, so that a certain amount of group culture existed, it seemed to me that the group as it was could never realize the possible potential that it had for the individuals who used it. The group was always dealing with separation issues with its constantly changing population. Anxiety was often very high in the group, adversely affecting people who were 'trying out' art therapy as well as affecting other aspects of the group, and staff anxiety was also high – it was never possible to know who was going to arrive or what might happen.

In my view the nature of an open group increases the possibility of splitting; an individual can off-load undesirable and uncomfortable feelings on to the group, leaving themselves free to invest another area or group with their 'good' feelings ('hit and run'). The peripheral position of the voluntary, open art therapy and psychodrama groups seemed to reflect a disproportionate dependency on verbal group psychotherapy, i.e. orthodox psychiatry in the medical model, and concepts of work as located in the work groups. The new groups that started in January 1987 arose out of several years of discussion and were finally agreed to by the staff group at a study day in September 1986. They were part of a number of decisions made on that day that had considerable effect on the programme. In three months the changes were instigated (see Table 3.1) which made the structure firmer and expectations clearer, as Rapoport had suggested.

The art therapy groups are group-analytic in orientation and approximately half the two-hour session is used for the image-making and half for discussion. I work with a co-therapist who is in both groups indefinitely, and a third member of staff in each group, who stay for six months. The staff teams of art therapy and psychodrama meet before each session for 20 minutes to discuss the previous sessions and also after the actual groups for half an hour in order to process the afternoon's work. All the after-groups at Henderson also have support, supervision and training functions. Every resident belongs to one of the two groups that meet one afternoon for art therapy and on another afternoon for psychodrama. A new resident is allocated in their first week according to the numbers in the groups and the distribution of men and women; so far the groups have had a maximum of 14 residents in each. Some residents belong to an art therapy group and the art work group.

Table 3.1 Table of changes, January 1987

Previous programme	*New programme*
Leavers' group: a voluntary open group for practical and emotional issues surrounding leaving the unit. On a Wednesday afternoon at the same time as psychodrama group and role play.	*'Leavers':* to take place at same time as small groups, for same issues as before but residents to join in latter stages of their stay, instead of continuing in their small groups (leaving to become a formal stage in the treatment programme).
Community meal: cooked by residents and staff, for whole community. Took place monthly on a Tuesday lunchtime. Evening meal provided by hospital.	*Cooking the evening meal:* to take place every evening. Voluntary rota of residents, some staff involvement. Introduced gradually and on a trial basis. Eventually very successful.
Psychodrama group: voluntary, open group. Seen as 'dangerous'. Wednesday afternoon.	*Psychodrama:* all residents to belong to one of two groups, two afternoons a week.
Role play group: voluntary, open group. Seen as 'fun' and/or 'silly'. Wednesday afternoon. Both groups actually did similar things, but role-play group offered training opportunities for new staff in a way that other groups did not.	*Role play:* ceased to exist but staff joined psychodrama group. Initially group called Psychodrama and Role Play.
Art therapy group: voluntary, open group. Thursday mornings at same time as three other groups – 'welfare', 'visitors' and an outside work project.	*Art therapy:* all residents to belong to one of two groups on two afternoons a week.
	Work groups: sessions reduced from four to three afternoons a week.

The art work group is a 'studio-like' situation, where all the members, staff and residents, do their own work or occasionally group projects, for one-and-a-half hours. After this there is a discussion for half an hour with a cup of tea, mainly focusing on interactions and how people have got on with the 'task' of the group, rather than focusing on the artwork as in the art therapy groups. Staffing is similar to the art therapy groups.

There are three work groups, the other two being 'cookery' and 'gardening and maintenance'. New residents spend a week in each and then choose one to stay in for the rest of their stay. The other groups have a similar structure to the art work group. These two 'work groups' are seen as producing things for the community, of doing real work that is necessary for the unit.

In a therapeutic community, staff have to become familiar with a constant shifting and blurring of roles as they move from one situation to another – from being therapist in a group one moment, to washing up with a resident from that group the next. However, it should be added that the transference and counter-transference have to be borne in mind all the time, for rather than being weakened or diluted, it seems to be intensified.

As art therapist in the two different types of groups for which I am responsible, I see myself in theory as having two fairly distinct roles although, as I have indi-cated, the issues involved are quite complicated when putting them into practice. The main apparent difference is that in the art work group I do my own artwork along with everyone else, and in the art therapy groups I do not take part in the art-making process although the other two staff do so. In the art therapy groups I see my main function and role as that of the 'door-keeper' in a symbolic sense, or guide who follows the group (I see the latter as a paradox rather than a contra-diction), one who is there to facilitate the 'journey' or process of the individuals and the group but who has to maintain a distance or objectivity from that process in order for it to take place for others.

In the art work group the containing or holding position I am describing is partly given over to the residents in order that the more sociodynamic function of the group can take place. In the art work group skills are shared amongst its members; for instance if someone comes to me wanting to learn to throw a pot on the wheel, I will usually suggest they ask a resident who has done some throwing to give them a hand. Staff, including myself, can be seen by the residents to struggle also with trying to master some process or problem, including the periodic 'lack of inspiration' which sometimes can also usefully be seen to accompany feel-ings that are being shared by the group as a whole. Ordinary fallibilities are apparent and the residents have the opportunity to see themselves as possessing particular abilities or qualities that a staff member might not have, and that everyone has their own particular areas of skills and experience.

In the art therapy groups transference issues sometimes emerge in how my not taking part in the art-making process is seen – for example, it may be experienced as holding and protective or it may remind someone of a particular incident when they were at school or in prison. In a situation like a work group, art therapists need to feel secure enough in themselves and their creative processes to expose themselves in their own artwork; also to feel free enough to be creative, whilst still being a key figure who has responsibility for, and has to maintain an awareness of, that group and its process. It is also important in this type of situation for the art therapist to be aware of and familiar with their own personal imagery and how this may be resonating with the group.

Phenomena relating to the context of art therapy at Henderson

In order to illuminate points I have discussed in this chapter, I include a descrip-tion of certain events that occurred in the ongoing life or large group of the community when it was in crisis. The time was the period immediately after the major fire in 1987 that ended the mother building – what had been Belmont Hospital.

The situation for art therapy had changed considerably with the introduction of the new groups. Further changes occurred as a result of the fire. The art and psychodrama and the gardening and maintenance workshops which were part of the old Belmont Hospital complex were rendered unusable due to demolition work. The management eventually agreed to provide us with facilities within our own building, which was separate from the old Belmont buildings. In the mean time, we had to cope with the emergency and much uncertainty about the future. For a month, not only were there no workshop facilities or staff library where the 'sensitivity' group was held, but there was no heating, hot water or cooking facilities (this was December). Many residents and all the staff were ill at some point, except the consultants and nursing officer; staff morale plummeted. We were worried about the residents and asked them if they wanted to make an emergency move to nearby empty NHS premises, but they were adamant we should stay, feeling that we would not get back in if we left the building (the staff felt the same). The art work group moved into three empty bedrooms on either side of a corridor, with a basic range of materials, the cushions and the easels from the old art and psychodrama room. After extensive and sometimes fraught discussions and negotiations within the staff group and with the management, plans were drawn up to convert most of one wing on the top floor into an art therapy department, and to roof over an area outside, situated in the middle of the building for the gardening and maintenance group, making a new workshop. These two new areas have the advantages of being *in* the building and so can be used at any time. Facilities for the staff were lost (the library and seminar room) and could not be reprovided in the foreseeable future due to lack of space. Psychodrama would have to take place in the '9.15' room.

One of the fundamental concerns throughout discussions was that of space and how it should be used. This relates to previous discussion in this chapter in that the staff team had to struggle with issues arising from its past culture when it came to making decisions of this kind. Many factors came into play and appeared on different levels in the community life; dilemmas surrounding central themes found expression and became located in particular events in the community. For example, for the first two weeks after the fire the art work group refused to use the third bedroom. For eight or nine residents and possibly three staff to use two rooms designed for a maximum of two in each seemed appalling to me (the cramped and freezing conditions made me think of the workhouse). But the group was resolute, saying that the physically split situation seemed difficult enough to cope with – not knowing what was happening in the other room, not being able to see everyone and wondering what someone was going to do if they left the room. They felt a third room would make the group even more fragmented. Further, they felt there would be anger from others not in the art work group if they used another room.

The motivating forces behind this reluctance to get basic needs met seemed to be fear of disintegration of the group, having lost the security of the art room and fear of attack from outside if they asserted a right to have adequate space to carry out their activities as a group – as if fearing disapproval of these activities, an envy or an ambivalence towards them. On an unconscious level, it seems that the group was playing out a situation that was occurring in the staff room. Whilst I was negotiating adequate permanent space for an art department, the group seemed to sense or anticipate our anxiety or anger about this. At the time I was under pressure from the staff group to accept a much smaller space than I felt was practical.

Eventually, the art work group decided to try a third room with the old art and psychodrama room cushions in it (familiar, comforting objects), to meet in there at the beginning of each group and have tea and the after-group there. There *were* grumblings about the art group using three bedrooms from others not in the group, but it was accepted.

Later, the size of art facilities for which I was negotiating was also accepted. However, at one point the issue concerning how to use available space became polarized in a conflict between the gardening and maintenance group staff, and myself. They wanted the same space as the art room despite having different needs as a group. At that time their workshop was only used three afternoons a week by a maximum of nine or ten people and then it was usually as a base from which they worked – whether in the garden or around the building. As referred to earlier, it is a group seen to be concerned with 'work' for the good of the community. One staff member from that group said they felt I was 'trying to push them out into a corner'. On one level it was as if the 'work' and sociotherapeutic needs of the community were seen to be in jeopardy, with strong feelings being aroused by the possibility of art therapy obtaining a bigger space in the building. It can be seen from this that the art work group appears to have unconsciously picked up a dynamic of the organization and acted it out before it emerged so clearly in the staff group.

Another situation that had been on-going for about a year came more into the open at this time. The community had agreed that the art work group would choose artwork done by residents to be put up with perspex and corner mounts around the unit. The work could be changed from time to time. Having chosen the work, there then seemed to be a paralysis when it came to putting it up on the walls. The gardening and maintenance group were too busy. The screws were too small. There wasn't enough work group time to do it, and so on and so forth. After many months an art group staff member finally managed to get up two in the main corridor on the ground floor. More months elapsed.

After the fire, the gardening and maintenance group staff were complaining that the group did not have enough work to do without the workshop. I reminded them about the pictures but they said now that the residents were refusing to put them up. And, as if to illustrate the discussion in the staff room, a gardening and maintenance group resident angrily said in the '9.15' community meeting that the art work group should put up the work themselves. However, soon after this I was away, and on returning was surprised to find that not only had the work started on the new art room, but the artwork was being put up on the walls of the '9.15' room.

Although there have been complaints that the art work group does not contribute or produce anything for the community, for over a year what it was offering in a concrete, visible way was effectively not accepted. With the new art room being physically created in the building, with manifest space for everyone that can be used at any time of day or night, suddenly the artwork was put up, as if it no longer posed a problem or a threat. Interestingly, the first picture to be put in the '9.15' room was a portrait of the new consultant, as if adding a touch of authority to the task. Also, the new art therapy groups started at the same time as the appointment of this consultant.

The phenomenon of the fire in 1987 forced change on the organization in a way that is difficult to conceive of happening without this outside event. In the January before the fire, art therapy was introduced into the formal programme and this major change was consolidated by the unforeseen circumstances of the fire, resulting in the art facilities, previously housed in the old Belmont Hospital, being moved into the Henderson itself.

Fire has figured significantly in Henderson's mythology in that it actually burnt down in 1977 and the unit was moved out of the Belmont Hospital into the present building – a nurses home. This fire resulted in connections with the mother building being partially severed, leaving what had previously been the rehabilitation workshops still in the original Belmont Hospital buildings. The 1987 fire finally severed these last connections. A new order could be seen to be coming out of the destruction of the old.

Conclusion

Henderson, as a therapeutic community, has evolved organically from its origins, where it was predominantly concerned with rehabilitation for work, to the present day where it offers an integrated treatment programme, including art therapy, for a specific client group. When I started at the unit, art existed in two forms: an established so-called work group, and a peripheral art therapy group. In this chapter I have postulated that there has been a resistance to art and art therapy in favour of work-oriented groups and verbal psychotherapy groups, involving a conflict of ideologies and value systems. The historical context illuminates the protracted influence of the work ethic, although there has been a steady development away from work-oriented rehabilitation. There has also been a continuing conflict in the area between what is seen as 'treatment' and what is seen as 'rehabilitation', which has manifested itself whenever any decision has to be made. Over the years there has been a gradual move towards specialized training, clearer structure and more explicit expectations. The events I have described took place at a particular time in the history of the Henderson. Since then yet other developments and dynamics have taken place which themselves have altered significantly the practice and position of art therapy within the organization and which perhaps can form the subject matter of some future work.

Thus, the organization in or for which an art therapist works will affect, by the workings of that institution and its underlying ethic, the functioning of art therapy and the manner in which the art therapist can practice. In an institution where verbal interactions predominate (which is most institutions), art therapy involves a shift to an unfamiliar area that may represent a potentially dangerous encounter. There can be a clash of ideologies when trying to introduce art therapy into an existing organization, but art therapy can provide opportunities not easily fulfilled by verbal methods. An awareness of this may contribute to the ambivalence felt by staff towards art therapy. Whilst current members of an institution may be unaware of its historical background, nevertheless residues of previous organizational preoccupations still exert a potent influence, albeit at an unconscious level. In many institutions where art therapists work, from social service day centres to the (ever decreasing) large hospitals, there is a danger that utility and the emphasis on social and rehabilitation issues might override the creative process at work in the individual. This is an area of tension not only between art therapy and work-oriented therapy, but also between the two tasks of therapeutic communities and other institutions that work with the mentally ill and handicapped, i.e. that which has external, outward-looking concerns of social adaptation and that which has internal, inward-looking concerns of personality integration.

Appendix: History of Belmont Hospital and Henderson Hospital

1853 'South Metropolitan District School' – a Poor Law School administered by Boards of Guardians to house, feed and educate 1,000 destitute children up to the age of 16. Built as a result of the 1844 Act requiring construction of 'schools' to train these children. An industrial training including: carpentry, shoemaking, millinery and farming 50–60 acres around the school. There was also music – some went into military bands on leaving.

1902 School closed after 1870 and 1902 Education Acts providing primary education for all. It was sold to Metropolitan Asylums Board and became a hospital for fever convalescents, which soon closed.

1905 Partly reopened as a home for 'mental deficients'.

1908 Whole building taken over to become 'Belmont Workhouse' for 1,200 men. Twelve London parishes sent the able-bodied paupers they were not able to accommodate themselves, supposedly their worst characters. It was famed for its repressive regime and in 1910 300 inmates rioted against the conditions. 'I am told by some who have been there that prison fare is much better and the men are all clothed in rags.' Occupations included wood-chopping, farming and oakum-picking.

1915 The workhouse closed to become a hospital for German POWs and a place of internment of enemy aliens.

1922 Reopened by Conservative Minister for Health, Sir Alfred Mond, as a workhouse 'Belmont Institution'. It was notorious for insufficient food and filthy, rat-infested conditions. '900 men herded together under the most hopeless and servile conditions.' There were accusations of it being a 'slave colony'. In 1927 a Stepney Poor Law Guardian is quoted when talking about the most work-shy in his borough as saying: 'We are going to send them to Belmont. They will have to work there, we will teach them to call Stepney "cushy".'

1928 It was renamed the 'London Industrial Colony'. Conditions improved and occupations increased to include painting, bricklaying and carpentry.

1930 Local Government Act of 1929 brought Board of Guardians to an end and Colony passed to London County Council. Renamed 'Sutton Training Centre'. Numbers were reduced to 685 and a more humane regime introduced. Occupations widened to include tailoring, boot repairs, car repairs and sign-writing.

1939 Became the 'Sutton Emergency Unit' for the treatment of acute combat neuroses.

1946 Became 'Belmont Hospital'.

1947 'Industrial Neurosis Unit' opened for young adult chronic unemployed in London area. 100 beds. Population proved to be composed largely of severe character disorders mostly from broken homes. Psychiatric training provided no treatment modalities but experience from previous years prepared Jones to listen to and learn from the patients. The staff admitted their limitations and asked for their help not only in 'treating' their problems but in keeping discipline. Name of unit changed to 'Industrial Rehabilitation Unit' and later to 'Social Rehabilitation Unit'.

1959 Unit became autonomous and renamed 'Henderson Hospital'.

References

Baron, C. (1987) *Asylum to Anarchy*, London: Free Association Books.

Bion, W.R. (1960) *Experiences in Groups*, London: Tavistock Publications, pp. 8–13.

Bridger, H. (1946) The Northfield Experiment, *Bulletin of the Menninger Clinic* 10(3): 71–6.

Carrell, C. and Laing, J. (eds) (1982) *The Special Unit, Barlinnie Prison, its Evolution through its Art*, Glasgow: Third Eye Centre.

Cole, P. (1975) Art therapy at the Henderson Hospital, *Inscape* 12: 6–10.

Edwards, D. (1986) Three years on: surviving the institution, *Inscape,* Summer: 3–11.

—— (1989) Five years on: further thoughts on the issue of surviving as an art therapist, in A. Gilroy and T. Dalley (eds) *Pictures at an Exhibition*, London: Routledge, pp. 167–78.

Fraser, D. (1973) *The Evolution of the British Welfare State*, London: Macmillan.

Hamer, N. (1989) Psychodrama in a therapeutic community, *Journal of the British Psychodrama Association* 4(1): 23–40.

Henzell, J. (1983) The institution as metaphor, in K. James (ed.) *The Institution*, Herts College of Art, pp. 14–16.

James, K. (1983) The institution as a living body, in K. James (ed.) *The Institution*, Herts College of Art, pp. 8–13.

Jones, M. (1953) *The Therapeutic Community*, NY, Basic Books.

—— (1956) The concept of the therapeutic community, *American Journal of Psychiatry* 112(8): 647–50.

—— (1968) *Social Psychiatry in Practice*, Harmondsworth: Penguin.

Kubler, G. (1971) On the colonial extinction of the motifs of pre-Columbian art, in C.M. Otten (ed.) *Anthropology and Art*, NY: Natural History Press, pp. 212–26.

Laing, J. (1982) The role of the arts in the special unit, in C. Carrell and J. Laing (eds) *The Special Unit, Barlinnie Prison, its Evolution through its Art*, Glasgow: Third Eye Centre.

Maclagan, D. (1985) Art therapy in a therapeutic community, *Inscape* 7–8.

McNeilly, G. (1989) Group analytic art groups, in A. Gilroy and T. Dalley (eds) *Pictures at an Exhibition*, London: Routledge, pp. 156–66.

Mahony, N. (1979) Chapter 9, in R.D. Hinshelwood and N.P. Manning (eds), *Therapeutic Communities*, London: Routledge and Kegan Paul.

Main, T.F. (1964) The hospital as a therapeutic institution, *Bulletin of the Menninger Clinic* 10(3): 66–70.

Malloy, T. (1984) Art therapy and psychiatric rehabilitation, harmonious partnership or philosophical collision, *Inscape,* **Summer**: 2–11.

Menzies, I.E.P. (1970) The functioning of social systems as a defence against anxiety, Tavistock. Institute of Human Relations Pamphlet No. 3.

Nowell Hall, P. (1987) Art therapy: a way of healing the split, in T. Dalley *et al.* (eds) *Images of Art Therapy*, London: Tavistock Publications, pp. 157–87.

Otten, C.M. (ed) (1971) *Anthropology and Art*, NY: Natural History Press.

Pomryn, B.A. (1953) Techniques in group formation, Chapter VI in M. Jones *et al. The Therapeutic Community*, NY: Basic Books.

Rapoport, R.N. (1956) Oscillations and sociotherapy, *Human Relations* IX(3).

—— (1960) *Community as Doctor*, London: Tavistock Publications.

Robinson, M. (1984) 'A Jungian approach to art therapy based in a residential setting', in T. Dalley (ed.) *Art as Therapy*, London: Tavistock Publications, pp. 82–95.

Schaverien, J. (1985) Creativity and the institution, *Inscape*, Autumn: 3–6.

—— (1987) The scapegoat and the talisman: transference in art therapy, in T. Dalley *et al. Images of Art Therapy*, London: Tavistock Publications, pp. 74–108.

Stanton, A. and Schwartz, M. (1954) *The Mental Hospital*, NY: Basic Books.

Stephen, I.B. (1982) The effect of the Special Unit on prison staff, in C. Carrell and J. Laing (eds) *The Special Unit, Barlinnie Prison, its Evolution through its Art*, Glasgow: Third Eye Centre, pp. 47–8.

Stevens, A. (1986) *Withymead*, Coventure Ltd.

Waller, D. (1983) Art therapy in Bulgaria, Parts I and II, *Inscape*, April: 12–15; October: 15–17.

—— (1984) A consideration of the similarities and differences between art teaching and art therapy, in T. Dalley (ed.) *Art as Therapy*, London: Tavistock Publications, pp. 1–14.

—— (1987) Art therapy in adolescence: a metaphorical view of a profession in progress, in T. Dalley (ed.) *Images of Art Therapy*, London: Tavistock Publications, pp. 188–213.

—— (1989) Musing cross culturally, in A. Gilroy and T. Dalley (eds) *Pictures at an Exhibition*, London: Routledge, pp. 179–88.

—— and Boyadzhiev, V. (1983) Art therapy and its relationship to psychiatry in Bulgaria, in K. James (ed.) *The Institution*, Herts College of Art, pp. 73–6.

Waller, D. and Gheorghieva, Z. (1990) Art therapy in Bulgaria, Part III, *Inscape*, Summer: 26–35.

Whiteley, J.S. (1980) A community study – the Henderson Hospital, *International Journal of Therapeutic Communities* **1**(1).

PART II

The practice of art therapy

Using art therapy with 'chronic' long-term psychiatric patients

CHRISTINE WOOD

Introduction

In September 1989 newspaper pictures of the mental institution on the Greek Island of Leros were shocking, but in some sense they conjured up an ancient universal idea about madness and the chronic mental patient. The pictures showed naked human beings with matted hair, dejected and submissive against a background of dark squalor. In Britain mental patients are certainly better dressed than their counterparts in Greece, but increasingly, numbers sleep in tent-city or in cardboard boxes under city bridges. There are now some two million people who are homeless in Britain, an increasing proportion of this total being people who have had to leave mental hospitals. These examples are contemporary ones and suggest that some significant issues affecting the lives of mental patients have not moved forward. Discussions about the relative merits of life in hospital compared to life in the community do not, in any real sense, manage to address the full range and breadth of difficulties likely to be encountered by someone dubbed a 'chronic mental patient'.

I began writing this chapter in my grandmother's living room some 18 months ago. My grandmother has since died and her death has made me think a lot about what she gave me during her life. I think that what I have tried to provide in offering sessions to my long-term clients has been quite strongly influenced by care that my grandmother gave to me. For me she had a safe presence, and the places in which I spent time with her, her kitchen and her living room, were orderly and warm. Even at difficult times I always felt welcome, her place being mine to share. For those of us who have a clear place in the world, our families and our friends help us to live; they give us a sense of our history within a network of relationships which is fundamental to our sense of security within the world.

Working with the long-term clients of the psychiatric services means being with people who no longer have available to them a network of family and friends. I have often heard my colleagues (fellow therapists and other psychiatric workers) talk about the trauma they experience when they make relationships with clients who are isolated from ordinary social contexts. What they glimpse of the loneliness and isolation of long-term clients makes therapists question what it is that they can provide. Sometimes therapists and psychiatric workers alike feel angry and upset about the limitations of what they can do. I have often heard fellow workers say, when they sit down after sessions with groups of long-term clients, 'What are we doing? Is this therapy?'

The way I think about my own work with long-term clients is that much of what I do has the characteristics of 'ordinary' caring, but I have no illusions about my ability to be a substitute for lost family and friends. I do work therapeutically with long-term clients and try to use all the basic tenets of therapy with them as I would with other clients, but the pace is slower and may need to go on over a number of years. Issues of dependency seem to me very pertinent to therapeutic work with long-term clients – therapists can sometimes feel dread at the possible length of a relationship and the dependency this will entail. As with other therapeutic relationships, the therapist needs help and support (hopefully from a clinical supervisor) in order to acknowledge and work with feelings about the length of a relationship.

The basic tenet of my approach is that I try to provide a safe place for clients. I think about the different ways in which I might enable my client to feel safely contained – basic work which must be done over a much longer period than that needed with other clients. It may then be possible for the therapist to begin some dynamic work of a more challenging nature but with long-term clients much that is about simple caring and containment will also need to continue. Because of the length of some relationships many aspects become quite informal, but it is still important for the therapist to be the gatekeeper and continue to ensure that meetings take place within the therapeutic boundaries of time and place. One positive aspect of long-term work is that as we get to know clients over a long time we not only meet those parts which are distressed and in pain but get a real opportunity to work with the healthy parts of these 'chronic' clients.

Art therapists have done a great deal to ensure that people who do not fulfil the 'normal' criteria for psychotherapy have access to art therapy. This has been done in a number of ways. The British Association of Art Therapists has campaigned long and hard to obtain recognition for art therapy within the public sector services where art therapists regularly undertake work with the elderly, mentally handicapped people, long-term psychiatric patients and prisoners. Much of this experience demonstrates both the value of including those normally excluded by class and status from psychotherapeutic work, and the impracticability and difficulty of working with such groups of people without acknowledging the material circumstances in which they have to live. Long-term psychiatric patients are not only to be found on those remaining back wards of large institutions, nor even within rehabilitation units. Increasingly there are new generations of people with long-term needs and they are to be found caught up in the revolving doors of the acute psychiatric services, the social services and charitable agencies.

To work with long-term psychiatric patients is to work with a group of people who are often presented as the cause of hard work with little reward. My purpose in this chapter is to demonstrate that not only is such work possible, but that it can be immensely profitable for all concerned.

The approach of art therapy

I do not think art therapists adopt any significantly different approach towards working with the 'chronic' long-term psychiatric patient than they do with any other group of the population. Possibly what is unusual is that art therapists do a good deal of such work. In Britain, people with a long history of psychosis are often deemed 'unsuitable' for psychotherapy, but given the range of illness which I regularly witness as an art therapist working for an inner city psychiatric service, I would like to see the emphasis for psychotherapeutic work in Britain shifting towards those who need long-term care. It is difficult, though, to anticipate just what the outcome of the political changes outlined in the second part of the government's White Paper (November 1989) will entail for the current long-term population of psychiatric, handicapped and elderly people. Nor indeed is it easy to anticipate which kind of services will be favoured by the different health authorities as a result of it. But it is important that art therapists continue to offer long-term substantial work with 'chronic' sections of the patient population rather than attempt to fit in with the whims of changing political circumstances. Of course there are risks in this approach, but to the present author it seems that there are more serious risks involved in losing sight of well-founded principles of therapy based on the collective experience of art therapists over some 50 years of work.

The pioneers

Since art therapists began to work in psychiatric hospitals they have worked most with those people who were said to be the chronic patients. In art therapy there has been a long tradition, perhaps first expressed by Prinzhorn (1922), of respecting the person and valuing their art, no matter who they are said to be. This is a good tradition and one worth being proud of.

In *On Art and Therapy* (1989) Martina Thomson repeatedly points to evidence that people in hospitals have made use of art long before ever they were invited to do so. The notion that there is something very receptive in people, to whatever it is in their art which can help them heal themselves, is one which persists today. However, Thomson is right to warn of the dangers of losing sight of this notion as art therapists gradually improve their psychotherapeutic skills. It seems important to me that neither aspect of the work is overlooked, neither the art nor its psychotherapeutic content.

When I worked as a newly qualified art therapist at Netherne Hospital from 1978, some of the patients remembered the art studio session run by 'Mr Adamson' in the 1960s. They remembered these sessions as being very quiet ones – everyone had their own place and their own materials, 'you worked in silence'. Indeed, Adamson's own descriptions of his work at Netherne in *Art as*

Healing (1984) suggest a gentle, unintrusive style full of respect for the people working in his room:

> My own method is to be as passive as possible. I never attempt to interpret a person's work, particularly when he or she is painting. I feel that this would alter the relationship between us . . . I try to avoid the word 'patient', or the medical terminology so beloved by some, which denies the person his essential individuality, and distances him, like a specimen.
>
> (Adamson 1984: 7)

Thomson (1989) describes the work of E.M. Lyddiatt, an art therapist to whom she had been apprenticed, and it is not difficult to imagine something of the receptive style which Lyddiatt favoured. She would encourage playing with a whole range of different art materials in the hope that clients might find something of inspiration for themselves.

It is interesting that both Adamson and Lyddiatt did not intervene in the artwork of their clients. Both had the idea that what is important is to provide a place and to be receptive. It is also interesting to note that both valued the strength of support given to their work by favourable medical backing. It is perhaps this and their now dated language which gained some art therapy pioneers the caricature of handmaidens to the medics. Yet undoubtedly it is the early art studios of people like Adamson and Lyddiatt which have so profoundly influenced the work of many contemporary art therapists in their use of open groups (see Chapter 1, this volume).

The same careful approach – some examples of contemporary practice

A great deal that has been written about the general practice of art therapy in Britain is relevant and helpful to people working with clients who have long-term needs. The literature shows that art therapists use the same careful approach to work with these clients as with any others. Dalley suggests that work with this group 'must be approached with a less curative emphasis, a more appropriate therapeutic objective is to use art for enjoyment, exploration and stimulation' (Dalley 1984: xviii). Although I understand why Dalley is saying this, I cannot agree with her emphasis because it could imply that art therapy with long-term clients is largely diversional. For too long rehabilitation policies have tended to suggest that what is needed is to keep these 'difficult people' occupied and by implication out of the way. I think that art therapists do considerably more than this with their long-term clients, and I know that Dalley would not wish to suggest otherwise.

In her article on using art therapy with the long-stay residents of psychiatric hospitals, Charlton (1984) gives a very readable account of some of the issues she considers to be important. She describes how art therapy can help reverse some of the processes of institutionalization, particularly through the use of the environment of the art room: 'The art room provides a setting where residents can experience trust, experiment with different behaviour, exercise choice and feel a sense of competence' (Charlton 1984: 175). Charlton considers that picture-making is central to helping a person discover a more positive self-image, in a manner which 'is defined by the resident's own inventiveness and level of ability'. She clearly makes use of a range of different group methods – all of which she makes efforts to match with the needs of the people concerned. As with group work she sees individual therapy with long-term residents, as opposed to acute admission patients, as having goals which are 'less specific in terms of time but possibly more directly concerned with personal fulfilment and self enhancement within the limitations of a hospital setting' (ibid.: 186).

Again, I understand why the purposes of long-term work are expressed in this way, but the emphasis concerns me. With long-term clients it is often supposed that the outcome of therapeutic work can be predetermined. I worry that if a therapist begins with a notion of having to find a positive agenda then some of the painful, messy feelings, which long-term clients undoubtedly have, could be side-stepped. This concern is something which Mary Watkins (1981) describes very clearly as the dangers of sweetening the image. I am conscious that much of what Charlton says of her practice is against such sweetening – her concern to acknowledge and respond well to testimonies 'of anguish and oppression' which she sees in the artwork of her clients is evident. Her experience of the demands of long-term work for the therapist is clear when she writes:

> The challenge is . . . to develop ways of working which prevent people from getting stuck in self defeating patterns but which avoid imposing unnecessarily patronising structures on them.
>
> (ibid.: 188)

However, she does add something which I have found repeatedly in my own experience of the work: 'Art therapy can have much to contribute to a new sort of environment that facilitates social and cultural life rather than destroying it.' (ibid.)

Molloy's article 'Art therapy and psychiatric rehabilitation – harmonious partnership or philosophical collision' (1984) is one which I have found very helpful over the years of working as an art therapist. It is clear that Molloy does not approach the work with clients who have long-term problems in an essentially different manner from any other group of clients. He uses the same careful approach to the work that might be appropriate anywhere. Initially he tries to help clients remember a sense of play and creativity from their childhood, seeing art therapy as 'a means or forging links between childhood and present life' (ibid.: 3) Such links, once made, can have many benefits – gaps in a person's sense of themselves can be filled and a feeling of self-worth and of safety in the world can improve.

Molloy is right to remind us that people with a long history of psychiatric illness may have particular difficulties with that part of themselves which Jung suggested is like a psychological shadow. He writes that they

> usually find themselves living in a narrower more restrictive world than the rest of us, in terms of opportunity, social freedom and financial stability. Their 'shadows' will thus loom larger. Add to this their emotional wounds carried by successive breakdowns and their decreased sense of independence

caused by periods of institutional care and a picture will emerge of a person who will experience great difficulty in confronting the more unacceptable aspects of themselves. Of course, it is quite impossible for anyone to be in total control of their unconscious mind and always able to confront their 'shadow'. But if a patient is to function even reasonably well in the real world then he is likely to need consistent help in this area.

(Molloy 1984: 4)

Molloy contrasts this with rehabilitation policies which focus exclusively on 'work training and practice in the tasks of daily living (ibid.: 6), and he suggests that it is in the area of a client's frightening and elusive emotions which art therapy can help most.

An article by Greenwood and Layton (1987), 'An out-patient art therapy group', describes a community group with ten 'long-term patients' all with a history of psychosis. As with Molloy both Greenwood and Layton feel that for these clients, 'Changes in self mastery are no mean achievement and learning to ride the surf of the unconscious better may be taken as our principal object in therapy.' (ibid.: 18) The article offers a helpful description of the form this group assumed, together with a practical guide to some of the theoretical ideas referred to. It seems clear from their account that the group assumed much importance for therapists and client alike. Despite the seriousness of their difficulties, clients' hospital readmission rates were reduced, and for the therapists there was the opportunity to work creatively and hopefully with a group of people who were rarely given such an opportunity. The paper provides a guide for the many art therapists and psychiatric workers who are having to make the transition from hospital to the community and demonstrates the breadth and depth of therapeutic work which it is possible to 'contain' in the community.

Other articles explore the practical steps needed in establishing groups for patients with long-term psychiatric histories. Both Lewis (1990) and Swainson (1990) describe and explore some of the group processes which they have seen emerging during the course of their art therapy practice. Lewis takes an idea from Donnelly (1988) of 'actively doing nothing' as a way of thinking about how therapists and clients can survive the long-term dependency needs which may arise in community-based rehabilitation groups. Swainson gives an honest account of repeated and continuous work needed in order to set up groups to which homeless people will actually come.

From the art therapy literature I do not have the impression of a 'blank screen' or 'faceless' therapist, which can be one caricature of poor psychotherapeutic practice. It seems as though there is something practical in the approach of art therapy which tends to protect art therapists from some of the dehumanizing possibilities which exist within all therapeutic work, possibilities which too often are defended against by making psychotherapy into an alienating theoretical construct. The dangers of losing sight of the importance of art in art therapy as a result of the quest for more psychotherapeutic skill is a discussion in which art therapists are currently involved. It seems to me that dangers posed to the art in art therapy are much more prevalent in the face of poor psychotherapeutic skills and reified theoretical constructs.

The basic principles of my own practice

I work as an art therapist for a mental health team in an inner city area, so I cannot avoid thinking about some of the broad political issues which affect it. The word 'chronic' has very particular connotations for me. I know who is meant to be indicated by the word 'chronic' – those people who get caught up in the revolving doors of acute psychiatric services, people with long-term repeated episodes of psychosis, people with repeated episodes of depression and anxiety, people with long-term eating problems or long-term addictions and people who suffer the effects of long-term unemployment. These are the very people with whom an art therapist in any of the adult public sector agencies is likely to work. The word 'chronic' implies a set of entrenched problems which seriously curtail the chance of change in a person's life. I do not pretend never to have used it myself, but 'chronic' is not a helpful word to apply to a description of someone's life and is not one I would encourage someone to apply to themselves.

In many ways the issue of whether or not we use a word like 'chronic' is pertinent to many problems about language used in the psychiatric services. One early attempt to avoid the stigma of madness was to describe various emotional problems as 'illness'. This well-meaning attempt has left in its wake a legacy of difficulties which confuse both the people with difficulties and those trying to help. It is a good example of how cosmetic changes to the language of psychiatry do not really touch the deep-seated, wide-ranging problems which bring people to psychiatry looking for help.

I have vivid memories of the indignation of a young woman (I will call her Wendy) with whom I work during her psychotic episodes. She had seen on the television an overgeneralized and patronizing account of 'schizophrenia' and had had a difficult shadow-fencing conversation with her relatives about programmes that generalize about people and call them 'schizophrenic'. Her relatives, by her account, had clearly felt uncomfortable (they themselves are members of the National Schizophrenia Association – because understandably they need the support) about the way in which the programme had made too glib a use of labels and had suggested to her that one solution might be not to use the labelling language. This suggestion had in no way eased the young woman's indignation – for her the difficulties and the level of alienation she experienced as a result of her psychotic episodes do not find much value in a polite change of language.

First meetings

When I had first met Wendy she was mute; she had not spoken for many weeks. A client's silence during a first meeting throws some of the issues of how best to introduce art therapy sessions into sharp relief. Many of the people who become my clients come with very few preconceptions about the nature of therapy. Most of them will not have any experience of therapy and for most it is unlikely that a notion of therapy will have been a part of their class or culture. It therefore seems reasonable that initially I offer some explanation of what might be involved. What I say is usually a response to what they tell me about themselves as well as some general issues. One of these issues, for example, is concerned with having choice because people (especially clients within the public sector) are not always clear that they have a choice about whether or not to make use of art therapy sessions. The question of choice is extremely important both in terms of the client's human rights and in terms of the client's inclination to begin therapy. Another general issue I raise is that whereas I am interested in how they see their difficulties and those things which have brought them into contact with psychiatric services, I am also very interested in their history as an artist as opposed to their history as a mental patient (Wood 1986). By that I mean that during the first stages of trying to get to know someone, I am listening very carefully to what they say about their lives and their difficulties, but in that listening I am trying to hear something of what it is that moves them. I am listening out for that spark in them that is their imagination. Many of my clients begin by telling me that they don't think they are very good at art – but few will say that they don't have an imagination.

Depending on who I am with, I try to find a way of explaining why I am so interested in their imagination. I might do this by suggesting to them that the part of them which remembers playing, looking at a picture or listening to a story as a child, is a part of them that might help them sort a few things out. At some point I will say a little about confidentiality. If possible I make my comments in relation to something they say, but if what they are saying doesn't touch upon issues of confidentiality I introduce the subject myself. I try to make it clear that I consider that essentially what takes place in the sessions between us will remain confidential and that I understand how unsettling it would be if they did not know this. I know that worries about confidentiality, especially in a hospital culture (but also in the social services) are very real ones – the issue of confidentiality is often returned to from time to time during the course of a relationship. At some crisis points in a client's life I might need to consult with colleagues working in the mental health team but I always first seek the permission of the person concerned. Only rarely would I act without that permission and even then I would act with due respect for my client's confidentiality.

I know that I am very fortunate in this, being attached to a small and supportive clinical team where client confidentiality is generally accepted as part of therapeutic work. Of course many psychiatric workers and therapists do not find themselves working in such an environment and without regular clinical supervision there may be dangers in not sharing with their colleagues. I share the broad general concerns of my work without discussing the details of the sessions. In this way I hope to demonstrate something of the way I work but also that I am open to learn from colleagues. Perhaps particularly with long-term clients it is important to remember how necessary it is to have effective team work, for clients have wide-ranging needs which cannot be met by once weekly therapeutic sessions alone.

Misconceptions about the nature of art therapy can range from the sublime to the ridiculous; art therapists have been stereotyped as mad mystics or more simply as people making astonishing interpretations of a person's meanest doodle. I readily acknowledge that as art therapists we have a responsibility to make our work still clearer, particularly when we introduce ourselves to new clients, for they too may have fears about magical powers of interpretation.

Of course first meetings do not always run smoothly. Nevertheless it is generally possible, even with very disturbed people, to make some sort of two-way introduction, although the pace at which it is done depends very much on the client concerned.

The rooms

The rooms in which I work can play a very helpful part in the introductions. When I first meet a new client I generally show them around the art room and the materials. I suggest to them that they can choose a place in which to work. I try to create an atmosphere in which my clients feel able to make a place for themselves – a corner or a section of the room which they can make their own. Some of the artwork made by other clients may be visible and if the new client asks me about it I am careful how much I reveal. I explain that much of the artwork which people make in art therapy sessions has a private quality about it and because of this it is put carefully away in portfolios and not shown to anyone (not even other staff) without the permission of the person who made it. Equally, some clients do want their work on the wall and I make it clear that this is their choice. If this has consequences for other clients I try to acknowledge and work with the feelings evoked. I think it is important to try to be sensitive to the differing needs of individual clients but I do not think the world is a bare place; I feel it is possible to work with and acknowledge any feelings which may arise as a result of what clients see and find in the art therapy room. In explaining these matters I am trying to suggest to a new client that they themselves will be afforded the same respect and confidentiality, should they decide to work with me.

There are many well-loved rooms in the history of art therapy – these therapy rooms are part of the tradition of artists' studios. They are also part of the tradition of art therapy work. I have already mentioned how the work of art therapy pioneers such as Adamson and Lyddiatt centred upon the art studio, and from descriptions I have read of their rooms, their art studios were an extension of their personalities and style of working. It is interesting to think of these rooms in this way, as art rooms, and the manner in which they are set out and decorated by art therapists and their clients has, as previously described, complicated therapeutic implications.

For many clients their first encounter with the art therapist's room can be a surprise. Art therapy rooms have been described as places where it might be possible to be 'absent minded' (Champernowne 1970). It is not quite right to say they are like nurseries or play rooms for adults, but there is something like this at the back of my mind when I am trying to make the art therapy room inviting. Perhaps with the increasing pace of life, it is not surprising that there are not words in our language with which to describe adult play directly.

I have visited a number of art therapy rooms over the years and all of them have helped me think about what is needed in such places. My first encounter was at Springfield Hospital in South London which I visited at the beginning of my art therapy training. After a number of circular tours along a confusing corridor system in the hospital I found the room, but it was deserted. I found everybody outside trying to attach a tin bath to an old car engine. The art therapist Robin

Holtom stood by, smiling. Eventually everybody returned indoors to the room and there I was shown the art materials and settled down to make some artwork. The room was a long one; patients who came and went had their own places in it. Some came to sit, others used the materials. At one point a young Indian man spent some time with me explaining his pictures; these covered the top part of one wall. The pictures were of doors; they were painted in light colours with different numbers on them and he wanted me to understand something about the numbers and his feeling about the different doors. To him they represented some of the different houses of relatives and friends. He had not been in Britain long. I think he found this country strange and he felt lost here. There was something about the room and the way in which the art therapist worked which meant that patients felt able to wander in and out, use the materials and talk. Much of the talk was not easily understood but there was an atmosphere of acceptance.

Another room I visited was run by the art therapist Britta von Zweigbergk at Bexley Hospital in Kent. This room had a different, lighter atmosphere and it was much bigger than the one at Springfield with several distinct sections. I did not meet Britta, but the art therapy room in which she worked suggested the enthusiasm with which she approached the work, or certainly the enthusiasm of the people who had worked with her. The room was literally encrusted with artwork; every available space on the walls and the ceiling had been pressed into use. The look of the place was vibrant and invited people to come in and try out some materials.

There is something of that quality of invitation in the art therapy room at Manchester Hospital. The room is in a building which is set slightly apart from the other hospital buildings. It is a very large, tall room with a lot of skylights in the roof. Tall shelving divides the room into several sections, so it is possible to find a place of some seclusion in which to work. The room is almost bursting with different pieces of artwork; it has an intriguing and inviting atmosphere, which, no doubt has something to do with the approach of the two art therapists, Pauline Mottram and Katherine Kennedy.

Other rooms which come to mind include those at Netherne Hospital in Surrey in which I first worked as an art therapist. There was the luxury of several rooms at this hospital, one of which was in the acute admission unit, John Reid House. It was slightly out on a limb of the building, away from the ward area with access to it down a long corridor. The room itself had windows on three sides, two of which were large bay windows which looked out over beautiful trees and grounds. The only other art therapy room I know of, which has such a well-tended view, is one in Hull at De la Pole Hospital – it too looks out over lovely grounds and a small hospital church. There is something about a room with a view which lends itself to reflection and exploration.

During October 1988 in a talk given in Newcastle, Bruno Bettelheim spoke at length about how much care and attention had been given to the environment of the Chicago school for autistic children. He described how helpful an interesting, cared-for environment could be in reinforcing the feeling for clients that they are people worth caring for. Many art therapists manage, sometimes against considerable odds, to offer their clients art rooms to which they wish to return. These rooms and the ways in which they are cared for provide safe places in which people can begin to reflect upon their lives. I know that when I am able to work in well equipped art rooms which are well cared for, well used and lived in, that it seems much easier for me to put my clients at ease. I think this is particularly the case with long-term psychiatric patients and this has implications for how art therapists will work in the community. As many of the old hospitals close down, the old buildings and the grounds associated with Victorian asylums disappear. Art therapy rooms will tend, as this happens, to have to move along with the rest of the psychiatric services into the cities and into local community buildings. There will undoubtedly be some advantages for the clients of the services as this occurs, but some favourable conditions will be lost too.

It may be the case that as art therapists move into the community they have to work hard to find suitable alternative premises. Although it may be possible to work in the client's home, the benefits of having a special place for them to visit and use will be something for which art therapists need to argue. The possibility of making artwork lies in the very surroundings. In a client's home there may be a number of things which make it difficult to work with them privately – the lack of space, children to care for and the simple fears of being overheard or making too much mess. There is also the very real question of whether or not it is actually possible for a therapist to create therapeutic boundaries in a client's home as essentially the client will be the host. The current psychiatric practices in crisis and community care teams mean that therapists will sometimes first meet clients at home, but when possible I think it advisable to move the sessions to an art therapy room.

The artwork and the relationship

The way I introduce myself to a client has much in common with the way in which psychotherapists work, but there are some differences, for, as I have described, not only am I inviting a new client to make use of me, I am also inviting them to make use of the room in which I work. This necessarily lends a degree of informality to the way in which the relationship is likely to develop. I might for example suggest materials for the artwork that they wish to make. Also, on the basis of what they say to me about their lives and how they feel, I might suggest particular themes to explore in their artwork. Thus, for example, when a young man (with a history of manic depressive psychosis) was particularly anxious about how angry he felt his father was going to be with him, I suggested that he try to make an image about his father. He chose to use collage and paint, taking pictures from newspapers and magazines of things which suggested to him aspects of his father's personality. With paint he then went on to draw the collage work into the body of a judgemental creature. Aspects of the finished creature contained things which terrified him about his father, but the overall look of this creature he had made was not so terrifying to him; indeed, there was something both sad and ridiculous about its posture. During the weeks which followed, the young man found that he began to see the picture in a different light. Other pictures were made (this time without the need for themes) and through his artwork and his conversations with me he began to understand and feel less afraid and less inclined to flee from his relationship with his father.

A long time may be spent in making a piece of artwork and it may involve several sessions. Sometimes people make artwork away from the sessions, but there is often a good deal of time spent in the company of clients while they are engaged in making their art. This quiet time often seems very important. With different people it has different qualities; some people talk for a little, some become absorbed in a way which means that they do not say anything, and others fluctuate in what they do, sometimes involving me in discussions about what to do next with their art, and sometimes not. Sharing the world with other people, even though not constantly involved in conversation, is something I have heard many people speak about. I know that this sense of human company can certainly be present in other forms of psychotherapy but I have the impression that this is a very important and immediate function of art therapy. Perhaps this is particularly important for work with people who have long-term psychotic problems, because of the containment it can provide.

As people get increasingly used to my presence and the room, they seem to find what suits them and ways to help themselves settle down to work – a space is cleared, they might rummage through their portfolio, gather materials, make a cup of tea, roll a cigarette and so on: things which most people would understand and recognize as part of the process of getting started and keeping going with something they want to do. The level of informality involved in settling down to make artwork depends on the nature of the relationship with the therapist. Different clients have different needs, and also in less structured open art therapy groups the processes are very relaxed. The messy needs of the art process generally lend a certain informality to aspects of the art therapeutic relationship and I imagine that other therapists who do not use art might find this surprising.

Ways of beginning therapy sessions depend on the client, but they could include asking them to remember how they used to play as a child, or indeed how they used to draw as a child. In the act of making remembered child-like pictures, all sorts of memories might come flooding back – the names of friends, people at school, older relatives, all manner of things which have made them the person they are, including perhaps a sense of play.

Sometimes people like to keep a special journal and scrap-book (like those kept by many artists), a place to record thoughts and feelings as well as pictures (pictures taken from newspapers, magazines, collages and pictures made by themselves). In *The Artist in his Studio* (Liberman 1969) there are numerous photographs of walls in studios which are decorated with old photographs, sketches, magazine cuttings and letters; these bits of wall are like pages from my clients' scrap-books. There is a long and honourable tradition in science and art of keeping such journals which record the periods of despair before change is possible. There could be a long struggle in getting to the point where the client feels able to make some artwork which mirrors so much else that takes place in therapy. This is why I wish to suggest that making art is sometimes only the beginning of art therapy but it can be a real sign that something is beginning to happen for that person.

With those people who have been long-term 'consumers' of the psychiatric services my approach in starting therapy is a little different from that suggested above, but things are likely to go at a much slower pace. Often the people concerned have a form of ingrained obedience (at least on the surface) to the behests of middle-class professionals, and so work might initially be needed to help the person feel that they have some choice about whether or not to use art therapy or to come to the sessions. If after preliminary meetings a person chooses to use the art therapy sessions, I generally discuss with them the options available in terms of individual or group work. For some, group work does not seem appropriate but I generally like to discuss the possibility with them because the number of people I can work with individually is limited, and given that such work may take place over many years it is important to consider what it is possible to sustain over a long period of time.

The following case-study illustrates how one client used art therapy.

Ruth

Ruth, whom I see individually, feels extraordinarily persecuted, to the point where from time to time she thumps the people she is with. They are usually unaware of the hostility she feels they are emanating until they have been thumped. Ruth is very vulnerable and almost constantly subject to her own persecutory feelings. However, because she sometimes gets angry enough to thump people, understandably enough others are often wary or even frightened of her. It is mainly because of her acute sense of persecution that I decided to work with her individually and not in a group with others who have a history of psychosis.

Ruth first had a psychotic breakdown in her early twenties at the time when she went away from home to work. Her descriptions of her first experience of being a patient on a locked ward in a large mental hospital, in a town away from home, are chilling. Pictures she has made of that time suggest how completely confused she was by the experience – even now, some 15 years later, she is unable to make sense of what was happening to her then and what is happening now. Sometimes the explanations we arrive at together seem to hold some comfort for her, but these moments of respite are fleeting before she slips back into wary confusion.

To some extent Ruth's life epitomizes the serious limitations of what can be offered by contemporary psychiatry. The medication she is offered, although it is regularly and carefully reviewed, does not really touch the seriousness and depth of her delusional system. She has sometimes said to me that 'It does not matter how much medication they give me, it will not stop me thinking and knowing what I do.' To her, the medication, which makes her very drowsy and which had contributed to her serious weight increase and blood pressure, only serves to add to her unhappiness and increase her suspicion of the doctors who are trying to help her. I too do not escape her suspicions; she has sometimes felt that I am not an art therapist but a psychiatrist in disguise. She worries that in addition to the oral medication (which she knows she takes), members of the multi-disciplinary team of which I am a part visit her clandestinely and administer additional medication while she is asleep. Attempts to reassure her that this is not so only serve to confirm her anxieties. She needs a lot of help and it is particularly hard for her to feel that even those people who try to offer her a safety anchor are not entirely to be trusted.

Patrick Casement (1988) discusses some of the problems inherent in the therapist's 'not knowing' quite what is happening to the person they are trying to help, nor what the way forward might be. Ruth, like many long-term psychiatric patients with an entrenched psychosis, is someone for whom the psychiatric services have very few and limited answers to offer at present.

My work with her involves meeting in the same place, for an hour, at the same time each week. It seems particularly important to provide careful boundaries for people as disturbed as she is as she needs to know what she can expect. Her general practitioner and her long-suffering parents feel that these meetings do help Ruth. There have been fewer crises over the three-year period than previously. It is not easy, though, to say what it is that I do – my relationship with Ruth does have the quality of 'not knowing' which Casement writes about.

Ruth comes to the art therapy sessions willingly – once she has taken off her coat and settled herself down with a cup of tea, she begins to talk. She tells me what has been happening to her in the preceding week; if she has been worrying (and she often has been) she tells me of her worries in a conspiratorial and sometimes brittle manner. Her explanation of her worries is quite elaborate and it involves a number of different themes which reoccur. The major theme is that of her betrothal to a Jewish man whom she feels she met many years before. He speaks to her every day – she hears his voice either in her mind or through messages sent through the voices of television and radio announcers. She desperately wants him to come and make a formal proposal of marriage to her, at her parents' home. That he (his name is Jeremiah) has not yet in some 15 years come to make his proposal is something which makes her deeply unhappy, but it is also something about which she has a series of complicated explanations.

One of these involves her feeling that she should make a sacrifice to please him. He tells her she should give away all her worldly goods and savings and then he will come to make her a proposal. Clearly this involves her in considerable conflict: she is conscious that her parents are elderly and that the day will come when she needs to support herself. Also, when sometimes she gets to the point where she feels she can no longer stand being single and so she begins to speak about giving away her savings, her parents understandably get worried and tell her repeatedly that Jeremiah does not exist. When this happens Ruth will often come to see me in tears and then will wish to paint a picture of Jeremiah. She has made a number of paintings of him, sometimes alone, at other times with him and her together. It seems very important that I accept these paintings and talk to her about them; after she has made them she seems to be full of a sense of sweet relief.

Sometimes she will ask me directly whether or not I believe in Jeremiah's existence. Knowing how to respond is a central question in work with people whose belief systems do not fit in with consensus reality. I make it clear to Ruth that I am willing to listen to what it is that she feels and acknowledge that her beliefs are sincerely held; but it also seems important to indicate that I see things differently. I talk about seeing Jeremiah as a part of her, a part which is created out of her deep desire to be married and have children. I also tell her I understand that my different way of seeing Jeremiah is not easy for her to accept and that it confuses her that I see things differently. Sometimes we manage to move on from this, to her feelings of sadness about not being married and her feelings of anxiety that her biological clock is ticking on and that the day when she will no longer be able to have children is coming closer. These are clearly very sad feelings and often cause her to weep. It seems important that I accept Ruth's tears and that I do not ask her to stop crying.

Another theme is Ruth's being followed and watched in a way which is malevolent. She has made many pictures in the attempt to show me what she feels about this. The pictures are often pencil drawings of people who, like the characters in comic strips, have bubbles coming out of their mouths which contain comments. Again when we talk about these pictures I try to show Ruth that I understand how persecuted she feels. At times when it seems possible for her to explore these feelings I suggest that they are again part of herself.

On one occasion, Ruth became screamingly angry with me. She clearly felt that I had become part of the world which persecutes her. I think I was not expecting much to happen in the session and she sensed this. Her anger woke me up and somehow she managed to stay in the room with me, although grudgingly at first. She talked herself through the anger, with my full attention. The episode was sobering for me and yet it was extremely valuable to our relationship because between us we managed to 'digest' the anger.

On another occasion, Ruth spoke vehemently about how she felt constantly on the verge of thumping someone. I did not feel myself to be a target but my heart did sink because I felt that perhaps things were getting worse for her. Her history of violence does mean that she is at risk of very long-term admission. Almost half-heartedly I asked her if she could show me something about the angry feelings and how they felt inside her by making a painting. Immediately she began to paint a huge black mouth full of decaying teeth (she remembered the mouth of an old woman she had once seen fall asleep with her mouth open). She added a lot of painterly detail to the mouth before transforming the painting by enclosing the mouth within a metal cage. She spoke to me about the intensity of her feelings and explained some of its significance while making the painting. Then after some 35 minutes she stopped. She said that the angry feelings had passed. Again between us we had digested the anger. For her, the session gave another demonstration that it is possible for anger to pass and for me it provided another sobering reminder not to be stuck myself with the idea that people are 'chronically' stuck and unable to move forward.

At other times Ruth has painted rich coloured patterns which contain many plant-like forms. She seems to derive a great deal of pleasure from making these pictures. They are part of the more playful and celebratory side of our relationship, as are the fairy stories which we sometimes read aloud together. This part of our relationship has inspired her to keep a journal in which she records some of her feelings through the inclusion of pictures, poems, quotations from stories she has read and occasional photographs. This journal has a very important place in her life, although as yet it does not record her sadness. Occasionally Ruth brings to me an account of a dream and it is in the exploration of her dreams that I think she comes closest to some kind of understanding about the nature of her condition.

Molloy (1984) describes proposals made in 1975 in a book entitled *Not the Same as You* or *The Salford Project* (Korer 1975). This book described a research project which was set up to investigate the possibility of a 'continuous care register'. The purposes of this register 'would be to monitor ex-psychiatric patients in the community, identify and locate instances of breakdown and provide a centralised service of intervention.' (Molloy 1984: 2) In work with people where a 'cure' or even substantial change are not immediately possible, it seems that 'continuous care' in the community would be an appropriate approach to the large section of the psychiatric population who have long-term histories of psychosis. Part of such treatment policy could certainly be individual or group art therapy.

Conclusion

At the beginning of the 1990s it does not take a radical consciousness to be aware of the dangers of institutionalization. In the late 1960s and the 1970s, writers like Goffman, R.D. Laing and Maxwell Jones helped create awareness of the dangers of this process and such awareness was at the forefront of psychiatric practice. The work of art therapists in large institutions at that time was largely pragmatic in that the existence of the institutions was accepted. Yet the more fruitful art therapy departments, together, of course, with the efforts of many other psychiatric workers, did a good deal to counter some of the worst effects of institutionalization. The push towards community psychiatry made in the later part of the 1980s is, on one level, the practical outcome of earlier efforts to counter this. Undoubtedly, from all they have learnt in the large 'mental' institutions, art therapists have a real part to play in psychiatric care in the community.

Unfortunately resources for community work are limited and the government's push for yet more work to be done in the community can be characterized as further evidence of economic 'rationalization' in the health service. Consequently, the face-to-face work between client and psychiatric worker is seriously underresourced in many places. It may be that the new Code of Practice which accompanies the new Mental Health Act can be used to strengthen arguments about improving after-care resources. Art therapists can make a useful contribution to after-care plans but it is important that they are backed up by a multidisciplinary team which can share responsibility for the problems of long-term psychiatric patients who have been so seriously marginalized by our society.

These patients are the largest section of the psychiatric population. This is true in Britain, as it is worldwide. Cohen (1988) in *Forgotten Millions* describes the size of this population in international terms. Despite being the largest group they are given least attention by professional workers. Therapeutic change with this group is slow, limited and gradual, and the contact needed with them is necessarily long term. Undoubtedly this section of the population is not a glamorous one to work with, and not liable to enhance a person's career prospects. Nevertheless, many art therapists (despite the small size of the profession) have undertaken much of this important work.

With the transition to the community, the social and economic context in which families and institutions have to survive can no longer be overlooked. The politics which have enabled art therapy to survive as a viable method of working to date need now to gain a wider framework which sees clearly the need for solidarity with other disciplines. If we get too caught up with ideas that suggest that what helps our clients is something to do with insular cures and magical techniques, we can become locked into professional rivalries and then the real contributions of care and respect (in therapy and in society) can be overlooked and lost.

References

Adamson, E. (1984) *Art as Healing*, Coventure.

Bettelheim, B. (1959) *Love is Not Enough*, USA: The Free Press.

Casement, P. (1988) On *Learning from the Patient*, London: Routledge.

Champernowne, I. (1970) Art and therapy: an uneasy partnership, lecture given for the Analytical Psychology Club and the British Association of Art Therapists at the Royal College of Art, London.

Charlton, S. (1984) Art therapy with long stay residents of psychiatric hospitals, in T. Dalley (ed.) *Art as Therapy*, London: Tavistock Publications.

Clark, D. (1989) Encounters, *Changes* **7**(3).

Cohen, D. (1988) *Forgotten Millions: The Treatment of the Mentally Ill on a Global Perspective*, London: Paladin/Grafton.

Dalley, T. (ed.) (1984) *Art as Therapy*, London: Tavistock.

Department of Health (1990) *Code of Practice*, London: DoH.

Donnelly, M.J. (1988) Psychotherapy and psychosis in out-patient setting, unpublished.

Goffman, E. (1968) *Asylums*, Harmondsworth: Penguin.

Greenwood, H. and Layton G. (1987) An out-patient art therapy group, *Inscape*, Summer: 12–19.

Killick, K. (1987) Art therapy and schizophrenia, a new approach, unpublished MA thesis, Hertfordshire College of Art.

Korer, J. (1975) *The Salford Project*, or *Not the Same as You*, Psychiatric Rehabilitation Association.

Laing, R.D. (1970) *Sanity, Madness and the Family*, Harmondsworth: Penguin.

Lewis, S. (1990) A place to be: art therapy and community based rehabilitation, in M. Liebmann (ed.) *Art Therapy in Practice*, London: Jessica Kingsley Publications.

Liberman, A. (ed.) (1969) *The Artist in his Studio*, London: Thames and Hudson.

Liebmann, M. (1986) *Art Therapy for Groups*, Beckenham: Croom Helm.

—— (ed.) (1990) *Art Therapy in Practice*, London: Jessica Kingsley Publications.

McNeilly, G. (1984) Directive and non-directive approaches to art therapy, *Inscape*, Winter.

Males, B. and Stott, J. (1984) Art therapy for people who are mentally handicapped, in T. Dalley (ed.) *Art as Therapy*, London: Tavistock Publications.

MIND (1983) Manifesto for a New Mental Health Service, *Common Concern*, Mind.

Molloy, T. (1984). Art Therapy and psychiatric rehabilitation – harmonious partnership or philosophical collision?, *Inscape*, August.

Prinzhorn, H. (1922) *Bildernei der Geisteskranken*, translated by E. Van Brockendorff, 1st English edition (1975), Berlin/NY: Springer Verlag.

Sedgewick, P. (1982) *Psychopolitics*, London: Pluto Press.

Smail, D. (1987) *Taking Care. An Alternative to Therapy*, London: J.M. Dent.

Swainson, C. (1990) Art therapy and homeless people, in M. Liebmann (ed.) *Art Therapy in Practice*, London: Jessica Kingsley Publications.

Thomson, M. (1989) *On Art and Therapy*, London: Virago.

Townsend, P. and Davidson, N. (eds) (1988). The Black Report, in the collection *Inequalities in Health*, Harmondsworth: Pelican.

Warner, R. (1985) *Recovery from Schizophrenia – Psychiatry and Political Economy*, London: Routledge and Kegan Paul.

Watkins, M. (1981) Six approaches to the image in art therapy, *Spring Journal*.

Wood, C. (1985) Psychiatrica Democratica and the problems of translation, *Inscape*, **1**.

—— (1986) Milk white panic – What do we do to people, when we ask them to paint and draw?, *Inscape*, **2**.

5

Art therapy with elderly people in statutory care

ROGER WILKS AND ANGELA BYERS

Introduction

This chapter is written with particular reference to the authors' own experiences of working with elderly people who live in statutory care: i.e. in council-run residential homes or in geriatric wards within psychiatric hospitals. It is based on work mainly with people who are over the age of 80. We will discuss theoretical issues concerning loss, death, organic disorders and the role and function of art in therapeutic relationships with the elderly in long-term care.

For the most part, the reasons why these people live in such settings are: because their mental ability to look after themselves is impaired to the point where they are a danger to themselves and others; or because they are no longer able physically to look after themselves; or because they suffer from extreme loneliness. All these reasons have social connotations because they result from dependence on other people and communities, and the availability or unavailability of help. The political trends at this time are aiming towards increasing the options for elderly people who need a lot of help, and hopefully this will result in their feeling that they have wider choices and consequently more say in their futures.

The group of people about whom we propose to write is composed of a great variety of personalities. However, there are certain common denominators which are relevant to any therapy undertaken with people who belong to this group. The most obvious, perhaps, is that they have all lived through the same period of history. They also share experiences which are unique to being old and in care; loss, of their parents, relatives and friends, of a home, of a job or occupation; the possibility of physical or mental deterioration; and the nearness of their own deaths. Many are in pain or feel ill.

In considering a psychological approach to elderly people in statutory care, the therapist has to appreciate the clinical and non-clinical factors in determining the most effective, but more importantly, useful type of intervention necessary in helping and understanding the elderly resident. As already implied, it is of paramount importance that the level of empathy the therapist has for the client should be the first stepping-stone in defining both a treatment method and objective in the therapy.

Although elderly people in care have many difficult emotional processes to go through, they still have time and life to be lived. The challenge for those who look after them is to create an environment in which they feel they can still engage with life and be of some value to others. This is a challenge which is being taken up by most care authorities, and is the subject of much debate. But one thing which is essential for these people is to have warm, caring and respectful relationships with others.

The relationships between the art therapist and his or her clients are a functional part of the therapy. Sessions are regular with limits or boundaries on the amount of time spent, and the clients have the full concentration of the therapist. For many people this may be the only relationship they have with such qualities of consistency and involvement.

Keeping an emotional life going despite the disintegration of the intellectual life is something that is familiar to other art therapists who have written about their work with elderly people. Rita Simon has described how valuable art can be in allowing room for mental growth in elderly people who have become withdrawn and deprived of much of their independence (Simon 1985), Jane Harlan (1990) similarly describes the importance of art therapy in promoting 'autonomous functioning' for dementing people, when the capacity for self-determination and meaning is being eroded by disease and social circumstances. She also mentions the concern that elderly people feel regarding failure, where the act of maintaining previous, more sophisticated levels of thought and ability has become increasingly difficult. Fear of failure, as a result of deterioration in physical or in intellectual skills, is an issue that occurs in much of the other available literature, as is the consequent need for the therapist to be actively supportive and consistent in encouraging a greater sense of self-worth (Harrison 1980, Wald 1983, Osler 1988, Harlan 1990).

Loss

Much has been written about bereavement (Murray Parkes 1972, Worden 1982). It is now accepted that bereaved people can experience strong emotions after their losses, and that this is considered to be normal and healthy. The intensity of the emotions reflects the significance of the losses to their personal worlds. The emotions are particularly those of denial, anger, guilt and sadness. As time passes these feelings become less intense and painful, and a bereaved person can gradually let go of the lost person as he or she reconstructs a new life without them.

Sometimes these emotions are repressed. This blocks the process of separation from the lost person, and inhibits the bereaved person's ability to lead a wholesome life once more. Sometimes the grieving continues for several years, and this is also a sign that something has blocked the ability to let go.

The bereavement process occurs when anything of significance is lost, such as those losses mentioned previously as having happened to elderly people in care.

Sometimes an elderly person will have suffered two or more very significant losses successively, such as the loss of a spouse, followed by deterioration in health, followed by a necessary move into hospital or council care. It is very difficult for such a person to adapt to a new way of life. The emotions aroused by such a cataclysm of events are intense and long-lasting. For example, Mr B. married late in life and consequently had no children. He had a stable working life after the war until he retired. Nothing of significance appears to have happened until his wife became ill and eventually died. Mr B. then became ill himself, was persuaded that he could no longer manage at home alone, and moved into a residential home. He has never fully accepted the home as a place in which to lead a reasonable existence, tending to be angry with people for most of the time, and says that he would prefer to die himself.

Reassessment of past life

Endings typically involve assessment of what has happened, been achieved, and not been achieved; they also involve anticipation of parting, loss of what has been, and anticipation of what is to come. Elderly people are in the last stage of life, and consequently they can be expected to be involved with these issues, albeit at an unconscious level.

Many elderly people are surprised at the clarity with which they remember things, and that their minds so often wander to certain events of a long time ago, even when their short-term memory is poor. This process is recognized as important and necessary, an unconscious need, and it is often called 'the life review process' (Birren 1964, Jacques 1988). Reminiscence therapy, in the form of sessions in which people are reminded about events and life-styles of the first half of this century, is frequently used now by those who work with elderly people (Age Exchange).

Jung (1960) compared life to the arc of the passage of the sun; in the first half, we are concerned with our own development, our place in the world and the bearing of and caring for children. In the second or downward part of the arc, he stated that we should be turning our thoughts inwards as we go towards death, which Jung insisted was a goal more than an end. This he said was a healthy pattern; if a person in the second half of life feels that he or she has not accomplished the tasks of the first half, that person will be looking back at life lived instead of looking forwards to death. Erikson (1979) also postulated that people in the last stage of life need to accept their lives as they were lived and as they related to man's historical development if they were not to feel despair.

But life review is a way of feeling again events of the past. It could be a way of trying to come to terms with what felt good and what felt bad, and as only some things are remembered, it seems very much to be governed by the unconscious. It may well be that it is a way of struggling with unresolved conflicts in order to be able to let them go. For example, Mrs H. had lost her mother when she was only a teenager. From that time she had had to cook, clean and wash for her father and six brothers, who restricted her life-style to a large extent. Because of this, she did not marry until she was 40. She was then unable to have children. She frequently talked about her resentment of what had happened to her, and it helped her when she could voice this resentment.

However, when positive events are remembered, it can give great pleasure. It can also be a way of raising the self-esteem for someone who feels that they have deteriorated from their former self. Mr D. had been confined to a wheelchair for about 30 years. Before he had become disabled, he had been a skilled worker and his work had involved physical stamina and expertise. He now used drawings and words to describe his work. He was interesting to listen to, and he felt pleasure and justified pride from his descriptions of his work.

Death

Most people are afraid of death, it is final, it is the end of life. In order to have the desire to live, we need the fear of death. Some elderly people say they wish they could die now. In the authors' experience these are always people who are very unhappy with their present lives, and who see death as the only answer to their troubles. Likewise, some people who assume they are no longer of any use to others feel that they might as well be dead.

Death is the ultimate loss, and with one's own death all is lost, left behind. Kubler Ross (1981), after interviewing many younger terminally ill people, realized that they go through the emotions of denial, anger, bargaining, sadness and then acceptance. It is possible that elderly people experience these emotions at times in relation to their own deaths. Often, they can experience ambivalent feelings, for example a longing to die to get away from pain, and yet a strong drive to survive illness and accident.

The work of Kubler Ross demonstrates her belief that people who are dying benefit from having someone who will actively listen to them. Many elderly people want to talk about how they feel about dying, at times of their own choosing, but it is difficult for them to find younger people who will not tell them to stop talking that way. In our society it is a taboo subject, and this taboo can prevent elderly people even from talking about it amongst themselves. The issue of their own death faces people with a particular loneliness.

Miller (1984) has written in depth about death in his paper on art therapy with the elderly and the terminally ill and discusses how feelings about their own death can be communicated by people in their artwork even when they themselves are unable to talk about these things.

Senile dementia

Many people disapprove of the label 'senile dementia', because it is vague and they feel it has a derogatory connotation. However, it is not derogatory and moreover it is a useful label to describe the severe and debilitating memory loss brought about by organic brain deterioration in elderly people. It is more usually people's attidudes which are derogatory because the conditions of senile dementia are so much to be feared by us all.

The two main conditions of senile dementia are Alzheimer's disease and cerebral arteriosclerosis. They both have a slow onset, such that degeneration could have been occurring for many years before diagnosable symptoms appear. Different areas of the brain may be diseased so that different areas of performance are affected. But in all senile dementias there is progressive memory loss, starting with the short-term memory. There can also be dysphasia, which is a disconnection between a thought and the choice of words with which to express it; and dyspraxia, which is a similar disconnection between thought or intention and movement. When there is a considerable loss of recent memory, a person lives his or her past memories, projecting the people and things of the past on to those around him or her.

Much has been written on deterioration and the slowing down or speeding up of it (Pitt 1974, Holden and Woods 1982, Gilhooley 1984). There are two areas of deterioration, organic deterioration in the brain, and the loss of social skills brought about by a decreasing awareness of reality. There is nothing that can alter the rate of organic deterioration, but this does not correspond at a consistent rate with the deterioration of social skills. The environment and the management of people with senile dementia can affect the rate of this last type of deterioration.

A psychoanalytical view of senile dementia is that it is a form of dying because it is a gradual disintegration of ego boundaries separating reality from fantasy (which is usually in the form of memories) and inside from outside worlds. There is no longer a reaching out for personal growth, which is seen by Eissler (1972) as the death instinct taking a dominant position over the life instinct. However, there are many people with senile dementia who are simply living, without any apparent thought about death. Whilst a person is aware of their deterioration, they will usually experience fear and anxiety as well as frustration. But once a person has lost their awareness, they may be happy or unhappy according to their basic personality. Emotions become more labile, and the person can be more easily distracted, but this does not mean that the feelings are any less intense or serious.

Senile dementia is particularly distressing to those around the affected person, for example to relatives who feel that this is a different person to the one they knew. This person can also be very demanding and disruptive as a result of the loss in social skills.

The role of the therapeutic relationship

Dependency on carers, and on the relationship with a therapist, can provoke a child–parent type of relationship. This brings up feelings within the dependent person which they had towards their real parents (transference) and responsive feelings in the carer or therapist (counter-transference). Sometimes, however, the transference and counter-transference can change, so that the therapist is seen as a son or daughter or even a grandchild. This is further complicated by the shift in the real relationship between the elderly person and their offspring, from being the carer to being the one who is cared for.

Brian Martindale (1989) has written about feelings of guilt which are easily aroused in the therapist (or carer) around real or imagined dependency, such as the fear and guilt in case he or she should ever have to leave the elderly person for good. Guilt, if not acknowledged and understood, can block the awareness of the therapist and the progress of the therapy.

Understanding transference relationships will help the therapist towards understanding a resident's reaction to the institution, staff and relatives, but as can be seen, they are complicated concerning this social group. However, the use of art within the therapeutic relationship brings in a third area which dilutes the intensity of the transference and provides an arena where some feelings can knowingly or unknowingly be exposed. For example, where negative emotions are expressed obliquely, or repressed, because residents are afraid of angering those whose help they need, art therapy can enable some expression of these feelings. In the spontaneous moments of making images, the choices of subject, materials, colour, shape, form and so on all reflect unconscious thoughts and feelings; just as fleeting thoughts, day dreams and night dreams do. The art therapist and the client can work together to identify, and thus bring to light, some of the feelings thus suggested.

Similarly, some people may be overwhelmed by the events which happened to them on their journey towards residential care. Losses may have happened one by one over a period of many years, or consecutively over a short period; they may have happened predictably or unpredictably. Some people will have grieved and adjusted themselves, others may have been unable to do so. Because there has been so much loss, there seem to be many different reasons for feeling one emotion. Thus it can seem overwhelmingly complicated, and difficult to acknowledge. It is helpful and positive for such people to be aware of what they feel and to know that the feelings are quite normal and understandable in their situations. The art therapist and the client can work together as described above, and thus find some identifiable threads of feeling in the tangle caused by the overwhelming events.

Some residents have no relatives and few friends. These people feel very alone and often worthless and are very much in need of good relationships. Others have families; sons and daughters who are unable to take care of their parents at home. Even when the reasons are fully understood and accepted on an intellectual level, this can be experienced as a rejection. The art therapist can accept these feelings without capitulation, such as the feared cutting down of visits.

Often the client in art therapy resists the idea that art expresses feelings, and will not work with the therapist in the way described above, but if he or she will make images or construct materials, there is a sense of a need to express, a struggle to express, and usually a sense of satisfaction at having done so. Or there is a sense of quiet concentration whilst the work is in process. This process allows for daydreaming. Unconscious thoughts and feelings affect spontaneous decisions over colour, form etc., whilst colour and form suggest associations and influence the daydreaming; a process usually acknowledged as 'satisfying'.

Frustration and shame can be felt at the loss of physical abilities, such as sight and hearing, mobility, ease of handling pencils. An art therapist must be particularly aware of the shame felt by a decreased ability in drawing. Mrs M. tried to draw a face and could not get the features in the right places. She knew it was wrong but could not improve on it, and she wanted to put the features in the right places. She was ashamed and refused even invitations to paint colour patterns.

Mr P. drew a face although he had protested that he was not able to draw. A nurse saw it and laughed at it; he refused to draw for a long time afterwards. The laughter, which could have been a joke to a younger person, reinforced Mr P.'s fear that because he was losing some skills he was becoming stupid. This fear is usually very strong in someone who has senile dementia, and this is why mocking laughter has such a devastating effect. A typical defence against the fear and the shame is to withdraw into oneself. Mr P. was in fact part of an open ward group which took place in the dining area of his hospital ward. It was thought that this would be a good venue for demonstrating what was available to people whose verbal comprehension is very limited and who do not move eagerly from one room to another, but as can be seen, this advantage had to be weighed against the disadvantage of the group being exposed to unfavourable comments.

In fact it is an added difficulty to doing art therapy with elderly people in care that the work often has to be undertaken in the place where the client lives and is looked after. Because of the physical frailty and dependence of many of the residents, it is usually impossible to bring them to a separate art room. Depending on the dynamics of the ward or home, it is seen as the territory of the staff, the staff and the residents, or the residents. The therapist is an outsider coming in, and does not have the same power as if he or she were working in their own art room. Traditional boundaries which enable art therapy to be effective, for example those of using a private room and having no interruptions, are more difficult to preserve and require some negotiation.

Living in a hospital or home where one no longer has to cook, shop or clean, it is hard to keep up one's self-esteem. All too often the residents feel useful no longer, for they have lost their work or home-keeping role, and have probably had to drop other roles taken on after retirement. Often, they lose pride in their bodies as they deteriorate from the peak of physical condition which our society so adores. Their sexual needs are there, but society does not recognize elderly people as sexual. They have probably lost people in whose eyes they mattered. They have lost their homes and with this a manifestation of their identity.

Some have enough ego strength to maintain their self-esteem, but most need anything which will help them to value themselves better; respect, usefulness, and good relationships at least. Art therapy provides them with a medium which expresses their individuality, an individuality which is accepted and valued, because the client is encouraged to make his or her own choices throughout the process, from choosing the materials to choosing what to do with them. This is a positive reinforcement of the value of that person as they are. The seriousness of the relationships between the clients and the therapist are also a recognition of the value of each client.

Also in art therapy, the past can be remembered and discussed. Images from the past can be depicted. Other images made can bring back memories through free association and discussion. The therapist and group members can bring fresh points of view to old conflicts.

Although the use of skills and the training of the eye would not be seen as belonging to art therapy, but rather as the stuff of teaching, it is inevitably important to one or two people in a group. This is beneficial to elderly people living in hospitals or residential homes, as it brings a new involvement with things outside their daily life, a daily life which has inevitably narrowed down. Because of the conflict between withdrawing into a passive wait to die, and the desire to have more than that, anything which encourages 'living' is vital. However, the therapist who responds to this need is walking on a tightrope. Hands have become shaky, eyes have lost their accuracy of vision: deterioration in the technique emphasizes deterioration of the body. Here, subtlety and sensitivity are of prime importance.

A big problem which is faced by art therapists working with elderly people in residential care is the common lack of motivation to do anything which is fairly active and a change to their normal routine. It is still normal to see a group of residents sitting in a circle asleep or gazing into space, none of them watching the television which is probably on. Of course the home or hospital can reinforce or challenge this situation, but there are other factors which pull these people to withdraw from social life.

Some are still grieving a lost spouse, and cannot accept living fully without him or her. Many grieve the loss of their own homes, and find it hard still to respect themselves now that they have lost so much independence. Many are so frustrated with their declining physical abilities, they lose the will to work at slowing the decline. Some suffer pain, which makes anything more of an effort. Some are afraid to take risks once they have lost their sight or hearing. Probably most are very afraid of having senile dementia, particularly those whose memory is getting worse, and of being seen as stupid (as with Mr P.).

There are a few for whom coming into a residential home marks a turning-point and a challenge, taking away the grind of loneliness and domestic chores; these people are motivated to make something of life in the home. But many seem to cut themselves off, as though the safest approach, perhaps the only approach, is to go passively through the rest of their lives until death comes to take them away. Yet they respond to attention, an interest in them. They can be very demanding of staff in indirect, often angry, ways. There is still the basic human need for more than this, except in the very few who have really decided it is time to die.

As well as this more general lack of motivation, it must be taken into account that there is a difference in attitude to life of the present generation of over 80s, to the attitudes of younger generations, certainly amongst working people. They suffered hardship during the wars, and often poverty or near poverty in childhood or later. Survival was hard work physically and often this helped the emotional well-being: 'you had to get on with it', as many now say. Exploring feelings, particularly negative ones, would be seen as a threat to the need to keep going; it is still seen as a threat although the situation is quite different. Most of the 'getting going', the physical work, is done by others; there is no such need for their participation any more, no demands, apart from their own needs and demands which they are used to denying. It is harder to want to change an attitude which worked for 70 years than to give in to a kind of depressed withdrawal from an active and creative involvement with life.

This lack of motivation can be very frustrating for an eager art therapist. What is important is that the residents' defensive feelings are respected, and that they get enough out of each session to want to return. Once the trust is established, suggestions about why the clients might feel like they do are slipped in and agreed with at ease. Often artwork is not so much analysed as digested, and the personality is felt through the style and content.

Thus art can be a gentle way for the clients to express how they feel about themselves, and it can be a way of discussing feelings evoked by loss, death and so on, or of talking about the past. It can also be a good way of responding to needs for relationship and better self-esteem.

Art therapy with residents of a psychogeriatric ward

The level of impairment one is likely to encounter in a continuing care ward of a psychiatric hospital, and particularly in a psychogeriatric ward, reflects the difficulty of establishing a way of working. The rudiments of the traditional insight-based, analytic approach, where the therapist is working very much in a reflective capacity and linking unconscious material with consciousness, may have little impact in such a situation. The confused, elderly patient whose level of functioning largely prevents a full comprehension of time and events and their relationship to himself, will have a poor ability to gain control and insight without suitable direction.

When having a conversation with a resident in a psychogeriatric ward, who is perhaps disoriented, confused, and has ceased to have any discernible relationship with the outside world, it will be found that his or her speech will reflect such internal disorganization by being jumbled and apparently irrational. The fragmentation of both internal and external worlds is often beyond the point where verbal psychotherapy would have any influence, although this does not preclude the psychodynamic framework of art therapy, where comprehension becomes visual within the artwork.

The trialogue that occurs in art therapy, whereby the artwork functions like a third person, as a receptacle for conscious and unconscious processes, facilitates a communication channel with the confused elderly person that words alone cannot create. Sometimes just the presence of art materials on the table are enough to arouse in the participant a curiosity and sense of play that may otherwise be inaccessible. The materials and resulting artwork, no matter how minimal this may be, can forge a link of communication between the client and the therapist in a definite and physical way, which stays visible in the real external world, rather than being lost in a torrent of disoriented thoughts. This 'staying' quality, or permanence, of the artwork can have a particularly constructive influence on the stability and continuity of the therapeutic discourse in progress, whereas the confused client may have tremendous difficulty in maintaining a continuity of his or her own. In this sense, the artwork is a point of reference which does not change by itself or disappear, but remains to confirm the efforts of its creator.

As a point of focus and permanence in the therapeutic relationship, the artwork fulfils a function which is similar to D.W. Winnicott's concept of the transitional object. This suggests that an object such as a doll can be regarded by the infant as a link between its own self and some other person. The transition which occurs from thought to external picture-making in art therapy echoes this idea, although with the increasing confusion of senile dementia, the image reflects rather a reversal of external reality building as opposed to the developing process of the infant.

Case-studies

The following two case-studies illustrate the role art therapy has to play in a continuing care ward of a large psychiatric hospital. The residents themselves are not individually referred by clinicians, as art therapy in this case is regarded as an additional component to ward life, therefore functioning as a facility for all residents. On a more diagnostic level, the ward caters for a variety of needs, housing residents with organic brain dysfunctions such as Alzheimer's disease and residents with residual schizophrenia. The level of intellectual functioning varies considerably with each resident as a result, and is reflected in the way the art therapy sessions operate, which is in the form of a group.

The focus of the group is aimed primarily at the individual needs of its members, rather than at the overall group dynamic, which is immobilized in the wake of such impaired comprehension. The group takes place in a designated room on the ward equipped with a variety of materials and is held on a weekly basis.

The first example described here is largely concerned with the non-verbal holding role of the artwork, with the account of some work undertaken by Roger Wilks (RW), with Mrs G., a lady of 93 now permanently resident in hospital with advanced Alzheimer's disease.

After a succession of progressively confused residencies in warden-controlled flats and nursing homes, Mrs G. was admitted to the acute psychogeriatric ward of the hospital. Then, having an increasingly poor ability to maintain self-care independently, she was transferred to the continuing care ward. She had become dependent on the hospital for both her mental and physical needs, having lost the ability to walk without supervision, and being frequently incontinent. Mrs G. would spend every day sitting quietly in the same chair. She rarely had visitors, her remaining family had moved some considerable distance away, and maintained minimal contact.

When engaged in conversation in the sitting-room of the ward, Mrs G. would find it very difficult to preserve any lasting consistency in the dialogue. This problem was compounded further by her apparent deafness, although physiological evidence did not confirm such a condition. She had no obvious relationship with any of the other residents, and relied totally on the nursing staff for nourishment, toileting and mobility. Despite such apparent isolation of both a physical and an interpersonal nature, Mrs G. would welcome the opportunity to chat with someone and hold on to them. Sometimes she would laugh and sometimes she would cry.

In art therapy, Mrs G. was always very keen to hold and investigate the objects on the table, which she would accrue until she had a complex assemblage of items comprising various types of art materials as well as everyday objects that were available, such as cutlery, teabags and an old alarm clock. Mrs G. would then set about arranging, rearranging and cataloguing the miscellany, until it conformed to the order that she sought to attain. Her level of involvement and commitment to seeing the process through made a stark contrast with her usual inability to stay with a consistent progression of thought. The physical being, and contact with the objects, reinforced her perception of the external world to a level which enabled a continuity to take place.

The experience of touch was of particular importance in shaping Mrs G.'s association with a concrete reality beyond her own internal confusion, with touching and feeling functioning as additional perception enhancers to her visual faculties in comprehension. At her request RW would often hold her when she was talking which, as well as aiding the continuity of her reflections and ideas, had the effect of strengthening her involvement in an interpersonal relationship. With her experience of touching and being touched, Mrs G. was developing a very real and quite literal hold on ideas and events that occurred within the sessions.

Mrs G. would regularly talk about apples. By all accounts from the nursing staff, this was a subject which was confined to art therapy, as she never spoke of apples elsewhere. She would become very animated at the thought of apples, and her 'deafness' which one would normally encounter evaporated in the liveliness of discussion. Often Mrs G. would recount her expeditions of scrumping on her way home from school in the south London suburb were she was brought up, with a cheeky relish, especially as she had to negotiate somebody's garden fence. There was a fluency in her descriptive recollections that did not accompany her short term memory and perception of the here and now. She could remember street names and a host of geographical features, some of which have long ceased to exist.

Quite by chance there are some apple trees adjacent to the art therapy room which Mrs G. was unable to see from her near permanent sedentary position in the wheelchair. This enabled RW to introduce some real apples into the conversation. The apples almost immediately became amalgamated into the assemblages and underlined the content of her thoughts. She was able to use and incorporate them into her own process of maintaining a stability, and this resulted in often consistent verbal exchanges in the session time. The apples acted as a catalyst on her creative faculties in tandem with her spoken comments. Mrs G. would write long, indecipherable words and add them to the objects, she would cut apples in half and underline them in paint and occasionally the apples would be eaten.

Although the example of Mrs G. is principally concerned with the role of the object in art therapy, it also illustrates how fundamental the relationship is in creating a process wherein the elderly and confused client can begin to establish an affinity with his or her surroundings and other persons. Long-stay wards for the elderly in large institutions are often socially and culturally impoverished, a factor which can exacerbate the already fragile capacity a resident may have in maintaining vital links with other people. Certainly one of the primary roles of the art therapist in such an environment is to address this by building up a rapport which will help to foster in the resident a sense of being involved. The hospital ward which houses severely impaired elderly people will usually be the last port of call, and will have a terminal quality which cannot help but influence the ability or inclination of the residents to interact with others. The dependence and also the level of regression which can be observed in many of the residents can provoke a parental response from workers within the ward, and can be strongly echoed in the transference relationship which develops with the art therapist.

In order to elaborate further on the theme of a parental transference, we give the following account of the case of Miss C., an active lady of seventy-nine, who has been resident in the hospital for over fifty years.

Miss C. had had a long hospital career moving around various different wards in the process. The diagnostic reasons for her admission are poorly documented, but an entry in February 1941 states, 'She is an imbecile with superimposed schizophrenia'. Over the years she had received a traditional assortment of psychiatric treatments, culminating in permanent medication with tranquillisers. Miss C. no longer had any links with anyone outside of the hospital, contact was lost with her family virtually on admission and there had been no new developments since.

As a resident in the continuing care ward, which was after a long series of moving to and from other wards throughout the hospital, Miss C. was physically independent, and maintained some capacity for self care. She was always clean and took some pride in her appearance, which was helped enormously by the installation of a dressing table in her own separate bedroom. She had certain obsessional tendencies, however, and exhibited some childlike characteristics in her behaviour which prevented her from separating from the institution and leading a life independent of hospital care. As was the case with Mrs G., Miss C. spent most of her day in the day room, as though she were waiting for something to happen. The stillness would be periodically punctured when she took a trip to her bedroom to check that her quilt and blankets were still on the bed.

Miss C. had formed a very close attachment with art therapy, although it would be more accurate to say that this attachment was primarily with the therapist (RW) rather than with a visual process. She attended every session that was available to her and had built up a collection of drawings illustrating the recurrent themes of houses and cats, which suggested a limited pictorial vocabulary. Miss C.'s main anxiety was her concern that WB, another female resident, kept taking the blankets off Miss C.'s bed in the middle of the night. This resulted in Miss C.'s permanent anger with WB and her need to keep a constant check on the state of her bedroom. In actuality, WB rarely ventured anywhere near Miss C.'s bedroom, but the act or fear of the act had been totally absorbed into Miss C.'s delusional belief system.

As the bonding between RW and Miss C. intensified over the months, Miss C. came to regard RW as a protective figure from whom she could seek reassurance and assistance in deterring WB. Initially her image-making, though not consciously connected with contemporary aspects of her life in hospital, centred around family life and depictions of the family home. These were often accompanied by early recollections describing how male members of the family looked after Miss C. as a young girl. She then began to link up such pre-hospital experiences with her present dilemma, by wondering what Uncle J. would have done about WB. Material also surfaced which drew a verbal portrait of L., Miss C.'s former 'husband' who gradually also became Mr C. her father.

Miss C.'s simple line drawings of the family home became interpolated with accompanying images of cats, sometimes in isolation and sometimes sitting next to the house. Initially, Miss C. would comment as she drew it that the cat lived in the house, but increasingly she would decide to draw Mr C., but employ the same visual representation of the cat, guarding the family home. In identifying the protective faculties of the cat, Miss C. began making connections with present events, depicting the cat chasing WB in order to 'give her a good hiding'. This was an action she was sure Mr C. would have taken, and in turn she surmised that in his absence it was the responsibility of RW to do the same. The process of such drawing gave Miss C. tremendous satisfaction whereby the image represented a form of substitute reality, in which ideas could be enacted that would be normally incompatible with a real situation.

The dual role of Mr C. as husband and father soon became displaced on to RW, whom Miss C. then regarded as an effective substitute for Mr C. She perceived RW as someone who should love her and keep WB firmly at bay. Miss C. also became increasingly concerned that RW did not share her intense dislike of WB, and this caused her in turn to seek regular confirmation that RW still liked her.

A split had developed, forming a core issue in the therapy, and moreover in the relationship between Miss C. and RW. She had idealized RW and polarized WB as an inversely bad counterpart, and recognized a strong need to keep the two opposing forces as separate as possible. In order for Miss C. to maintain such a split, she persistently sought to convince RW of WB's wickedness, both verbally and in pictorial form, by making drawings of RW or Mr C. giving WB a smacked bottom. This, like her other imagery, had a poignant association with the past. She would sometimes reflect on what Uncle J. used to do to her when she had been mischievous at home. A spanking it seems, by her account, was commonplace.

The failure of RW to enter fully into a collusion with Miss C. over WB did little to jeopardize the symbolized father–daughter relationship, however. As Miss C.'s need to internalize something good overran her more negative impulses, she increased the investment in her relationship with the therapist. Gradually, despite her persistent scorn of WB, Miss C.'s sense of humour began to emerge, and encouraged by RW, her anger and fantasies of WB soon became more a source of amusement rather than irritation for her within the sessions.

Through the strong level of attachment she had formed in the present, Miss C. had found herself referring increasingly to pre-hospital, mostly family-centred experiences, which seemed so influential in the therapy. Interestingly, she had little recollection of the intervening hospital years, as though time had stopped emotionally on separation from her family only to be reactivated again in art therapy. She often commented that she was fourteen, having been sent to hospital by her mother quite recently. Her life review still involved a large part of con-structive reorganization of her present and she had effectively blocked off the notion that her life was in its twilight years. Miss C. reminded RW to send her a card for her fifteenth birthday on frequent occasions.

Perhaps the most influential way in which art therapy made an unbearable situation more bearable for Miss C., was the effect the therapeutic relationship had in promoting a reconstruction of a parental model. The nurturing quality of such a model enables the therapist to promote a comfortable enough situation for the client, whereby self observation and its bond with the artwork becomes a creative process. The dual mirroring role of Miss C.'s relationship with the therapist and with her own creativity amplified the difficulties she was experiencing within the containment of the sessions. Ultimately Miss C.'s verbally expressed anxieties regarding WB, and her picture making became fused together as one process, alleviating some of the difficulties encountered by her own decision making in isolation.

Although there are distinct social and pathological differences between Miss C. and Mrs G., the extent of a dependence on statutory care is of equal necessity for both of them. The art therapist therefore addresses similar needs, in enriching the experience of living in a hospital that had become the home.

Conclusion

Demographic studies indicate that the number of people over the age of 65 within the total population of the United Kingdom is set to rise over the next 20 years (OPCS 1989). If mental health is to be reflected in such figures, they may also be a corresponding rise in the prevalence of Alzheimer's disease and other debilitating conditions which affect the elderly. In the provision of services for the elderly dependent on statutory care, there will continue to be a need for psychological support in tandem with care of a physical nature.

In this context art therapy has an important role to play, not only as a resource in the psychodynamic understanding of the elderly, but more importantly as a resource fostering some greater understanding for the elderly themselves. As we have already described, work with elderly people in care is not without difficulties. The lack of motivation and level of dependency can provide the therapist with sizeable obstacles in establishing an effective method of therapy. But perhaps the cases of Miss C. and Mrs G. reflect the rewards of such work by restoring a sense of value in the individual and a continuum of emotional engagement which beyond all else is so important in maintaining a desirable quality of life.

References

Age Exchange Theatre Company: specializes in reminiscence work. Their address is: 11 Blackheath Village, London, SE3.

Birren, J. (1964) *The Psychology of Aging*, Englewood Cliffs: Prentice-Hall.

Eissler, R.S. (1972) *Death Drive, Ambivalence and Narcissism. The Psycho-analytical Study of the Child*, NY: Quadrangle.

Erikson, E. (1979) *Identity and the Life Cycle*, NY: W.W. Norton.

Gilhooley, M. (1984) The social dimensions of senile dementia, in I. Hanley and J. Hodge (eds) *Psychological Approaches to the Care of the Elderly*, Beckenham: Croom Helm.

Harlan, J. (1990) Beyond the patient to the person: promoting aspects of autonomous functioning in individuals with mild to moderate dementia, *American Journal of Art Therapy* **28**(May).

Harrison, C. (1980) Creative arts for older people in the community, *American Journal of Art Therapy* **19**(July).

Holden, U. and Woods, R.J. (1982) *Reality Origins*, Edinburgh: Churchill Livingstone.

Jacques, A. (1988) *Understanding Dementia*, Edinburgh: Churchill Livingstone.

Jung, C. (1960) The structure and dynamics of the psyche, in *The Collected Works, Vol. 8*, London: Routledge and Kegan Paul.

Kubler Ross, E. (1981) *On Death and Dying*, London: Tavistock.

Martindale, B. (1989) Becoming dependent again: the fears of some elderly persons and their younger therapists, *Psychoanalytic Psychotherapy* **4**(9).

Miller, B. (1984) Art therapy with the elderly and the terminally ill, in T. Dalley (ed.) *Art as Therapy*, London: Tavistock Publications.

Murray Parkes, C. (1972/1975) *Bereavement*, London: Tavistock; Harmondsworth: Pelican.

Office of Population Censuses and Surveys (1989) *Population Projections 1987–2007*, Series PP2, No. 16, London: HMSO.

Osler, I. (1988) Creativity's influence on a case of dementia, *Inscape*, Summer.

Pitt, B. (1974) *Psychogeriatrics*, Edinburgh: Churchill Livingstone.

Simon, R. (1985) Graphic style and therapeutic change in geriatric patients, *American Journal of Art Therapy* **24**(August).

Wald, J. (1983) Alzheimer's disease and the role of art therapy in its treatment, *American Journal of Art Therapy* **22**(January).

Winnicott, D. (1971) *Playing and Reality*, London: Tavistock.

Worden, J.W. (1982) *Grief Counselling and Grief Therapy*, London: Tavistock Publications.

6

Art therapy with people who have severe learning difficulties

ROBIN TIPPLE

Introduction

Since the beginnings of art therapy in Britain art therapists have been working in the larger Mental Handicap Hospitals. These institutions, though smaller now, still provide a home for a broad range of society's casualties. They are the homes for those people who have, through the lack of education and opportunity, been unable to care for themselves. Their behaviour is seen as deviant in some way and a lack of intellectual skills has burdened them with the label of mentally retarded. The Mental Handicap Hospitals also provide homes for those who lack language and have communication difficulties; those who have suffered brain and central nervous system damage or whose neurophysiological development has been delayed or injured in some way. This includes people with concomitant physical disabilities and sensory deficits.

This chapter is about the work that art therapists in Britain have developed with the more severely disabled members of this group. Such clients may be severely or even profoundly mentally retarded and have associated learning difficulties. They may not have any speech. They may be withdrawn and exhibit stereotypical motor patterns, rocking and so on. They could, perhaps in part because of years of institutionalization, present with bizarre, anti-social and aggressive behaviours including self-mutilating acts. As can be imagined and as is well known by all professionals working in this field, it is very difficult to help this client group. Establishing stable and positive relationships with these difficult and unattractive individuals is difficult. When artwork is possible, it appears that the client has merely repeated a series of simple motor movements with the crayon or marker and the resultant work may seem banal and of little value.

I first began working with mentally retarded people at Leytonstone House in North East London. I soon became impressed by the richness and variety of the art products made by a range of clients who used many different processes, sometimes in very inventive ways. I was also puzzled by some of the behaviours I saw and intrigued by the use made of art materials in the work of the more severely disabled and handicapped clients. In my next post, at Leavesden Hospital in Hertfordshire, I was able to study the mark-making or scribbling of severely disabled clients more closely. I saw these clients in both individual sessions and in a small group which I organized for a number of neglected individuals who enjoyed mark-making. I realized, especially after I displayed some of the work produced by this group, how each individual was capable of using her or his own mark in a very creative and expressive way and that the work, far from being impoverished and banal, was full of incident and variety. I also began to pay much more attention to the behaviours of these artists during the group and I reflected on the ways in which the scribbling and marking was affected by the atmosphere, mood and disposition of all the members of the group, as well as by the individual's own state of being.

Much of this chapter is about the importance of mark-making for the severely disabled person. I shall include a brief account of the work of other art therapists who work in this area, look to the theoretical background to their work and consider the relationship of the scribbling or marking of this client group to the scribbling of infants. I will then give the reader some indication of the origins of my own ideas and delineate in more detail the way in which I see mark-making as being expressive. Following this there will be some case material which I hope will show something of how I work and how a particular client made use of the opportunity to paint in a therapeutic relationship.

Art therapy approaches to working with severely disabled clients

Over the years art therapists have adopted many different ways of working with the mentally retarded. Much of this work can best be described as 'studio based' – that is, the art therapy department offers open sessions where the client comes and uses the art materials and space for creative work. This style of work has been developed and extended by art therapists Joaquim Catala and Sue Hammans at Leytonstone House. Here the art therapy department functions like a small creative community within the larger institution, an asylum in the true sense, where residents or clients can find sanctuary or retreat from the pressures of life in the institution. Clients can use the art materials how and when they choose, create their own environment and seek support and encouragement. The therapist is available to help with all practical tasks as well as ensuring that one person's freedom does not impinge on the activity or security of another's. Art products and processes can be shared between residents or clients, as well as presented to the therapist as communication. In this milieu it is usual for the art therapist to work in what has become known as a 'non-directive' way, that is she keeps her interference, her interventions, to a minimum and does not seek to determine the direction that the work takes. A 'non-directive' approach does not imply that the therapist makes no interventions and does not interact with the client; rather it indicates that the initiative remains with the client and the therapist seeks to encourage his or her creative endeavours whatever form they take.

A directive approach is described by Stott and Males (1984). Central to their work is the concept of stages of development in comparison with children. 'There are similarities between the drawings produced by children of "normal" intellect and mentally handicapped adults' (p. 117) they write, and 'drawings will reflect the particular stage of development' that the artist has reached (p. 118). The art therapist 'must observe the stage of development' that his or her mentally handicapped client has reached and then make the 'intervention' that gently guides or directly encourages her client towards the next stage. They suggest that it is important to recognize that the mentally handicapped person may not be able to reach the next stage in drawing development and that the art therapist must ensure that the individual can succeed. Stott and Males describe how an individual who repeats the letter 'A' is encouraged by the art therapist reproducing the letter upside down to see the letter afresh as pattern and shape.

Some art therapy departments run small closed groups, sometimes in addition to the open groups I have described. A closed group could consist of between three and nine members. The members of the group would meet regularly once a week, at the same time and in the same place. The membership would remain stable over time and each member would be expected to attend regularly and stay for the duration of the session, which could be, for example, one-and-a-half hours. The art produced in such a group is seen as communication between the membership. The therapist would seek to understand the behaviour within the group (the group dynamics), to interpret the artwork in the light of the group dynamics and to reflect this back in some way to the group. A number of art therapists work this way; Coral Driscoll and Les Trewin at Leavesden Hospital in Hertfordshire have developed considerable expertise in this area. Sue Strand (1990) gives an eloquent account of working within the group analytic framework.

Almost all art therapists working with mentally retarded clients will have some knowledge and understanding of psychotherapy and will be acquainted with psychodynamic theories. In a series of articles in *Inscape* (the journal of BAAT), four art therapists working at Leybourne Grange in Kent presented case-studies and argued for the need to develop psychotherapeutic models of art therapy with mentally handicapped people. Most of these case-studies were concerned with mildly or moderately retarded people. Rose Hughes (1988) has worked with more severely disabled clients and has developed a technique and style of work influenced by the theories of Winnicott. It is the work of the art therapist to create and maintain a 'facilitating environment', writes Hughes. This is an environment where the individual can work playfully and find or create a 'potential space'. The 'potential space' is an intermediate area between fantasy and reality where an individual may experience herself moving from being in fantasy to being in reality. The movement between fantasy and reality, between subjectivity and objectivity, is achieved through the use of objects. In this case the object is the art product, perhaps just a piece of paper that has been marked according to desire. This is the 'transitional object' (Winnicott's term) which gratifies through fantasy, but also reflects back its otherness, its separateness from the self. Hughes argues that handicapped individuals who have experienced social and psychological deprivation can, through the use of such an object, created out of their own needs, begin to regard the world in general more positively, because it is a relationship to an object that is satisfying, not experienced as frustrating or punitive in any way. The art therapist in this approach is likened to a mother who can allow her child to be 'contentedly separate' through the 'assistance' of transitional objects (in this case art materials) whilst at the same time the child remains in her mother's presence.

For Rose Hughes, the task for her severely handicapped or disabled clients in art therapy is one of moving from an infantile subjective state to a more objective adult orientation towards the world: a coming to terms with the otherness of the world and perhaps recognizing its disappointments. Her approach implies that the adult mentally handicapped person with severe disabilities does not have a capacity to recognize the otherness of the world, that they have a poor sense of self. It implies that the artwork produced in an art therapy session by such a client does not serve as a direct communication between the client and therapist. The artwork serves rather as 'a positive reinforcement', an object that can be experienced as satisfactory or comforting. Although Hughes recognizes that a drawing can 'mirror' a client's 'state of being' she does not describe in detail how particular works are produced, at what point in time and how they might relate to previous behaviours. Her use of Winnicott's theories and observations of child develop-ment parallels the use that Janie Stott and Bruce Males have made of theories of drawing development. My feeling is that some art therapists assume a state of delayed development of ego and/or of self in the more severely disabled groups of mentally handicapped people and that their productions and behaviours are best treated as if they were developing infants; in my view this can result in some communications being overlooked or ignored. I will expand on this idea as I proceed. None the less such parallels are drawn and it necessitates a consideration of the differences between the drawings or markings of mentally handicapped people and children's productions through discussion of the literature on the 'scribbling stage'.

Children's drawing

Rhodda Kellog (1969) analysed and compared approximately a million drawings done by young children. She identified 20 kinds of markings which she labelled 'the basic scribbles' and then considered the placement of scribbles on paper and categorized these into 'placement patterns'. The relationship of figure to ground in these placement patterns demonstrated to her the growing aesthetic sensibility of the infant. 'Line formations in child art are the result of motion', she writes, and 'when the hand moves to make the scribbling gesture characteristic of early childhood a record of the hand movements is left on some surface' (Kellog 1969: 250, 253). There is a 'mental association', she believes, 'between the flow of lines on a surface and the movements of the body'. 'Art Gestalts' therefore have a 'physiological effect' on the viewer who can consequently feel the movement. Kellog's comparative method led her to develop a complete classification system for all children's drawings whether from the pre-representational stage or later, a system which has been used by others to categorize and describe children's drawing.

Lowenfeld and Lambert Brittain's large comprehensive text (1970) is designed for parents, teachers and others who have an interest in children's art, and it incorporates many research findings. They suggest that developing sensory awareness of the environment in the early months is the prerequisite background to the production of art, the child usually making his or her first mark around 18 months. Lowenfeld and Lambert Brittain divide scribbles into three categories: disordered scribbles, controlled scribbles and named scribbles. The disordered scribble may contain many accidental results; fine muscle control has not yet developed and crayons and sometimes held upside down or sideways with the child even looking away as she or he works. According to Lowenfeld and Lambert Brittain about six months after starting to scribble a child will discover the relatedness between the motions and the marks on the paper, leading to controlled scribbles. Often a child at this stage will fill the whole page and the lines may be repeated in order to gain mastery as more elaborate scribbles emerge. Naming of the scribble follows at 3½ years. There will not be any visual representation of the subject to which the child refers, but naming the scribble is important because it demonstrates that a new way of thinking has occurred in relation to the child's drawings.

Lowenfeld and Lambert Brittain have some interesting things to say about colour. Colour plays a 'subordinate role' in the scribbling stage when the child is establishing motor co-ordination. The authors quote a paper by Corcoran (1954) who found evidence that three-year-old children used colours in sequential order when painting, i.e the colours were used left to right or right to left on the easel or palette. During the scribbling stages colour may provide an opportunity for exploration, but the creation of lines and forms may be more important. 'It is quite apparent that scribbling is a natural part of the total development of children, reflecting their physiological and psychological growth' (Lowenfeld and Lambert Brittain 1987: 191).

Gardner (1980) observed the drawing behaviour of his son from his first marks begun when he was 18 months and three days old and is careful to place the first marks in the context of the developing infant. The infant has at this stage acquired knowledge of objects, the world has become more predictable and the young child has the possibility of using tools as demonstrated through his understanding of the use of the marker. The drawing becomes a communication – an object to be shown to others for approval or acknowledgement. These first marks, argues Gardner, add to the growth in autonomy at a time when the child is gradually breaking away from its caretakers. The detailed description of the drawings demonstrates the development of a variety of marks, gestures and designs – for example, the attempt to move lines in different directions and the use of dots on their own and within circles. This scribbling is compared with a child's night-time babbling; it is experiments with words that enable it to make a language. Further drawings result (at 2 years, 1 month) in the production of 'a face', that is a circle containing marks representing features.

Matthews (1986) also emphasizes descriptions of the child at work, but greater stress is given to the context in which drawing behaviour takes place. To understand this context is to understand the development process as a whole which leads, Matthews argues, to a revision of our adult notions of representation. 'Researchers', he writes, 'have been and still are, primarily concerned with configurative drawing, that is drawing which encodes the shape of objects' (ibid.: 13).

If an infant's marks fail to measure up to this configurative standard, then, the author argues, it is dismissed as mere scribbling, resulting in the neglect of an entire area of 'symbolization'. Scribbles or drawings are seen as part of a 'family of expressive and representational behaviour' that children use to organize their world, for example 'action representation' where the movement of a brush represents a car turning the corner and disappearing.

A mark carries with it the history of its making. It reflects the movement made by hand or arm. Kellog says the viewer can feel the movement, and this enjoyment is clearly one reason why marking or scribbling is such an enjoyable experience for the infant and the severely disabled person. I am not sure that Kellog's passion for classification is always helpful as many of the marks made by scribbling infants and severely disabled clients do not fit easily into the 'basic scribbles' or 'placement patterns' which she delineates. One reason for this is because the early scribbles or marks, as Lowenfeld and Lambert Brittain have observed, are very chaotic or 'disordered'. Howard Gardner's account of his son's markings shows how experimental and dynamic children's scribbling can be, but a period of control and repetition does supervene. These more 'controlled scribbles', as Lowenfeld and Lambert Brittain have called them, are similar to the markings of severely disabled clients. However, their markings tend to be more conservative, often with a strong perference for certain kinds of marks which will be repeated and elaborated. These clients are less likely to mirror or describe structural properties or things in their markings in the manner in which Mathews describes, but sometimes a representational or symbolic element can enter into the work. Lowenfeld and Lambert Brittain have stressed how children's reactions or interactions to art materials reflect aspects of their physiological and psychological growth. The same can be said for this client group. Their response to art materials, the processes and strategies they adopt, tells us much about them as individuals.

Art therapy research

A detailed and exhaustive account of the mark-making of four severely mentally handicapped male subjects can be found in Dubowski's research dissertation (1985). Dubowski's method of research and descriptions were influenced by this adoption of ethological techniques. (Ethology is the study of animal behaviour and ethologists are, or have been, chiefly concerned with non-human species, and the relevance of their work to the understanding of human behaviour may be questioned (Hinde 1982: 202). However, their methods and techniques may be useful in helping to clarify descriptive concepts or 'to provide principles whose applicability to the human case can be assessed' (ibid.).) Dubowski wanted to compare the mark-making of normal children, at the pre-representational stage, the mark-making of retarded adults and the mark-making of chimpanzees. He believes his descriptions show that the pre-representational stages are more complex than the previous literature has suggested. During his experimental procedures and observations Dubowski purposely interfered with the mark-making conditions for each of his four mentally handicapped subjects. He concluded that his four subjects had in common a 'basic response' to mark-making, formulated in terms of rules in the same way as Desmond Morris attempted to establish 'the biological principles of picture making' (Morris 1962).

All four subjects produced a controlled scribble but whereas a normal child would experiment with types of mark, these subjects limited their type of mark. Physical comfort, lack of initiative and attention to the marks and the boundaries of the paper characterized their work. When the mark-making situation was manipulated by the researcher the response was limited, all of which suggested an inherent conservatism. When reading Dubowski's dissertation I found the transcripts of the videos of the subjects at work the most interesting, and though he has determined the limitations of his subjects' mark-making, one feels that the formulation is a little barren. (He does not however err in the other direction, as Morris does when he declares that there are six principles which cover all picture-making which, when examined closely, only confirm Morris's own aesthetic prejudices.)

Mair Rees also used ethological methods in her research and suggests that art therapists should concern themselves with the 'pervasive effect of the ward social system on the individuals drawing endeavours' (Rees 1984: 22). Her work attempts to establish a link between behaviour patterns on the ward and the form an individual's mark-making or similar activity may take. Rees places great importance on the ethological constructs of territoriality and dominance in studies of ward social systems and quotes Esser, who writes, 'chronic mental patients seem unable to simultaneously focus attention on all group relations and they often have to establish and protect their status in one-to-one dominance encounters with others' (Esser 1976, quoted in Rees 1984: 28).

Rees discusses her study of patients' behaviour on the ward and observations of some of the same patients when they attend art therapy sessions. She gives short profiles of six subjects to show how the two sets of observations link and seeks to establish the relationship between the marks and an individual's social functioning.

In a later paper Rees argues that many individuals with severe learning difficulties use territorial strategies in order to gain 'some definition of the limits and boundaries of "self"' (Rees 1989: 1). In painting, which, writes Rees, is the preferred medium of many of these clients, 'The individual's central aim seems to be the filling in or reinforcing the boundaries of the page' (p. 4). This mirrors the way in which such clients relate to the physical and spatial aspects of their world, in order to maintain a relatively stable psychological state and emotional life. Rees describes a young man who spits on his hands and sweeps them along the floor pushing furniture aside to reach the edges and corners of a room. In his painting, he paid most attention to the edges and corners of the paper. The use of space in the painting may therefore be 'a symbolic statement' about an individual's emotional and psychological needs (Rees 1989: 11).

Rees's work is important as she demonstrates how marking and non-representational painting can relate to an individual's social functioning. What I miss is descriptive detail of the process of making paintings as it is clearly here that, in my view, emotions can often be most clearly expressed. It is through the gestural application of paint or the way material is handled that other areas of mental life, apart from spatial intelligence, may be communicated. In the final product, gesture may be lost in the accumulation of paint, especially when the aim is to produce a homogeneously filled-in sheet.

Dubowski gives a clear and objective description of the 'basic response' of some clients to mark-making; Rees has demonstrated how important the use of space in the painting can be; and Hughes seeks to reveal how the art product may enable the individual to progress towards a more complete experiencing of the world. Before presenting some case material, I want to reflect a little more on mark-making and painting as communication. That is, in what way could the marking or painting express or reveal emotional states or embody the feelings of the artist?

Emotional expression and painting

By concentrating on feelings or emotions, I do not want to suggest that thoughts or ideas are not involved in the mark-making activities of intellectually impaired individuals, but because many of these clients do not have speech and their ability to symbolize is severely limited (as far as one is able to judge), it is more difficult to disentangle or isolate ideas and thoughts from emotional states, and in fact it may well be that thoughts and ideas, even elaborate and sophisticated ones, can never be entirely divorced from feelings.

For my definitions of feeling and emotion, I have adopted Bowlby's (1975) view. I have found his writing useful in many ways when considering the difficulties of working with the severely mentally retarded person as he combines the insights of ethologists with the knowledge gained by psychoanalytic observations. Many of our clients have experienced rejections and lossess from an early age and have had great difficulty in forming lasting attachments. Bowlby's central concern is with attachment and the behaviours that result from separation and loss. His definition of feeling is helpful because he is careful to separate out the feelings or, more accurately, feeling states from the words we use to describe them and to show how they are connected with our apprehension of the world; further, the possibility of communicating feeling to oneself and to others without the intervention of words is made apparent. Bowlby links feelings to 'appraising processes', processes whereby an individual evaluates sensory data from an internal state and sensory data from events in the environment. It is these 'intuitive appraisals', Bowlby writes, that have 'the very special property of being experienced as feelings, or to use better terminology, "as felt" ' (1975: 104).

Feelings or emotions should not be thought of as discrete entities. Feeling is rather a phase in a physiological process. Bowlby quotes S. Langer, 'When iron is heated to a critical degree it becomes red: yet its redness is not a new entity . . . it was the phase of the iron itself at high temperature' (p. 104). This analogy shows how a physical or physiological event can reach a phase of being felt. Sensation is often experienced in terms of value – pleasant or unpleasant – nice or nasty or if very unpleasant, as pain. If environmental stimuli or sensory input from the environment activates instinctive behaviour then the subject is likely to experience emotion – alarm, anxiety, hunger, anger and so on. The appraisal or monitoring of current behaviour may elicit a range of feelings, for example exhilaration when things are going well, or frustration when things go badly. When the consequences or behaviour are assessed, then it may be felt as liked or disliked or as disappointing – satisfying, and so on (Bowlby 1975: 104).

Bowlby suggests that emotions have a function in communication with others and with oneself. As social animals we need to be able to detect and gauge emotions in others to assess their disposition or intentions. We all recognize that emotions are conveyed by facial grimaces and movements; bodily postures; gestures with arms; the play of hands; leg movements and so on. We respond to many such subtle signals daily. We may never verbalize or clarify the exact meaning of a given sign, but we understand it instinctively. Sometimes we misunderstand and get it wrong, but especially in encounters with those we know well or when the situation is a familiar one, we do not often make a mistake. Our own bodies communicate too, sometimes consciously, often unconsciously. We witness ourselves in movement finding a way around a difficult encounter, choosing or not choosing the right movement, the best way of achieving our aim, communicating honestly or dissembling.

Does emotional expression have a structure? In what way can material products, the plastic arts, embody feelings? Apart from the representational value (the ability to evoke the presence of an absent object), can the materials of art, used without intention of picturing, embody or contain an emotional message?

Arnheim (1954) has argued that all things, objects animate and inanimate, as well as human beings, have or contain expressive qualities. Take, for example, the tree we refer to as the weeping willow: this tree does not in itself feel sad, neither does it make us feel sad, but because of its form, the passive hanging of its long slender branches, low and brushing the ground, it mirrors the structural properties of the mood or feeling, and sadness is communicated. These expressive qualities of objects have been called physiognomic properties and are seen as directly perceptible; it is for Arnheim 'the primary content of vision in daily life' (ibid.: 455).

Rycroft says that no one has experiences that are sensations and nothing else (Rycroft 1985). Consciousness and, more particularly, self-consciousness induce us to reflect on experiences, to assimilate 'all sensational events' – 'into that continuum of being that constitutes our "Identity" ' (p. 160). Any event depends for its experience upon the psyche of the perceiver and their 'age, sex, education, occupation and health' could all play a part (p. 162). This is especially true, he argues, with works of art. There are repressed elements, too, in the self, and part of the psyche will want to keep those hidden, and in consequence the individual may wish to avoid events or sensations that 'might revive or resonate' these elements. "This leads inevitably to impoverishment of both sensation and experience' (p. 164). When considering 'our imaginative as opposed to literal' response to perceptions, Rycroft argues that objects are reacted to as though they were 'substitutes or representatives' of 'people and bodies or parts of bodies'. Thus 'tall buildings, particularly if they lack windows, are austere and forbidding and houses with bay windows and wings coming out to meet one are inviting.' In reacting in this way, we are reacting 'as though they were people who might embrace, ignore or cold-shoulder us' (p. 165). This ability 'to endow the sensory world with symbolic meaning' is important, writes Rycroft, 'although it would be rational to be immune to the pathetic fallacy and perceive scenery as only geological formations, buildings as only bricks and mortar, paintings as only pigments on a canvas' (p. 165). Rycroft concludes that these 'symbolic resonances and meanings hark back to infancy' where objects were not recognized

> as entities in themselves but were still regarded as extensions of ourselves or our mothers and when all pleasurable sensations were interpreted as evidence of her love and all painful ones as evidence of her neglect or hostility.
>
> (ibid.: 166).

There are therefore inherent structural properties in objects which communicate or carry expressive meaning, or that expressive meaning is perceived in objects because we endow the object with human attributes or seek the structure of the human body in its form. Bowlby, Rycroft and Arnheim make it clear that the perception of expressive content is a common experience. It was the perception of the expressive content in objects that led some artists in the twentieth century towards abstraction and eventually to non-representational paintings: paintings whose inherent properties and internal structures would communicate without any reference to absent objects, without resorting to picturing the world.

I believe it is this kind of art product that severely disabled clients are making, and although less sophisticated than the products of more intellectually able artists, the possibility of communication remains inherent in the work. I am not assuming that because of the symbolic resonances we feel before these paintings that they have self-consciously encoded messages that the therapist or others are expected to decode. Rather, what takes place during the painting or marking is an apprehension of feeling, an emerging awareness of felt states.

Internal and external stimuli and physiological events that are felt can only be labelled when they enter the public domain or become visible in gesture or movement. It has been suggested that facial expressions sensed by the individual as she or he make them helps that individual determine their own emotional state (Tomkins 1962–3). Midgley (1979) has also noted this aspect of communication

> throwing something down on learning a piece of news does the same clarifying job, both for the thrower and for others, as swearing. It manifests his feelings not just as an undifferentiated flood, but as a certain kind and degree of annoyance, indignation, despair or whatever. In such ways do we make ourselves understood both to ourselves and each other.
>
> (ibid.: 246)

So it is with expression in art. Artists do not necessarily know what it is they are about to communicate. The severely retarded client using art materials in an art therapy session in a direct way seems to be communicating in a manner analogous to the methodology or philosophy employed by American painters in New York in the 1940s and 1950s, as described by Harold Rosenburg:

> The painter no longer approached his easel with an image in his mind; he went up to it with material in his hand to do something to that other piece of material in front of him; the image would be the result of this encounter.
>
> (Rosenberg 1959: 25)

In this 'gesturing with materials' an individual can begin to perceive or apprehend his or her own emotional state, however dimly, and however far from words such apprehension may remain.

I hope this complex process, whereby art materials are manipulated and reflect the mood of the individual who manipulates them, will become more apparent when I describe the individual at work. However, I must first say something about the nature of painting itself since this is the activity with which my case material is chiefly concerned.

Painting is quite a different activity to drawing. There are many differing elements that can determine the marks in painting, most importantly the type of paint in use and its particular quality. If, for example, the paint is very thin and watery, it will be absorbed more by the paper, producing even, matt surfaces and the movements of the brush, the gestural element, may well disappear. Paint that is too thick can be difficult to spread and the colours can remain on the brush, contaminating the next colour, or the brush dry too quickly, thus changing the mark produced. The type and size of brush in use will also determine much about the nature of the mark made. Clearly, a small sable brush is good for control and painting a small area neatly or for using with water colours, but a large hogs-hair brush can hold more paint and produce a considerable effect in one sweep. Using water with the paint can enable an individual to change the nature of the paint, and if a selection of brushes is available, more variety can be obtained. There will be many accidents with paint drips, runs and smudges not intended; bleeding of one colour into the next; mixing of colours by accident in the water tub or on the paper itself. Often people get into a mess inadvertently, but it is in these messes that discoveries are made and the happy accident can be accepted as part of the process. Paint provides an elemental, sensual pleasure to its user. In this way it is like water, but paint is also (if it is of reasonable quality) vivid colour. It has greater covering power than crayon and can be spread around quickly. Paint is a flexible medium that responds rapidly to any change in movement and it can absorb many manipulations. When dry, it can still bear the traces of the artist's hand and arm or indeed fingers and, I believe, in consequence is able to transmit the structure of emotions without describing forms or depicting objects.

Case-study

The subject of my case-study I shall call Alfred. He was seen individually for one hour's art therapy a week for 30 months. The sessions usually took place in side rooms on three different wards, though there was a period towards the end of treatment when he was attending the art therapy department. My observations are based on notes written shortly after each session.

Alfred's mother is unmarried and of Caribbean extraction. Alfred was born in September 1964. In 1966 Alfred was referred to the local children's hospital because of his slow development. He had learned to walk at 18 months and also began teething at 18 months, but at two years had shown no sign of speaking. Dr I from the children's hospital described Alfred as a 'mentally retarded child with some superimposed emotional disturbance'. In 1967 Alfred attended a specialized day nursery, and the staff reported that he 'makes animal noises, screams frequently, is incontinent of urine and faeces. Spits out his food and spits on floors and walls and has caused a lot of damage to toys and furniture.' Alfred's only brother was also born in 1967. An attempt was made at this time to conduct a formal intelligence test but results were inconclusive and the information insufficient to be of any value. The hospital where Alfred presently lives was approached to see if Alfred could be admitted for a short while until a place could be found in a training centre, and he was admitted for a short stay from January 1969 to October 1969. The Physician Superintendent regarded him as a 'severely subnormal child with consequential emotional disturbance including psychotic features'. Alfred was readmitted for another short stay in March 1970. A report from the social worker said that the two boys were living with their unemployed mother in a medium-sized room which contained a double bed and a cot and was heated by a paraffin heater. Alfred, who slept in the cot, was causing problems because he screamed, was very active and sometimes interfered with the paraffin heater. Alfred was again in hospital in December 1970, until January 1971, and readmitted in October 1971 when it was agreed that he should receive 'informal long-term care'. In 1978 a progress assessment chart of social development was compiled. It showed that his self-help skills were good and that his dexterity and agility were also good, but he was very poor at initiating or making any communications of his own and his understanding of the communications of others was below average. He also showed below average ability or willingness in socializing. Two years later in 1980, Alfred was transferred to a smaller hospital, but attacks on fellow patients and staff in 1986 led him to be returned to the larger institution.

Alfred was referred to art therapy just after this readmission. No single reason for this referral was established at the time except that there was a feeling that it was important that attempts should be made to form working relationships with Alfred, and an art therapist might help in establishing a way of communicating with him or in understanding Alfred's behaviour. So it was without any clear programme, rather to assess Alfred's ability to use the situation, that art therapy was begun in August 1986.

Alfred is a tall, handsome black youth. He is broad and well proportioned, but is well known for having very large feet, and his walking is characterized by a slow, ponderous quality, sometimes holding his arms outwards as if balancing. The movements of his arms and hands, though sometimes slow and measured, are, by contrast, much more graceful, and this grace is accentuated by his large, long-fingered hands. I took with me to the ward (where our sessions were to be held) a basket containing two palettes of paint, a selection of brushes, crayons, pencils, plasticine and markers. The palettes each contained six pots of colour. Usually I ensured that each palette contained the primary colours (i.e. yellow, blue, red, green, white and black paint). Occasionally, one of the palettes contained a pot of orange or light blue and so on, instead of black or white. There was a selection of paper available, the largest size (25" × 20") being the one which Alfred usually chose.

It was clear from the start that Alfred was familiar with paint. He began straight away using red paint and covered the central area of a large sheet of paper. He chose a hogs-hair brush with a small handle which he held in his left hand with thumb, forefinger and middle finger extending down the handle and the top of the brush nesting in his palm. After having painted approximately half-way across the paper, he transferred the brush to his right hand. The patch of colour did not extend completely to the edges of the paper. Alfred also used markers in this session to cover smaller sheets of white paper (20" × 15"). The majority of marks moved from the bottom left to top right; these were executed with the right hand but more open zig-zag marks in the opposite direction were made with the left hand.

Alfred is able to use both hands equally well but as his painting progressed, a preference for the use of the left hand developed. When using the marker, Alfred extended his marks right to the edge of the paper, using smaller zig-zag movements to extend the patch. In this first session, Alfred was listening for other noises in the ward (or seeming to) and making shrugging movements. He also copied my pointing in an exaggerated form and towards the end of the session, held out his hand to mine. In the second session, Alfred painted right up to and over the edge of the paper, ensuring that the sheet was completely covered. The resultant picture was without much incident, being composed of one even colour, and it is typical of Alfred's early paintings when he was able to find sufficient colour for one sheet. This is the kind of painting that Rees (1984, 1989) has observed. Alfred's painting does not seem to have any other aims – that is, conscious intentions – apart from the filling in of the sheet of paper. His adoption of a comfortable posture and attention to the marks fits in with Dubowski's notion of 'basic response'.

I wanted to test Alfred's thought processes in some way, to see how he regarded paint; if he could or would respond to other boundaries apart from the edges of the paper and if he could make choices about colour. To this end I gave Alfred a sheet of paper on which I had outlined an orange circle. He responded by colouring the circle in orange, allowing some of the paint to go just beyond the edge of the circle. On another sheet of paper, I painted first a green circle, which he completed in the same way, and then a purple and black circle which were also coloured in turn. Alfred seemed to enjoy this game but returned to painting the blank paper in one colour all over. When I presented him with other marked or painted sheets as the weeks progressed he continued to respond in a similar fashion, but not always with the same colour; and he eventually indicated that he would prefer not to participate and he painted the marked paper as he would if it were a blank sheet. He clearly had no difficulty in recognizing colour and he also seemed to be aware that colour could be confined to a limited area.

After four months I decided to hold the sessions in the art therapy department where I felt there would be less distracting noises and Alfred would be freer to choose from a larger range of materials. By this time I was beginning to recognize some of his characteristic behaviours and communications. When excited or sexually aroused, Alfred rubbed his hands together under the table. When aggressive or angry, Alfred rubbed his head with both hands, moving his scalp in short, jerky movements, backwards and forwards, making short 'ah . . . ah . . .' utterances. If it was allowed, he would squeeze my hand very hard and dig his nails in, sometimes drawing blood. One of the mistakes I made in the early part of the therapy was to assume that when Alfred held out his hand towards me this was friendly and positive. In fact, usually it meant all was not well! The progress of his painting was often interrupted by lengthy pauses. He would sit poised, adopting a listening attitude, brush held out in front of him, hovering over the water jar or paper. It seemed that he was listening to noises on the ward and he may well have been at times, but since I observed this action more and more, I am now of the opinion that Alfred was reacting to his own internal bodily sensations and/or thinking in some way, endeavouring to apprehend the feelings and thoughts that were emerging. During these pauses, he often played with the brush in the water pot, pushing the brush into the pot and then scraping it against the sides and watching the drips, repeating this many times and looking at the bristles. This kind of action would be repeated from time to time with the paint and it might be only after many such actions that Alfred would be satisfied that the brush held a good quantity of paint. As a sign of affirmation, 'yes' or 'OK', or when he completed a painting, Alfred tapped his chin with the back of his right hand.

When the sessions began in the department, I was able to witness Alfred's love of water (the nurses had previously told me how he spent long periods in the bathroom). He became engrossed in scooping water from one hand to the other and letting it trickle over his fingers and running it down his forearms, and so on; it was difficult to get him to leave the sink and return to the ward. Unfortunately, Alfred's jealousy was aroused through an incident on the ward just before escorting him to the department and this resulted in him attacking me. It was difficult to escape from him and it became necessary to lock him in the department and seek help from the nursing staff. After this, it seemed prudent to return to holding the sessions on the ward, which I did.

After eight months, in the hope of influencing Alfred to explore the possibilities offered by colour, I painted some separate pictures in the session while he painted. Apart from being smaller (this was necessary because of the space on the table), the essential difference in my paintings was that they were clearly divided into two contrasting colours, for example yellow and blue. Though Alfred seemed quite happy to see me paint alongside (he laughed and tapped his chin), he was not immediately influenced to change his own painting in any way. Nevertheless, Alfred did not remain incapable of changing his desires with regard to paint and as the sessions progressed, his work became richer. Usually it was his practice to work through the colours in the palette one by one and because he used paint liberally with a brush heavily laden, his pots of colour soon became empty and it was then necessary to move on to a fresh colour. The second colour was usually brushed into the first to achieve the homogeneous surface he desired but, in time, he grew tolerant of contrasts and accepted the change of colour and occasionally three or four colours were used as he rapidly moved from pot to pot, not always emptying each one completely. There was not any deliberate choice of colour combinations, and his movement through the palettes was usually from one adjacent pot to another (much as Corcoran [1954] describes). Only once or twice did he ever seem to change his mind about a colour and break his usual series of rhythmic movements, remove the paint from his brush by scraping it on the side of a pot and then change colour. Alfred also began to tolerate drips made as the brush travelled across the paper from the palette. In contrast, he would take up his brush to paint an area of spillage that had occurred outside the boundaries of the paper, for example on the table and once on the floor.

I would now like to present the brief narrative of the two separate sessions and hope I have chosen two sessions where Alfred's prevailing mood was explicable and where he was able to show his feelings in some way and that a connection between his emotional life and his painting will be described. The first session took place a year after the start of therapy. Alfred had before become sexually aroused during an art therapy session and there was, I believe, a sexual element in the transference; that is to say he saw in me the likelihood or the possibility of sexual gratification (not consciously). In this session, the frustration he felt was clearly demonstrated. He began by painting a black picture. From the beginning he made regular noises and wanted to squeeze and twist my hand, which I refused to allow. The black painting was evenly painted except he left very tiny areas of paper which normally would not have been left. His noises continued and he slid the table backwards and forwards. He returned to the painting but then rubbed his head, moving his scalp. I began to take the second black and green painting away because Alfred had indicated that it was finished, but as I did so, he held it back with his finger and then lifted the painting back up again from the table to show me that he wished it to be taken away after all. This green and black painting was painted with his left hand; the palette was placed to the left of the sheet and drips occurred as the brush was carried across to begin the rhythmic push and pull of the brush, moving up and down and curving towards the base of the sheet. Finally, to complete the picture, the drips and runs were painted in but again he left some tiny patches of white paper showing. I remarked to Alfred that he seemed not to know what he wanted to do and was frustrated. He tapped his chin quickly.

The next green and black painting was made with the same movement but he covered the paper completely, though he left some drips at the bottom on the left. A green and yellow painting followed which was carefully finished; a grey patch was added to cover a spot after contemplating the painting for a short while. Next, he completed a yellow and red painting with curved strokes across the surface done by the right hand; he spilt water from the water jar on to the painting. More scalp rubbing took place after this painting and his face began twitching and he banged the corner of the table with his fist. However, he commenced a final painting, brushing on blue paint with the brush in his left hand. After more banging on the table, he moved his chair back and took his penis from his trousers and showed me his erection. I stood up and suggested, whilst holding the door open, that he went to the toilet adding, when I had collected myself a little, 'you're showing me how you're frustrated, but if you want to masturbate, you should go to the toilet'. He covered himself again but after a short while exposed himself once more, this time crying out. Finally, he was able to put his penis back in his trousers and continue with his painting. Red and white were freely added and he left the drips and runs as they occurred. Before leaving the session Alfred washed his hands in the water jug, slowly and calmly.

It was clear from the noises he made at the beginning of the session that all was not well, and his emergent feelings acted as a distraction to the painting process. Consequently there were tiny white patches of paper left in the first two pictures, but he established his usual rhythmic way of using his left hand. The third picture was painted after an increase in frustration and sexual arousal had animated the painting process, resulting in the application of more paint, and leaving a puddle or reservoir of paint and drips on the surface of the paper. Alfred was unsure about finishing this painting. There was a lull and the next yellow painting was painted confidently and energetically, as were most of his paintings, using the paint liberally. It had more finish than the previous one. He then spilt water on the next picture, which was out of character, and the banging sequence followed. The rise in excitement or the presence of strong feelings were disrupting the painting process again. The last picture looked more dramatic than the previous paintings but it is hard to determine how much the sexual feeling directly influenced the result. Accidents were left that normally would not have been tolerated and there is altogether less concern or care for finish. There is more energy in the marks and for this painting Alfred used more paint (See Figure 6.1).

The second of the two sessions took place 14 months after we had begun. Alfred was in a happy mood throughout, making coughing, gasping sounds and knitting his shoulders together followed by soft 'ah . . . ah' sounds. He was working very rapidly using short vigorous strokes mainly with his right hand. The first picture contained red, green and blue. There followed a pause and he seemed to be

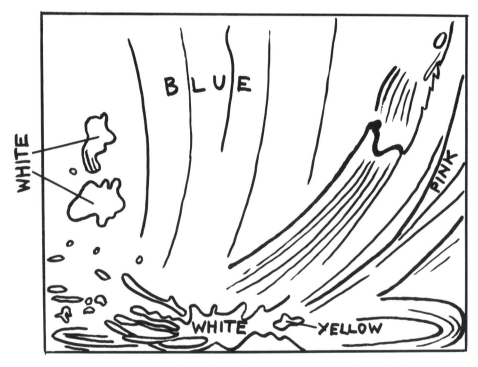

Figure 6.1 (line drawing made by the author from photograph of the painting). Alfred painted this painting at the end of the session in which he experienced considerable sexual frustration. It was painted using the left hand and a pool of white, white blobs, spots and runs, have been left to dry. The palette is positioned on the left of the paper and the brush is swept along the bottom and pushed up into the top right-hand corner. Red and yellow have been mixed with the white and blue along the right-hand edge. There is, I believe, considerable energy and drama in this painting.

listening to the rain. The second picture was like the first except he changed the red for an Indian red or brown and the predominant strokes changed direction. Alfred's happy mood was maintained because he had seen that coffee and sandwiches were being served in the day room and I allowed him to go and get some. On his return he continued to work rapidly and in the next picture he splashed green over black. A black, brown and yellow picture followed which was unusual because of the clear divisions between the colours. He agreed when I suggested this picture was good – tapping his chin. There followed some more hunching of shoulders. The next painting was finished by some close zig-zag brush strokes moving across the surface diagonally. The final painting of the session was finished in a similar fashion with the addition of horizontal marks along the edge (Figure 6.2). On leaving the room with Alfred, I asked him to stop and look at the work which was spread out over the floor to dry; he moved his arm in a gesture of dismissal.

The speed with which he worked in this session was due to his happy and

Figure 6.2 (line drawing made by the author from photograph).
This painting was painted at the end of the second of the two sessions I described. Alfred used his right hand this time. The blue was laid down first, followed by the white and then the red. The colours were brushed into each other; what is most striking is the movement of the brush, zig-zags and loops that move across the surface of the painting. The energy in this painting is looser and has more of a dance-like rhythmic quality which is altogether different from the long pushing and pulling that produced the marks in Figure 6.1.

confident mood and most of the gestures in the paintings were quite different in quality from the long sweeping movements made when using the left hand. It is important, though, not to imagine that Alfred was in any way self-consciously representing his mood or creating a symbol for his feelings. The pleasure derived from the painting is in the greedy use of the paint pot and the covering of paper quickly and efficiently. The delight is in expressing his manipulative skills and making controlled, rapid movements. That is why he can dismiss the paintings drying on the floor because it was the free play with the materials that was important.

Alfred's violent behaviour in the sessions disappeared as art therapy progressed, and challenging behaviour in the ward diminished. He was able to attend other day-care departments and I again offered him the use of the art therapy department where there was more quiet, less distractions and access to a larger choice of materials. Alfred stuck to paint, though, and he did not change his method of working. He did some brief experiments with dots and also painted the paper when placed vertically, but an emphasis on the reduction of contrasts and an achievement of a homogeneous finish remained. I grew bolder in interpreting his movements and moods and spoke more to him in the sessions. For example, three months before the end of the therapy I wrote the following note: 'You're watching me look at your painting.' He taps his chin, in affirmation. I ask if he is wondering what I am thinking. He taps his chin. I say I like his paintings, and he taps his chin. Then I go on to speak about the paintings above the yellow door and he waves his hand for me to be quiet. There are people walking past and he sits and listens to their talking. I say that he wanted me to be quiet so he could listen to the people. He taps his chin.

In this instance Alfred showed understanding and seemed to hear what I was saying but at other times, when I misunderstood or misinterpreted the situation, he did not seem to know what I was saying. The real focus of the art therapy sessions with Alfred was the painting. He worked freely and in a relaxed way, enjoying the fluid and responsive qualities of the paint. How Alfred saw his paintings is difficult to tell, but his gesture that seemed to dismiss the work that was drying on the floor suggests that the process, the encounter with the materials, was of much more importance to him than any finished product.

Art therapists have had to work hard at creating and maintaining a therapeutic environment, a bounded space where the severely mentally retarded or severely disabled client can feel secure enough and confident enough to use the art materials supplied. This space can be an area where a degree of autonomy could be experienced, where choice could be exercised. The mark-making or scribbling that ensues is accepted and seen as an important activity. Some art therapists equate this with the early scribbling of children, others prefer the concept of the 'Good Enough Mother' allowing child/client to find contentment and satisfaction in the free play with the art materials. Research by Dubowski (1985) resulted in a clear description of the drawing behaviours and the processes of mark-making, and Rees (1984, 1989) focused on the use of space in the painting or drawing, discovering a relationship between her clients' artwork and their behaviours in the hospital ward. I have suggested that bodily movement betrays or expresses emotion, and that emotion can be communicated through the movement of the paint brush or marker. This hypothesis draws on theoretical material I have incorporated into this chapter. I hope the description of how paint was used by Alfred has enabled the reader to see that representations and symbols are not a necessary prerequisite for expression in art.

I hope that art therapists will continue to provide a service for this neglected client group. Maybe, as we gain in confidence, we will begin to make more use of the sensibilities we have developed as artists, growing ever more responsive to our clients communications and more able to interpret and unriddle the meaning of the gestures and manipulations of art materials that we witness daily.

References

Arnheim, R. (1954) *Art and Visual Perception*, University of California Press.

Bowlby, J. (1975) *Attachment and Loss, Vol. 1*, Harmondsworth: Penguin.

Chance, M.R.A. (1977) 'Social cohesion and the structure of attention', in M.T. McGuire and L.A. Fairbanks *Ethological Psychiatry*, London: Academic Press.

Cole, P. (1986) Art therapy as psychotherapy with the mentally handicapped, *Inscape*, February.

Corcoran, A.L. (1954) Colour usage in nursery school painting, *Child Development* 25(2): 1907.

Dubowski, J. (1985) An investigation of the pre-representational drawing activity of certain severely retarded subjects within an institution using ethological techniques, Abstract in Research News – *International Journal of Rehabilitation Research* 8(3): 355. (Doctorial thesis available, Library of Hertfordshire College of Art and Design, 7 Hatfield Rd., St Albans, Herts.)

Esser, A.M. (1976) Interactional hierarchy and power structure on a psychiatric ward, in S.J. Hutte and C. Hutte *Behaviour Studies in Psychiatry*, Oxford: Pergamon Press.

Gardner, H. (1980) *Artful Scribbles – The Significance of Children's Drawings*, London: Jill Norman Limited.

Hinde, R. (1982) *Ethology*, London: Fontana Paperbacks.

Hughes, R. (1988) Transitional phenomena and the potential space in art therapy with mentally handicapped people, *Inscape*, Summer: 4–8.

Kellog, R. (1969) *Analysing Children's Art*, California: Mayfield Publishing Co.

Lowenfeld, V. and Lambert Brittain, W. (1987) *Creative and Mental Growth*, 8th edition, London: Macmillan.

Matthews, J. (1986) Children's early representation: the construction of meaning, *Inscape* 2: 12–17.

Midgley, M. (1979) *Beast and Man*, Hassocks, Sussex: Harvester.

Morris, D. (1962) *The Biology of Art*, London: Methuen.

Pearson, M. (1986) Art therapy as psychotherapy with the mentally handicapped, *Inscape*, February.

Rees, M. (1984) Ethological constructs of territoriality and dominance and their implications for the practice of art therapy with institutionalised mentally handicapped patients, in *Art Therapy as Psychotherapy in Relation to the Mentally Handicapped?* Proceedings of the Conference held on Thursday 29 and Friday 20 November, 1984, at Hertfordshire College of Art and Design, St Albans.

—— (1989) Territories of the self: the use of physical space by people who have severe learning difficulties and challenging behaviour, from Proceedings of Day Conference on Art Therapy for people with severe to marginal learning difficulties held at Charles Frears School of Nursing, Leicester, Wednesday 29 November 1989.

Rosenberg, H. (1959) The American action painters, in *The Tradition of the New*, NY: Horizon Press.

Rycroft, C. (1985) *Psychoanalysis and Beyond*, London: Chatto and Windus/Hogarth Press.

Stott, J. and Males, B. (1984) Art therapy for people who are mentally handicapped, in T. Dalley (ed.) *Art as Therapy*, London: Tavistock.

Strand, S. (1990) Group art therapy with people with learning difficulties, *Group Analysis* **23**(3).

Tomkins, S.S. (1962–3) *Affect, Imagery, Consciousness*, in M. Arguile (ed.) (1984), *Bodily Communication*, London: Methuen.

7

Art therapy with families

MICHAEL DONNELLY

Introduction

Art therapy, with its primary heritage in the psychoanalytic tradition, has tended to focus its attention on the intrapsychic functioning of individuals, whether seen as individuals or in groups. The challenge of formulating ways of looking at the family as a whole has been addressed by a number of art therapists, but, as yet, no clear independent function for art therapy has emerged, except perhaps in facilitating better communication within the family. This is still a growing area of endeavour for art therapists to explore, and often the struggle is for the art therapist to leave behind their individual heritage and to develop the use of images which fit more appropriately with the goal of looking at the family as a whole, rather than its individual members.

In this chapter I will review the principal theories of family therapy and the practice of family art therapists as described in the literature, and suggest ways in which art therapy may contribute to improved communication within a family setting.

Theoretical context

Family therapy is an umbrella term for the theories about families that have arisen and been refined in the last four decades. Prior to this the family as a unit of psychotherapeutic intervention had received little attention; there were some psychoanalytic family studies and some interest was shown in the areas of child therapy and child guidance. These tentative explorations with all or part of the family did not give rise to any theories that accounted for the ways that families functioned, and more importantly what happens when families become dysfunctional. It was not until the end of the Second World War that new ideas and ways of thinking began to emerge, particularly in America.

This new body of ideas developed at the same time as the burgeoning social sciences movements which was encouraging the study of small groups: animals were observed in their natural environment instead of in the zoo or laboratory; businesses began to be thought of as complex systems that interrelated; mental hospitals were studied as total institutions; ecology developed as a special field with man and other creatures looked upon as inseparable from their environments. This concept of man being seen as inseparable from his context is central to all the theories of family therapy that emerged from this period. These ideas and theories were developing at a time when the principle response of the psychiatric establishment was the treatment of the individual by removing them from their context.

During the early 1950s much work was done on the observation and understanding of the reciprocal behaviours of groups of intimates who shared a history and would have a future association together. A principal outcome of this activity was the understanding that if psychotherapists and psychiatrists were going to become more active in intervening at the level of the family, different concepts of change than the existing individual or group theories were going to be needed. Indeed, the unique nature of the family as a social grouping demanded a new look at ways of bringing about change. The problem was how to change the interpersonal environment of the person while not taking them out of that environment. The therapist wishing to work with a family needed a way of conceptualizing the functioning of the family group as distinct from understanding the individual members that make it up.

Family therapists have pressed into use various theoretical models designed to assist them in understanding the working of family groups; while some have adapted psychoanalytic models, the most significant and widely accepted model for explaining how families function was General Systems Theory. This was proposed by Von Bertalanffy (1968) as a general theory of the organization of parts into wholes. The ideas which family therapists have developed from systems theories are centred on the structural and communications functions of a system.

This new viewpoint of a family as a functioning system gave rise to a number of theoretical assumptions about families that are drawn from General Systems Theory. Systems are made up of sub-systems, and themselves are subject to and are part of supra-systems – an example being the family as a system, with the children as a sub-system and the grandparents and other extended family members as the supra-system. The relationships between the various parts of the system, sub-system and supra-system are, it is generally accepted, most usefully understood in terms of circular causality rather than linear causality. Thus, for example, a child's attention-seeking behaviour is explicable as a result of its interaction with the parents (circular causality), rather than the child being bad or suffering from an illness (linear causality).

Every system has a boundary and the properties of these boundaries, whether they are permeable, open, closed, one-way or non-existent, are important in the therapist's understanding of why the family may have problems. Most family therapists are interested in establishing, changing or respecting the boundaries that mark the different functional components of the family system.

The communication and feedback mechanisms are recognized as being of equal importance as the structural features of the family system. Communication is seen as more than what is said, it is also a matter of posture, gesture and tone of voice. The emphasis is on how family members relate to each other, and how family systems individuals are defined in terms of their interactions. It is hypothesized that not only do communications convey information, they also define the relationship between those who are in communication.

There is, in addition, an assumption that family systems naturally tend towards achieving a steady state, where change is resisted until circumstances require the family system to adapt. While growth and evolution are possible and very usual, the way that the family system copes and responds to change is an attribute of the system that the therapist would be concerned to establish and understand. As circumstances dictate, the family system must be able to change its preferred patterns of coping. There are three major sources of change that inevitably occur because of the nature of family life. First, there are the developmental changes to the individual members; changes which occur between birth and maturity, in the use and perception of authority, independence, sexuality and productivity. Second, there are changes between family members; such as between a husband and wife before the birth of a child and after having a child. The illness or injury of one or the advancing age of family members are also examples of the sorts of changes that happen between family members. Finally, there are changes which are demanded by the social environment, a new role or job, a change of school, change of neighbourhood or the enactment of new laws. As change always has to be coped with, a family that does not have any functional ways of assimilating and adapting to such changes will encounter difficulties when natural or artificial forces prevail upon the family.

We have so far seen that the family is not one system but is a number of different kinds of system, the parts of the system have boundaries with particular properties and ways of communicating and receiving feedback, and that given no pressure to change families will evolve into a steady state. The mechanisms for adapting to change are important features of the family system. All these are attributes of the natural group called a family and are the focus of family therapy interventions.

It is necessary to recognize that systems thinking does not always give rise to the practice of family therapy. It may mean that we continue to see people as individuals or see them in groups, but with a greater understanding of the familial and social pressures and constraints that are operating and limiting the range of responses that the individual has open to them. More importantly the introduction of systems thinking to the clinical setting has expanded the range of formulations that can be used to understand the problems that are presented to us as clinicians.

To illustrate how the formulation changes if one thinks in different units, let us, for example, take an adolescent boy who is repeatedly caught stealing. He is a boy from an ordinary background and is not in any other form of trouble. When we try to explain his motive for the act, the explanation will differ with the unit of observation. If our unit is the boy, we must explain that he stole because of something about him or his nature. We may say that he is immoral, or that he has a weak conscience, or that he is expressing feelings of rebellion against the establishment, or that he lacks impulse control. We could also explain it in terms of his needs or thoughtlessness, or we could consider what the stolen object might mean to him symbolically. The variety of causal possibilities would necessarily involve only him since he is defined as the one with the problem. If we extend our thinking in terms of a dyad, we could include at least two people in our description. We might say that the act was done in relationship to a peer, or we could say that his mother or father was not firm enough in giving him proper discipline. His mother had been too permissive with him, or his father encouraged this kind of behaviour because he got vicarious satisfaction out of the boy's misbehaviour. Our explanation can vary, but the problem would be defined as between the boy and one other person.

Should we make our descriptions in terms of three people, we could describe the act as part of a triangular interchange. For example, many family therapists report that when a marital couple is about to break up, the couple's child will get into difficulty in some way. The parents pull back together to deal with the problem child and the marriage stabilizes. From this view, the child is helping to hold the family together by his or her delinquent acts. This is only one of the many possible triangular explanations of his behaviour.

The major models of family therapy practice are derived from either psychoanalytic theories, behavioural theories or systems theories. The systems theory models are structural family therapy, strategic family therapy and systemic family therapy. All these are variants derived from systems thinking, each with a different emphasis on aspects of family functioning. For clear descriptions of these therapies the reader is directed to work by Minuchin and Lishman (1981) and Bentovim *et al.* (1982).

The reality of clinical practice is such that the distinction between the differing models becomes less clear. This is mainly because of the complexity of family life; the size of the treatment unit, the type of problem presented and the developmental status of the family will all require the therapist to have a basic orientation, but also to be capable of a range of responses from different models and theories.

The much expanded range of formulations open to the clinician provides a rich field of possibilities for therapeutic interventions and are a means of appreciating the relevance of family relationships in the understanding of many emotional and developmental problems. When it is recognized that family therapy is not only a method of treatment but also an orientation to the human dilemma, it is clear that any number of methods may be used to intervene in family systems. Such a wide range of possibilities can, nevertheless, be described as family therapy because they are based on an attempt to understand and to seek to change the total family system rather than its individual members.

Family art therapy

The use of art therapy in a family therapy context is generally first credited to Hanna Kwiatkowska. Both Landgarten (1981) and Wadeson (1980) describe her pioneering work in the 1960s introducing methods of art therapy treatment and evaluation of families. From this original work others have branched out to develop new and different methods for using art therapy with many kinds of families in various treatment settings, and with various combinations of family members. Some have focused their work with the children only, others on the couple dyad only, and some on working with the whole family, including grand-parents where appropriate.

In her paper 'The child's participation in conjoint family therapy' (1975), Guttman offers some ideas about the way she sees drawing being useful within a family setting and considers it most useful when trying to engage children in a greater participation in the family sessions. She quite rightly points out that the child's participation is often on a non-verbal level and they will not usually respond to direct questions which focus on the family problem. It is here that the voice that art expression gives the child is considered by Guttman *et al.* to be its most important function; giving the child the opportunity to have their 'feelings and experiences shared and acknowledged by the rest of the family'. Unlike other therapists who would also encourage the whole family to draw, Guttman suggests that those who have used art therapy to facilitate and clarify family interactions often neglect to integrate the child's experiences and feelings into the treatment of the family. Here like many therapists she chooses to see drawing in a family setting as a source of intrapsychic material, for interpretation and integration back into the family rather than exploiting the interactional possibilities of drawing in a family setting.

She described two differing roles for the therapist in relation to the child's drawing: one is a passive approach of observing, drawing attention to or inter-preting the young child's spontaneous productions, while the other role is more active, with the therapist asking the child to draw a picture of the family engaged in some activity such as at work or at play. Guttman gives an example of such a use of spontaneous drawings with a six-year-old girl: 'She drew a picture in which there was a tiny girl in the distance whom she identified as her 12 year old brother, and a larger person in the foreground, who she identified as herself.' (p. 490) This drawing, Guttman suggested, reflected the parents' perceptions of her being more independent and mature than her overprotected, diabetic brother. Later in treat-ment, this girl drew another picture which had her brother as the large figure in the foreground. This, the therapist inferred, reflected a substantial improvement in his independence and maturity. Even with Guttman's good intentions in using drawing to make the child feel more part of the family, she reluctantly concludes, it seems, that as often as not the child's presence is not really serving a useful purpose and asked that they be left at home for future sessions; from then on the therapist concentrates on the older family members.

In her book *Art Psychotherapy* Wadeson (1980) reviews the various applications of the use of drawings and art expression with couples and in couples groups. She outlined a number of general benefits to be expected as a result of art therapy activities with couples: these are genuineness, immediacy and sharing, which a purely verbal approach may not always facilitate. The pace of the session is dictated by the therapist, who introduces a number of themes which are intended to highlight the expected benefits of genuineness, immediacy and sharing, and make them available for the family to work upon. Immediacy is defined as the therapist being a witness; he or she may make observations and ask questions about what has actually been seen or heard, and not just heard about. Genuine-ness is seen to be present because picture-making is a less familiar mode of expression than talking; as a result over-rehearsed patterns of interaction within the family may be undercut by this approach to communication. Sharing is seen to be a product of an activity which enables those with differing points of view to share them at the same time.

The themes that the art therapist introduces are generally along similar and well-defined lines, with adaptations for the particular couples in question. These themes, as well as encouraging genuineness, immediacy and sharing, generally seek to solicit emotional and experiential release between what are hypothesized as emotionally blocked couples. One theme, for example, asks the couple to develop one well integrated picture together, without verbal communication. The process of development of a joint picture is as important as the content of the resulting image. Thus, the emerging pattern of interaction that leads to the subject, the organization and execution of the picture brings to light in a direct way evidence of dominance, submissiveness, collusion, passiveness, aggression, openness and so on. Wadeson cites an interesting description of the work of one couple, Mr and Mrs K:

> Mrs K. began with a sailboat in a pale colour, Mr K. went over her lines in a darker colour, she made small fish in the water and he made a large fish eating them up as well as someone on the boat fishing. She made people on the beach and he put hats on them all and umbrellas over them and a life-guard to look after everyone. Finally she made the sun in the sky, and he responded by constructing a lighthouse with a light far brighter than her sun.
>
> (Wadeson 1980: 287)

She comments that the picture-making enabled him to see that his intrusiveness was a result of his own needs.

In another regularly used theme each partner in the couple is requested individually to draw an abstract picture of the marital relationship. The focus here is not on the pattern of interaction but on its emotive content; it is the word 'abstract' that suggests that the therapist is interested in what the relationship feels like, encouraging representation of their differing experience of the marriage. Wadeson describes this as a way of 'focusing on poorly perceived feeling states by examining the mood of the picture rather than the consciously intended content' (1980: 289)

Another task, which can be criticized as potentially being a negative experience is one where the therapist instructs a couple to make a self-portrait with the paper placed vertically, to fill the whole page, and make it as realistic as they can; and when they have finished to give the self-portrait to their partner. 'When they have thus symbolically given themselves to each other by exchanging pictures, they are told that they now have their spouse and can do anything they want to them.' (p. 292) Wadeson considered the most important outcome of this task as being the immediate expression of affect. The opportunity to do whatever one wants to your spouse can have a catalysing effect as well as allowing for anger to be directed at the other person. The last theme, very much in the psychoanalytic tradition of art therapy, is where the couple is requested to make free pictures, without any instruction. Wadeson comments that 'these spontaneous images produce a rich field for exploration and understanding' (p. 298).

The use of artistic expression with whole families owes much to the efforts of Hanna Kwiatkowska (1971). Her theoretical stance underlies much of what is vacuously called family art evaluation, family art therapy or family art diagnosis. She describes the use of art as

> most fascinating, because it provides a continuous learning-experience, enabling each of us (the therapists) to empathize ever more readily and more intuitively into the secrets of symbolic communication expressed through the creative art of family members.
>
> (1971: 138–51).

She considers that there are three main functions of art expression with families, first as an adjunct to family therapy, second as a primary method of family treatment and third as a form of family art evaluation or diagnosis. She describes her approach as being based on psychoanalytic concepts, aiming to elucidate the immediate experience as projected through the families' pictures and interaction. We can rely on what we observe rather than on what we can infer, the original objects of emotional investment or conflict are present and taking part in the therapeutic process.

Kwiatkowska uses a set of procedures combining spontaneous art expression with standardized tasks; these are repeated with each family in order to make comparisons possible. The main task is one where easels with six drawing pages each are set up for each member of the family. They are offered chalks or crayons and are asked to respond to six themes – a spontaneous drawing, a picture of the family, an abstract picture of the family, a free scribble drawing, another scribble drawing, a collaboration by the whole family on one of the scribbles chosen by them, and finally another spontaneous drawing – and are asked to give a title to each image they make. She asks us to consider some of the unique characteristics of using such themes with families; these she calls defence-detouring and generational-levelling. The act of defence-detouring occurs when the language used is not verbal, as in the case of art expression, 'this being a more primitive mode of communication, is less burdened by the conventional defences that family members have developed and masterfully use in their verbal repertoire' (1971: 140). It is proposed that this use of art expression to detour or avoid the families' conventional defences produces a new situation with the family engaged in looking at their usual patterns of behaviour and interactions, as if, temporarily, they were able to stand to one side and observe themselves. Kwiatkowska goes on to suggest that strong feelings can be expressed without somehow producing intense feelings of guilt, while family members are gradually able to develop conceptions different from their habitual and sometimes stereotyped images of each other.

The second concept of generational levelling is described as a process brought about by the simultaneous expression by family members, so that those with differing points of view can have uncensored access to the therapist. It can also enable disengaged or peripheral family members to be seen much more on a peer level, so that to some extent each of them can experience a sense of mastery within the family (Kwiatkowska 1971).

Other therapists have developed these basic concepts of defence-detouring and generational-levelling as ways of confronting the family with its own unresolved emotional conflicts and needs. Muller (1966) describes a process in which the family is asked to produce drawings on themes such as 'something about the past', 'feelings about the future', 'feelings that are unpleasant' and so on. These themes were based on the hypothesis that the individual family members had undisclosed or unapproachable needs that required communicating to other family members so that, 'for a brief period through the use of shared creativity, they (the family) could communicate with one another' (ibid.: 138). She suggests that the family begins to learn to replace coldness and rejection for warmth and affection as a result of this sharing. Sherr and Hicks (1973) have adopted standardized themes and have directed their activities towards uncovering the core problems of a family. They assumed that most families tend to revolve around one or more core problem areas, and that if these problems were present in a family they would be made manifest in the family's drawings.

They describe a confrontative form of family therapy which exploits the defence-detouring and generational-levelling characteristics of art expression with families. The therapists encourage the family to produce images that they can use to induce a family crisis and to start the process of change. They conclude that the family drawing session appears to be a useful diagnostic tool, unveiling crucial dynamics in a dramatically short time. In addition, it may be a catalyst for change when the therapist can 'follow-up the vivid confrontations presented to family members in their drawings' (Sherr and Hicks 1973: 449).

Jenkins and Donnelly (1983) suggested that a significant role for creative and art therapy activities is to enable the therapist and family to find a common language with which to articulate and consider the family's needs and concerns. Often the family has to translate its experience into the language offered by the therapists, with failure to adopt the therapists' language and consequent view of the world being interpreted as resistance to the treatment being offered. They propose a way of working which emphasizes the family's assumed ability to initiate the therapeutic material, drawing on their own creativity and resources, producing their own shared material from which to work, being guided by the therapist who is accordingly less central. They suggest that in those families where engagement appears to be particularly difficult, the placing of emphasis on the family producing its own material to work on may result in a greater commitment by the family, since these activities tend to be more concrete, relying less for their impact on sophisticated intellectual processes (Jenkins and Donnelly 1983).

The three activities discussed in the paper are 'sculpting', genograms and family drawing. In the family drawing, pairs of themes are used, such as 'your family as you see it now' and 'your family as you would like it to be', the focus being on the family's own perception of itself, the development of images and language that the family accepts as standing for its difficulties or problems, and the concentration on the differences between the two sets of images.

In a previous paper (Donnelly 1989) I have taken the view that the intention of art therapy interventions is to enable the family to learn about itself, in order that the whole family system is illuminated for both the family and therapist, with the goal of either clarifying the nature of the system or of generating change in it. I suggest that when using consecutive themes, themes that follow one another, the purpose is to encourage the family to appreciate the impact of changes that may have happened, and to consider changes in the future. Such linked themes are usually in pairs but can sometimes be three or four themes. Such pairs of themes may be 'life with husband/father', and 'life without husband/father', or 'family life before things began to go wrong' and 'family life now'. Here the therapist concentrates not on the individual images but on the differences between them. Themes which require the family to look forward, such as 'family life with our problem' and 'family life in the future', can often provide the family and therapists with information with regard to the motivation for change, what the family sees as a solution to its difficulties and the outcome the family members may wish to see.

The art therapy contribution to the development of family therapy concepts is in its potential as a medium of communication. This attribute is of even more importance in the family setting than the content of the communication, as the content (what the image means or signifies) is negotiated between family members. Art therapy can provide a means whereby all family members can take part, relatively equally, in a language considered less likely to be either censored by the family system or slip into the habitual and redundant exchanges of families in difficulty or crisis. It creates a circumstance where the family's own resources can be mobilized, particularly its creative resources and its healing and therapeutic potential. There is an assumption that all family members are able to draw, or are able symbolically to represent their experiences, relationships or insights, and communicate these to others. Even the blank paper, or unformed material, seen in systems terms, is a comment about the way the family functions.

There are a number of goals that the art therapist will have in mind when working with a family and which would be generally agreed; these are:

1 that art therapy enables members of the family to have access to each other and the therapist;
2 to act as a diagnostic or assessment procedure for understanding the family's difficulties or problems;
3 as an engagement technique, where the activity enables the therapist to join, either empathically or using the same language, with the family;
4 to establish goals or at least speculate how the future could be;
5 to provide a means of catharthis or containment for repressed or feared emotions and ideas within the family or couple;
6 to illuminate the family process and transactional patterns for both the therapist and the family;
7 to encourage the family to have a greater awareness and understanding of its own symbolic expression;
8 to enable the family and therapist to develop a common language.

Whatever the assumptions and goals of art therapy in a family setting, one common theme is the art therapist's ability to take whatever material the family offers and to create opportunities for the family to perceive itself differently.

The therapist who approaches the family with a set 'game-plan' in mind will transmit their consequent anxiety when the family treatment takes an unexpected turn; at this point the dissonance between the therapists' plan and the family expectations can lead to a failure of therapeutic engagement. The therapist is required to be sensitive to the family's needs in order to be able to assist family members to generate the flexibility and energy to help solve their difficulties. To this end the therapist becomes directly involved in attempting to develop flexibility into the lives of his clients, and will find that they too must develop their own flexibility and willingness to experiment so that the art therapy activity can produce a new encounter by the family of itself.

Case-study

The practice of art therapy and family therapy is an area of activity that demands of the art therapist not only the ability to work with the images or art products made by the family, but also to be able to work with families in general and all that they present. The art therapist needs to be thoroughly grounded in the principles and practice of family therapy, lest his or her role becomes one of the therapist who is constantly looking for opportunities to introduce one of a number of set responses to the family, rather than working with the family to develop ways that complement and extend the work that the family is wanting to do. The descriptions of the activities of the art therapists practising within a family context have tended to focus mainly on the mechanics of theme-setting and delivery, and pay little attention to the essential skills of being with the family, of enabling the family to make use of its own resources, and of encouraging the family to use its products as a way of encountering itself.

The following case-study arises from the author's own practice. The family therapy team in the clinic was made up of a number of NHS disciplines: two psychologists, a social worker, an occupational therapist, an art therapist and three doctors, one a consultant psychiatrist. The therapists for a particular family were chosen so that there was one person of each gender as part of the co-therapy pair, the remainder of the clinic taking on an observing and supervisory function. The setting of the clinic was in a purpose-built family therapy suite, which had a large treatment room with domestic style furniture, in one wall of which was set a one-way mirror. This enabled those members of the clinic team not engaged in seeing the family to follow the course of treatment. They are able to hear what is going on in the main treatment room via a series of microphones and are able to make video recordings for review between sessions as well as for teaching purposes. No audio or video recordings were made without the explicit written permission from all family members.

Mr and Mrs R. were referred by their general practitioner (GP), who had been trying to help them for some time. The GP described them as both suffering from depression, which had originated in part as a result of an accident at work which had profoundly affected Mr R. The GP was asking for an intervention at the family level as he had exhausted all that he could by treating them as individuals. The first session was arranged, and Mrs R. aged 35, Mr R. aged 37 and Guy aged 10, their son, attended. The various features of the room were explained, as was the presence and purpose of the other members of the team in the observation room. They did not wish to be the subject of a video recording.

The intent of the first meeting was to begin to establish the version of events as seen from each member of the family and what, if anything, their expectations were. It transpired that some eight years ago, Mr R. had been the subject of an attack at work. He had been the head of a Physics Department in a large comprehensive school when two angry ex-pupils entered his classroom and hit him over the head with a laboratory stool. Only the prompt action of the hospital saved his life. As a result of his injuries he suffered some brain damage, leaving him with impaired use of his limbs on his right side, causing him to limp. He had difficulty in concentrating, some interference with his speech and an inability to sustain prolonged mental effort. Since the attack there had been little or no change in his condition. All this information came from Mrs R., who would finish Mr R.'s sentences, correct his mistakes and translate his words. He was not able to speak uninterruptedly. Guy was not invited into the conversation by his parents, and sat a little apart.

Mrs R. described the effect of the injury on their family life as disastrous. Immediately after the accident all had been well with Mr R. making a limited recovery and returning to work in his old school, not as the head of the Physics Department, but as the assistant to the person who made the visual aids for the school. Mr R. increasingly became remote and would spend all his time in his room at home on his own. Eventually he had all his meals in his room; there was little communication with his wife and he had nothing to do with his son. Mrs R. had responded to this by accommodating his solitary behaviour. Their social life was non-existent, Guy had few friends and never brought them home. Neither of their parents were still alive. Mrs R. was finding it hard work, both physically and emotionally, looking after Mr R. She had approached the GP for help, saying that she thought the marriage would break down if nothing were done. All this information came from Mrs R., with little contributed by Mr R. and nothing from Guy.

The therapists did communicate with Mr R. but found that verbal questioning tired him. He found difficulty in remembering the question and would, for example, sometimes get half-way through his answer and then forget the original question, would ask to be reminded of the question and then be unable to remember where he was in his answer. It was very slow, Mr R. made it clear that he was pessimistic that this sort of therapy would help and he saw himself as having no future. The therapists acknowledged his difficulties and also his view of himself and the therapy.

It was during the fourth session that the use of art therapy was introduced. During the first three sessions the therapists had continued using a verbal approach. This had been much slower than was usual, as the therapists had matched their pace to that of Mr R. Mrs R. had remained central and a little dominant and Guy had begun to join in, mainly in agreeing with his mother.

Discussions with other clinic members between sessions had reminded us that although we had received much information from Mrs R., we did not have a comprehensive view of the family from which to work and that we were in danger of making assumptions about how the family functioned. Both Mr R. and Guy had not really contributed to the discussion of the family problem. At the beginning of the fourth session, the therapists shared their observation that in this family not everyone was able to communicate at the same place, leaving some with responsibility for talking on behalf of others, and some not taking part at all. The therapists suggested that the family's use of the art materials might help them overcome this difficulty and enable everyone to have a say. Since the first session the art materials had been present and clearly visible in the room and had been commented on by the therapists during the initial introduction of the room when the family first attended. It is considered important that the materials are not suddenly introduced, but that they should come naturally to hand so that when the right moment arose the family or therapists could suggest using them. Accompanying the art materials were a number of boards that could be put across the arms of the chairs they were using to provide a place to work. The therapists encouraged the family to depict themselves, 'to use the materials to represent the family as they saw it'. It was anticipated that this act of simultaneous expression would give previously silent or disadvantaged members a voice. The therapists also expected that by having their views and perceptions entered into the family dialogue, this would enable all members of the family to take part more fully.

The therapists took pains not to mention the word art, as this appears to set a standard on the resulting product, and has been the cause of difficulty with some families who find themselves facing another event at which they may perceive themselves as failing, as well as the difficulties they bring to the therapy setting. The practice that evolved was to encourage the family to 'talk with its hands' or 'to use the materials to represent . . .'.

The family accepted the task, but got off to a slow start, particularly Mr R. The therapists offered no further instructions, other than they should represent themselves, and did not comment on whether the family should talk together or show each other their work. How the family sets about the task as well as the result are of equal importance at times. Mr R. used pencil only, and no colour, Mrs R. did the same, Guy drew a pencil outline, which he then proceeded to colour in. Both Mrs R. and Guy finished quite quickly, with Mr R. taking a considerable length of time. When the pictures were completed the materials and boards were put to one side and the images placed on a low table in front of the originators, and visible to everyone. The therapists were careful not to pass any judgemental comments about the images or to do or say anything that might lead the family to think that they were going to interpret the images. The role of the therapist at this point is to encourage and facilitate discussion of the images by asking each person to describe their picture and to describe why they had drawn it to the other members of the family. The therapist should constantly enquire about the responses of the others to the descriptions given, and to compare and contrast themes in all or some of the images. It is necessary at times for the therapist to restrain members of the family from taking over control of the meaning of the images, without alienating the controlling person. This is not always easy.

The following descriptions of their images are offered as a guide to the reader. It is understood that such descriptions cannot be considered a replacement for the images themselves. Mrs R. used her paper in the landscape format, and filling the whole page, drew the outline of a house. Within this outline, in the top left hand corner of the house she drew a room, with Mr R. in it. In the bottom right hand corner of the outline she drew a room with herself and Guy in it; this was the kitchen. There were no other marks, and there was a vast empty space between the two rooms. She said that this was the way they lived, spending their time apart. Guy had also used his paper in a landscape format, and he had divided it into two horizontally. In the top half he drew his father in his room, the bottom half he divided into two equal parts, on the left hand side he placed his mother, at the kitchen sink peeling potatoes, and in the right-hand side drew himself lying on his bed reading a book. He described that they lived apart, and that he spent much time on his own and did not spend any time with his father, which he would like to do. Mr R. drew, in a rudimentary way, the outline of a modern kitchen, on the left-hand side drew himself preparing to paint the door to the kitchen, with a pot of paint on a chair. On the other side of the kitchen at the cooker he placed Mrs R. cooking and between them Guy, playing on the floor. He described that he had no real place in the family and was reduced to being the man who did the odd jobs, while he felt that real family life went on between mother and son.

The therapists encouraged the family to discuss the images for some considerable time, and concluded with the family that their encounter with themselves had enabled them to see that they all lived separate lives, with mother and son having more to do with each other than with father. Mr R.'s perception of being the odd-job man was not so far wrong. Both Mrs R. and Guy said they went out of their way to make things easy for him and only to get him to do small jobs as a way of shielding him from the stress of more complex tasks. They all agreed that the atmosphere at home was unpleasant and difficult. These first images, while confirming for the therapists their own observations and intuitions about the family, are important as they are often the first time that the family will have looked at itself in quite this way.

During the next session, the family was invited to use the materials to represent how they would like to see the family. Mrs R. and Guy drew, while Mr R. did not attempt anything, but sat waiting for the others to finish. Once again the images were arranged in front of the originators for all to be able to see. The therapists asked each person to describe their image. Mrs R. drew a beach scene, with the paper in a landscape format, with Guy throwing stones in the sea, and Mr R. and Mrs R. sitting together having a picnic; all this was drawn in colour using the wax crayons. She described how she hoped they could be a family again, as they used to be, going out together and being at ease. Guy, once again, divided the paper into two, horizontally; in the upper part of the picture he drew himself with a pair of binoculars lying by a pond, bird-watching. The lower section was divided into two; in the left hand he drew his father gardening, and on the right hand drew himself and his father in a car going out together. He described how he wanted to spend time with his father again, to go bird-watching, do the gardening and go on outings with him. Mr R. said his blank piece of paper said how he felt, that there was no place for him in this family any more and he could not see any future for them together. These pictures provoked intense discussion, with the focus being on the apparently positive commitment of Mrs R. and Guy to the family having a future, and Mr R.'s negative and unhelpful approach. It was confirmed that Mrs R. had been arranging for many of the routine household maintenance tasks to be done for Mr R. but, she said, in order to help him and make life easier for him. The therapists concluded with the family that it seemed that there were differences as to the way they saw the future and that this would be the focus of the next session.

Between sessions the therapists, and the rest of the clinical team discussed what had happened. This was mainly around why Mr R. should behave in such a negative way and what it was in the family system that maintained this. One of the observations was that the images of Mrs R., the family out together at the beach, and Guy, wanting to bird-watch with his father, garden with him and go out with him, were not about the future – how they would like to see the family – but about the past – how the family used to be. The implications of this were that perhaps Mrs R., and to a lesser extent, Guy, had not accepted the changes that had occurred to Mr R. During the next session, the images were arranged in front of the originators and discussion encouraged about the images. The therapists shared the observation that the pictures may be about how the family used to be, and not about how they could be. Mrs R. replied that it was both, she wanted to get back to the way things used to be, that she worked so hard to free him from worry and stress about the family in the hope that he would eventually get well. Guy also said that he wanted to help his father to get well. At this point the therapists explored with the family what they knew about the injuries that Mr R. had sustained. Mr R. said that he was not the same, that was why he did not fit into the family any more, he could not be the man he used to be. Mrs R. said that someone at the hospital had said that if he took it easy he would make a good recovery; she had taken it to mean a total recovery. She had been unable to accept that he would not return to his usual self. Mr R. said that this had been the problem all along, with Mrs R. not accepting that he was not the same. He had accepted it, and he realized that he could not be the husband or father that they wanted him to be.

The agenda for the sessions now became the issue of the changes that had occurred to Mr R. and the denial by Mrs R. of their impact. The therapists encouraged the whole family to move nearer and nearer to the realization that they had to grieve the loss of the previous Mr R. and to develop ways to accept the 'new' Mr R. as he really was.

Conclusion

In this case-study of a family treated through family art therapy I have shown how the images enabled the family and therapists to encounter directly the denial and defensive mechanisms of Mrs R. in hoping that he would get well, and Mr R. by withdrawal to demonstrate his changed nature, and to a lesser extent Guy, whose support for mother's point of view alienated him from his father. The images were effectively used to give all members of the family a voice and access to each other and the therapists. They acted as a means of illuminating and therefore eventually detouring the family defences; that of having the past as a goal for the future. Most importantly it gave the opportunity for encounter, that act of looking afresh, in a language chosen by the family and respected by the therapists.

References

Bentovim, A., Barnes, C. and Cooklin, A. (eds) (1982) *Family Therapy: Complementary Frameworks of Theory and Practice* (2 vols), NY: Academic Press.
Donnelly, M. (1989) Simultaneous and consecutive art expression in family therapy, in A. Gilroy and T. Dalley (eds) *Pictures at an Exhibition*, London: Routledge.

Guttman, H. (1975) The child's participation in conjoint family therapy, *Journal of American Academy of Child Psychiatry* **14**: 490-9.

Jenkins, H. and Donnelly, M. (1983) The therapist's responsibility: a systematic approach to mobilizing family creativity, *Journal of Family Therapy* **5**: 199-218.

Kwiatkowska, H. (1971) Family art therapy and family art evaluation: indication and contradictions in conscious and unconscious expressive art, in I. Jakab (ed.) *Psychiatry and Art*, vol. 3, Basel: Karger, pp. 138-51.

Landgarten, H. (1981) *Clinical Art Therapy*, NY: Bruner/Mazell.

Minuchin, S. and Lishman, H. (1981) *Family Therapy Techniques*, Cambridge: Harvard University Press.

Muller, E. (1966) Family group art therapy: treatment of choice for a specific case, in *Psychiatry and Art, Proc. IVth Int. Coll. Psychopathology of Expression*, Washington, pp. 132-43.

Sherr, C. and Hicks, H. (1973) Family drawings as a diagnostic and therapeutic technique, *Family Process* **12**: 439-60.

Von Bertalanffy, L. (1968) *General Systems Theory: Foundations, Development, Application*, NY: Brazilier.

Wadeson, H. (1980) *Art Psychotherapy*, NY: John Wiley.

8

Art therapy with children
and adolescents

ROGER ARGUILE

Introduction

There are those who think of art as a form of relaxation, and in school it is usually viewed as a recreational subject. While there is some truth in this, in my view it is important to realize that most art of any worth is born from some kind of need, anguish or difficulty. The expression of art often defines the anxiety in some way. The painter Kandinsky fashioned a definition of art based on it being an outer expression of an inward need. The psychoanalyst D.W. Winnicott spoke of the 'potential space' as being where we play, and that is where outer and inner realities meet. In Kandinsky we have art and in Winnicott, therapy. It is easy to see the similarity in the two statements. Thus, art and therapy seem well matched. If we place art and therapy in a particular room with a therapist and a client, the clinical practice is given life. The art therapy session may last for perhaps an hour. It will begin and end, and in the space of the session events will occur. Like a fine painting, there will be a sense of life.

Theoretical context

The literature concerning art therapy with children is fairly extensive, reflecting that aspect of art therapy which grew out of the 'child art' movement of the late nineteenth and early twentieth centuries. As a result of pioneers of that movement (Cizek, Viola, Richardson *et al.*) children's drawings and paintings began to be taken seriously and to be seen as vital to their development. Psychotherapists working with children tended to have art or play materials to hand, finding that the art process offered the child a non-verbal, symbolic language through which to tell their story (Pickford 1967, Lowenfeld 1971, Winnicott 1971, and many others). Matthews, an art educator, has studied the origins and nature of representation and expression in early childhood, focusing special attention on very young children's drawings (Matthews 1983, 1984, 1986, 1988, 1989). He describes his work as being concerned with:

... the genesis of representation in early childhood, when the meanings of images, events and objects are constructed by the child. When we try to appraise the qualities and meanings of artworks, pictures and other vehicles of representation, the forms out of which these are composed embody those spatial specifications and relations attached to them in early childhood.

(Matthews 1989: 127)

On the basis of an analysis of his highly detailed observations made over 15 years, he notes that the drawing process forms part of a holistic programme generated by the child to form descriptions of events and objects:

These studies show that very young children are making graphic experiments of their own, in which actions, lines, marks, shapes and colours are often part of exquisitely orchestrated spatiotemporal events. In these episodes children monitor a series of alternating representational possibilities, which are not usually elicited in the experimental setting.

(ibid.)

He concludes that children's drawings are literally recordings of their vitality and life: the drawings are structures in themselves, yet simultaneously refer to events and objects outside themselves, and it is to this dimension of 'meaning' that therapists – and educators – should attend.

In a recent British publication specifically about art therapy and children, ten art therapists have addressed theoretical and clinical issues in work with a range of emotionally, mentally and physically impaired children (Case and Dalley 1990). Dubowski, like Matthews, argues for respect to be given to children's non-representational art – i.e. their 'scribbles'. He suggests that as the child's linguistic abilities develop, the more complex uses of language emerge:

The use of metaphor allows for the exploration of complex ideas. We usually associate the metaphor with spoken language. However, pictures can also operate on a metaphorical level. When this occurs we have a clear relationship between two modes of expression, the iconic and the linguistic. Another example of this same relationship occurs when one asks a child, engaged in drawing or painting 'what is it?' Here the request is that the child 'translates' the iconic mode of expression inherent in the picture to the linguistic by giving a title or other explanation.

(Dubowski 1990: 8)

Dubowski notes that in his work with profoundly handicapped and neurologically damaged children, even the most severely impaired can grasp an implement and direct it towards a picture surface, which is the start of making a statement about his or her own individuality.

Vasarhelyi (1990) suggests that it is difficult to justify art therapy as a viable and legitimate option in the treatment of children within a multi-disciplinary team, since opinion has it that children are supposed to be able to draw without much inhibition and can do so with anyone, given a reasonably relaxed situation. This of course assumes that for children, drawing is a natural activity, without any specific investment of the child's inner world in these pictures. Vasarhelyi argues that the symbolic content of the images produced in a well-defined and contained therapeutic space is not just playful or arbitrary but rather allows insight into the dynamics of the child's unconscious world and 'the privilege of seeing hidden processes which would otherwise remain largely inaccessible to exploration' (p. 54).

Sagar (1990) also refers to the 'safeness' or contained space of the therapeutic environment in her work with sexually abused children. She discusses the manifestation of secrets, codes, mess and guilt in the artwork of these children who are 'trapped in a painful vow of silence' under threat from their abuser. She also notes that art therapy provides an opportunity for 'cleansing and purification. The child seeks for rituals which will perform these functions.' (p. 110) Other authors emphasize the need for a 'contained space' where the child may feel safe to explore, make a mess, participate in rituals and test boundaries (Lillitos, Rabiger, Case).

Rabiger's work has mainly been in a school for children with severe learning difficulties (SLD), making the distinction between this concept and that of 'mental handicap', a category which she considers too broad in the range of conditions it encompasses. In 'Art therapy as a container' (1990) she describes working with children who have little or no sense of an 'as if': children with SLD do not normally draw, and even those who can use simple mark-making implements (such as pencils) are often not able to be symbolic or even figurative in any way. Rabiger maintains that it is necessary to establish at what level the child is functioning and what medium may best suit him or her. The therapist should not expect realism or figurative subjects, nor pretend that something may be representational when it has not been indicated by the child, but should encourage a more concrete interaction with the materials themselves.

In an interview with the author in 1990, Rabiger stated that many of the children were apathetic and unaware of how to use various materials or tools, or they could be hostile and aggressive. She found it helpful in such cases to encourage the making of marks, or imprinting shapes on a lump of clay, or rolling a ball or sausage shape with clay or playdough, which often led to awareness of, or even interest in, the therapist. She noted that if one could wait patiently and be attentive to the child – that is, allowing the child to take its time – it could result in a greater creative expression, more effort and involvement. On the other hand, the tactile experience of handling various substances could be seen as being as important as the sand and water activities in a nursery school.

Rabiger stresses the importance of firm boundaries and structure, together with encouragement for self-expression and choice, conformity or assertion (or both). Apparently small changes could be big steps for many SLD children which could help their attitude to their whole environment. In her experience, the art room offered a good opportunity for assessment, being a place where a child's 'true intelligence' could reveal itself:

> Many children who seem overwhelmed by a class of as few as six can show great potential in their practical intelligence in the art room and an even greater developmental ability than previously revealed. A child who

appears not to talk or understand can attempt a face or a figure, or even speak a few words or a single sentence in this quieter, more contained environment. One child made it clear to me that he was profoundly deaf, not mentally handicapped and so was able to be moved to a more suitable school.

(interview with author)

Motivating children who are determined to avoid interaction is an exhausting and sometimes defeating challenge. The child's resistance could stem from his or her suppressed rage or impotence. In such a situation, allowing the child some kind of autonomy, as in clay or finger paint, where marks could be saved or obliterated at will, could release some feeling or intent. Such activities could sometimes lead to a heightened symbolic awareness.

Goodall, interviewed by the author in 1990 about his work in a psychiatric adolescent unit also points out the value of encouraging the children to use a wide range of media within a contained environment: one in which structure and safety in the form of direction and support are given, but where care is taken to ensure that space is allowed within which personal choice and a high degree of spontaneity may flourish. In Goodall's view, art therapy and art education are part of a continuum. Although an art therapist, he is employed as an art teacher in the unit, where art is part of the school curriculum and each child spends at least two to three hours a week in the art room. Goodall rarely discusses the artwork with overt reference to the children's personal problems, but employs strategies such as story-telling based on their images, as an oblique way of exploring personal issues.

Dalley (1990) points out that the practice of art therapy within a school can run in conjunction with, and indeed facilitate, the educational process. The art therapist works alongside the teachers, sharing the same overall objectives. Unlike Goodall, Dalley does not work as a teacher and indicates the difference between an art therapy session and an art lesson. She too emphasizes the importance of art materials for self-expression, and the necessity for firm boundaries for the safe containment of the child.

From this most recent literature and from interviews with a number of art therapists working with children in different settings, several features of a session emerge which are endorsed by all the practitioners: there is a secure environment (the art therapy room), the therapist, the child and the art materials. The art-making process plays a prominent role in the context of a relationship with the therapist

The art therapy process

When a child first comes to art therapy the therapist normally begins by stating the boundaries of the session. This would involve explaining that the time and regularity of the session is set and consistent. Also, the child may be told not to leave the session until it is over. Some therapists mention other boundaries, such as the child is not to damage the room, the therapist or themselves. It is most important to state the basic limits of time and space to the child because it makes the next part of the introduction possible. The therapist, having explained the simple but absolute boundaries, usually would go on to state what is appropriate in that the child is free to draw, paint, make or say anything he or she likes within these boundaries. Such permission immediately seems to spark off the session. Some children feel a sense of liberation. Here, at last, perhaps after feeling much pressure from the self, parents, teachers or peers, they find a freedom, safely held. For other children the sense of freedom can be a restricting or frightening moment. Suddenly they feel exposed or lost or alone. To operate freedom on such a level without the secure boundary would be a therapeutic disaster. Feelings would be expressed into a limitless formless space. Equally, to have the secure boundary but no sense of free space for the child would be counterproductive. As art and therapy seem matched, so boundary and freedom are complementary.

Thus, the child knows there is the potential in the art therapy session to explore, create and play, but all things happen in the presence of the therapist and so a relationship develops. This is the second major dynamic to consider. The relationship is usually a psychotherapeutic interaction. The therapist's task is to be a facilitator and at all times the essence of the relationship is accurate empathy. A child faced with a therapist often feels a little unsure. Is this person a teacher? Should I be good at art? Shall I play up? Is he a doctor? Is she a social worker? He reminds me of my dad; she seems quiet like my sister . . . he has a beard like my uncle. I do not like my uncle: she blinks a lot, like me when I am worried, so perhaps she is worried. Shall I ask her? Er, no I'll do some work . . . is she a teacher? I'll make him a gift.

So many questions and fantasies abound because of the uncertainty in the child as to the role of the therapist. It is not necessarily the therapist's task to calm and clarify these wonderings. It is his task to allow the child the space and time to do that. Sometimes this means talking and sometimes it means silence. Just as there are degrees of speech, so there are rich qualities of non-verbal communication and silence. The therapist monitors the atmosphere while at the same time being part of it. Feelings the child has about people are usually focused on to the therapist just as they may be visualized in a picture. Often powerful feelings about someone may be transferred in therapy on to the therapist, so that the child may, for example, become uncomfortable or angry at the therapist. The relationship then enters a deeper level, where the therapist's task is to maintain and contain the situation safely. In time, the child begins to understand his anger and its source. Some children may push the relationship to a limit. They may attempt to destroy it. In therapy it is permissible to go to a limit so that a feeling is wholly expressed. The security of the boundary makes this possible and the psychotherapeutic relationship deepens and evolves. The child finds she can explore her most frightening or murderous feelings safely in this relationship. By doing so the child treads a tightrope, but the process allows the child to learn powerfully and clearly about an area of her personality that had before been unclear or misunderstood. Such a direct and unavoidable learning process becomes a vital experience enabling the child to gain a degree of self-confidence and understanding she previously lacked or vainly searched for.

Of course, such a relationship exists in what can be called an art framework.

The art object and the art-making processes are the key factor and provide a focus for the developing relationship. In an art lesson at school a child may, for example, draw a house, and the teacher may give advice on how to make the drawing better, by shading or adding more colour. In therapy a similar image may be produced. The therapist may approach the image from a different viewpoint. He may say 'I wonder who lives there'. By saying this the therapist moves straight into the picture. Now the child feels a response. She tells the therapist who lives there; or she tells a lie, or thinks the therapist should not ask so soon, so gets agitated or sullen, or she feels pleased the therapist has entered the picture and senses it is therefore all right to open up a secret fantasy about a house. The responses are endless, but by the art playing such a prominent role the therapeutic flow begins. The therapist accepts the child's picture without judgement. He perhaps comments or questions it as if it were a new addition to the world. In that sense there is the idea of life, the feel of things developing. Responding to the here and now with accurate empathy to facilitate growth is the task of the art therapist.

Through the psychotherapeutic relationship in a safe space, using art, children can, over a period of time, resolve often overwhelming problems. The art objects can be saying all manner of things. Of course anyone can read all sorts of meanings into art so the therapist is careful in the area of interpretation. Sometimes the interpretation of work becomes quite clear after a number of sessions. The meanings of the first drawing become clearer after a number of weeks. Links and parallels can be observed in the work or in its making. It may be that an interpretation is clear but there could be reasons for not explaining this to the child. Sometimes the act of making art pieces in therapy is enough and to interpret meanings to the child would be counter-productive. Then at a different time the moment would arrive when interpretation would be proper and wise.

Pictures can be indicative of different moods. Some children may be using the art as a way of avoiding some difficult issue. Others may have things to say and the only way is in symbols and codes. It is a way of saying something special or secret employing a similar technique to some of the more sophisticated advertisements we see where the name of the product may be hidden, buried in a code or symbol that only certain people will pick up on – the people at whom the advertisement is aimed. The feeling is a desire to communicate something – to make contact. Then there are children whose work is a discovery for them. They find a means of making visible a productive and highly original imagination. They will tell stories in pictures and become lost in the language of art, alone in the presence of the therapist.

The unconscious is given expression in art therapy. Some images are unconsciously produced. That is to say that the child is unaware of the meaning and reasons for some of the images. They can sometimes become quite surprised or shocked when they realize what they have produced, or why they have made an image.

The children's work is personal and usually the therapist would tell the children that the pictures or objects would be safely kept in the art therapy room and only seen by other people with their own permission. This makes a distinction with classroom art, and indeed in schools there is no reason why art therapy work should clash or interfere with classroom art or art prepared for examination purposes.

Art therapy for children and adolescents takes place on an individual level or in groups with specific children. With groups there exist of course, the strong psychodynamics that always occur between all the members. In some groups, the children will work individually while other groups will produce a single group art piece, which can then be responded to by the group. Sometimes the therapist may have set a theme. In individual or group art therapy there are often strong dynamics concerning ritual and mess. The regularity of the session can create elements of repetition, where children reveal their need for security and containment, or find links between art materials (for example plasticine) and food. The process of using paint has links with infant nappy-wetting and soiling. Such links are sometimes very much part of the sessions and children with eating disorders and obsessional disturbances can find in art therapy a way of diverting their rituals and obsessions. They can begin to confront and resolve much of the problem. For many children, the messiness of paint takes them back into their infancy. They sometimes learn how to play for the first time. Making a healthy mess with paint fulfils a useful function. It can fill a gap, or make a long-needed connection for the child. They can 'let go' in safety. There is something primitive and universal about making lines and marks. Infants begin to explore texture and see the effect of running their fingers through their food or dribble.

Art therapy, then, is a relevant and useful resource in helping with a variety of problems such as personality and emotional disturbances and disorders, speech and language disorders, sexual and violent abuse, deprivation in childhood and bereavement, to name just some. It is a fascinating process for anyone who wants to understand themselves better, and their place in the world.

Case work

I concentrate now on my own place of work and some of the children I see. I am employed at St Mary's School for Children with Special Needs in Bexhill-on-Sea in East Sussex. The school is for up to 90 boys and girls who for various reasons cannot be placed in their local authority. Children come from all over the south of England to this residential school, which is of independent status, with fees being paid by the different educational authorities sending children there. Some children stay for perhaps a year but many stay for several years and ages range from 7 to 16. In addition to the care staff and teachers, the school has a visiting consultant child psychiatrist, a visiting careers adviser, a social worker, recreational staff, nurses, a physiotherapist and speech therapists.

The school takes children with learning difficulties, unusual syndromes and personality disturbances and disorders, epileptics, asthmatics, diabetics, children with speech and language disorders, emotional problems and some physical handicaps. Many children have various major problems to deal with and for that reason they cannot be placed locally so would come to St Mary's. The school is a member of NAIMS – the National Association of Independent Maintained Special Schools. I came to the school in 1982 on the recreation staff, providing various out of school activities but with an emphasis on art for groups of about five children. The principal and the governors seconded me to train in art therapy at Goldsmiths College in 1984–5 on the agreement that I would return and set up art therapy within the school.

As I write in 1990, art therapy is a thriving resource at the school and there is a constantly full timetable of referred children. Since 1986, each year an art therapy student has been placed at the school from Goldsmiths College, London. Referrals come from any of the care, nursing or teaching staff but go through the principal and psychiatrist and on to me. I liaise with all areas of the school and art therapy is accepted throughout the school with no conflict between art in therapy and art in class. All children have art in class but I am a full-time art therapist and do not teach. The children understand the boundary and do not confuse art in class with art therapy. The art therapy room is used almost entirely for individual work though there is one group for the youngest children. The room is divided into two halves: the first half is the area where the sessions happen and the other area is my office/studio space. The children can go into that part but generally do not.

While I may see some children for a short series of sessions, many continue on a weekly basis for up to two years and sometimes more. During that time, the powerful themes that arise in the art processes are confronted interpreted, worked through and often resolved. Because of the large variety of children and adolescents at the school I feel it may be of interest briefly to discuss several cases to see how the therapeutic flow alters in quality with time and with different children.

I start with all cases by introducing the boundaries of time and space, then go on to state that the time, space and art materials are for their use, to draw, make or talk about anything, should they so wish. From this consistent and simple origin things begin to happen. Some children draw, some paint, some chatter, some fidget, some move into spontaneous drama. I do not set themes. I do not need to. Themes evolve in the sessions quite naturally. However, I do sometimes intervene quite directly – almost as if to throw a spanner in the works. Children can sometimes lock into a particular style of drawing or behaviour. Now this may be a defence, a compulsion or it may be automatic but there sometimes comes a point where it feels like the child needs 'dislodging' if he or she is to make progress. And so I intervene if the child becomes stagnant in therapy. I do this in various ways. Either I talk 'to' the child as opposed to 'with' the child, or I suggest a new media or image. Sometimes I suggest a drawing game. I make several marks and ask the child to respond to the marks through drawing. The marks are a dot, a line, an angle, a squiggle, a circle and a match-stick figure. I find this an interesting exercise, especially when assessing a child for therapy, as I am often asked to do. Much can be gleaned from their responses. Using this technique in the middle of a series of sessions, however, is merely a diversion and I rarely use it. Some art therapists working from a more 'analytic' stance would probably not intervene in such a direct and perhaps unsettling way. I believe, however, that from the art point of view, intervention is an intuitive art-making dynamic. The artist will look and will see. The artist will make a mark and then make another mark. There will sometimes be sudden changes. In therapy, the art therapist is working in relation to another creative being and can intervene just as the child can intervene. So I use intervention as an art process. It is a way of making a mark – in therapy. I do not make an intervention to push some hypothetical theory I may have about the child.

I use it to facilitate a creative dynamic in the child. Art interrupts our way of seeing. We see from a new angle and reassess what we thought we knew. For some children who have grown dull through circumstances, the language of art allows them emotionally to grow anew.

A large number of the children at the school have speech and language disorders, and I see two such children. One of them, Rebecca, is physically unable to speak. She can make squeaking sounds with expression, however. Art therapy has been most liberating for her. She uses her time to draw elaborate documents of her weekends, family or school outings. She likes me to guess the names of everyone and what they are doing. She knows it all and I know nothing! She has great fun trying to tell me through squeaks and pictures her weekend activities. In the early sessions her drawings always included me and there were always images of extending arms with huge expressive fingers, stones being thrown, often at me. She expressed her frustration, anger and determination. She expressed her confusion about not speaking. The art becomes a mediator for communication both visual and non verbal. We are on one level. She fills each session and we both end up exhausted. She enjoys being able to teach me and being able to get cross with me as she casts *me* as the person with the problem of communication. It seems like role reversal.

The other child with language problems, Bridget, is also partially deaf. She has used the art more unconsciously, creating pictures that are loaded with meaning. It is as if she uses the language of art to re-evaluate her own feelings and in doing so her unconscious feelings emerge too. For example, one picture is of a house. From one of the windows is a purple ghost whom she called mummy. Over the house there is a sun with a sad face. Out of one of the ears of the sun hot blood pours down on to the ghost. Bridget is an angry girl inside. Perhaps she was unconsciously expressing a feeling of anger and confusion or blame towards her mother for the fact that she is faced with such a severe hearing and language disorder. She loves the art therapy. Again, she enjoys being somehow in charge. Over the time of seeing her, her anger has gradually lessened and she has grown more at ease with herself and others.

A young adolescent called Robert has very slowly built up quite a strong rapport with me in therapy. He finds making any kind of trusting relationship difficult because of his background. He has been let down by family events all through his life and is at present fostered. Added to that he has a muscle and bone degenerating disease and sees himself very slowly getting weaker at a time when the rush of puberty should make him vigorous and stronger. These two issues seem to be simmering behind a series of cartoon drawings he has recently produced. They involve two people in the Armed Services. One is called Robert who is 'youngish' and the other is an older person called Roger (myself). Robert is always in charge of Roger. They do not like each other but always seem to end up working together. One day during an exercise Roger crashes out of an aeroplane and Robert saves his life and says he would like to be friends (see Figure 8.1). These were just a few drawings but in art therapy such images take on a strong significance. They involved the two people in therapy and they acted as a platform

Figure 8.1 Drawing by Robert, 'Before going into the de-aging machine'.

for Robert to gain confidence in a relationship. They also expressed preconscious feelings about rejection and need of a father figure. Towards the end of the series both Roger and Robert went through a de-aging machine. This seems in some way to be about Robert's preconscious wonderings regarding his physical degenerative condition. To interpret these things would have seemed wrong at that stage. The time may come in therapy, as often can happen, when the child will interpret the meaning. The therapist therefore needs to be a holding container to sustain a feeling of safety in the session for the child. The work continues with Robert.

With some children, the problems they are going through are entirely conscious but it is in art therapy that they find an acceptable and clear mode of expression. This enables the child to view their problems more objectively and to understand themselves better. Some children use symbols and secret codes to re-create their concerns. Others, as in the case of John, use figurative models and narrative. John has had art therapy for over two years now. He is 14 and copes with a vast amount of problems. He has a partial cleft lip and palate (corrected surgically), impaired sight, poor co-ordination, spatial difficulties, speech, language and learning difficulties, hearing loss on the left side and dyslexia. John also had physical difficulties at birth which resulted in a long series of bowel operations.

He tells me he has had 18 operations and they have not yet finished. His urethra is being reconstructed in order to allow urine to flow directly through his penis. John's great dream is to 'go for a pee standing up' like other boys. His feelings about his physical problems are particularly strong now he is in puberty. He expresses anger and frustration in his artwork but uses plasticine wonderfully well as a means of maintaining an understanding and acceptance of his problems. John makes robots and figures usually with phallic horns or hair styles. He includes them in amazing stories he invents about people being attacked and chopped in half. Parts of their bodies are removed, reshaped and grafted on again. Fathers, sons, mothers, daughters, wolves, monsters, all interweaving a web of anger and desire to improve things. Sometimes John talks openly about the operations on his penis but usually the plasticine is enough for what he needs to say.

Imaginative energy poles are fixed to the robots. Extending tails and endless skin grafts are made and carried out. He is aware that much of his work relates to his abdominal condition. He works for an hour, lost in this most vital creative sublimation. I am there. That seems to be enough. Sometimes he gets off the chair and extends the story into the rest of the room, throwing the robot high in the air where it then falls on to a knife. Part is cut off. Then thin layers of plasticine skin are carefully wrapped and secured on to the robot again to repair perhaps an elaborate phallic-looking head-dress. The horror of the knife and the mutilation is made safe by being on the level of fantasy cartoons but the undiluted feelings are saturating every second and every inch of the session. He makes sense of himself as a person and not just his physical self. It is pure art therapy. He is there, alone in the space where outer and inner realities meet, in the presence of a therapist. It is an ongoing process of steady emotional personal growth and adjustment.

Another child I see is called Ben. He is a 14 year old who has been at the school for several years. Ben has Asperger's syndrome. Asperger was a Viennese child psychiatrist whose work led him to define a group of children for whom normal interrelating and communication on socially accepted terms was impossible or very difficult. Asperger's syndrome comes somewhere close to infantile autism. The child may be aloof and indifferent and have specific and time-consuming idiosyncratic interests. Social contact may be bizarre and awkward. The child may use language freely but fail to make appropriate social adjustments. Such children wish to be sociable but fail to make satisfying relationships with peers. They may be clumsy and have impairments in non-verbal expressiveness.

Ben's behaviour had first given concern when he was four years old. He developed interests and questions that seemed odd, and he seemed separate from his peers. He is now 14 and for the past two years he has had weekly art therapy sessions. In the first session I was immediately struck by how fluently and spontaneously he drew a line pattern. There seemed to be some element of automatic drawing in the way he worked. Later he went to the sink and played with the water, filling cups and emptying them. He spoke about the colours of paint, asking questions like, 'What would you say is the brightest, yellow or red?' and 'How bright is the brightest colour?'

Over the many sessions there has been no fundamental change, but rather he has changed in his response and adaptation to circumstances, and he continues his constant pursuit – to question. To question the concept of endings and beginnings, life and death, love and hate, good and bad. Such big questions. It is as if he gravitates from one extreme of any subject to the other, but whereas most of us fit in to the spectrum at some point which is socially appropriate, Ben is constantly searching for a place; but because he has always viewed life from just outside most people's experience he always has to settle for another question, another line of enquiry.

Ben has various interests: colours, letters, words, numbers, emotive phrases, film stars, celebrities who have died, lists. He has more conceptual fascinations linked to his interests: decomposing bodies, moments before death, moments into life, fatal diseases, time, balance between being full and overflowing, percentages around zero often in relation to disappearing substances such as paint, cutting, chopping, hacking in relation to bone, hair, skin, using plasticine. He is interested in the differences in meaning and sound of obscene words, usually written down. He is also fascinated by letters and particularly the number of times that any one letter may appear in the same word. Such an extraordinary array of interests obviously causes some degree of isolation even though he is actually a likeable and popular boy with staff and children. His lines of enquiry to us make rather horrific reading, yet for Ben they are ways he creates to make sense of what, to him, he cannot experience emotionally. He has no feeling of security or well-being in relation to himself, his peers or the world.

In art therapy, Ben finds he can explore these issues to a greater level of involvement than he can anywhere else. His drawings often appear surrounded by vertical lists of words or dates and numbers. He produces inverted container shapes which are actually one continuous freely drawn line. So the shapes appear whole and secure but are not. One is never sure which is the interior or exterior of the shape because of the inverted curves – rather akin to the autistic 'me' and 'not me' confusion.

Ben seems to find himself surrounded by a sea of emotions and feelings, and while he senses these things and even understands them objectively he is impervious to them on a personal emotional level. Yet his endless quest for an experience of 'experience' is slowly bearing fruit.

I will now focus on my notes from a couple of Ben's recent sessions.

Sessions with Ben

Again concerning humans, life-support machines and death. Ninety-nine to one was life and zero was death. He wrote 99 to zero getting ever closer to zero. As he did I intervened using drama to increase the experience of his enquiry from a list of numbers and words to related reaction and movement. I asked who was dying and he said, 'It's me' so I said, 'Right, when you reach zero, collapse and die.' This was a concrete instruction rather than an offered suggestion because he responds better to concrete fact or instruction. Having understood my instruction I knew he would either accept or reject it. He accepted it. I was next to him and he collapsed into my arms dead weight and so I put him safely on the floor and pronounced him dead. He lay there dead. Then he got up smiling and I praised his participation in drama and stated the importance of what he had done. On other occasions he had thrown paint to be dramatic but this time he had been 'in' the drama using imagination. He is beginning to 'feel' the quality of his enquiry. He was relating rather than merely reacting. In the following session (number 77), he continued the interest in life and death by emptying three bottles of paint down the sink. For another child, such an action would be a waste or unacceptable behaviour, and should Ben do such a thing in school, that response would apply, but he knows that art in therapy is different to school. It is not a waste, to him it is a game where the concept of life and death is to the fore. He emptied the paint, then swilled the bottle over and over again until all trace of colour (or life) was gone. He said the white was milk, red, blood and the blue was the sea, but all were alive and finally dead. He asked me to guess the percentage amount of colour of life left in the bottles as he swilled them out. It became a game. We both got wet and so did the floor. He was aware that I had entered his game and I was aware that he accepted that. The game lasted for about half an hour and was sustained activity with a dual empathy for cause and effect in relation to getting wet. He seemed to feel and be involved on the appropriate social level for such a game. A game that had its equivalent in terms of, for example, adults at a fancy dress party or carnival; a sense of permissibly being just outside what is normally acceptable. Ben seemed to experience this created dual mess as a more whole experience than is often the case. He is usually locked into quantifying elements and grading events. Today, while he did that, he also seemed to be reacting with subjective and accepted social emotion. I praised him verbally at the end and explained simply why, by stating what had happened.

Ben may not fundamentally change. Questions such as, 'If a poacher shot a Rhino how long would it take for the Rhino to fall on the ground?' and 'If "A" is the skin of an apple and "Z" is the very centre, what letter would the pips be?' – questions such as these may remain, but Ben does show some degree of adaptation to life, which is most rewarding for all concerned – not least Ben, who enjoys a growing sense of social belonging.

For many children, using art within a psychotherapeutic relationship gives an arena for the illumination of exciting and questioning worlds of imagination. One of the children I see is a girl of 14 who used to get into terrible fits of confused anger over minor problems. Using art she has opened up her swirling thoughts and feelings of persecution, in drawing. She has worked that through, and proceeded to explore her fantasy thoughts. She invents rectangular rooms leading into other rooms. She sees articles of clothing, coloured lights, pop stars, and goes back in time by self-hypnotism. All of this is safely achieved, and the 'trance' she evokes is performed as a dramatic addition to her images. The point of all this is the fact that she is able to be so openly creative, then is able to understand some of the usually simple reasons behind it all. She is now less anxious and is more calm when faced with confusions or irrational worries.

Finally, I will mention Terry, for whom snakes have been a consuming fascination. For well over a year he has painted, drawn or made snakes. He seems attracted by their brooding power. Occasionally, he will suddenly shout out or lunge forwards, seemingly snake like. His work and behaviour strike me as having a primitive quality and his snake image may be seen as an archetype. He frequently copies the snakes but no matter what the picture in the book looks like, Terry's snakes are usually positioned round as a containing line. I have said to him how good I thought his paintings were. I asked if they could be exhibited, 'No! They're safe in here. They would be harmed out there', he said. Such is the feeling of safety in art therapy. As he works I am there with him. He works mostly in silence – a creative silence of therapist and client. This is the emotional holding environment that Winnicott spoke of. Often in art therapy, the presence of the therapist is enough. The child knows what is good enough. The therapist must be good enough.

Children and adolescents seem to need just that. Enough, is enough.

References

Case, C. and Dalley, T. (eds) (1990) *Working with Children in Art Therapy*, London: Routledge.

Dalley, T. (ed.) (1990) Images and integration: art therapy in a multi-cultural school, in C. Case and T. Dalley (eds) *Working with Children in Art Therapy*, London: Routledge.

Dubowski, J. (1990) Art versus language, in C. Case and T. Dalley (eds) *Working with Children in Art Therapy*, London: Routledge.

Lowenfeld, V. (1971) *Creative and Mental Growth*, NY, Macmillan.

Matthews, J. (1983) Children drawing: are young children really scribbling? Original version of paper presented at British Psychological Society International Conference on Psychology and the Arts, University of Cardiff, Wales, September.

Matthews, J. (1984) Children drawing: are young children really scribbling?, *Early Childhood Development and Care* (18).

Matthews, J. (1986) Children's early representation: the construction of meaning, *Inscape*, Summer: 12–17.

Matthews, J. (1988) The young child's early representation and drawing, in G.M. Blenkin and A.V. Kelly (eds) *Early Childhood Education: A Developmental Curriculum*, London: Paul Chapman pp. 162–83.

Matthews, J. (1989) How young children give meaning to drawing, in A. Gilroy and T. Dalley (eds) *Pictures at an Exhibition*, London: Routledge.

Pickford, R. (1967) *Studies in Psychiatric Art*, Illinois: Thomas.

Rabiger, S. (1990) Art therapy as a container, in C. Case and T. Dalley (eds) *Working with Children in Art Therapy*, London: Routledge.

Sagar, C. (1990) Working with cases of child sexual abuse, in C. Case and T. Dalley (eds) *Working with Children in Art Therapy*, London: Routledge.

Vasarhelyi, V. (1990) The cat, the fish, the man and the bird: illness behaviour in children, in C. Case and T. Dalley (eds) *Working with Children in Art Therapy*, London: Routledge.

Winnicott, D.W. (1971) *Therapeutic Consultations in Child Psychiatry*, International Psycho-analytical Library no. 87, London: Hogarth Press.

9

Art therapy in the treatment of women with eating disorders

MARY-JAYNE RUST

Introduction

In the following chapter I will begin by reviewing the literature on art therapy and eating disorders, then discuss the psychodynamic approach to treatment that appears to be used by the majority of art therapists writing about or working with this client group. I will explore the particular role played by the art object within the therapeutic relationship, and end with a case-study from my own practice in which I have used a model deriving from object-relations and feminist psycho-therapy.

I shall not address here the complicated questions regarding the recent increase in the incidence of eating problems amongst women and its links to societal pressure on women to conform to a particular image. My own view is that this pressure stems from the wider context of living in a patriarchal society where the power of a mature woman is experienced as very threatening. The female images portrayed around us are of thin, somewhat boyish and generally adolescent girls. They appear as cold and untouchable, and their darker sexuality embodied in a more voluptuous shape is split off into a pornographic image where the woman is portrayed as powerful but needing to be captured, dominated and harnessed. These two images could be seen as madonna and whore. Chernin (1981) writes:

> The body holds meaning. A woman obsessed with the size of her body . . . may be expressing the fact that she feels uncomfortable being female in this culture.
>
> A woman obsessed with the reduction of her flesh may be revealing the fact that she is alienated from a natural source of female power and has not been allowed to develop a reverential feeling for her body.
>
> The body holds meaning. The fact that this thought takes us by surprise itself reflects significantly upon a culture that is seriously divided within itself, splitting itself off from nature, dividing the mind from the body, dividing thought from feeling, dividing one race against another, dividing

the supposed nature of woman from the supposed nature of man. As part of this division we have come to believe that only those things that concern the soul and the spirit, the mind and its creations, are worthy of serious regard. And yet, when we probe beneath the surface of our obsession with weight, we will find that a woman obsessed with her body is also obsessed with the limitations of her emotional life. Through her concern with her body she is expressing a serious concern about the state of her soul.

(1981: 2–3)

The issue of 'bodily meaning' plays a central role in the psychodynamic art therapy on which this chapter focuses. First, though, I will clarify the way in which I am using the term 'eating disorders', noting that the three categories outlined are rather artificial and that no woman belongs in a hard or fast way to any one of them: rather, she might pass from one to the other at different phases of her life.

Anorexia nervosa

This is self-imposed starvation in which the sufferer will exist on as little food as she possibly can. The problem usually begins before the girl has left home, around the time of the onset of puberty although it can continue well after this.

The anorexic tries to build a world of her own where she relies as little as possible on others for her dependency needs, thus her relationships mirror the deprivation of food. She denies her hunger both literally and symbolically and in doing so she numbs her whole range of feelings. Within the therapeutic relationship she finds it equally hard to take in anything from the therapist. Lawrence (1984) points out that an interpretative approach feels extremely threatening so that in the first instance the anorexic needs to feel that the setting is safe enough for her to begin to tell her own story in her own time.

The image I have for describing the anorexic is of a young waif-like girl, very thin, and the feeling that she is barely of this world. She is shy, says little and seems very frightened. It is as if she is behind a sheet of glass: someone who is hard to reach.

Bulimia nervosa

Bulimic women binge on large amounts of food and then purge themselves of it either by vomiting or taking laxatives. A sufferer will often begin by going through a mild anorexic phase in her teens but cannot sustain the rigid denial of her hunger. She then breaks out into uncontrollable binging on food that she would label as 'bad' – that is, any food that is forbidden in dieting such as rich, creamy or sweet things. She then feels revolted at herself, guilty for having taken so much and very frightened of growing fat, so she purges herself. In the extreme this can be done up to 40 times a day but generally speaking the bulimic woman will go through phases of purging herself once or twice a day.

As with the anorexic, the bulimic woman's relationship with food is mirrored in her relationships with those around her. She will be eager to 'take in' from others – care, support, good feelings and so on, but finds it hard to hold on to anything and will then reject it. In the therapeutic relationship she will be very keen to begin, very precise in her timing, wanting as many sessions as possible. But when the slightest thing happens to make the experience, in her terms, less than perfect, she will want to opt out without a struggle, purging herself of what she feels to be a bad situation. She might organize her life so that the therapy can only last a limited period of time so she does not have to struggle with the prospect of a long-term relationship (as in the case-study described in this chapter). She hates her emotional 'mess' which symbolically gets flushed down the toilet in secret.

One of the tasks is, then, to enable her to express the mess within the session times. Keeping the boundaries of the sessions is of the utmost importance so that she can feel safe enough to do this (see Dana and Lawrence 1988).

The image I have to describe the bulimic is of a young woman, older than the anorexic. She is a slim, wiry, city-slicker, someone who appears on the surface to be very successful and in many cases is holding down a good job. Of all three eating problem 'types' her problems are the hardest to see.

Compulsive eating

The compulsive eater alternates between binging and dieting or starving. This pattern usually begins on leaving home. She will attempt to diet, thinking that she is too fat, but like the bulimic woman she cannot sustain the denial of her hunger. She binges and feels disgusted with herself but unlike the bulimic she can hold the food inside her and tolerate the fat on her body. Even though her ritual binges are done in secret, the effects of this behaviour are visible to the outside world via her body, even though at the time she is not conscious of her fat having any positive value.

In the therapeutic relationship she will be eager to take in as much as possible but finds it hard to spit out what she does not want. She will go to great lengths to avoid conflict which tends to get separated or 'split off' from the relationship and metaphorically 'swallowed'. The task is, then, to encourage her to feel and express her full range of feelings within a safe and boundaried setting.

The image I have of the compulsive eater is one of tremendous hustle and bustle. She is always on the go, either rushing from place to place or talking, eating or working – often in one of the 'caring' professions. She often appears rather stout – 'a little overweight' according to our cultural norms.

For all their differences in body sizes, personality types and backgrounds, the one thing that these women have in common is their fear of getting fat and their longing to be thin. It is not merely a question of losing or gaining pounds of flesh but of changing from being one woman to another. The thin place is where everything is going to be 'all right' and the fat place is where it goes 'all wrong'.

Review of the literature on art therapy and eating problems

Many papers and books have been written on the subject of eating disorders in general but few have specifically addressed the possibility of using art therapy as a treatment. Crisp (1980), in a book about anorexia and its treatment, gives a description of the use of projective art therapy with hospitalized anorexic patients. Each week these young women are given a theme to work with by the art therapist; their artwork is a response to this theme and together with the art therapist they talk about these responses. This is in contrast to a non-directive way of working where the client has a set time to spend with the therapist each week in which she can paint or talk as she wishes. The role of the therapist is then to comment on the process of this interaction both between the client and her 'making of things' and within the relationship itself. In my experience there are differing views about these ways of working. Using a directive theme-centred approach can be felt to be more containing when the client experiences a high degree of anxiety. It can also be felt to be more controlling.

Levens (1987, 1990) describes a non-directive approach. She draws attention to how the process of painting mirrors the woman's relationship to her body and to food. For example, she writes:

> Katy, an eighteen year old woman suffering from anorexia would paint herself in white paint on white paper effectively making herself invisible. Her terror of beginning to express something for herself was very real. As with many anorexics she felt her mother had always known exactly how she felt and what she thought. Katy felt transparent within her family with no substance. She felt the need to control every relationship. By remaining invisible (on the paper) she felt that others would be less able to control her.
>
> (1987: 3)

Murphy (1984) pinpoints several ways in which art therapy is particularly useful as a form of treatment with anorexics. She writes:

> Concentrating on a painting in an intensive psychotherapeutic relationship removes the focus from the patient and provides a safer, less threatening arena for therapeutic work. Pictures can therefore facilitate personal exploration for example, fantasies, self-image, and can also provide a safe vent for feelings such as anger, depression and fear. In the same way pictures can be used to express and thus clarify love–hate relationships and other ambivalent feelings which predominate in most adolescent experience.
>
> . . . One of the most important aspects of art therapy is that the patient must participate in her own treatment and thereby her own recovery . . . the actual process of painting helps to break down the defensive/defiant mechanism that operates particularly in the early stages of treatment. The initial commitment to paper is a commitment to therapy.
>
> (ibid.: 101)

Waller (1983) discusses a group for eating-disordered women which formed an element in a research project to investigate the effectiveness of the treatment. The women found it extremely difficult to attend regularly and alternated between 'binging' and 'vomiting' in the group. They would 'starve' themselves by not attending just as they were beginning to gain some positive value from the process. Waller describes the difficulties of working with this group, which was characterized by ambivalence about change and in which the therapist was alternatively overwhelmed by love and then punished. Many of the images reflected the 'ideal' self, compared with the self that the patient saw – that is, fat, ugly, worthless.

Schaverien (1989) describes how the image becomes a most important mediator between the therapist and anorexic client, where the client can begin to unlock her frozen, imaginal world. Because the anorexic needs so much to protect her vulnerable sense of self, she experiences any transference interpretation as an intrusion and thus a threat. She fears that if another person 'gets inside her' she will lose control and, more importantly, her sense of self. The therapist, Shaverien feels, must maintain a safe distance and allow the client to use the image-making process as a place in which she can unfold in her own time. In this way, painting can be exchanged for food:

> The picture may exhibit the imaginal world of the client and it may become a talisman in the therapeutic relationship standing for, and carrying transference feelings.
>
> (ibid.: 14)

Schaverien concludes that verbal discussion may or may not be necessary in this process as the relationship may be carried in the pictures for a long time and progress may be made without recourse to verbal interpretation. She notes that in psychoanalytic terms this may be seen as encouraging a defence which should be worked on, and that this would be true if there were no pictures:

> But in art therapy the pictures reveal far more than is consciously put into them and so the unconscious content is assimilated without verbal interpretation. Ideally the additional understanding gained from some verbal discussion is helpful in fixing meaning and understanding but with this client group this may not be beneficial.
>
> (ibid.: 1)

The question of whether or not verbalization needs to take place is an important one and I shall return to it later in the chapter when discussing the role of the art work.

Woodman (1980, 1982, 1985), a psychotherapist, has written about the importance of images whether painted, danced, written or spoken in the therapeutic relationship. She uses Greek myths to illustrate the archetypal figures with which these women identify, and to show how a transformation out of this process is possible.

The psychodynamic model and art therapy

This is the model currently in use by the majority of art therapists writing and working with eating-disordered clients, so I shall give here an outline of the model and explore how it is seen to be of particular value to this group of clients. The model rests on the assumption that there is a constant dynamic interplay between aspects of the personality and between each person and the world in which she lives. The way in which these dynamics take shape depends to a large extent on a woman's early relationships, which are in turn shaped by the culture into which she is born. As she grows and develops, certain aspects of these dynamic interplays will become repressed into the unconscious if the tension between them becomes unbearable. These unconscious forces will make themselves known through dreams, bodily symptoms, behaviour and relationship patterns. An eating problem can be seen as one such pattern of behaviour – as an unconscious expression making itself known through the woman's body.

This idea was first suggested by Susie Orbach in *Fat is a Feminist Issue*, where she links the cultural pressures and expectations within a patriarchal society together with patterns from early experience to form a gender-based psychodynamic theory of eating problems. She and Louise Eichenbaum develop a feminist psychoanalytic theory in their later books. They suggest that '. . . the mother will *identify* with her daughter because of their shared gender . . . (she) also *projects* on to her some of the feelings she has about herself (Orbach and Eichenbaum 1982: 32–3, author's emphasis). Furthermore, because of the mother's own unmet needs, she 'prepares' her daughter not to expect too much by limiting the care she receives as a baby. This may imply that the baby girl will be given less emotional nurturance within the earliest symbiotic relationship. This withholding of care is symbolized in terms of food. The mother may delight in the appetite of her baby boy whilst continually curbing that of her daughter. This is how the links are made from a very early age between emotional care and feeding.

So whether the daughter experiences being overwhelmed and overfed by mother, or not having had enough, she will be left feeling hungry for what she really wants, or stuffed so full that she has no room left to feel. As the daughter reaches puberty and begins her journey into womanhood she also begins to separate from mother and to feed herself. It is at this point that her eating problem seems to manifest itself. If she does not feel she had enough mothering and has not learned how to listen to her own needs, she will be both hungry for more and at a loss to know how to feed herself, both literally and metaphorically. As a compulsive eater, she blindly attempts to respond to all her needs with food. She is left still hungry and takes all the emotional feeding she can get, without being able to discriminate. Then she feels overwhelmed and lost, cuts off feelings and tries to find herself again by going on a diet to empty herself. As an anorexic, she tries to cut off altogether. Any feeding is experienced as intrusive and overwhelming; it feels to be undermining to her sense of self. As a bulimic, she takes the food inside but can only hold it in for a short while before it feels bad and must be cast out again.

Within the therapeutic setting we would expect the client to re-experience the very early relationship she had with mother. In an attempt to get what she never found with mother, she will create the therapist as 'all good and nurturing'. Then the therapist feels to be overwhelming and she must get away to protect herself. The therapist is then felt never to be good enough and that she cannot *really* understand. As the client does not have a sense of what her own needs are, she keeps asking the therapist what it is that she feels inside, imagining that she holds all the answers. The client swings from pole to pole, from fat to thin, from all good to all bad. A typical stance from one of my clients is: 'This isn't any good . . . it isn't working because I'm still compulsively eating. There's no point in my coming any more until I decide to do this properly.' In other words, I was no good as her therapist ('this isn't working') or she was no good because she was not 'doing it properly'. A paradox is contained within these two sentences, the point being that she could not conceive of a relationship working between the two of us whereby a gradual understanding of her problems could emerge.

Another example is of a client relating what her mother had once said to her as a little girl: 'You see, you have your Sindy doll, just like I've got mine.' She was, of course, referring to her daughter as her Sindy doll. The daughter was an object, a longed-for pretty doll in her mother's inner world. She was not given a separate identity as a person growing up and therefore had little sense of what a relationship between two separate people felt like. Little wonder that this woman found her mother's presence overwhelming and consequently had to keep her at arm's length. At the same time she had left home yearning for more and came to me exasperated and confused by her continual binging.

It is difficult to convey the full complexities of this process. The task of this relationship is to enable this woman to find her own sense of identity which she can only do in a safe space which she does not experience as too overwhelming. Gradually, with the aid of insight into what her eating problem and body image symbolizes, she can begin to express her needs and feelings through images and words rather than through her behaviour and her body. As the eating problem diminishes we would expect a period of chaos and turbulence as the painful feelings and memories that have been repressed for so long bubble to the surface.

What of the image and art therapy? I will now attend to what is unique about this approach to therapy.

The role of the art object in art therapy

There are many ways in which using images in work with women who have a damaged sense of self may be particularly helpful. Art therapy provides a different kind of space from verbal psychotherapy where inner processes are normally articulated in words. Of course, all analytic psychotherapy makes use of the image: free association and dream analysis are central elements. But this approach assumes that the client can to some extent bridge the gap between the image *inside* as felt and conceived, and the image *outside*, given form to and embodied in the spoken word. Art therapy, however, makes it possible to produce a non-verbal vehicle for that inner image as the art object, which may in time be spoken about or may be a complete expression in its own right. Art therapy also implies a 'making process' within the session time, which may be considered as a form of waking dream, or an alternative to lying on the couch and free associating. The art object produced is of course different from the spoken word; it is concrete and can be kept from week to week. As something which is external to both client and therapist it could be seen as producing a three-way system of interchange within the session:

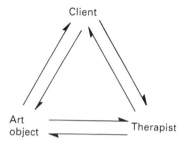

The art object therefore acts as an intermediary and in this sense can carry some of the transference. For a woman with eating problems, this can be of value in several different ways, as follows.

The art object as intermediary preconscious messenger

In outlining the possible difficulties in the mother–daughter relationship, I have indicated how hard it is for a woman to have a sense of herself as separate from her mother. Consequently she has difficulty in really knowing her own needs and feelings. Even when these are felt, she has difficulty in expressing them directly for fear of damaging the already damaged-and-in-need-of-protection mother. She will, instead, 'swallow' these feelings and only let out those that will protect and nurture mother in order that she will continue to get the hoped for nurturing she needs. As she grows older this pattern will continue to be played out in her close relationships. She will feed and nurture others in the hope that she gets fed in return.

Within this dynamic it is her body that unconsciously expresses that for which she cannot find words. Her body becomes an intermediary between her inner and outer worlds. As such she uses something concrete and literal rather than something symbolic. If she is feeling overwhelmed by mother, her small body is saying: 'I'm all right, I'm a normal size, don't notice me; I have no needs.' Her anorexic body, much smaller, is saying: 'I'm as frail as a bird, I can't grow into a woman, it's all too frightening. I still need to be taken care of.' Her large body says: 'I'm eating too much because I feel very needy but it's all right, don't come too close, the food has taken care of my needs. You don't have a place here. I'm big because I want attention but also because inside I feel so small and vulnerable that it has to have protection and I don't know any other way of getting it.'

Part of the therapeutic work is to enable the client to bridge the gap between inner feelings and words. It is as if the gap is too wide. Her body feels numb whilst her head may know all the theory there is to know.

From the literature and from my own experience, it seems as if the art object may fill an intermediary role, giving the unconscious a form before it reaches consciousness and can be articulated. It is more concrete than dreams and words. It not only survives from week to week but inside and outside of sessions too. It has an external life and form and as such acts as an extension to the woman's body. It becomes a container for unconscious material instead of her body and it is preconscious.

The art object can be used to express something literal or it can move towards the symbolic. For example, a woman might paint herself eating many different types of foods to express her feelings about a binge she had during the week. She might, alternatively, move deeper into these feelings where she paints herself as a huge mouth which consumes both good and bad objects which are expressed in a more abstract way. At this point she may begin to understand what her behaviour symbolizes: her need to take things in and her inability to distinguish between the good and the bad object.

By referring to the art object as an intermediary I am implying that it is part of a process and that the end may be an articulation in words. At times it does seem necessary for this verbal articulation to take place so that the insight is fully integrated within the personality. But there are other times when the art object is an expression in its own right and does not need any further step for its meaning to be integrated.

The art object as a means of reaching the gut

As previously mentioned, a woman with an eating disorder has difficulty knowing what she is feeling. She often arrives knowing much of the theory surrounding her problem and can explain what her difficulty is, and even to some extent why she starves and binges. What is lacking is a connection with her 'gut feelings'. For example, she starts by describing the 'logical amount' she 'should' eat but recounts time after time of eating when she knows she is not physically hungry, and not being able to stop when she is full. Her mind is able to tell her when she should be hungry but either she cannot detect her bodily signals or her mind simply overrides them. Likewise she is able to understand logically when she should be angry with someone but in the heat of the moment she is unable to feel this or express it directly. The feelings are then stuffed down with food and the anger is expressed via her body. She becomes angry with herself rather than anyone else.

As she begins to paint, she interacts and plays with physical materials in an activity using her body. As she makes images she is faced with a range of experiences. Sometimes the art object appears as a raw intensifying of what she feels, as with the aforementioned example of a woman depicting a binge scene. With the help of this image she can bring these feelings into the here and now of the session and begin to reflect on what happens that is so frightening.

At other times the art object may contain a very powerful sense of meaning which cannot yet be linked to anything she understands. A simple colour or shape may make her weep, and through feeling like this she gropes her way to a fuller understanding of the issues. I recall watching a woman cover her hand in clay. At first she wept as she stroked this clay hand; then she convulsed into laughter at the sight of this huge, rather clumsy-looking object. Again she cried, again she laughed. Eventually she talked about the memories of her mother's hands on her, feeling the sadness of her loss but also the joy of being stroked. The materials evoked a very powerful memory of an early experience that connected her with her body.

For this woman to trust feelings is crucial as for years she has tried to eat as 'they tell her to', or as she feels she 'should'. The needy little girl inside her becomes shut out. The activity of painting and making things brings back early memories of playing and the little girl has a space in which to come alive, to vent her frustration towards a mother who was not emotionally available enough, to express her joy, her sadness, her anger and fears.

The art process as an arena for making a transitional space

A woman with an eating problem has great difficulty in allowing 'space' – that is, empty or unstructured time – in her life. When she has this, her anxiety and difficult feelings emerge. In order to control them, she fills up the spaces with food, with activity, with words. This is reflected in group or individual sessions by her need to 'gobble up' all the time. She 'binges' with words (does not stop talking) and makes it difficult for interaction to deepen. Then she feels guilty for taking up too much space and, as it were, goes on a diet by keeping quiet for a while. When she is faced with time to paint or make, it is as if she has time alone to reflect, which is contained – rather like a child playing knowing that mother is there in the background. This is a transitional space where she can begin to test out feelings rather than act them out. Of course she can metaphorically binge in this time by painting as many pictures as possible, or filling up all the space on the paper. But she is alone with this, being faced with the reflection of the binge rather than stuffing it back down inside. She will often speak of how painful it is to be alone. As these are frequently the times when she turns to food, it is very important and revealing for her to have the experience in the sessions of being silent and not interacting with another, but being engaged with herself.

The art object as a tool for enactment

Alice Miller (1979) writes:

> There are children who have not been free to experience the very earliest feelings such as discontent, anger, rage, pain, even hunger and, of course, enjoyment of their bodies. Discontent and anger aroused such uncertainty in their mothers about their role, pain had made her anxious. Her children's enjoyment in their own bodies aroused her envy, sometimes her shame about 'what other people would think'. Thus a child under those circumstances may learn very early what she is not allowed to feel lest she runs the risk of losing her mother's love.
>
> (see also Dana 1987: 55)

A woman with eating problems stuffs those unpleasant feelings down with food, turning her rage inwards. But she also at times turns them outwards or acts them out. For example, she might become involved in destructive relationships or other such dramatic situations where her feelings are played out in the world around her.

The making of an art object gives her the chance to have an arena where her feelings may not be experienced as so destructive. She may not be ready to vent fury at her therapist whom she feels might be destroyed if she really let rip. On the other hand, she needs an outlet other than the one she is used to. She can be murderous in her making, use dripping red paint to express the violence she feels. She can scratch round in blacks and greys in her stuck and depressed times. This is a realm of feeling that has an instant and malleable vocabulary. Her words may take some time to catch up. The place of making and its process become her own theatre and play where her dramas can be put into form and enacted in an active way between inner and outer worlds.

The art object as a mirror

In her early experience the baby girl looks to mother for some kind of reflection of herself. The mother acts as a mirror to discover her own identity. To quote Miller (1979) again:

> Mother gazes at the baby in her arms and the baby gazes at her mother's face and finds herself therein, provided that the mother is really looking at the unique, small, helpless being and not projecting her own needs onto the child. In that case the child would not find herself in her mother's face but rather the mother's own predicaments. This child would remain without a mirror and for the rest of her life be searching for one in vain.
>
> (see also Dana 1987: 52)

Dana (1987) argues that this continual search for the mirror manifests itself in two ways:

> It is looking for approval and acceptance from other people, looking for other people to mirror her, define her, tell her who she is and create boundaries for her. At the level of the actual mirror she may continue to try to define herself in terms of her reflection. Her body will become the focus of her search for identity both because in society her body represents her commodity and because it is what is reflected in the actual mirror.
>
> (ibid.: 53)

In the therapeutic setting the woman with an eating problem will look to the therapist to gain a reflection of herself both in outer and inner terms, how she looks and who she is. In a group she will also look to the other members for this purpose.

The making of art objects provides another dimension in this interaction which offers the woman an opportunity to find a reflection of herself. But instead of trying to find it in another she is faced with a reflection of her own inner world on a more figurative level. She can also experiment with depicting herself as a range of sizes. In a group she has the opportunity to have feedback on where she really is in all this. Having a range of magazines available is important so that she can begin to play with the images of women she is envious of, threatened by, idealizing, is drawn to or repulsed by and so on. She can begin to understand how these different images mirror the many different aspects of herself, rather than needing to identify with any one of them.

The art process as a contained out-of-control space

Control is a key issue for this client group. The woman feels out of control in her life, which is expressed through her very out-of-control eating habits. She feels at her best when in control of her body and food and when eating only the 'good' foods and having a 'good' body. Asking her to get in touch with these split off unconscious feelings is like throwing her into the deep end of a binge. She needs to feel in a safe and contained space before she can allow those feelings to surface and be explored. In art therapy she is the active maker of art objects and can contact some of her unconscious feelings whilst fully awake. The art object has a boundary and therefore can contain whatever feelings of chaos may be expressed within it. (Interestingly I have noticed a great reluctance on the part of group members to engage in a group painting which I feel reflects their need to maintain their boundaries for fear of losing their sense of self. The chaos would then feel over-whelming.)

An image once spoken of in a workshop describes the different parts of the woman being locked up in separate boxes inside her which she could only open up one at a time. The other group members immediately identified with this image. When I asked why they needed to keep the contents of the boxes so separate she replied: 'If I opened them up together they would get all mixed up and there would be chaos.' She feared she would lose herself and there would be a battleground where parts of her would be destroyed. In working with art objects these different aspects of the self can maintain their separate identities but be held together at the same time within a framework.

The art process as a means of reaching a metaphorical way of perceiving

Images, dreams and stories are all a window into a metaphorical way of perceiving. A woman with an eating problem finds it difficult to engage in metaphorical thinking or in symbolizing. For example, a dream becomes something literal. She cannot grasp its varied layers of meaning and that it may point to something beyond the apparent. In the same way, she sees her fat body as just extra fat because she has been a greedy pig, not that it might have meaning. It is indeed frightening for her to take this on.

The art object as a metaphor contains an element of transformation. I am thinking of one woman's image of a tree. The roots were shown under the earth and amongst them was painted 'black shit'. She described the tree as portraying herself and that she felt her early experience to be 'full of shit'. How could she, she asked, make something of her life when all there was at the beginning was bad? The rest of the group puzzled over this dilemma. Then they struck on the idea that plants thrive on shit and that it fertilizes them. The tree could transform the shit and use it in its strong, healthy growth. Through this image she began to see that she could use her experience in different ways. Instead of cutting off from her anger and sadness about her early experience she could feel it and use it to help her understand and distinguish her current needs and behaviour patterns.

Another example, again a tree image, is from a short-term workshop. A woman painted a series of three trees to depict her feelings about being fat and thin. On the left was a tree painted in blacks and greys. The branches were bare. There was a magazine image of a rich, sweet pudding in the corner. She had also included an image of a very fat woman, placing this in the tree trunk. This felt to her a dark and barren place, depressing and stuck. The middle image was a tree in leaf, its surroundings in green. She had included a magazine image of food she felt she 'should' be eating: a dry biscuit with cottage cheese. This image was where she felt herself to be at that moment: really trying to be positive about herself and her life, eating only the 'good' foods, feeling in control. The image on the right was a tree surrounded by yellow, gold and orange. The tree was bearing fruit and in the corner was a magazine image of bubbling lasagne. This image depicted the place where she wanted to be: able to eat any food she fancied in the midst of fruition.

In describing these images she wanted to be only in the final one and to be rid of the other two. The group reflected on the images as showing the different seasons of the year. 'If only', she said, 'it could be summer all year round.' I commented on this, asking how it would feel to be rid of winter. Indeed, could we survive without a period when the energy goes downwards and inwards? The group used these images to explore whether the darker periods of their lives, when they felt fat, could hold some value. Did they actually need to get fat to feel depressed, they wondered, rather than feeling depressed *because* they were fat? What were the feelings that were being de-pressed? They began to see how their large bodies housed all their difficult feelings whilst their thin bodies were all sweetness and light. They began to explore their fears about having these feelings inside and to see how they were not able to be expressed within their families.

In this part of the chapter I have suggested ways in which the art object may prove an essential element in the treatment of women with eating problems and illustrated the theoretical points with case examples. In the following case-study I shall describe how the model was used in the treatment of a bulimic woman in individual art therapy.

Case-study

It is indeed a challenge to present a case-study about the art therapy process without also presenting the images concerned. I feel this raises some interesting questions about the need we have as art therapists to capture the art object itself rather than to speak of the image etched on our memory. There are other questions here about confidentiality and the requesting of permission from the clients concerned to publish material. I do not wish to discuss these issues at length; suffice to say that I welcome this opportunity to attempt to write about the images in this way.

I wish to write about a woman whom I shall call Jan. She came to me with the presenting problem of bulimia and we worked together for a year on a twice-weekly basis in a private setting. On arrival she stated that it was her intention to move abroad in a year's time, automatically time limiting our relationship. This made the ending her own decision rather than something we arrived at together. Part of my decision to describe this relationship is just because of this: it is common for bulimic women to want to control the ending in this way so as not to face the possibility of being abandoned by the therapist and preventing the relationship from developing too deeply. In this way she can protect us both from her ambivalence about forming a dependency. Neither need she face her disappointment with the situation; she can edge her way out for 'external' reasons. It is a complicated set of issues for the therapist and client to face.

Jan was in her early twenties when she came to see me. On the face of it, she could cope very well in the world. She held down a well-paid job in the City in order to fund further studying abroad. She was well dressed and neither fat nor thin. In other words, from her outer appearance it would appear as if nothing at all were wrong. She had a wide number of aquaintances but had difficulty in sustaining long-term intimate relationships.

Her presenting problem of bulimia began when she was 16 years old alongside a drink and drug problem. At that stage she sought help from a therapist and her difficulties improved, leaving her with a mild compulsive eating problem. She came to see me because she had begun to make herself sick again and was worried that this would escalate. She was also seeking help from a number of other sources such as Overeaters Anonymous and co-counselling sessions.

Jan had survived a difficult childhood. She grew up in different parts of Asia as the only white child amongst black children. Her early memories of her parents describe a mother and a father with great difficulties. Her father was tall and fair whilst her mother was small, dark and fat. Her father jibed at her mother's body, calling her an elephant. She remembers them arguing a great deal. Her relationship with her mother was very cosy, one in which she was allowed to do anything; she could never say 'no'. She felt that her father set the boundaries telling her what was 'right and wrong'. However, when Jan was five years old her father was suddenly killed. She had few memories of this. Afterwards her mother began to live a nomadic life-style, forming brief relationships with a stream of lovers, some of whom made passes at Jan. She developed a drink problem and it seemed that Jan became the carer in this relationship, clearing up mother's mess and being the go between in her mother's failing partnerships. As Jan grew older they began to share lovers. At an early age she left this situation to live with a boyfriend. When this failed she found a family to lodge with and at this point her eating and drink problems began. She has continued to move from place to place, from lover to lover and from therapist to therapist.

When Jan came to see me she described her binging and vomiting as 'the only bit of her life that isn't right'. She could not understand her reasons for her behaviour and was enormously frustrated with this apparently greedy, messy, unruly, unattractive and out-of-control part of herself. She was very articulate in describing her problem but very out of touch with and very frightened of this needy little girl inside who was very deprived and despairing. She had become her mother's mother from an early age and had not been allowed to express her own messy feelings or feel them to be contained.

Within the first few weeks of our relationship Jan forged an immediate rapport with me and I quickly became the good mother and the person who held all the answers. She imagined that I lead a very settled life, that I had a very good long-term relationship and that I was happy and fulfilled. My mess must be clearly out of sight and preferably a thing of the past, no longer here.

She talked constantly and described the various dramas of her life, of which there were many. She focused on the problems in her current relationships, one with a woman abroad with blonde hair who was seen to be the person who could save her and one with a woman here with dark hair who was an ex-lover. This had been a difficult relationship. We talked about this in relation to her parental differences and began to explore her feelings towards myself, a woman with blonde hair, whom she saw as the person who would rescue her. The question was whether she could feel that both these aspects could reside in the same place without annihilating one another.

Jan took some time before she could settle to any painting in the sessions. She needed to talk and have eye contact to maintain an intensity in our relationship. This seemed to protect us both from a sense of being stuck or depressed. She tried to keep these feelings of deadness out of the room.

Her first images reflect this level of intensity. She painted pictures of herself drawing blood on her skin and more abstract images of razor cuttings. There emerged a series of images centring around the theme of red blood appearing on white paper. Unknowingly, she came to the sessions dressed in these colours. The images seemed to reflect many different issues. One was her need to 'get inside' and 'to get under her skin'. It mirrored her need to take in food and throw it out, to pull something from inside out. It is interesting to note here that this cutting and drawing blood is something I have heard other bulimic women describe. Sometimes this is acted out, usually in hidden places on the body, which I feel reflects the secret nature of binging and vomiting.

These images also heralded her transition from, in her words, a 'white virgin to a red menstruating woman'. She talked about this transitional period in her life as being laden with conflict and ambivalence: how difficult it seemed to grow into a woman when she had not had enough of being a child and when her mother presented such an inadequate female role model.

The images also seemed to reflect a 'quiet violence', a sense of murderousness without the rage. She was not able at this stage to bring these feelings into the room except via her images. At this stage her eating patterns had begun to shift. She had started to lose weight and had not been sick for some time. I saw this as a temporary respite whilst she experienced me as the 'all good saviour', and could express her feelings through the images. The binging would probably return (and did) when I became the opposite, and settled down to a slow recovery as I could gradually be experienced as the mother who could be both good and bad at the same time. Nevertheless, this initial shift was important and gave her confidence in eventually finding a way through.

The images changed to include herself vomiting what looked like green mucous coming out in a long strand. Other images showed herself scratching at her face with long nails, blood coming from her cuticles, mouth and gums, both places being the boundary between something hard and something soft. It felt significant that these boundaries were under attack. Certainly she began to test the boundaries by arriving late to our sessions, oversleeping or taking longer holidays than myself. It was hard for her to see that this behaviour could be a means of her expressing her anger towards me; but as we talked she challenged and confronted me and realized that I did not retaliate nor get destroyed by her feelings. She spoke of her envy towards me, how much she imagined I had, but at the same time trying to prove to me that her journey abroad next year would become her 'promised land'. This made it very hard for her to stay with her current sense of deprivation and feelings of disappointment, except in a few sessions.

The images of mucous seemed baffling. On the one hand they were a literal representation of her inner mess; but why this green slime? It occurred to me that mucous was the lining of the digestive system and is thus the substance that forms a protective layer between inside and outside. Did she want to destroy this boundary also?

Her images continued in this vein, at times becoming a literal sequence of before, during and after the ritual binge and vomit sessions. It seemed as if she was needing to know whether I could really see her mess with her, in what felt to be its most barren state. It had always been her very own, her secret ritual, and now she was exposing it.

She began to paint images of herself in black lace underwear bringing her sexuality into the room in a very strong and particular way. She talked about her close relationship with her mother and how it had bordered on becoming sexual. It was clear she was again testing my boundaries to see whether I could be seduced by her or whether I could give her clear limits within this situation.

As time went on and the date of her departure came close this became a predominant feature of our sessions. She at times felt relief at the thought of escaping our relationship; this would often be expressed in the form of escaping 'Thatcher's Britain', that cold, stuck, dark and depressing place. But she also got in touch with the fear and the sadness she felt about losing this relationship she had become involved with. Her images reflected this ambivalence.

For a short period of time she actually allowed herself to explore the possibility of delaying her plans to leave in order to continue seeing me. However, it seems that she was not yet ready to face the rock bottom sense of despair inside, and her move might perhaps enable her to do this eventually. I am not the person to say what was right or wrong in this situation but it does seem that our time spent working together helped her to integrate a little more the sense that her intolerable mess inside could be witnessed and held with another person.

Her binging and vomiting became worse as the ending date approached and this gave her the opportunity to *feel* a separation and its links with her eating problem for perhaps the first time. She described her constant moves in childhood as being without emotion. Her pattern was to cut off from the feelings of loss, looking only at the hope of the new place much as she might view the promise of being thin.

There are many details of this relationship I have left out, one being the conflict between Jan's parents and how this reflected her difficulty in bringing opposing sides of herself together in a relationship without destruction. She talked to some extent about her father's death but I was left feeling there was a mound of buried issues here for her to explore, as with many aspects of her life.

My intention here has been twofold: first to illustrate the value of images as containers of extremes of emotion expressed in a non-verbal way and in a form that feels less threatening than making an attack on the therapist; and secondly, to illustrate that despite her premature leaving, Jan was able to gain some insight into her eating problems. In a paradoxical way it is precisely the separation issue that she most needed to work with, and if nothing else I believe that our relationship gave her the opportunity to form an attachment in order to work through an ending that was felt. This raises many questions about both working with bulimic women and their immense fear of commitment, and how one negotiates contracts at the starting point of a therapeutic relationship.

Conclusion

In this piece of writing I have attempted to illustrate how the image and the process of image-making can hold particular meaning for the woman with an eating problem. As a concrete entity the image can help to replace the need for a woman's body to express that for which she cannot find words. The client can use this boundaried space as a means of communication with the therapist without necessarily needing to translate into a more literal form what is taking place inside her. She can therefore feel more privacy and protection of her vulnerable sense of self and yet feel that her inner world is revealed, held and survived.

A woman with an eating problem, on entering a therapeutic relationship, inevitably uncovers that chasm of emptiness; there is no experience of 'woman' there, as there was no experience of mother. Once this emptiness, this black hole, this state of utter despair can be reached and held we can begin to 'make a soul'. And what better way, I feel, to do this, than to build it in images and in words.

References

Chernin, K. (1981) *Womansize: The Tyranny of Slenderness*, NY: Harper and Row.
Crisp, A. (1980) *Anorexia Nervosa: Let Me Be*, London: Academic Press.
Dana, M. (1987) Boundaries: one way mirror to the self, in M. Lawrence (ed.) *Fed Up and Hungry*, London: Women's Press.
Lawrence, M. (1984) *The Anorexic Experience*, London: Women's Press.

—— (1987) Poison is the nourishment that makes one ill. The metaphor of bulimia, in M. Lawrence (ed.) *Fed Up and Hungry*, London: Women's Press.

—— (1988) *Women's Secret Disorder – A New Understanding of Bulimia*, London: Grafton Books.

Levens, M. (1987) Art therapy with eating disordered patients, *Inscape*, Summer.

—— (1990) Borderline aspects in eating disorders: art therapy's contribution, in D.E. Waller (ed.) Special Section: Group Analysis and the Arts Therapies I, *Group Analysis* **23**, 3 September.

Maisner, P. and Turner, R. (1985) *The Food Trap*, London: Unwin Paperbacks.

Miller, A. (1979) *The Drama of the Gifted Child*, London: Faber and Faber.

Murphy, J. (1984) The use of art therapy in the treatment of anorexia nervosa, in T. Dalley (ed.) *Art as Therapy*, London: Tavistock Publications.

Orbach, S. (1978) *Fat is a Feminist Issue*, London: Paddington Press.

—— and Eichenbaum, L. (1982) *Outside In and Inside Out*, Harmondsworth: Penguin.

Rust, M.-J. (1987) Images and eating problems, in M. Lawrence (ed.) *Fed Up and Hungry*, London: Women's Press.

Schaverien, J. (1989) Transference and the picture: art therapy in the treatment of anorexia, *Inscape*, Spring: 14–17.

Waller, D.E. (1983) Art Therapy as a Treatment for Eating Disorders: Report of a Research Project, in J. Henzell (ed.) Proceedings of the British Psychological Society International Conference 'Psychology and the Arts', Wales: University of Cardiff.

Winnicott, D.W. (1971) *Playing and Reality*, London: Tavistock.

Woodman, M. (1980) *The Owl Was the Baker's Daughter – Obesity, Anorexia Nervosa and the Repressed Feminine*, Toronto: Inner City Books.

—— (1982) *Addiction to Perfection: The Still Unravished Bride*, Toronto: Inner City Books.

—— (1985) *The Pregnant Virgin – A Process of Psychological Transformation*, Toronto: Inner City Books.

10

Art therapy in the treatment of alcohol and drug abuse

JACKY MAHONY AND DIANE WALLER

Introduction

In this chapter we will discuss critically some theoretical issues on art therapy and substance abuse. There is an abundance of American literature on art therapy and alcoholism and drug abuse, but a marked paucity of British literature on the same subject, although little to indicate why this should be.

Many methods have been used to help people who have problems with drugs and alcohol, but it appears that controlling and punitive elements enter into a number (e.g. Synanon, Daytop) and that there is emphasis on confrontational tactics. Moore (1983) reviewed the American literature (approximately 20 papers) and found a wide range of orientations in the treatment of substance abuse by art therapists, but found that special assignments and special art techniques dominate the therapeutic approach. However, apart from two art therapists – Head (1975) and Kaufman (1981) – Moore (1983: 258) states that none give reasons for their chosen structured approach but all felt their work was 'therapeutically effective'. Also criticized was the lack of dissemination of ideas: 'in literature spanning three decades, only two art therapists cited another art therapist's work on substance abuse' (ibid.: 259). It seems to us that examination of the literature on the therapist's counter-transference and a critical analysis of methodology are essential in therapeutic work; its absence leaves a real gap in the theory on art therapy with alcohol and drug abusers.

Theoretical and conceptual perspectives

Psychoanalytical models

Many art therapists appear to use psychoanalytical concepts to underpin their understanding of states where drug and alcohol abuse is a feature, although few give evidence of using theory to inform their practice. In many instances theory seems to bear little relation to the structuring of sessions or the role of the art therapist. Several use the term narcissism in relation to addiction, but apart from Albert-Puleo (1980) none give any indication of understanding the notion of the 'curative transference' and how this might affect practice. This is discussed succinctly by Albert-Puleo and forms the basis for her model of art therapy applied to drug abuse.

Albert-Puleo describes the narcissistic defence of those addicted as a 'withdrawal into euphoria' (p. 43) in an attempt to avoid externalizing rage and other feelings that are experienced as overwhelming. This way of handling feelings is seen to originate in the first six months of life when there is an undeveloped ego and the baby is unable to produce the required response from an excessively frustrating environment. 'To protect the much-needed love object from overwhelming rage, the infant internalizes or blocks the heightened aggressive impulses' (ibid.). Albert-Puleo considers that:

> Art is particularly useful in treating narcissistic patients because of its non-verbal nature. Since developmental frustrations theoretically occurred prior to verbalization, many narcissistic patients are unable to verbalize feelings.
>
> (ibid.: 48)

Albert-Puleo bases her theoretical approach on that of Spotnitz (1967) who developed Freudian theory in order that there could be successful treatment of the narcissistic patient. Freud considered that there could not be any object transference in the narcissistic patient because a sense of 'other' is not yet developed, hence there can be no interpretation of the transference – the basis of Freud's technique. Spotnitz developed techniques that were aimed at encouraging what is termed the 'narcissistic transference', where the patient experiences the therapist as indistinguishable from the self. Albert-Puleo reports that the 'narcissistic transference occurs frequently in my art therapy sessions' (p. 45), and considers that it must be worked through, giving examples of its manifestation in the artwork of her clients. Strengthening the ego is seen as important in order that aggression can be discharged appropriately and without the destruction that the patient expects, and Albert-Puleo considers this can be achieved through the artwork.

Virshup (1985) describes drug abusers as having 'early narcissistic conflicts' and as being resistant to verbal forms of treatment. Addiction is described as an attempt to 'compensate for developmental and structural defects originating in the non-verbal oral stage'. Also described are traits including 'nonlinear, non-logical appositional thinking and impulsivity (which makes it difficult for them to pursue a topic or sustain a constructive and maturational line of thought in both individuals and group processes)' (ibid.: 153). Virshup concludes that these traits seem to be responsible for the 'positive response to the process of art therapy in group settings' (ibid.) but unfortunately does not explain why this might be. However, earlier, Virshup and Virshup (1981) had described the characteristics of substance abuse as:

> deriving from early, narcissistic conflicts which are difficult to treat verbally because of their origin in the nonverbal oral stage. The addition of art therapy allows a controlled regression to the stage of fixation, permitting the individual to explore the conflicts nonverbally.
>
> (ibid.: 371)

It is regrettable that this argument is followed by a more questionable statement about the function of the right brain:

> If the addict is, in this process, using right brain functions, then we have a physiological basis for the use of art therapy and other nonverbal therapies.
>
> (p. 371)

Robbins (1987) attempts to present a cohesive theory of art therapy based on object relations in conjunction with principles of aesthetics. His premise is that 'all psychological phenomena have their aesthetic counterparts and that incorporating those elements facilitates the therapeutic process' (ibid.: 22). To illustrate:

> it is the artist in the therapist who keys into deadness in color or form and then looks beyond the hollowness or lack of energy to ascertain the psychodynamics being reflected.
>
> (p. 23)

The basis of his technique is to diagnose the developmental level of the patient and if intervention is necessary, to intervene according to the level of object-relatedness. For example, he considers that the use of finger paints with a borderline patient could 'reinforce a regressive pull towards fusion' (p. 41): in object relations terms the borderline patient is stuck in the separation-individuation phase (normally at about two years old), the dilemma being wanting to separate but needing to be held.

Robbins' short mention of substance abuse looks at the phenomena in developmental terms. He says that substance abusers 'can be quite slippery in their use of negativism, avoidance, withdrawal, or evasion' (p. 55), making diagnosis difficult. He states that:

> The substance-abuse population represents a wide range of personality problems that demand different treatment procedures. Some patients fall within the neurotic range, some present character problems, and some are defending themselves against a breakdown into a psychotic state.
>
> (ibid.: 55)

Luzzatto (1989), working in Britain, presents short-term work (between ten and twenty sessions) with two patients who have drinking problems. She uses the terms 'withdrawal' and 'clinging' around which to centre the discussion and says that they are seen in object relations as 'early defences against an unsatisfactory relationship with an absent, or threatening, or impinging, primary figure in childhood' (ibid.: 207): the young child is seen as trying to re-establish a harmonious situation that is free of conflict. She also says that they are seen as two basic emotional positions of patients with addiction and particularly alcohol problems where the young child's way of coping with a frustrating relationship is resorted to in the adult through the use of drugs or alcohol. Within the short-term plan Luzzatto focuses on particular images of the client as being possibly more meaningful than others and works on these images with the client using certain interventions based on Winnicott's theory of 'play', Bowlby's concept of 'exploration' and Sartre's ideas about imagination.

Disease model

Our understanding of the disease model is that the addicted person is seen to be suffering from an illness or disease which they have to come to terms with and adjust to, rather than addiction being seen as a symptom of underlying emotional problems. Thus, with the disease model a didactic approach might seem appropriate, teaching the addicted person about their illness and educating them about how to modify its effects. Alcoholics Anonymous uses this model.

Like Virshup (1985), Adelman and Castricone (1986) see the addicted population as being mainly resistant to treatment, particularly verbal group therapy, manipulative, and having a high incidence of narcissism. They seem to use a psychoanalytic framework. They state that the objectives of their model 'are congruent with the treatment goals of the disease model of addiction' (ibid.) although this is not explained.

Allen (1985) describes the primary objective of the three-week alcoholism treatment programme at her place of work as 'breaking down resistance to treatment' (p. 10). Other staff members were initially concerned about art therapy as they viewed it as psychoanalytic and thereby potentially detrimental to their view that drinking is the primary problem. In order to integrate art therapy into the programme, Allen provided an art lecture once every four to six weeks and found its didactic nature 'invariably enhanced participation' in the group that occurred the same week. The groups were 'highly structured' in order to be compatible with the rest of the programme, despite Allen's preferred 'non-directive' approach.

Concept model

This model has been developed at 'Concept Houses', which are sometimes known as therapeutic communities and are based on the Phoenix Hotel model as developed in the United States. They incorporate the concept of self-help by ex-addicts who graduate through the system and after a period 'outside' return as staff members. The programme is highly structured and designed to help residents learn to cope with emotional, work and social situations and conflicts. There is a strict hierarchy in a Concept House. A newcomer starts at the bottom and has to do menial tasks, such as cleaning. He is under the supervision of a resident on the next level, who reports on progress to the community. The resident has no say in what task they are given and may not question the authority of the supervisor. If he or she is able to perform the given task well and conscientiously, then they may move upwards to a more responsible task. Residents may move up or down the various levels according to their attitude and their general progress – which includes the ability to abstain from alcohol or drugs. As residents succeed at each level they eventually reach senior staff positions and have much responsibility for running the community.

The favoured form of treatment is group therapy, although individual therapy may be included. Some communities include psychodrama, gestalt therapy, encounter and, rarely, art therapy. The aim is for residents to express their feelings and to accept responsibility for them.

Not all people can benefit from the highly confrontative and structured routine of a Concept House. For instance, it would not be suitable for addicts who are also psychiatrically disturbed or severely depressed, or for people who are not verbally articulate or cannot tolerate the high pressure daily routine. Foulke and Keller (1976) claim that:

> Many addict rehabilitation programs fail to meet the addict's need for integration of the life of feeling with the life of cognition and action. We have found that art can further a beginning synthesis of unconscious thought with conscious behaviour in that it provides a safe form of expression that allows the addict a glimpse of his authentic self.
>
> (ibid.: 75)

Their therapeutic community programme includes: 'Gestalt, encounter, attack therapy and didactic approaches' but 'art therapy plays a major role' (ibid.). They consider that art therapy can offer the former heroin addict opportunities where a sense of control over feelings can be experienced, and that it is a medium of expression that does not lend itself to intellectualization and rationalization. They appear to consider that confrontative techniques are necessary in the treatment process: 'Exploratory psychotherapy, stripped of confrontative aspects, has also been notably unsuccessful in therapeutic work with addicts' (ibid.).

On the basis of conducting non-confrontative art therapy groups with addicted young people in Concept Houses, we would not agree with this statement. The nature of these groups came as a surprise initially, but the introduction of materials into an interactive model of groups caused early disturbances to be reactivated and catharted, and the group members discovered vulnerable, sensitive areas of self which had previously been disowned (Waller 1989).

Relationship of theory to practice

In 1983 Moore pointed out that the majority of authors in the art therapy and addiction literature used structured methods in their practice with this client group. This continues to be the case in the literature we have examined, as will be seen.

Projective techniques and theme based assignments

We were particularly curious about Virshup's (1985) technique in her work with drug abusers which ran for two and a half years in a waiting room with a changing population similar to the British 'open group'. Virshup, though, uses the group dynamics and process for therapeutic purposes.

Whilst waiting for their daily dose of methadone, six to twelve clients voluntarily produce drawings:

> In the lobby is a large newspaper covered table . . . in the center of which are boxes containing soft pastels and two bottles of black poster paint. In

addition, there are half a dozen 'chop sticks' with 12 inch pieces of kite string
tied like a fishing line to each, plus 11 inches by 17 inches paper.

(ibid.: 154)

The kite and fishing line imagery brought to mind hooking/catching/hanging on
to rather unwilling and elusive clients. There follows a description of how these
implements are used – the string is dipped in the black ink and dragged across the
paper making marks of a random kind, and the clients look for images within the
shapes, adding colours with the pastels. They are then asked to title the work and
to write an explanatory story. This is reminiscent of Winnicott's 'squiggle' technique or a game for children. Virshup comments that it is similar to the Rorschach
test using inkblots and the Thematic Apperception Test. Was this an attempt to
validate the art therapy process using a method drawn at least in part from
psychology? Virshup concludes that the 'Lobby Art Therapy Program is a successful mode of therapy for the drug-abusing population' (p. 158), but gives no
evidence for this, leaving a puzzling lack of information as to the rational behind
this strange technique.

Adelman and Castricone (1986) use art therapy 'techniques' in what they call
an 'Expressive Arts Model' for substance abuse group training and treatment
alongside techniques drawn from psychodrama and music therapy. Their model
is extremely structured and didactic. It seems to be used both for training workers
and as part of in-patient programmes. Sample sessions with staff are described;
for example, the first session – in the 'Art Mode' of art therapy – consists of the
group being presented with the idea that the image of a wall represents a barrier or
defence and they are invited to draw their own wall with personal graffiti.
Adelman and Castricone state that the goal of the session is to 'help each person
become aware of his/her own isolation and resistance' (p. 54).

The other exercises are similarly didactic, using the medium as an educational
technique. The medium (art or music) seems incidental to the didactic process,
the main goal seeming to be facilitating an identification or empathy with the
client group and teaching how the group process reduces isolation, though negative feelings were discouraged.

Similarly, Robbins (1987: 56) recommends a 'tough mirroring approach' as
being more effective than a 'softer, more responsive stance' (ibid.) with this
patient group. His intervention also seems prescriptive in that he asks patients to
depict something in particular, e.g. the mother and father.

The example Liebmann (1984) uses of a group from an alcoholics unit is
prescriptive but more structured than the approach of Robbins, who only intervenes when he feels it is necessary. In the unit referred to, undirected art therapy
sessions provided a contrast to the rest of the programme, which was
'educational', 'direct and confrontative'. For reasons that are not discussed,
another art therapist is invited to 'lead a structured art therapy group . . . to see if
it might be of value to the clients' (ibid.: 164). In this example, 'warm-ups' and a
main theme decided by the two art therapists are used and all the staff join in
'trying to be as open in their work as they expected the clients to be' (p. 165).

In a later publication (1990) Liebmann describes 'strip cartoon' assignments as
a narrative technique for working with probation service clients, in order to help

them explore events leading up to their arrest and to see patterns in their offences. In the 'Alcohol Education Group' a comic strip sequence is used as an educational technique that 'helped to bring home to them in a personal way the connection between their drinking and the resulting offences' (ibid.: 146).

Donnenberg (1978) found that the initial format for the art therapy group in a therapeutic community did not work to her satisfaction – i.e. individuals talked about their individual productions and there was little interaction as a group. Donnenberg's response was to introduce a new format – that of producing murals. She considered that 'individual sheets of paper symbolically confirmed to the residents that they were individuals and not part of the group' (ibid.: 39). She says art therapy was provided at 'Turning Point' because it was seen as offering the residents a way of expressing themselves non-verbally in a 'non-threatening, socially acceptable manner' (ibid.). It is clear from the description of the resulting murals that she viewed a co-operative, well-organized mural, with members given specific duties, as desirable and congruent with the culture of the unit.

Foulke and Keller (1976) provided three hour art therapy sessions twice a week to their residents. Group members were asked to complete a series of assignments aimed at facilitating expression of feeling about some aspect of their lives. The therapist remained mainly supportive, offering little interpretation or discussion of content. With regard to resistance, rather than trying to 'break down the defences' like other methods, Foulke and Keller's 'provides them with the security of a non-committal, but supportive, environment within which they can tentatively test the feared rush of emotions from a painful past' (p. 80).

In her discussion of brief therapies, Luzzatto (1989) points out that brief art therapy does not aim for deep personality change, but links behaviour and feelings and encourages exploration of alternatives to the defence. The therapist is very active and it is again a structured approach. However, in this case the images and creative process seem to be used in a psychodynamic approach, although there are also didactic elements in that certain interventions are made based on Luzzatto's perceptions of what would be helpful for the client to address.

Spontaneous art-making

Albert-Puleo (1980) describes, in what is termed 'Modern Psychoanalytic Art Therapy' how an easel and comfortable chair is used in a similar way to the traditional psychoanalytic couch, with the art therapist instructing the client to paint 'anything' (ibid.: 49). In this paper, practice is linked directly to theory providing a different model for the treatment of drug abuse from those suggested so far. 'Some analytic modifications to traditional art therapy' (p. 52) are suggested:

1 Delay interpretation until the narcissistic transference is worked through.
2 Limit verbal interaction to guard against overstimulation, deprivation, or counter-transference.
3 Explore all contact made by patients (questions or comments to the therapist).
4 Channel all actions (of the patient) into words or graphic expression.

5 Decrease use of ego-oriented questions and increase use of object-oriented questions. (e.g. Instead of 'how to you feel about . . .' use 'I wonder what is causing . . .')
6 Encourage, work with, and welcome resistances.
7 Use the easel in place of traditional visual interaction.

(ibid.)

In contrast to didactic, prescriptive and confrontative approaches, Albert-Puleo considers that resistance needs to be nurtured, understood and worked with, basing this approach on the assumption that the defence will be dropped when it is no longer needed. The limited verbal interaction allows transference to unfold, with the amount and timing of intervention determined by the client.

Discussion

Half of the art therapists described in this review of the literature use psychoanalytical concepts in some way to try and understand the client group in question. All except for Albert-Puleo use some kind of structure in their therapeutic technique, whether in a minimal way, such as Robbins who only intervenes when necessary to the highly structured didactic approach of Adelman and Castricone. None consider the literature on group analysis, transference and counter-transference and a few seek to ally themselves to psychological testing techniques and neurobiology. Apart from Albert-Puleo, none appear to have given any consideration to the implications of using structure in their therapeutic technique, although Allen was concerned with the integration of art therapy into an overall treatment programme and Adelman and Castricone refer to congruence of models. However, there seems to be a lack of critical analysis of technique and its relationship to theory and practice.

In this examination of the literature, as well as there being an emphasis on highly structured methods as described, there also seem to be situations where the art therapist would be unsatisfied with a particular technique or situation and change to another without apparently considering the implications of the change or exploring why the technique was unsatisfactory (Liebmann, Donnenberg). The didactic approaches usually meant that the therapist decided what the client should learn about themselves, from the design of whole programmes to themes aimed at imparting this information.

There seem to be few art therapists working with drug and alcohol abusers in this country. Could it be that there is a difficulty in integrating art therapy into existing treatment settings (as Allen discussed) and that this accounts for the large number of structured approaches? Perhaps art therapy based in psychoanalytic theory which follows the client's lead is perceived as being too liberal for this client group?

Considerations of technique and counter-transference responses

Albert-Puleo's discussion of transference illuminates what seems to us to be a major theoretical issue in working with problems of drug and alcohol dependency:

i.e. resistance, narcissism, manipulative behaviour. Other art therapists described seem to approach these difficulties by employing controlling, structured and confrontative methods, without conceptualizing a framework to rationalize their approach. Whilst intuition and pragmatism may provide what the client needs in a treatment situation, unless there is a conceptual framework to provide a rationale for interventions and therapeutic technique, the therapeutic relationship is open to misuse and abuse.

In a paper appearing in the *International Journal of Therapeutic Communities*, Donnellan and Toon (1986) attempt to look at concerns about the Concept model of treatment – concerns they say have not been examined in depth before. Donnellan and Toon challenge some of the therapeutic techniques as being potentially counter-productive, suggesting that sometimes staff are inadequately trained in their use. It seems the Concept approach has been seen and experienced as 'overly harsh and punitive' (ibid.: 184) at times and it has not been a popular method of treatment in Britain. We have already mentioned the hierarchical nature of Concept Houses and the treatment methods used, and as Donnellan and Toon point out:

> Many of these techniques are personally very intrusive, particularly if residents do not have the right to decline to participate, as they often do not in Concept Houses.
>
> (p. 185)

They refer to 'the power staff have over residents' (p. 187) and how this is often used to 'exaggerate their own self-importance as therapists' (ibid.). Referring to a high drop-out rate, they suggest that a modified approach with more emphasis on 'what is acceptable to the drug abuser rather than on what staff think is appropriate' (p. 188) may improve outcome.

Donnenberg (1978) says that none of her clients were voluntary and all were unmotivated for treatment which may explain some of the language she uses: 'the resident is forced to confront . . .' and so on (ibid.: 37–41). Naturally, this presents considerable difficulties but further discussion and description would have been useful.

Luzzatto (1989) says she is not attempting deep personality change but the therapy seems so brief as to avoid any risk of 'clinging' and 'withdrawal' in the transference – no danger of dependence. Could it be that there is a dynamic arising out of the counter-transference of the art therapists working with this client group, perhaps in response to clients who appear to be demonstrating such a lack of control?

From the literature so far, it seems that the response from the therapists to the client group involves taking control in what is sometimes an intrusive way and also that there are punitive and omnipotent aspects to the response. The therapist decides or makes assumptions about what the client should do, learn and so on. Disappointingly, we could find no exploration or examination by art therapists of their response, which surely must involve counter-transference, apart from Albert-Puleo. In this case, there is no discussion but there is a recommendation that verbal interaction is limited in order to prevent the therapist acting on counter-transference. Moore (1983) refers to the lack of specified reasons for the wide use of structure by art therapists with this client group and wonders whether 'this was due to the response of art therapists to this population' (p. 257).

What is it about this client group that elicits this kind of response? In order to get a view from an allied discipline, we turned to a paper which addresses some of these issues from a group analytic viewpoint within an in-patient setting. Knauss and Freund (1985) start their paper with a somewhat pessimistic view:

> An ever-increasing number of alcoholics and drug addicts are being con-fronted with an increasing number of psychotherapists of various schools, many of whom feel frustrated and disappointed by this group of patients, and treat them with reluctance. Therapeutic nihilism when faced with addicts is particularly widespread among psychoanalysts.
>
> (ibid.: 124)

This is an interesting contrast to Moore (1983: 258) who pointed out that art therapists 'consistently felt that their work was therapeutically effective'.

Knauss and Freund claim their model is that of object-relations, assuming that the addict has suffered 'severe narcissistic wounds' (p. 124) which they 'try to heal and overcome through a slow process of destroying themselves and significant others' (ibid.) by the substance abuse. Also significant is the splitting of objects into good and bad, involving devaluation and idealization. Knauss and Freund see certain conditions as being essential in the treatment situation in order that all may survive in 'primitive aggression and narcissistic rage' (p. 125) of the patient. These include structure, clearly defined boundaries, a certain activeness on the part of therapists, and constant supervision by an outside supervisor. These conditions have a protective and containing function in the face of strong transfer-ence distortion and primitive defence mechanisms.

Knauss and Freund state that for successful therapy the following two points are essential:

(1) The sadistic attack against the early maternal object must be transferred onto the group and/or the therapists, giving rise to a split between a devalued and an idealized object.

(2) The therapists must not act out their counter-transference, either sadis-tically or indulgently, in order to be able to survive the attacks of the patients psychologically.

(ibid.: 126)

The last two points of Knauss and Freund seem important in terms of thera-pists' response to this client group whilst a structured approach dominates the picture. They have conceptualized it within a model, thus clarifying what other-wise may have been potential dangers in the treatment situation. These two points could also explain the predominance of controlling treatment methods that are sometimes intrusive and punishing. Whilst some kind of structure or modified approach seems to be indicated in order to contain and protect the treatment situation, if there is no examination or understanding of the counter-transference and response to the client, there is the potential for acting it out, possibly, for instance, through the model or therapeutic technique that is employed.

We have included a case-study of an alcoholic patient treated successfully in an out-patient clinic to demonstrate that with this patient at least, the object-relations model was a helpful one for the therapist in making sense of the experience and in trusting the art-making process within securely held boundaries. It also helped her survive the patient's verbal attacks and to avoid retaliation, thus enabling him to develop and change.

Case-study

The following is an excerpt from a case-study of a patient, Ben, treated in an out-patient psychotherapy clinic over four years. Ben's presenting problems were agoraphobia, recurring alcoholism and depression. He had already spent several periods of time in psychiatric hospitals as a result of severe depression and alcoholism. He had started drinking while in the Navy, as it was part of the 'macho' culture to do so, and he was drinking around a bottle of whisky a day when referred. His treatment in the clinic was to be a combination of art therapy and small group therapy, but he could not tolerate the verbal groups, finding them 'threatening'. He was therefore admitted to art therapy in both individual sessions and open group, as his sole psychotherapeutic treatment. After a few sessions with Ben, and thinking about his particular problems, I thought that the object-relations model, particularly the work of Winnicott and his concept of the 'transitional object' (see Chapter 1 of this volume, and also Knauss and Freund 1985, mentioned earlier in this chapter), would be helpful in my own theoretical understanding of Ben's experience. I felt that some of his difficulties may have arisen from very early childhood trauma (Virshup 1985) and that, as Albert-Puleo has pointed out (1980: 45), the making of art-objects could enable threatening material to be expressed and contained, without the destruction that the patient expects.

Despite Ben's wish to be in art therapy, we spent the first few sessions talking as he was very scathing about the art materials and despite gentle encouragement ignored them. His attitude to me was faintly patronizing. He made it clear that women should not be taken seriously and he indicated to me that I had better not start psychoanalyzing him as it would no doubt be useless. Nevertheless he attended regularly and established a space for himself in the art room, where he left various things. This space was very near to where I usually sat, so I felt he wanted to make contact but it had to be in his own time. He got furious one day when another patient, coming to the art room for the first time, sat in 'his' space, and this resulted in a burst of sarcasm towards myself for letting it happen and a verbal fight in the art room about space, territory, feeling invaded by a certain violent patient who had come into the day hospital and might have got into the art room and destroyed people's work.

Ben strenuously denied feelings of anger, and indeed any feeling except contempt for doctors and therapists in general. He claimed that all his problems had begun after an accident in which he fell off a ladder while painting a house and he merely wanted to be as he was before the accident, which he claimed had changed his personality. I had no means of knowing whether or not this was true as his history before admittance to the clinic was hazy. However, it was true to him so I did not question his claim as I increasingly felt his vulnerability and that the macho manner and sarcasm was a huge defence against depression and despair.

One day he showed me a painting he had done on his own, when I was away. It was divided into two parts with a section in the middle, which Ben described as follows: the shapes on the left-hand side of the picture reminded him of masks and snakes he had seen in Africa when in the Navy, and the shape in the middle was him on a ladder. The right-hand side, which was a blur of colours, represented his agoraphobia and the present time. I felt that on the one side was the (idealized) past (and alcohol) and on the other the misery of agoraphobia. I had the idea that this painting represented a crisis in Ben's life when the Navy (perhaps representing an all-containing parent) had failed to satisfy him, so he left. Yet he did not know what he wanted to replace it and had 'solved' the conflict through becoming agoraphobic, but had brought the alcohol in from the past. I simply asked him if the ladder could be a crossing, and it seemed to me that a person was standing in the middle, not knowing which way to go. I made a connection between the ladder in the picture and the ladder from his accident. Ben seemed rather upset by this painting and totally ignored my comments. He went into a long description of life in Africa, the jungle and the variety of animals and reptiles he had seen. He discussed the picture only in aesthetic terms.

In the group later that week, another patient wanted to make a cobra and Ben tried to help him mould the clay into the correct form. The rather crude object looked like one of the forms in his first painting. With the compliance of the other (male) patient, Ben took over the cobra and stuck it into a pot where it remained throughout his treatment. I felt that the cobra might have acted as a symbolic reminder of the ambivalence he felt towards the Navy – i.e. the good and the dangerous together. He made it safe by planting it in a pot. It was interesting that another man had started to make it.

Several weeks later Ben made another picture, of two trees, one with much foliage and deep roots and the other somewhat dead-looking. He had painted a large sun in the middle. By this time he was talking quite freely about his alcoholism and how he tried to keep it under control. He restated that it was as a result of being in the Navy and indicated that he was a bit proud of his capacity for drink. Sometimes a friend would call and they would drink a whole bottle of whisky in a couple of hours, resulting in Ben collapsing, drunk. But he seemed to be defying me to be shocked and annoyed and seemed to want to provoke me by his persistent boasting and degradation of women. He treated me as one of the boys and wanted me to join him in his verbal abuse of women. I felt him to be trying to punish me, at the same time as make me a close 'pal'. I maintained a laid-back attitude towards his appallingly sexist remarks, but he was usually challenged by younger women in the group, whereupon he would laugh and go back to his painting, or his newspaper. After finishing the two tree painting, Ben got very upset and tore the picture into two pieces, throwing it in the bin. I asked him why he had done that and he said he couldn't paint the trees the way he wanted to and it was 'useless'. He continued with his denigration of women and made ribald remarks about a female therapist in the day hospital. He equated feminine with being weak and brainless and boasted of his sexual conquests and of the women who pursued him. Somehow the ripping of the tree picture into two made me wonder if Ben was split in his sexual identity, and if he was not happy with either aspect. In object-relations terms, this problem would stem from very early childhood. I looked again at the first picture and wondered if this contained a question about sexual orientation – i.e. which way to go. However, I fed none of these thoughts back to him, sensing that he would leave treatment if I made even the slightest interpretation or indeed suggestion as to unconscious content (see Klein 1990).

I did intervene and rescue the tree picture from the bin but left it in two pieces, suggesting he might repair it. He did so, apparently amused that I had done this. After this incident, he began to paint with enthusiasm, using a piece of paint roller he had brought in instead of the large brushes provided. He had an image of a tree which he said came from a painting he had once seen and it seemed very important that he should be able to re-create this image. He took great care over the preparation of the paper before painting and many days over the actual painting. He was not happy with the result as it was not as he remembered the picture. I noted that the tree was black and dead and the landscape appeared cold. There was a large moon dominating the sky. However we just talked about the technicalities of mixing paint, light and shade and so on. The next attempt at painting the tree, this time against the background of an orange sky and huge red sun, also failed to satisfy him, although he strove long and hard to reach the desired effect. I had a feeling that the moon and the sun might represent male and female elements, neither of which nourished or satisfied the tree as it was already dead. My counter-transference was of feeling useless and sad.

Ben next attempted to paint a mountain and as usual prepared his paper carefully. However the result looked more like a rock than a mountain. He said he had failed because he did not know about perspective and blamed me for not teaching him this, as after all I was supposed to be an artist, wasn't I! He tried to amend the situation by adding an extra piece of paper at the top, but the result still looked rock-like. He was very disappointed and angry. I had to struggle not to rush in and help him, but decided to talk to him about proportion and perspective and so on. In the course of this 'teaching' session, I gently made an equation to him between his painting and life: in painting one had to proceed slowly and it took a long time to achieve what you wanted. Ben wanted to have the skills of a professional artist when he had only been painting for a few weeks. I said something vague about starting to climb rocks before mountains and that perhaps he expected too much of himself. He laughed and told me to teach him how to paint.

Ben was much more relaxed within the art room after this, and made strong, friendly but rather rivalrous relationships with two men who had recently joined the group. These men had sexual identity problems which had manifested themselves in depression and obsessions. The three of them made many attempts to cause trouble between myself and the other art therapist by complaining about each to the other. Although we came in on different days and tended to see different patients, these three were particularly keen to set up rivalry ('splitting' their objects into good and bad, involving devaluation and idealization). Ben had fixed me as the male and my colleague as female (we could not both be female, apparently) and I was supposed to protect them from interference from other male patients who used the art room. Generally speaking, Ben ignored the women in the group except for fetching some lunch for the oldest woman who was sometimes too scared to go into the kitchen.

The theme of protection by myself had become very important for Ben in order that he could, in object-relations terms, survive the 'primitive aggression and narcissistic rage' (Knauss and Freund 1985: 125) that he felt towards me. I felt I had to protect his defences until such time as he was ready to acknowledge the deep, painful conflicts which had led him into alcoholism and agoraphobia. In this respect, the artwork was essential as we could both relate to it on the 'concrete' aesthetic level, while at the same time being aware of its underlying message. Our communication was oblique, much time being spent on the technicalities of the artwork and particularly in the last period of treatment, in preparation of clay and glazes and firing work in the kiln. At this point, I was in the background, while Ben was increasingly able to 'play'.

Ben's ability to work through his conflicts through artwork was probably a life-saving one as he gradually gave up alcohol and began to go out to parks, shopping and so on, and eventually started a small business doing electrical repairs. In the last few months of treatment, he began to make elaborate ceramic objects, which caused him to be much admired by other patients and increased his self-esteem. He took all his paintings when he left, after allowing me to photograph them with him holding them. From this I inferred that he owned, albeit non-verbally, the conscious and unconscious parts of himself. It is several years since his admittance to the clinic and he continues to be well and not using alcohol.

I have used a similar approach to other patients having problems with alcohol and drug abuse, both individually and in groups, and have found similar responses: i.e. initial reluctance to acknowledge any value in the artwork while being attracted to the process; dissatisfaction with one's ability to paint and so on and tendency to blame the therapist; fear, and feeling overwhelmed by the image and wanting to destroy it; dependence on the therapist and subsequent rage; coming to terms with the images and wanting to experiment; love for the objects produced and ability to relate to the therapist as 'good enough' (Winnicott).

It is initially difficult for an art psychotherapist when working with a group where the culture of the institution is 'confrontative', as the persistent non-confronting of defences is unexpected and even anxiety provoking for the patients and other staff. As the patients relax into making images, they often feel overwhelmed by very early 'primitive' emotions and have a tendency to rush into intellectualizing or interpretation as a way of dealing with the anxiety. By setting clear and firm boundaries and remaining non-judgemental and non-confrontative, the somewhat punitive super-ego of the individual and the group is modified. They can then begin to experience the sadness, despair, hurt and emptiness which has made them want to block out the world through alcohol or other drugs and find support for self-reparation.

This is a different attitude to treatment from many examples found in the literature, which insist on confronting the patient's defences and provide a controlling regime. This may actually prevent the patient from finding their own way through to the point where they neither want nor need the drug – as opposed to living in fear of taking a drink and once again being at the mercy of events.

Conclusion

In this chapter, we have examined how art therapists approach working with clients who have problems with drugs and alcohol and how far they formulate their ideas with regard to theory and practice. It appears that art therapy has a unique contribution to make to this field in offering a vehicle for the exploration and expression of feelings that are experienced as overwhelming. However, it would seem from much of the literature that the majority do not relate their technique to their theoretical ideas. If this is a problem only with this particular client group, further research would need to be done to ascertain the reasons.

References

Adelman, E. and Castricone, L. (1986) An expressive arts model for substance abuse group training and treatment, *The Arts in Psychotherapy* **13**: 53–9.

Albert-Puleo, N. (1980) Modern psychoanalytic art therapy and its application to drug abuse, *The Arts in Psychotherapy* **7**(1): 43–52.

Allen, P.B. (1985) Integrating art therapy into an alcoholism treatment program, *American Journal of Art Therapy* **24**: 10–12.

Donnellan, B. and Toon, P. (1986) The use of 'therapeutic techniques' in the Concept House model of therapeutic community for drug abusers: for whose benefit – staff or resident?, *International Journal of Therapeutic Communities* **7**(3): 183–9.

Donnenberg, D. (1978) Art therapy in a drug community, Proc. 8th Int. Congr. Psychopath. Expr., Jerusalem 1976, *Confinia psychiat.* **21**: 37–44.

Foulke, W.E. and Keller, T.W. (1976) The art experience in addict rehabilitation, *American Journal of Art Therapy* **15**(3): 75–80.

Head, V.B. (1975) Experiences with art therapy in short-term groups of day clinic addicted patient, *The Ontario Psychologist* **7**(4): 42–9.

Jellinek, E.M. (1960) *The Disease Concept of Alcoholism*, New Haven: College and University Press.

Kaufman, E. (1978) Individualized group treatment for drug-dependent clients, *Group Analysis* **2** 22–30.

Kaufman, G.H. (1981) Art therapy with the addicted, *Journal of Psychoactive Drugs* **13**(4): 353–60.

Klein, J. (1990) Patients who are not ready for interpretations, *British Journal of Psychotherapy* **7**(1): 38–49.

Knauss W. and Freund, H. (1985) Group-analytic psychotherapy with alcoholic inpatients, *Group Analysis* **XVIII**(2): 124–30.

Liebmann, M. (1984) Art games and group structures, in T. Dalley (ed.) *Art as Therapy*, London: Tavistock, pp. 157–72.

—— (1986) *Art Therapy for Groups*, Beckenham: Croom Helm, pp. 75–6.

—— (1990) Introduction and Chapter 8, in M. Liebmann (ed.) *Art Therapy in Practice*, London: Jesssica Kingsley.

Luzzatto, P. (1989) Drinking problems and short-term art therapy: working with images of withdrawal and clinging, in A. Gilroy and T. Dalley (eds) *Pictures at an Exhibition*, London: Tavistock/Routledge, pp. 207–19.

Moore, R.W. (1983) Art therapy with substance abusers: a review of the literature, *The Arts in Psychotherapy* **10**: 251–60.

Naumburg, M. (1966) *Dynamically Oriented Art Therapy*, NY: Grune and Stratton.

Robbins, A. (1987) *The Artist as Therapist*, Human Sciences Press, Inc., Chapter 2.

Spotnitz, H. (1967) Techniques for the resolution of the narcissistic defense, in B. Wolman (ed.) *Psychoanalytic Techniques*, NY: Basic Books.

Virshup, E. (1985) Group art therapy in a methadone clinic lobby, *Journal of Substance Abuse Treatment* **2**: 153–8.

—— and Virshup, B. (1981) An art therapy approach to the drug abuser, correlating behavioral, narcissistic, and laterality theory, *Imagery* **2**.

Waller, D.E. (1989) Art therapy in Rome: working with drug addiction, *Artia: European Journal of Arts and Disability*, Summer.

11

Brief art therapy in acute states: a process-oriented approach

SHEILA McCLELLAND

Introduction

This chapter presents an approach to art therapy with acute states associated with non-psychotic disturbances that is based on the process-oriented psychology of Dr Arnold Mindell (1982, 1985, 1988). The focus is upon how an art therapist might work with individual clients in the course of acute episodes, and describes a way of working which I have developed over the past three years within an NHS Acute Psychiatric Unit. It represents an interpretation of some of the essential ideas of process work, exploring and developing ways in which process work and art therapy might interface.

Acute states are typically characterized by 'languaging' other than verbal. My choice of process work as a model is for its practical 'tools' and concepts for working with a broad spectrum of human communication signals in a very dynamic way, and for its valuing disturbing states as something inherently creative in that individual's life. For many reasons, not the least of which are limited time resources, the distress and even danger that is often occasioned by an acute episode, and the concept of using crisis as an opportunity for movement to a more constructive level of personality organization, this chapter also explores structures for time-limited therapy. In this I draw from both process work and from the personal construct psychology of G.A. Kelly (1955), specifically the concept of a 'creativity cycle' as the basis of all therapeutic change.

The art therapy department which I manage is autonomous and is located in a purpose-built unit within a large hospital complex. The unit houses an acute admission unit, a day hospital and an out-patient department and is staffed by a multi-disciplinary team. My department provides a service to clients referred from within the unit by consultant psychiatrists and members of the team, by the Department of Psychology, and by general practitioners. In the context of an evolving community psychiatric service, which addresses many acute states at the primary care level, the unit may be seen as a specialist service which can offer a level of containment and support which is not possible in the community for clients who are more seriously disturbed, for example suicidal states, severe depression, anorexic states, drug-induced states, acute panic attacks and actively psychotic states. In psychiatric terms, clients display a characteristically wide range of psychopathology, averaging 25 per cent psychotic and 75 per cent psychoneurotic-type disturbances.

In this setting clients are often referred to more than one treatment modality whose goals and methods may be at variance. The process-oriented approach entails searching for some underlying principle which ties the various treatment modes together (Mindell 1988) and using tensions and conflicts in groups to create a greater sense of meaning and community. I address this issue by co-working with my clients together with their key workers or other members of their care staff, and through teaching and research. In this way the work can be more co-ordinated, differences in approaches clarified, and a broad focus negotiated. Issues such as admission to and discharge from the acute unit, levels and types of medication are discussed in relation to the total therapeutic programme by the team and with the clients.

My art therapy room reflects its function. It is spacious, allowing plenty of room for movement. Large sheets of paper may be placed on the walls, floor or the one table, and comfortable mats and cushions in primary colours are piled on the floor, offering flexible seating arrangements for individuals or groups. A full range of basic art materials is available.

But just what is an 'acute state'? Psychiatry speaks in terms of a sudden, critical, psychologically disturbing, even dangerous situation which requires urgent attention. Other definitions refer to 'severity', or to being 'overpowered'; all definitions imply an 'intensification' of some sort. Process work refers to an acute state as an 'altered state', altered, that is, from the customary state of consciousness. Everyone has them, for instance, when gripped by a 'big' emotion. Psychosis is conceptualized as just one end of a spectrum of states, at one end of which is consciousness and control and, at the other, literally no awareness or control.

In the course of researching this chapter one of my consultants, Dr Tom Ravenette, posed several questions which helped me think alternatively about 'acuteness'. The first two questions – 'To what set of circumstances might this (acute) state be an appropriate response?', and 'Who has the acuteness?' – placed 'acuteness' in a wider context and invited me to consider for whom the 'acuteness' might be meant, whether I would need to work also with a partner, family or community. They also invited me to consider my involvement in, and responses to, 'acute' work. The third question – 'How do you recognize acuteness and how, as an art therapist, do you work with this?' – triggered me into being personal, descriptive, more of an artist than clinician. I found myself saying 'I study the form'. A flow of images was released of clients in the grip of extreme states, faces variously flushed or pale, sweating, etched with pain; bodies shaking, violently acting out; loud weeping, shouting and screaming. Or conversely blank, apparently emotionless faces; bodies rigid, crumpled up, motionless or seeming to drift around in a trance, and silences. . . . Sometimes the acuteness was in myself, my responses ranging from fear and apprehension that my intervention could trigger an even 'worse' state, to a chilling horror or hopelessness, as someone sat calmly planning their suicide.

The tendency in our culture is towards the suppression of acute states; we generally fear and avoid them. An art therapist will seek the image and enable people to give shape to some strange, apparently terrible and even wonderful states. Let us consider just a few images 'characteristic' of these states. One whole category is the 'blanks' and 'fogs' – blank sheets of paper, or greyness and blackness covering the whole sheet; the person says 'I can't do anything, it's just a blank' or 'it's all black', or 'a fog'. Another category is the 'tangled messes', where jumbles of chaotic lines fill the page; the person may say 'It's just chaos'. No sense can be made of anything. But the most common and striking category comprises the extremely polarized images, wherein the person is victim of an attack of some sort, either from within or without. Typically a small vulnerable figure is confronted by powerful, threatening elements, for example huge waves, sharp instruments, webs, bars, heavy weights, animals or 'ogre' figures, described variously as 'overwhelming', 'attacking', 'intruding', 'trapping', 'pressurizing', 'devouring', 'fragmenting'. The client identifies with the victim side of the polarization, describing the other side as 'happening' to him, or conversely, may identify himself as being a terrible figure, and doing deeds which are quite abhorrent to him in his normal state. There are no viable pathways for action; either chaos or no energy, a paralysed victim or evil aggressor of some sort. But I have found that when clients are supported to give shape to their experiences, in a form which closely matches that of the disturbing state, something starts to happen. How process work can inform art therapists, illuminate this process, and work with the polarizations of 'me' and 'not-me', is the subject of this chapter.

Theoretical context

Although this chapter is informed by the literature of brief therapy and ideas which led to its inception (in particular those of Bateson 1972 and Watzlawick *et al.* 1974), space does not permit a detailed account of the literature. The interested reader might consider a review of brief individual psychotherapies by Ursano and Hales (1986), or Gustafson's *The Complex Secret of Brief Psychotherapy* (1986) which explores psychoanalytic, interpersonal and systemic models. However, the intake criteria of most of these approaches would exclude many clients who are experiencing acute states. The work of Yalom (1986), and the cognitive analytic therapy of Anthony Ryle (1990) are notable in offering brief therapy to a wide spectrum of clients.

In the literature on art therapy, work towards defining theory for working briefly is rare. Much 'brief' work is done with acute states in 'open' and closed groups and in individual sessions, but time is not used as a dynamic factor. One recent publication describes brief art therapy in the area of substance abuse (Luzzatto 1989). Work in progress in the art therapy department of Guy's Hospital, London, is concerned with developing art therapy along cognitive analytic therapy lines.

The history of process work itself is relatively short; it has been developed over the past 20 years by the Jungian analyst and physicist Arnold Mindell, together with his associates in Zurich and Oregon Institutes. It was introduced into this country in 1987, prompting the establishment of a Research Society. This has resulted in a growing core of practitioners who are working towards integrating and developing the model in line with their varied practices. This is the first publication in the area of art therapy based on process-oriented psychology.

The rationale behind the process-oriented approach is that the person is a form of motion: both the world and human beings are in a state of flux. 'Process' is defined by Mindell as 'the perception of the evolving flow of signals as they appear in various perceptual channels' (Mindell 1985: 11). Psychological disturbance is said to arise when a person acts 'as if' she and the world are not in a continual process of change. How a person 'freezes' is largely a function of the way in which she identifies herself; to 'go with the flow' implies having the ability to be fluid in revising and elaborating the ideas and constructs we have about ourselves and the world, but we may be threatened by the notion of a constantly changing self. Such resistance needs to be kept constantly in mind so that as art therapists we do not 'push' for flow when the process is to resist in order to conserve the 'core' identity.

In process work terms, acute states are regarded as 'frozen' parts of a larger experiential pattern which is trying to express itself in an individual's life. Far from being chaotic, these states are said to contain inherent patterns of creativity which, if assisted to unfold, contain the seeds of their own resolution. This is a view of events which considers the implications of the acute state for the future, as distinct from the causal tradition which looks towards the past for sources of current problems, and seeks to alleviate symptoms by substituting more 'healthy' patterns of behaviour.

Linking philosophy with theory is a range of attitudes which are essential to the practice of process work. These include 'tough compassion', by which all parts of the process are supported; curiosity and the ability to have a 'beginners mind', through which all preconceptions are suspended, and 'what is' is observed; playfulness, humour and creativity to participate in and negotiate processes; and courage to dare to stay at difficult edges.

Mindell's formulations are a descriptive tool which helps the therapist order his or her perceptions in a way that prescribes action. In this model the concepts of 'conscious' and 'unconscious' are redefined as these terms imply the presence of a 'meta-communicator', or a part which is present, aware of its awareness, and with the ability to communicate about that awareness. Mindell found that this part is absent in psychotic episodes and also in states which we all experience from time to time, for example when in a rage (Mindell 1985). He speaks instead of primary and secondary processes. Primary processes refer to the process of identifying with certain behaviours, gestures, feelings and thoughts; secondary processes are all the verbal and non-verbal signals in an individual's expressions with which they do not identify, and which conflict with the primary identity. Secondary processes are the spontaneous things which are described as 'happening' to one and which may be denied, projected or found in acute states or in the body in the form of symptoms. In process work going into these areas of experiencing is what makes the difference.

Defining the boundary between primary and secondary process is an element termed the 'edge'. Edges are the belief systems which differentiate processes closest to our identity (primary) from those further away from our identity (secondary). They mark off what is relatively known from all that is experienced as uncontrollable and threatening. At the edge the person 'double-signals' – one part of the personality does this, another part that. The client has something he would like, or needs to do but cannot, because his belief system is against it, and he does it unconsciously. In imagery, edges are frequently represented as impenetrable barriers, or the person pictures herself standing on a cliff edge; what is both on and over the cliff gives valuable information about the identity crisis. Edges exist to create awareness of what we are actually doing.

Let me give an example of a polarization of primary and secondary process and the accompanying edge. A woman drew an image of herself as a weak victim, pressurized by a one ton weight; she also painted a powerful image of a huge black knife, dripping with blood. She identified herself as 'depressed', fearful of people and pressurized by her family (the ton weight). About the knife she said nothing. Her primary process was of someone 'weak' while the polarized secondary process looked like a powerful 'heavyweight', incisive personality (the knife). Other people observed 'strength' signals in her stance and voice tone, but she had little or no awareness of these. The secondary process was also expressed in the form of a disturbing, explosive sensation in her stomach which she said she needed to let out, at the same time making a fist. The edge to doing so was that she 'could not hurt people', and a fear that she could murder someone as she 'didn't know how to channel it'.

Process signals are said to express themselves through channels, a term drawn from modern communications theory. A 'channel' is a pathway of perception along which process information flows. Mindell designated six of these as being most commonly used; visual, auditory, proprioceptive (body/felt sense), movement, relationship and world. Each channel has both inner and outer aspects. For example, in the visual channel we see objects in the outer world, but also see dream images in the inner visual channel. The latter two, relationship and world channels, are also said to be 'composite', or an irreducible combination of all of the others (Mindell 1985).

The client's problem of channelling her anger and strength lay partly in her lack of awareness of the 'felt sense' of these processes. When we identify with particular channels, when our access to them is easier and we have a sense of control, they are termed 'occupied'. In unoccupied channels it is as if we are not doing the perceiving; we feel victimized by our perceptions which are described as 'happening' to us, outside of our control as in the above example where secondary processes express themselves in terms of movement – feeling 'volcanic', 'explosive', 'pressurized' – in her proprioception, and in the 'dripping' blood/red paint.

The therapy process

In my view acute states can only be dealt with by going right into them: one works by supporting them as experiences which the client somehow needs, but because he has little awareness within them, they express themselves in destructive and painful forms. The therapist obtains very detailed information as to how the client is perceiving the disturbing state by having him focus his awareness within the channel in which it is occurring. An initial hypothesis is then constructed about the major polarizations of the client's identity, his edges and the relationship of his awareness to the various processes.

The therapy process might best be summarized by outlining four categories of intervention which are used in working with non-psychotic states (Audergon and Audergon 1990):

1 determining the roles;
2 completing the existing process;
3 channel switching;
4 re-creating an acute state that is being talked about.

Determining the roles involves picking up on the constant attitudes which the client is displaying and the roles which are constellated in the therapist in response. Rather than remaining polarized in one of these roles, for example help-less patient and a 'doctor' who will look after everything, the roles are brought into awareness and the client supported to develop the polarization.

In completing the information contained in the existing process, a major tool for working with unoccupied channels is that of amplification, which refers to supporting the client to focus on and intensify or exaggerate what is already happening there. Is the client's 'panic attack' experienced as a burning sensation, or a movement like shaking or falling, or what? The therapist shows the person how to amplify, for example seeing a vision even more vividly, bringing a small movement into the entire body, and may go into it with them. For a while the acute state may seem worse. But, when amplified, process can flow, cross the threshold of awareness, complete itself and reveal its purpose.

When a secondary process is amplified the client usually reaches an edge: they stop, there are long pauses, or they may somatize after doing something strong. There are many ways of working at the edge (see Goodbread 1987). Careful atten-tion must be paid to clients' feedback; not to do so may be dangerous. How a therapist works is always a function of client feedback: failure in therapy is fre-quently attributable to insufficient work with phenomena at the edge – 'who', or what value system is working against what is emerging? The work consists of eliciting more information about the primary identity for whom this secondary process part is meant, finding out how they relate together, and what a creative combination might be. The differentiation of primary and secondary parts by really going into them is the beginning of awareness and gives rise to further awareness, that of the meta-communicator, which can reflect on and communi-cate about both states.

When a process is amplified it may switch channels, but the therapist may also request a channel switch. One example is when a person is, metaphori-cally, 'drowning' in an unoccupied channel, say having an overwhelmingly disturbing feeling (see Mindell 1985, 1988). In this case it is vitally important to work with the process in an occupied channel: for example, a client could be asked, if very visually oriented, to 'see, very vividly an image that would represent that feeling', and even paint it. Another occasion for a channel switch is when the process has gone as far as possible in one channel, and the information can only be completed by 'fleshing out' the emerging part in as multi-channelled a way as possible.

The final intervention refers to that point when the 'acuteness' has gone 'underground' without the information contained within it becoming useful. The client talks (or even draws) 'about' the state. These processes have a tendency to recur, and client and therapist can make a decision as to whether to re-access the state, based upon the client's potential for achieving and maintaining some awareness and control, in order to work with it as described above.

Art as a channel

Image-making can be regarded as a composite channel as the process may engage all major channels in a complex, interwoven way. Each art material has its own intrinsic properties which, in interaction with tools (brushes, hands, knives and so on) access and carry forward a specific range of communications. I have noticed that in acute states people often use the solid malleable qualities of clay to bring out their physical strength – to grasp, squeeze, push against, cut and throw. These movement processes often lead into, or are accompanied by, strong emotion. If there are indications of a vivid visual experience, coloured pigments may best carry the process forward. Textural qualities of the pigments may be centrally important for some processes; for example, finger paint tends to evoke powerful tactile processes and early memories. By contrast pencils are frequently used to stab and score, charcoal to represent experiences of darkness and despair.

Art therapists usually offer a broad range of materials to clients, inviting them to use the materials in any way they wish. This is a sort of 'blank access' and may carry the emerging process forward. Conversely, the client may need to have her process amplified in another channel (for example, movement) prior to engaging with the 'art channel', and if the art therapist is not comfortable with this, the work may get stuck. If work with materials is slow or stereotypic, the client may simply be working from their primary process and not using materials in a fluid way that encourages new awareness in unoccupied channels. In this situation, process work skills in picking up various secondary signals, together with art therapists' intimate knowledge of the qualities of art materials, may combine to structure interventions which:

1 suggest materials which may best 'fit' with what is emerging;
2 assist natural amplifications within the image-making;
3 bring awareness into the 'artist body'.

I shall give an example. A client who had been severely sexually abused and who had presented several sessions previously screaming 'don't touch me, don't touch me', began to experience sensations associated with anger and excitement, but found them 'unsettling'. She made a spontaneous drawing with charcoal of a jagged line, looked at me questioningly and asked, 'Am I patching over the cracks?' I asked her what might be behind the cracks and she looked intently at some red and yellow finger paint. As her fingers were also moving I suggested she might use the finger paint on a sheet of paper pinned to the wall. She said that she did not like red and yellow, identifying herself with the colour blue, which represented 'calm'. I encouraged her to experiment with the red and yellow, and she got into increasingly vigorous movement with one 'yellow' and one 'red' hand. The emerging image was filled with sinuous flowing rivers of what she termed 'firey' colours, as I encouraged her to feel her feelings and the rhythm of her movements even more. Then she hit an edge! She reached for blue paint and began to cover the fiery forms, so I attempted to amplify the secondary process by taking over the primary process of the blue (calming) colour, painting blue on the back of her 'yellow' hand and on her image, and challenging her by saying 'don't be like that; don't be a lively, firey woman . . . just get yourself together'. This intervention triggered her into elaborating the image of her excitement and anger more fully. With encouragement she became aware of her 'artist body', experiencing and enjoying those sensations and movements. She gave the 'artist' a name, the 'fat fairy' who was spontaneous and assertive, exploring where she needed more of this quality in her life. The earlier integration of the 'red' and 'yellow' with the 'blue', which she attempted in the image-making, might not have been as useful as pushing the polarization further.

Image-making is also very much characterized by 'relationship' in the sense that a 'feedback loop' is set up between the artist and their image. The image may become 'embodied' and an object of transference (Schaverien 1987). An example from my own practice would be a client who depicted her husband as a figure bound by a thick black line filled with mucky red paint; she scored deeply into it with her nails, and said '. . . where else could I have put this feeling? He was too ill, and I was furious; I could have really torn him with my fingers, just like that.'

This client was developing somatic awareness of a powerful, angry process which could not, in this instance, be expressed in her relationship, and the image was clearly useful in facilitating a satisfying expression of the affect, while helping build a pattern for this behaviour. In many instances the therapist will need to connect the 'artist' with their image-making process as they work. This occurs through drawing the client's attention to the channels which the 'artist' is momentarily occupying, for example by mirroring the client's art-making behaviour, or having the client notice all of the visual, movement, proprioceptive and auditory signals very closely as he works. Often there is little multi-channel awareness in both the creative and the destructive act.

The therapist's process

Considerable demands are made on the therapist, both within and outside sessions, to work on her own edges. Three important edges are likely to pose problems: the therapist's least accessible channel, working with chaotic processes and the relationship with the client (Goodbread 1987).

If a therapist is customarily visual and encounters a client with a process which is expressing itself strongly in movement, the therapist may stress methods which emphasize the visual components of the process and exclude methods such as creative movement or art-making processes which would amplify the movement directly. Questions which help locate the therapist's edges are, 'What is it that I cannot do, see, hear, feel with my client?' If client and therapist are blocked in similar channels the work becomes static. In my view, working on one's own edges relieves the client of the need to conform to the therapist's preferred model.

Working with chaotic processes is a major difficulty faced by beginning therapists. Process work deems the 'chaos' a function of a lack of therapist skills in picking up a wide range of communications. In practice, the therapist needs to develop both a high level of perceptual skills for the process as it jumps from one channel to another, an acute sensitivity to her own responses in the moment, however unrelated to the client's process they seem, and an ability to record them in as detailed a way as possible. In this way the inherent pattern of meaning can eventually emerge and become clarified.

Process work also brings in the therapist as a person. If the client's strongest signals are manifesting within the therapeutic relationship then the information can only be completed within the relationship. The relationship (in process terms, another channel) is worked with as is any other channel, that is by the therapist retaining his awareness. Process workers are also reformulating the transference/counter-transference situation and the emerging model is much more interactive. For example, if the therapist misses a client's edge, he may become a channel, and be 'recruited' to enact the client's secondary process. If the therapist remains unconscious of the situation the process will remain polarized and stuck. But if he can become aware, the process may be consciously embodied and thereby valuable information gained about the client's process structure as a whole.

This brief account of the therapist's process indicates that the potential fluidity of boundaries between client and therapist demands a multi-levelled and broad awareness on the part of the therapist.

Working briefly

Put at its simplest, time-limited therapy involves having a theoretical structure for beginning, middle and end phases of therapy, and for using time as a dynamic factor in the therapy. A time 'frame' determines what may be dealt with in the sense that a realistic focus must be established.

Several elements are common to most brief therapies. These include:

1 the need for a rapid establishment of rapport through meeting the client in his own 'languaging' system; this involves the therapist in experiencing the world from the client's perspective and communicating this to the client;
2 the necessity of establishing and maintaining a focus while retaining the broad viewpoint of the initial consultation;
3 an active and assertive therapist style which keeps the work alive to new processes;
4 anticipating the ending in a concrete way throughout the therapy.

With regard to working briefly I am informed by personal construct psychology, in particular the concept of the therapeutic enterprise as a 'cycle of experience' which has a creativity cycle at its centre (Kelly 1955, Epting 1984). I also draw on the work of Ravenette (1988) where a creativity cycle is completed in each session.

Assessment

Prior to establishing a contract I do a consultation of one-and-a-half hours in which I consider the following questions. What is the crucial identity which the person must preserve? Is the client flexible enough to allow experimentation and creative 'cycling'? (Kelly 1955, described below). Can I challenge their 'edges' without undue risk of pathological response? Is the person motivated to change, in contrast to seeking simple alleviation of symptoms, and is she likely to support the new processes through independent work? How might the work affect the client's life?

A further area of enquiry is concerned with relationships. Has the person had, or does she have, at least one meaningful relationship? Can she engage meaningfully with me? Have I got the skills to make contact? Will the client be able to disengage without excessive trauma being triggered, and what were previous responses to loss? What is the nature of the client's awareness, does she respond to feedback and can she meta-communicate? If the answers to these questions are mostly affirmative and constructive, and if no really dangerous reactions are anticipated, I go ahead and establish a contract.

Beginning phase

This phase starts by locating the client in terms of the channels wherein the process is flowing and with rapid establishment of rapport via that mode of communication. The client's complaint is established in her terms as the therapist comes to know the world from the client's standpoint and communicates this. A working hypothesis is set up as to the nature of the process structure, short-term processes are sorted out from long-term and a focus is established.

Middle phase

In this phase the creativity cycle is engaged; this is concerned with the creation of new meaning, so that the way the person is currently making sense of the world can be elaborated. The working through of a creativity cycle refers to alternating between 'loosening' and 'tightening' one's meaning system. Loosening refers to adopting a 'what if . . .', propositional attitude in order to experiment and 'play' with new ways of being in the world. Tightening refers to clarification of the new conceptualizations and exploration of their implications for the client's present meaning system, and her life and relationships (Kelly 1955).

End phase

Whereas the creativity cycle is concerned with the creation of new meaning, the work now moves into a cycle of action (Epting 1984). If this part of the cycle is not engaged the client is, at best, left with a better understanding of life without any model for putting that understanding into practice. Having experimented, the sequence involves choosing one new dimension of meaning which has emerged and testing it out in the therapeutic relationship and in life. In this the client exercises personal control by making a choice and taking some action; this involves risk, for both client and therapist.

In the following case these attitudes and structures are applied over a number of sessions (time-limited therapy is described as anything from one to 35 sessions). However, it is important to note that the cycle of loosening–tightening and testing in action may be applied to one consultation, or to a number.

Case-study

Ann

An increasing number of women who are presenting in acute states, and who carry a wide range of diagnoses, are disclosing early sexual abuse. Media coverage of this issue is often reported as the 'trigger' of their disturbance. The details of this case are particularly horrific. I have included it to show not only how art therapy might address such extremity but also because work with a wide range of acute states is marked by similar experiences of dissociation, disorientation in time and place, extreme mood swings and suicidal feelings.

My client, Ann, was referred by the psychology department. She is 51, married and has raised a family of five. She presented with crippling agoraphobic, obsessional and bulimic symptoms. Initial work with a psychologist revealed that she had been severely physically and sexually abused between the ages of three and twelve years. She had been having 'flashbacks' in the form of images and distressing body sensations accompanied by fear and panic, and increasingly felt suicidal. The severity of her symptoms and the extent of the early trauma did not indicate a time-limited therapy, but she said she needed to 'go back to the past to feel better about it and to do it quickly' before it overwhelmed her.

Ann was clearly motivated to change. Her tough, independent nature suggested that she would not become too dependent on me, and she had meaningful, if somewhat difficult, relationships with her husband and family. Following an interview with a consultant psychiatrist in the unit and one assessment session, we considered her to be at risk, but even when suicidal she would not consider admission to the 'funny farm', as she called the unit, nor would she have medication. I therefore accepted her on an out-patient basis and we targeted a time limit of four months, with flexibility for one or two sessions per week.

I shall give a few details of her early experiences. She was the only girl child in a small, close-knit rural community, and now considers she was abused by the entire community as injuries from the severe physical and sexual abuse were very visible, and no one intervened. Her mother rejected and beat her as she was illegitimate, and the abusing continued with rape by her natural father at six years, and almost daily physical and/or sexual abuse by a psychopathic stepbrother, and subsequently by neighbours. Ann often walked the parapet of a bridge over a main railway line; she said 'I used to think that if the wind blew strongly enough, it would take me to dreamland' (the tracks). At the age of ten she attempted suicide. To survive she 'went away' by 'drifting into another body'. She said 'I could see them down there doing things to me; I felt the pain, smelt the smells, but part of me was gone, was mine'. The rape was often collective: she said

'It's bad enough for one man to rape you, but two or three . . . they used to watch one another, laugh, urge one another on . . . it destroys your soul, your spirit, your innocence. You might as well be six or a hundred and six.' She said 'the little things were the worst . . . a kiss like that smothers a child . . . the weight of bodies . . . the taste . . .' Until she went to school she thought her name was 'hey . . . you!'.

Beginning phase: Ann's doodles and animals

Ann had brought a series of drawings to the assessment session in which grids and squares covered the entire surface of the paper. I was reminded of cages. She said 'I've got to make them: they are always exactly the same'. Process work seeks to represent what is in the background and I began to hypothesize a figure saying 'do not dare to change anything'. Ann told me that she needed to go back to the past 'to feel better about it'. Establishing a rapport had a lot to do with appreciating her disgust with her altered states of panic, weeping and inability to function – 'I should be able to control them . . . it's weak!' – but also actively respecting and supporting them. The initial consultation triggered a 'compulsion to paint', and gave her an acceptable way to explore her experiencing.

To the second session she brought an amazing image. The entire surface was covered in strange animal heads, some with tongues and teeth, painted in brilliant, clear colours – blue, red, yellow and green. All were interlocking, and defined by a heavy black line, which 'could have been one inch high'. She kept insisting 'I know exactly what to do: this is exactly right!'. Here a background figure might be saying 'you know nothing!'. She identified herself as 'dirty, different from other people', and said the animals were how she wanted to be, 'clean and bright'. The black line was 'the strength', without which the animals could 'slip out'.

The process structure

The state she was in most of the time had a meta-communicator, but often during sessions, and sometimes outside, there was none ('I went away'). Sometimes the extreme states persisted for hours and several times she 'found herself' on the edge of the local railway station platform, not knowing how she got there. Her primary process was to be 'strong', meaning 'in control' (it is 'stupid not to cope, to crack up'), but also to be a second-class citizen, 'not like other people, dirty, a nut'. Ann's secondary process was to have animal strength and teeth. Secondary processes expressed themselves also in the proprioceptive channel as distressing burning sensations, and as internal movement experiences of shaking and of 'something entwined inside, swallowing me up'.

Where to take a hold? It appeared likely that proprioceptive and movement processes would characterize the work. I began also to build a hypothesis that boundary-making would be important – the black outline which needed reinforcing and kept the red animals from 'slipping out'. Who might they want to 'slip out' at? Seeking the past in the present I found a pattern of extreme compliance – dominance in the marital relationship, where she had an edge to being assertive

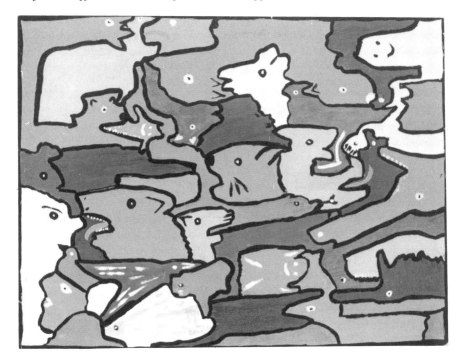

Figure 11.1

'for fear of making things worse'. But working with the couple was not an option as her husband considered she should just pull herself together and actively opposed her engaging in therapy. On the intrapersonal level, we found the 'husband' in a part of her personality that termed her tears and her fears 'stupid'. A very disturbing dream, which she brought to the next session, pointed the way forward.

Middle phase: Fighting back

In this phase the first task was to unravel and bring awareness into an aspect of the secondary process. Dreams offer access to loosened constructions, and Ann spontaneously reported a recurring nightmare of a man who pursued her and pushed her down a lift shaft; she fell in terror, never reaching the bottom. She also dreamt of her mother standing next to her in a supermarket queue and of stabbing her in the chest. Recounting the dreams she went deeply into a very altered state and turned away from me, her body crumpling up, but at the same time her hands were opening and closing, one pushing strongly against the other. Ann was primarily the hurt child/victim, but in the dreaming process of the body there was a 'pusher' (like the male dream figure) in the movement of one hand against the other. That her movement channel was unoccupied suggested that this could be a place to take hold.

I tentatively placed a ball of clay in the 'passive' hand, and got immediate positive feedback. I suggested she keep doing what she was doing with her other hand, and to notice what happened. She began to push and stab the clay and I helped her amplify the process by supporting her increasingly violent movements, and offering a sharp tool which she grabbed. She began stabbing, gouging and shouting 'I've killed him'. The work moved on to her making phallic shapes, and repeatedly chopping them up and reforming them (her step-brother's abusing stopped short of killing her, as if he were saving her up for the next time). She looked agonized as she worked, and subsequently felt vulnerable and panic stricken. I continued to support the tendency to push and stab, validating it verbally, mirroring the behaviour and calling attention to the narrowing and glaring of her eyes. This was the first hint of retaliation, arising out of the state itself, and accessed through her movements. At the end of the session she said that she did not know she could be so aggressive. The edge to her aggression would have to be crossed many times before she had a model for this behavior.

In a subsequent session Ann made images of terrifying mouths swallowing her. She began re-experiencing, as if in the present, physical trauma similar to the abuse. It is likely that if we had only worked with these experiences in her proprioceptive channel she could have remained in a disassociated state, but she spontaneously began to dramatize the scene by picking up a toy bear that was in my office, appearing to pin it to the arm of her chair. When I drew her attention to this she said 'I have to do to him what he did to me'. Her step-brother's torturing had been ritualistic. He had a case containing rope, a candle and a sheath knife. He tied her by the limbs and neck until she almost hanged and then burnt her with a knife. She began to draw detailed images of the abusive scenes.

She asked me to make a figure to represent her step-brother ready for the next session, saying that if she made it herself she couldn't destroy it. It had to be big enough to take hold of and she 'had to see the evil in it'. Her hands moved a lot as she spoke and so there were indications that she needed to do something strong – the drama needed to be amplified. I made the figure in tough material to offer resistance, stuffed it with 'heart' and 'guts', and represented the genitals. She brought the 'ritual' ropes to the next session and began to tie the figure to a chair. There followed a long and agonizing process wherein her hands tore the figure apart, violently, while her 'child' part crouched on the ground with eyes averted, shaking and whimpering 'just like it was'. She came to a number of edges to the violent strength in her hands, fearing retaliation, hesitating, falling back and stopping. I worked by alternately encouraging, challenging, suggesting she stop, and by requesting a switch to a more occupied channel, i.e. if she could not continue being physically strong, to go inside and visualize herself tearing him apart. I maintained physical contact by exerting a light pressure on her arm in the rhythm of her breathing, which she later said had held her 'in the now, making it possible to go back there'. Paying close attention to my own responses, I found that I had a real fear that she could get stuck in a state of terror. I also had a strong urge to push her to go all the way, but wondered if I was becoming 'dreamt up' to be an attacker. As she had so carefully planned this session I followed my instinct and urged her on. She did go 'all the way', even moving right out of the 'victim body', and congruently ripping 'him' to shreds. After this powerful work there was a clear body shift; she appeared and felt relieved, relaxed. As she had little awareness of the process, I mirrored some of it for her. The point of this work is not catharsis. 'Tightening up' involves establishing awareness of and a connection between all parts of the process structure. She said that if she had stopped she would have been 'lost for ever'. That night she dreamt she was in her stepbrother's room in their house, and that he had gone from it. Physically she felt as if he had lost his hold.

Having gone over her edge to her power and aggression she began to assert her need for emotional support in the marital relationship. When this was not reciprocated she began to express her pain and also to recall and work on feelings around her mother's abusive behaviour, which sounded quite crazy. As 'mother' she 'never existed' for Ann, who now experienced deep hurt and anger. Around this time she brought a drawing of a witch-like figure with claws saying 'I don't know who drew this; I found it in my sketch book, so it must have been me . . . it's horrible'.

The work of this phase of therapy is also concerned with tightening up and bringing primary and secondary parts into better contact with one another. As Ann did not identify with this figure or display any awareness of the image-making process, I encouraged her to consider when having teeth and claws like that might be 'just right'.

Over the next three sessions, she began to work with the same broad, fluid strokes with which she had painted the 'swallowing mouths' of the earlier sessions, feeling compelled to paint with red and black and engaging in increasingly physical contact with the paint. A figure resembling the witch began to emerge as if from a fire. At first she rejected it but gradually became fascinated by its transformation into a quite wonderful, wild looking figure who grasped a sword in her hand, the final image saying 'fuck you all, I will be me!'. Ann named her 'Mrs C'. She said:

> My life . . . that's what I've got to do. I've to have her strength to bury them (the abusers' power over her life). Her hands . . . that's her strength . . . she can crush you up in her hands. She feels part of me . . . as if she's part of my being. She's really wild. I used to think other people thought me mad, but I couldn't care less now. Part of her gets burned up, but she just gets her claws out. . . .

'Mrs C' also had a kind side and 'only kills the right people'. To build up more of a model for this 'personality' I invited Ann to show me 'Mrs C' then and there, to act, move and speak as her, and to have her deal with any issues which she might have with me. I also enquired who else this figure might be meant for. She now began to test the new part out in her marital relationship, finding her 'black line' in asserting her boundary – 'he used to think my body belonged to him; I started telling him to back off, that I was not just part of him'.

In following sessions, amplifying more sensory processes, she explored the strength in her hands ('I have to wait for it to come into my body'), imprinting them boldly with thick finger paint, red on black, black on orange, and inscribing 'I AM ANN' on the images. She said that her name now belonged to her.

It is not unusual in this work for the therapist to be affected deeply. On occasion I found myself gripped by powerful emotions, with tears streaming down my face.

Figure 11.2

I encountered my edge as a therapist and I imagined being thought not to have worked with my own pain enough, the more so as my behaviour angered Ann, who 'needed me to be strong'. I worked with my reactions by bringing awareness into them, by sharing this with Ann, and in supervision. I owned that some of the feeling was personal, but had a very strong sense that I was responding not only personally but also as a member of the wider community, who had never acknowledged her suffering. I considered also that I was experiencing a 'dreamt up' reaction to her matter-of-fact attitude towards her past, encapsulated in her phrase 'that was just how life was'.

The eventual outcome of my personal response was that she began to feel that someone really cared about what had happened, and she came to see me as 'not just a therapist, but a person, and a woman'. This seemed vital for before this she 'had no pattern for relating to women with affection'. At this point in the therapy she came to another major edge – to her sensitivity. She experienced a recurrence of a disturbing body sensation: she felt as if she were tied at the wrists. I asked her to work on it very directly with me.

End phase

Increasingly the work moved into a cycle of action. I invited Ann to take over the secondary figure who 'tied people down', actually to do it to me and while doing it, to find out in what way might she need to do so. With some encouragement she did, and it emerged that she thought I had too high expectations of her that she should be strong; that often she felt nothing but hurt. In a very moving process she slowly reached for my hands, placing them one by one around her neck, and holding them there. I guessed this was very important as she had told me that if I ever touched her neck, she'd put me 'across the room'. After a while I felt prompted to say 'you have the control; you can choose who may touch you and who may not. Do what you need to do.' Later she told me that she was pleased to have been direct with me. She also said:

> All of a sudden I just needed you to touch me . . . something I've never experienced, like a baby wrapped in warm. Once the body knows it's not going to be hurt, and there are ways of touching, that's part of the healing. Then that part will be buried, the part that was tied up.

The meaning that emerged was something like 'standing up for one's sensitivity versus fulfilling the expectations of others'. The end phase had to do with selecting one aspect of the process, and moving into a cycle of action, testing out, and integrating (or rejecting) that part. Ann began to bring her sensitivity into sexual aspects of the marital relationship, anticipating that this would be difficult. It was. She explained to her husband that although she loved him, she did not like sex and that sometimes her body would freeze up 'as if someone had thrown a switch'. He felt rejected and angry. Paradoxically, she began also to have sexual experience which she enjoyed. She said 'all the body knows is sex and pain: the body doesn't equate sex and love'. When one member of a couple goes over their edge in a relationship, this brings the other partner to theirs. His was to acknowledging and expressing deep feeling, but the couple began to move in this direction, with him also giving her more space to be an individual.

Of 'Mrs C' she said: 'I don't need her any more on paper; I have her. It still hurts to know what happened to me, but the fear that used to rise up inside is gone. I feel like someone different, more confident.' At the same time she said: ' "Mrs C" doesn't always work, as Ann has always shied away, and has to learn a new set of rules.' There was still a part that was frightened, felt different and a bit lost. All of the obsessional symptoms had disappeared. At the end of this time-limited therapy, this extremely creative woman indicated her longer term 'mythic' pattern as she said. 'The animals showed me what it's going to be like: they are the animal strength, and they are eternal, from my mystic part. I don't know if I shall ever paint them again, but when I do I shall be me.'

Conclusion

In this chapter I have explored a central idea of process work, i.e. that acute states contain inherent creative patterns for their own resolution. My aim has been to convey a range of possibilities for addressing such states in a language which 'fits' and enables their expression, transformation and integration. I have described some aspects of art therapy and process work, and shown how the model is an appropriate one for working briefly in acute psychiatry.

Limitations of space have not allowed for the elaboration of many important aspects of process work and art therapy, for example how judgements are made as to whether or not one supports, challenges or clarifies a client's edges at any point. In working closely at the edge to these states I would stress that considerable training is needed both in extending perceptual skills and in working with many channels in order accurately to gauge at what point to support what is primary, or what is secondary, or to enable and educate a client to switch to more occupied channels, thus gaining a measure of control. I would also stress the necessity for personal, in-depth engagement with art-making processes as a prerequisite for accuracy with minimal cues, and the creativity which is the hallmark of both process work and art therapy.

For art therapists who wish to work briefly this chapter suggests a model for an active therapeutic style based within creativity theory which, paradoxically, is a model of minimal intervention as it aims to draw forth what is already happening. It also allows the art therapist to explore the interface of various arts therapies in relation to channel theory, encouraging the development of ways of moving fluidly and interactively both within and beyond image-making. Art therapy and process work invite us to be both perceptively accurate and creative in our work with disturbance and conflict. The best methods are yet to be invented.

Acknowledgements

Thank you to all those who have made this chapter possible: to all my process work teachers, especially Arlene and Jean-Claude Audergon, and to Arny and Amy Mindell; to Dr Tom Ravenette for his ideas around consultation; to the editors, for their encouragement of this new approach; to my family and friends and to my professional colleagues on Villa Unit, for their support; and to my clients, who have taught me so much by their courageously choosing change.

References

Audergon, J.C. and Audergon, A. (1990) Seminar on process-oriented psychology: interventions in psychiatry, St Francis Hospital, Haywards Heath, Sussex.
Bateson, G. (1972) *Steps to an Ecology of Mind*, NY: Ballantine Books.
Epting, F.G. (1984) *Personal Construct Counselling and Psychotherapy*, Chichester: John Wiley.
Goodbread, J. (1987) *The Dreambody Toolkit*, London: Routledge and Kegan Paul.
Gustafson, J.P. (1986) *The Complex Secret of Brief Psychotherapy*, London: W.W. Norton.
Kelly, G.A. (1955) *The Psychology of Personal Constructs*, NY: W.W. Norton.
Jung, C.G. (1969) The structure and dynamics of the psyche, in his *Collected Works, Vol. 8*, 2nd edn, Princeton: Princeton University Press.
Luzzatto, P. (1989) Drinking problems and short term art therapy: working with images of withdrawal and clinging, in A. Gilroy and T. Dalley (eds) *Pictures at an Exhibition: Selected Essays on Art and Art Therapy*, London: Routledge.

Mindell, A. (1982) *Dreambody: The Body's Role in Revealing the Self*, London: Routledge and Kegan Paul.

—— (1985) *River's Way: The Process Science of the Dreambody*, London: Routledge and Kegan Paul.

—— (1988) *City Shadows: Psychological Interventions in Psychiatry*, London: Routledge and Kegan Paul.

Ravenette, A.T. (1986) Transcending the obvious and illuminating the ordinary, unpublished paper.

—— (1988) A drawing and its opposite, unpublished paper.

Ryle, A. (1990) *Cognitive Analytic Therapy: Active Participation in Change*, Chichester: John Wiley.

Schaverien, J. (1987) The scapegoat and the talisman: transference in art therapy, in T. Dalley *et al. Images of Art Therapy*, London: Tavistock.

Ursano, A.J. and Hales, R.E. (1986) A review of brief individual therapies, *American Journal of Psychiatry* **143**(2): 1507–17.

Watzlawick, P., Weakland, J. and Fisch, R. (1974) *Change: Principles of Problem Formation and Problem Resolution*, NY: W.W. Norton.

Yalom, I.D. (1986) *In-Patient Group Psychotherapy*, NY: Basic Books.

PART III

Training and research

12

The training of art therapists: past, present and future issues

DIANE WALLER

Introduction

This chapter is written in the light of a major review of art therapy training being conducted under the auspices of the British Association of Art Therapists' (BAAT) Training and Education Sub-Committee. In 1990, this committee recommended to the Annual General Meeting of BAAT that art therapy training should be extended to two years full-time equivalent instead of the one year which had been approved by BAAT and the Department of Health in 1982 (PM/82/6). It also recommended that the training should be:

> . . . rooted in psychotherapeutic principles, which recognises the need for a considerable period of clinical practice to produce art therapists who are able to perform at a high standard and assume positions of authority and respect in the agency in which they eventually come to work.
>
> (Donnelly 1990: 4)

The necessity for art therapists to be engaged in their own personal therapy, at least for part of the course, was also felt to be essential if the 'psychotherapeutic' base of the work was to be credible. The nature and style of this engagement has not yet been worked out – that is, whether intending art therapists should be in personal *art* therapy or verbal therapy. The problem of continuing with one's own therapy whilst on a course in a town far from one's home is one which has to be grappled with.

These proposals were approved by an overwhelming majority of members and the committee was charged with making recommendations for implementing the new policy – a task which, at the time of writing, is still underway. In the mean time art therapy training lasts for one year full-time and is open to graduates, normally in art or design but exceptionally in another subject or having professional qualifications, who must also have at least a year's working experience in an area relevant to art therapy before the course starts. In practice, most applicants have at least these qualifications and many have several years' working experience and also have engaged in their own personal therapy. The three courses approved by the British Association of Art Therapists and by the Department of Health and National Joint Council are at Goldsmiths' College, University of London, Hertfordshire College of Art and Sheffield University.

In the following chapter, I shall give a brief sketch of the history of art therapy training, showing how it has developed within the British higher education framework, paying some attention to the issue of professional ideologies. I shall also discuss the current position and in particular the implications for British training of the European Community directive on the recognition of professional qualifications (89/48/EEC).

Some contextual background and early views on training

Recent and past literature concerning art therapy training remains scarce, with the majority of critical writing in Britain being produced by the author herself (Waller and James 1984, Waller 1987, 1991a, b), or incorporated into articles on the theory and practice of art therapy (for example, Birtchnell 1977, 1981, 1984), most of which have been published in *Inscape*, the journal of BAAT. One of the earliest references to training in art therapy was made by the art educator Marie Petrie in *Art and Regeneration* published in 1946. Petrie was ahead of her time in suggesting that art therapy should have its own training, separate from occupational therapy under whose aegis it had emerged during the rapid development of rehabilitation services during and after the Second World War, and her ideas were subsequently taken up by working parties formed by the National Association for Mental Health in London from 1949 onwards. In 1979, many years and many meetings later, the deliberations of the BAAT Registration and Training Committee were published in *Inscape*, together with recommendations for a 'core course' of training which would enable the three then existing programmes at Hertfordshire College of Art and Design, Goldsmiths' College and Birmingham Polytechnic to be approved by BAAT, and a 'blueprint' to be available for future contenders. I shall discuss the content of this important document later in this chapter.

In 1979 and 1980, two further issues of *Inscape* were devoted to descriptive articles by the leaders of these programmes. Articles by ex-students of Herts and Goldsmiths' College, describing their experiences during training, were also included, together with a letter by a graduate in her first job, deploring the 'competitiveness' which she experienced between students trained at different colleges. In 1980, Byrne followed up his article in the previous issue of *Inscape* with a thorough exploration of the content and methods of approach to teaching art therapy at Birmingham Polytechnic (1980).

Organization of training

From the late 1940s until the mid 1950s, various committees and working parties organized by the National Association for Mental Health had tried to decide what would constitute a suitable training for the practice of art therapy. Especially problematic were issues to do with who should gain entry to the training, or, conversely, who should be excluded. I have drawn attention to Petrie's view that the training of art therapists might be separate from occupational therapy. In discussing the value of art with emotionally and behaviourally disturbed children, she commented:

> To trained eyes, definite symptoms of whatever psychic difficulties, fears or inhibitions the child is suffering from will here emerge, documented not only by the choice of subject, by the content or absence of content of the drawing, painting or model, but as much or more by the general handling or by the means employed. I hasten to add that these trained eyes do not as yet really exist, or exist perhaps only in a few isolated cases, for any really reliable diagnosis would demand not only the experience of the trained child psychologist but also that of the trained art teacher.
>
> (Petrie 1946: 77–8)

A prominent contributor to the development of art therapy in Britain, Dr Irene Champernowne, founder of the Withymead Centre for Psychotherapy through the Arts in 1942 and a Jungian analyst, firmly supported her position. Champernowne is recorded in the minutes of the early working parties as feeling that occupational therapy, being concerned in the post-Second World War period mainly with rehabilitation in a practical, activity-based framework, was a very different process from art therapy. She thought that the art therapist should be an artist or an art teacher who had experienced their own psychotherapy (as had the artists working at the Withymead Centre which she directed) in order that they could become deeply involved with the patients' image-making process and be empathic to the patients' condition. Other committee members (Adrian Hill and Edward Adamson, for example) felt that being an artist was important but that personal therapy was not. Yet others felt that the art therapist should not be an artist at all, but rather an occupational therapist or a doctor or psychologist.

Although such matters were debated throughout the 1950s and early 1960s, it was not until the formation of BAAT in 1963 that the matter received serious attention. Basic philosophical conflicts had obviously emerged but were left unexplored. A definition of art therapy was also lacking. BAAT's mission was a complicated one, encompassing aims appropriate to a learned society, a professional association *and* a trades union. It included a commitment to devising 'suitable programmes of training'. In 1965, BAAT entered discussions with the London Institute of Education over a proposal for an Advanced Diploma in Education which was to encompass art, music, drama and movement therapy and to be taught at the Institute. This course fitted into BAAT's then current strategy for career development, which was to acquire a structure for art therapists under the auspices of local education authorities equivalent to that of graduate teachers. As it happened, the course did not get off the ground, probably because it had a complex programme and demanded a high level of staff–student contact, making it expensive to run; it was multi-disciplinary and required sophisticated timetabling and total co-operation from different departments; art therapy was not officially defined and the other arts therapies were at different stages in organization and establishment of identity. Finally, there were territorial questions, in that it was not clear which discipline would be in control of the course.

Despite the frustration of being involved in such long drawn-out discussions and negotiations (these lasted from 1965 to 1972), there was a positive side for BAAT officers in that they gained much understanding of the politics of higher education and insight into the position of other arts therapists, particularly music therapists with whom art therapists worked closely during negotiations for a place in the Whitley Council structure.

At the same time as these talks were going on, an option in art therapy had been introduced into the Art Teacher's Diploma (ATD) course at the School of Art Education, Birmingham, in 1969, and a Certificate in Remedial Art had begun at St Albans School of Art (now Hertfordshire College of Art and Design) in 1970. These were very different in structure and in philosophy. The Birmingham option was introduced by Michael Edwards who had spent many years at the Withymead Centre, following a training in art and art education. Edwards was employed as a lecturer in art education, but with his background in art therapy, and experience gained in child guidance work at the Tavistock Clinic, he was able to develop the work already begun in special education by Lea Elliott and extend it by enabling the ATD students to do part of their teaching practice in hospitals, clinics and special schools. They also had to do the statutory amount of practice in mainstream education, making for a very full programme. Some of the ATDs went on to work full time as art therapists.

In the mid-1970s, art therapy was included in the MA in Art Education, and by 1979 two students had been supported to research to M.Phil. level in art therapy by the then Social Science Research Council. By this time Edwards had left and Peter Byrne, an artist who had worked as an art therapist at St Barnards' and Maudsley Hospitals, had joined the staff. The programme at Hertfordshire College of Art (then St Albans School of Art) differed in that it was a discrete one-year full-time course entitled 'Certificate in Remedial Art', a name which was designed to overcome the ambivalence with which government departments, especially the Departments of Education and Health, regarded the term 'art therapy'. John Evans, who became course leader and eventually head of the art therapy department at Herts College, noted that the word 'therapy' seemed to generate fear and suspicion amongst many people, particularly within art schools where the notion that art could be therapeutic was seen as insulting to the serious pursuit of Fine Art. Importantly, because the college was small and needed the approval of the 'establishment' it was felt necessary by the college's management to gain the support of named psychiatrists (and therefore of the medical 'establishment') to give it credibility with government departments (Evans 1979: 6).

This strategy, and to some extent a clash between the two parties over course philosophy, lead to a rift between BAAT and Herts College, as BAAT was identifying itself with art education not only from the point of view of employment possibilities but also in order to prevent art therapy being caught up with the 'medical model' of psychiatry. Indeed, many of BAAT's prominent members of the late 1960s and early 1970s were much influenced by the 'anti-psychiatry movement' and were reluctant to see art therapy being allied to psychiatry.

However, as Evans pointed out in reflecting on the close links which the Herts course made with the psychiatric profession, for a college which needed the approval of orthodox psychiatry in order to survive, it was not surprising that it should take this stance and have to distance itself from BAAT, which represented, at least through its more vocal members, the ideological position which saw psychiatry as a 'mystified technique for regulating behaviour which challenges the existing social structure and ideology' (Ingleby 1972: 71). There was also the question of admission to the course. BAAT (and Birmingham, as the art therapy programme was an option within an art teacher's training) stipulated an art degree or equivalent. Herts College was prepared to admit non-art graduates, including occupational therapists and nurses as part of its strategy for moving closer to the professions allied to medicine. BAAT felt that this would dilute the process of art therapy which relied on sophisticated understanding of visual media *and* therapeutic skills. This issue could not be resolved, as it was more serious than a question of admitting a few exceptions to the art graduate norm: it was, again, a fundamental difference of position. It was, therefore, debated at length by the Registration and Training Committee of BAAT, but without recourse to the kinds of arguments I have outlined above.

In 1974, Goldsmiths' College (in the person of myself) introduced an option in art therapy to the postgraduate art teacher's certificate (ATC) course. At the same time I was part-time art therapist at the Paddington Centre for Psychotherapy, an NHS clinic which was unusual for its time in treating patients entirely through psychotherapy. Its day hospital had a radical approach to treatment and accepted patients for whom psychotherapy would not normally have been indicated: i.e. those with 'psychotic' or 'personality' disorders, being addicted to drugs, including alcohol.

The Goldsmiths' option grew up in a department already influenced by Evelyn Gibbs, well-known exponent of 'child art', Anton Ehrenzweig, author of *The Psychoanalysis of Artistic Vision and Hearing*, and which had a tradition of teaching art teachers through encouraging them to continue to engage professionally in their own artwork, ostensibly because it was felt that this would make them stimulating and enthusiastic teachers but perhaps unconsciously out of a desire to retain a 'fine art ideology', which I shall discuss further later on.

In the 1970s, Goldsmiths' ATC had the highest number of applicants of all such courses, and following the introduction of the option, the application rate increased so that at initial interview a selection process was eventually made to the option itself. After two years, the College began the long and very difficult process towards a discrete Diploma in Art Therapy, drawing on the option which was gradually separating itself from the ATC course. The problems were made more acute by the fact that both Goldsmiths' and Herts College came under the Regional Advisory Committee (RAC) which was a body charged with assessing regional training provision and need. As there was already one course in existence in the South-East, the RAC initially refused to approve another – even though the Herts course was the only one in Britain and no other college was attempting to start a training! The problem was eventually resolved by demonstrating that there were sufficient jobs for graduates, and through the Goldsmiths course calling itself 'Diploma in the Therapeutic Application of Art for Children and Young People' in order to be sufficiently different from the Herts course. This unwieldy title continued until 1979 when the course was approved by the Department of Education and Science as a Diploma in Art Therapy. By the time that the Goldsmiths proposals were with RAC, Herts College had changed its course title from 'Certificate in Remedial Art' to 'Art Therapy'.

Throughout the early 1970s there arose the question of which course or courses should 'own' art therapy training. Herts College felt their claim was more justified than either Birmingham or Goldsmiths because they had a one-year full-time course labelled 'art therapy'. But the latter felt equally entitled to ownership because their options had grown out of a long-standing link between art education and art therapy, and because they were elements in BAAT's strategy to avoid being absorbed into the paramedical grades, and especially into occupational therapy. The options had strong identities within the departments in which they had grown up, but nevertheless neither were able to award a discrete art therapy qualification.

By way of trying to resolve this issue, a Registration and Training Sub-Committee was established at the BAAT AGM of 1976, having representatives from all three colleges and from practising art therapists. The committee aimed to arrive at a 'core course' which all training establishments would have to deliver. The resulting 'core course' did not specify that the training had to be under the formal umbrella of a discrete 'Diploma in Art Therapy', but the committee decided that this should be the aim for the future. In January 1978, the recommendations of the committee were published in *Inscape*. They stipulated that the training should consist of a balance of theoretical, clinical and experiential learning, with a minimum 60-day period of practical placement. Entry requirements were for art graduate status, but were left open, exceptionally, to others who could demonstrate 'ability in and commitment to the practice of a visual art'. As far as the theoretical input was concerned, this consisted of a long list of subjects for study, obviously impossible to achieve in a lifetime, let alone a year. For example, under 'An introduction to and study of basic theories and models', the list included such diverse models as 'psychoanalytical, behavioural, biological, anthropological, social, semiotic, aesthetic . . .'. This was intended to give each institution the opportunity to develop its own 'theoretical style' rather than restrict the development of art therapy to one or two models.

In a descriptive chapter about art therapy training, Waller and James (1984) note:

> Although there is much agreement within the existing courses about structuring, content and standards, these are healthy differences which reflect the growing profession . . .
>
> The colleges are, however, faced with a daunting task of having only one year full-time or two years part-time to train an artist in 'the therapeutic application of their art skills'. It must be stressed, though, that this year is not simply 'tacked on' to the first degree but is an integral part of the whole education of the art therapist. Failure to perceive this means that the one year is dismissed as being impossibly inadequate by all concerned, not least by students and staff and by other professionals
>
> (1984: 196)

By the time this chapter was published, the Goldsmiths option had developed into a full-time Diploma in Art Therapy and the Herts course was validated by the

Council for National Academic Awards (CNAA), the validating body for polytechnics and colleges of further education. That college had also mounted an MA in Art Therapy intended mainly for qualified art therapists. The Department of Health had issued a personnel memorandum listing the programmes at Birmingham, Herts and Goldsmiths as 'approved', but had given only provisional approval to Birmingham, which by 1982 remained an option in the ATD course. For many reasons which seem mainly to do with the politics of higher education in the early 1980s and despite the fact that Birmingham had included an art therapy mode within its MA in art education, the option did not become a discrete Diploma in Art Therapy and approval was withdrawn in 1985. This was a loss to the profession as the option was grappling with the central issue of the role of art in art therapy and how to teach art graduates to become therapists. In addition it was supplying art teachers who could readily work with children having special needs in mainstream education.

In 1985, too, a new diploma course emerged at the University of Sheffield, under the aegis of the Department of Continuing Education, which gained approval from both BAAT and the Department of Health. This course was later incorporated into the Department of Psychiatry. John Henzell, a founder member of BAAT who had completed M.Phil. research in art therapy at Birmingham, and Christine Wood, a practising art therapist and graduate of Goldsmiths, were the first course tutors. Several other course proposals found their way to BAAT's Training and Education Committee but for a variety of reasons did not get off the ground (see Waller 1991b: 253–57).

The emergence of a 'fine art' ideology in training

Waller and James (1984) discussed some of the problems experienced by BAAT and the training colleges in gaining recognition from the Department of Health. We drew attention to the argument put forward by BAAT that art therapists should be first and foremost artists – that is, having a degree in art and design prior to entering art therapy training. The rationale was presented to the Department of Health by Gilroy and Waller on several occasions and summed up in a letter in October 1977, which drew attention to the 'considerable understanding of art processes and proficiency in the area of non-verbal communication' which an art training would confer. This position has been criticized by Birtchnell (1977, 1981), who assumed that art graduates would exaggerate the importance of art in art therapy out of a (mistaken) belief that making art was in itself therapeutic and that the professional association's insistence on art graduate status was nothing more than 'political expedience'. Birtchnell was correct in assuming a strategy behind the demand for art graduate status but this was by no means the whole story. Indeed, the intention (or perhaps the hope) was that the students would arrive at a *synthesis* of art and therapy from which to develop as art therapists.

The fact that art therapists in Britain mainly come from an art background, as opposed to a medical or psychological one (as in some parts of Europe) cannot be seen merely as a 'political expediency' but as demonstrating a powerful ideology.

This issue cannot be overlooked when discussing any professional training. Pateman (1972) brought together a number of articles which clearly demonstrate that behind all training courses lie ideologies which are not usually visible to trainers or trainees but which have an effect on the way that the future professional will function. Professions discussed were medicine and social work, but some courses were also examined for ideological content (for example, English Literature, Mathematics and History).

Dyne (1985), writing about psychotherapy, also points out the importance of training in shaping the future of an occupational group or profession:

> A training must generate those authorities who will hold the subsets of the field together and thus maintain the therapeutic society. Training is an act of faith, in which the teachers must hope to create and work to realize a family, some members of which will go further than have their teachers – their parents – who can then learn from them.
>
> (ibid.: 127)

Part of the way that the ideology is passed on is through language. Silman, in writing about the 'language' of medicine in 'Countercourse', notes:

> . . . anyone can examine a person and notice that his heart has stopped. It takes five years of special training to diagnose a cardiac arrest. To qualify as a doctor, it is not sufficient to know medical science and its corresponding language; one has to learn the language of confusion, the language of the profession, the language that imposes itself by pretending to be science but which is not science because it is the language of the mediator.
>
> (1972: 268)

(By mediator, Silman is referring to those who mediate between authority and the world: for example, the lawyer mediates between the authority of the law and its world, the church between the authority of God and his world. He suggests that there is a confusion between the role of the authority and the role of those who represent that authority.) Silman goes on to argue that it is certainly true that doctors undertake to cure patients by diagnosis and treatment, but there is more to it than that. There is the imposition of a social order on the basis of a sacred authority. This order has rites: it creates two ritual social identities, that of 'doctor' and that of 'patient'. In relating this statement to the training of art therapists, it is necessary to examine the fact that, in Britain, art therapists are normally required to have a degree or equivalent in art or design before taking the Diploma in Art Therapy, the mandatory qualification for practice in national health and (recently) social services departments. Occasionally non-art graduates are admitted to training, but all course entry requirements specify they have to demonstrate 'a long standing commitment to and ability in the practice of a visual art'. (The same applies to music therapists, who have a first degree in music and must go through an audition as well as an interview as part of their application to train.)

The requirement for training in art therapy was only laid down by the Department of Health in 1980. Between 1966 and 1980, the Department had required art therapists to possess 'a qualification in art obtained after two years post-A level study'. This was, in fact, the Intermediate Certificate in art and design which had ceased to be awarded in 1964! This was a half-hearted recognition that art therapists needed some art training (although not to the level of the National Diploma in Design or a degree) and that was seen as sufficient to define them as 'therapists'. The implications of this failure to recognize the need for a 'therapy' training led to a public perception of art therapy as a recreational, activity-based intervention, which well intentioned amateurs could provide (see Chapter 1 of this volume).

How, then, did this 'art base' come about? The art base of art therapy has a long history and the involvement of artists in work with hospital patients began in Britain in the early 1940s with pioneers like Adrian Hill (1945, 1951) who were engaged in the developing post-war rehabilitation movements. It continues today under the umbrella of 'hospital arts', and 'art therapy' (see Chapter 2 of this volume).

There came a point, around the mid-1950s, when these artists who had been teaching patients about painting or appreciation of pictures in the same way as they would have taught adults in evening classes, started to define themselves as 'therapists', and therefore as being engaged in 'treatment'. As the artists became art therapists, so the pupils became 'patients'. But once the artists had defined themselves as therapists, they needed to be 'trained' to learn the language of *therapy* in order to take their place in the professional family. However, they did not wish to lose their artist role so tried to resolve the problem through a process which Ben-David and Collins (1966) referred to as 'role hybridization'. This process may account, in part, for the emergence of a new professional role, in that the individual moving from one role (for example, that of artist) to another (for example, that of therapist) is placed in a position of conflict. This can be solved by giving up attitudes and behaviours appropriate to the old role and adopting those of the new, hence ceasing to identify with the old group. But if the individual does not want to give up this identification they might attempt to solve the conflict by *innovating*; that is, by fitting the methods and techniques of the old role to the materials of the new one to create an entirely different role – in this case, art therapist.

One may ask why artists found it necessary to innovate in this way. One possibility is that career opportunities for art graduates, in particular of fine art, were limited and that these particular graduates were searching for a socially valid role other than that of teaching. To elaborate on this theory a little, it appears that the goal of many art students on entering art school was and is to become full-time artists. Their tutors encourage, if not insist upon, such an aspiration. Failing this, only art college teaching may be seen as a reasonably respectable alternative, yet such posts were and are very limited.

The socialization of the art student

Madge and Weinberger, in *Art Students Observed* (1973), touch on this issue, which centres round the socialization of the art student by asking 'Socialization into what?'. They studied the functioning of a large British art school over a period of three years and the relation between the hopes and expectations of the students taking the Diploma in Art and Design and their expectations and reactions over the period of the course. They found that art students, particularly Fine Art students (from which discipline most art therapy trainees have emerged), were being socialized into a role of 'artist' which was extremely fluid and ill defined compared with, say, medical or law students. They pointed out that:

> . . . the art student – and especially the Fine Art student – is pushed or pushes himself as far as he can go towards the unlimited, untrammelled role of artist in all its creative unpredictability, and in this lies the drama and the pathos of his situation.
>
> Some young people may turn towards the role of artist, or art student, as a means of avoiding more conventional occupational roles, of contracting out of the industrial society.

(ibid.: 20–1)

A group of postgraduate art education students (including the author herself) at Goldsmiths' College took up the question of socialization in a pamphlet entitled 'In pursuit of change in education and society' (Flavell *et al.* 1974). In an article entitled 'Diploma in Art and Design: The Process of Seduction', they pointed out that most art college prospectuses stressed the importance of their courses as training grounds for the professional artist or designer, but in reality, very few graduates earned their living practising fine art full time. Therefore, the fine art model as propagated by colleges – and art students – was a pseudo-professional one. However, it was a powerful model because its falseness was not often discovered, or admitted, until most people had left college:

> Most people enter (art school) believing – or wanting to believe – that it is going to be a professional way of life and in this way it is acquired and confirmed implicitly, without realising, as one goes through the system. The extent to which this system is successful can be measured by the number of students who internalize the role of 'professional artist' and identify with other aspects of the dominant philosophy. Such an identification helps to create a contradiction later, especially if the 'fine art' student finds that he has to change his 'role' into 'teacher'.

(ibid.: 5)

(It is important to note that the 'professional artist' is not a 'commercial artist' but one who responds to their own muse and not that of advertising or industry or fashion: in fact, a rare category in our present society.)

The authors go on to say that the 'fine art ideology' emphasizes the nurturing of the individual and 'uniqueness'. In an elitist sense, students were led to believe that art is unteachable, and that the artist's talent must be allowed to grow, unharmed by outside influences. There was also the notion that the artist was, perhaps, someone who had a streak of madness. In other words, art was something which was not influenced or caused by social and economic developments around it.

They traced this concept back to the mid-nineteenth century when industrialization and technological developments were causing changes in society. In the alienation of worker from his work and place of work, the 'artist' became separated from the 'craftsman' who took the role of making and manufacturing while the artist was seen as someone above this vulgar concern with materials.

One can see how 'art therapy', as it was practised in the 1960s and 1970s, would have appealed to those art graduates who had partially absorbed the fine art ideology but who had neither the inclination nor the ability (as with the majority of art students) to earn their living as full-time artists but who did not wish to teach in schools nor to enter industry.

In the 1940s and onwards, many hospitals opened studios for recreational art activities, and working in these studios with adult patients in 'open groups' rather resembled the artists' own experience of art college (i.e. quiet atmosphere, tutor moving around the studio, peering over shoulders, whispered conversations, emphasis on individual artwork). However, the patient-pupils who came to hospital art studios were not art students: they came either at the request of the medical or ward staff or to escape from the regimentation of the rest of the hospital into a place where individual attention was available but there was little pressure, and where they could have access to a form of 'free expression', or just a cup of tea and a chat. Many of the patients were long-stay, diagnosed as 'chronic' or 'psychotic' (see Chapter 4 of this volume). In some cases the resulting paintings were used by psychiatrists as possible diagnostic aids; in others, they remained in the studio and were eventually taken away by the patient or kept by the art therapist or ended up in the basement. A few patients found that painting opened a new world for them and, in the case of long-stay patients, this gave a new form of communication, sometimes quite a dramatic change in self-esteem, as well as a creative way of spending the days in hospital.

Gradually, then, the artist-teacher role was modified and the artists got more interested in the meaning of the art for the patients, and in the relationship they could develop with them. They started to redefine themselves as art therapists. From those individuals working in isolation throughout the country came the impetus to organize themselves, and hence the British Association of Art Therapists was formed in 1964. For many years – until 1977 – art therapists remained closely linked with art education and some were employed under the auspices of local education authorities and seconded to hospitals (for a detailed historical account of this period see Waller 1991a).

It is my impression, on the basis of interviewing candidates for art therapy training from the mid-1970s on, that many of them wanted to reject the 'fine art ideology', in the same way as the group of ATC students who wrote 'In pursuit of change', although they were perhaps not fully conscious of this. They perhaps had a view of art as being about 'play' in its importance to human development and had found this so in their own development.

During the course of art therapy training they would have to arrive at a *synthesis* of art and therapy, in which the operation of the imagination is an essential element. The ability to synthesize is also essential in undertaking psychotherapy training. As Dyne put it:

> . . . each (psychotherapy) student must become a researcher in order to develop his or her personal skills and system, and the essence of this process is the imagination. Synthesizing is an imaginative exercise disciplined by

thought; it is in the use of the imagination that coherence and novelty can be joined so that the student's personal knowledge can have that necessary quality of proper conservatism which is part of the healthy performance of guardianship of the field.

(1985: 128)

He goes on to say that he feels it is reasonable for students to undertake the burden of synthesizing, so long as the teachers themselves display and facilitate the process. Whether this was a reasonable aspiration for art graduates, given the 'fine art ideology' to which they may have been subjected, has not been fully debated to date. (It can be noted in passing that these issues are being explored in depth by Andrea Gilroy in her current research from the point of view of the new 'world view' that psychotherapy, and art therapy trainees take on in order to enter their respective professions (Gilroy 1992).)

In 'Art therapy in adolescence: a metaphorical view of a profession in progress' (1987) I noted that there was a tendency among some art therapy educators to wish to enrol non-art graduates in greater numbers than before, ostensibly in the interests of having a multi-disciplinary student group, and that such a tendency was considered by the profession, as represented by BAAT, to erode the art base of art therapy and to dilute its potential. Byrne's paper (1981) gives excellent theoretical explanations of the reason for admitting primarily art graduates to art therapy training, given that understanding and relating to images, as well as to a patient, is central to the practice of art therapy. This issue is still unresolved and will be raised again later. I also drew attention to the apparent contradictions inherent in training artists to become therapists. One can see how difficult it would be for anyone who had absorbed too thoroughly the fine art 'ideology' discussed earlier on to take on the mantle of therapist, especially if it had an allegiance to a 'medical model' of treatment. It became clear that the association of art therapy training with art education rather than with psychiatry, which was made by two out of the three emerging training courses (and by BAAT), was one way of trying to avoid this conflict.

The position today

At the time of writing, BAAT has made a submission to the Council for Professions Supplementary to Medicine (CPSM) for the state recognition of art therapists. State registration gives a safeguard to the public in that it regulates the activities of members of an occupational group. One of the requirements for registration under the CPSM Act is that the profession has 'reached maturity' and that it has a 'recognised course of training over a substantial period', that its examinations are 'adequate' and properly conducted and that a minimal educational standard is enforced for all entrants.

Establishing art therapy as an academic subject has been a slow and often painful process, as is the case with all new disciplines (see Goodson 1981, for example, discussing Geography). Approval of the Herts College of Art's Diploma in Art Therapy in the late 1970s by the CNAA was a very important landmark in the 'establishment' of training, as was the approval of the Masters degree in Art Therapy at Goldsmiths' College by the University of London's Board of Science in 1989. Art therapy can now claim to be an 'academic subject' as well as a form of practice.

Another criterion of the CPSM Act which BAAT has to meet is: 'having a body of knowledge which can be examined'. Given that art therapy is now taught at Master's level in Britain, this criterion can be said to have been met in that much attention has been paid by validating bodies to the way in which the content of the course is examined, and to the status of the examiners themselves.

But what does, or should, this 'body of knowledge' actually consist of? Such was the problem that faced the BAAT Training and Education Committee, when it attempted to re-examine the 'core course requirements' in the light of perceived shifts in the organization and philosophy of training among the three approved centres since the first set was published in 1978. (For example, two centres operated continuous placements throughout the course of approximately 80 days while one operated a mixture of block and continuous; one centre [Goldsmiths] emphasized object-relations/group dynamics theories, while another [Herts] gave some prominence to developmental psychology.)

Over a five-year period, this committee reviewed the existing requirements and found that, indeed, many changes had taken place. In trying to reflect these changes, and again to take into account the differences in training philosophy among the three centres, the committee arrived at a series of recommendations which was presented for approval to the BAAT AGM in 1990. Among other things, the report stated:

> The committee established two basic and enduring principles that have permeated its thinking. Firstly that the existing one academic year of training was not sufficiently long enough, and secondly, that the basis of the training should be a psychotherapeutic one . . . the principle aim of the training is to enable graduates to undertake the clinical practice of Art Therapy in which Art and the process of making images play a central role in the context of the psychotherapeutic relationship.
>
> (p. 2, para. 5)

It continued:

> The knowledge, understanding and experience of psychotherapeutic relationships is central to the practice of Art Therapy. The possibility for clients to make personally significant objects or images within the context of clearly defined relationships with the Art Therapist is of primary importance in Art Therapy. It is shared, discussed and valued. The Art Therapist therefore must acquire considerable experience, knowledge and understanding of the nature of psychotherapy in theory and in practice, as well as in in-depth knowledge of symbolic communication, be this in words, pictures or through the making of objects and the rituals accompanying the act.
>
> (p. 6, para. 8)

The members of the committee found themselves in agreement over the structure and content of the training but, in the same way as the previous committee members, were unable to concur over the entry requirements. Most members felt strongly that entry should normally be limited to art graduates with at least a year's relevant working experience prior to entry to the training, but some wanted to include non-artists in greater numbers than before. This issue is unlikely to be resolved until a more strenuous debate is conducted which takes into account some of the questions of professional ideology which I mentioned earlier on.

It is worth noting that whereas unanimous agreement was reached over the 'psychotherapeutic' orientation of art therapy, the model or models of psychotherapy to be studied were not defined. An important change had occurred, however, in that the *relationship* between art therapist and client had been highlighted, and defined as a *psychotherapeutic* one, implying that it had significance for the process as well as the artwork itself, whereas in the past, it was the artwork alone that had prominence. If we consider the historical origins of training, we can see that Irene Champernowne's concept of art therapists has emerged strongly, with the important difference being that they now perceive themselves as *key figures* in the treatment process as opposed to 'midwives', as Champernowne was prone to call them, who related only on the level of the artwork and left the deeper exploration of feelings and emotions, including transference phenomena, to the psychotherapist or psychiatrist.

David Maclagan, an art therapist and lecturer, points out that the increasing 'psychotherapeutic' dimension poses problems for the art therapist:

> . . . I think there is a shadow side to Art Therapy, whereby a trust in the intrinsic healing power of psychic processes mediated through art is compensated by adherence to a strictly conventional psychotherapeutic framework, as if to give official respectability to what would otherwise appear wild or woolly.
>
> (1989: 10)

He feels that there could be a tendency to translate the pictorial image into an interpretative idiom:

> . . . whose mode is essentially alien to that of the image itself: ie a technically psychological language, such as 'good mother' or 'anima figure'. This may take the form of what I shall call an 'iconographic prejudice', in which the picture is scanned principally in order to discover symbolic representation of one kind or another . . .
>
> (ibid.)

Maclagan's work is important in drawing attention to the need for a language suitable for art therapy (or art psychotherapy) and one which does not merely adopt what he calls the 'convential therapeutic assumptions' that have their origins in verbal psychoanalysis.

If art therapists are to be mindful of these arguments and to take a role in which they may be key therapists, able to work with all levels of the process from the complexities in the relationship between themselves and the patient, including transference, to knowing when to help with the practicalities of painting and making, entering into the symbolic and metaphoric world of the image, and so on, then it follows that training must be sufficiently rigorous in theoretical, clinical, experiential and personal terms to enable them to carry out this innovative work. Add to this the necessity to understand and relate to the changing nature and organization of the institutions wherein art therapists practise, the necessity to prove oneself 'cost effective' and the burden of being pioneers in a still new profession, and it is clear why a longer training has been agreed.

The problems involved in 'role hybridization' have merely been touched on in this chapter, but it may be that it is increasingly difficult, given this workload, for the art therapist to hold on to their 'art' base and certainly, for those who wished to, to maintain a 'fine art ideology'. (The question of the continuing importance of art-making to a practising art therapist is currently being addressed by Gilroy, who noted in a recent paper that working as an art therapist may result in the therapist sacrificing their own self-expression in the service of the patient's creativity. But she notes:

> . . . for those who maintain a relationship with their art outside their work with patients the rewards are inestimable, both professionally and personally. It maintains the uniqueness of the discipline and of the individual. If we hang on to our own art, even though we might do it only occasionally, no one will take the art out of art therapy.
>
> (1989:9)

It is hard to see how non-art graduates can 'compensate' for a whole four or five years' worth of intensive study in a few days of media workshops – even if such people have demonstrated a 'long standing commitment to the visual arts' at interview.

What is clear is that trainees on the one-year full-time art therapy courses have little time to assimilate the wealth of theoretical psychotherapeutic material and experience provided which would lead them to feel secure in the role of art therapist. Many graduates do, of course, return to regular supervision either in their training centres or elsewhere and we may find that it is usually these people who stay in the profession, go on to higher degrees and senior posts or develop new approaches to clinical work.

In the near future

The task of BAAT, together with the training centres, is now to implement the new structure. The financial climate has never been favourable for art therapy (nor indeed, one might say, mental health or mental handicap services generally), and intending trainees are faced with ever increasing fees and the likelihood of having to acquire loans to pay fees and maintenance while on course. Some trainees are successful in gaining discretionary awards from their local education authorities, and a rare few gain secondments on full pay, or at least get their fees paid by their employer. A longer training will necessitate increased expense and it will be important to ensure that candidates are not excluded from participating because they cannot afford the fees. In this respect art therapy trainees will be in the same position as many other postgraduate and post-experience students.

There are obviously some risks in extending the required period of training:

some people who now feel able to take 'time out' for a one-year full-time course may baulk at a longer commitment, especially with the additional funding to be found (and the present government's higher education policies do not give much hope that fees will be subsidised); a one-year commitment which ends in realization that art therapy is not the career one wants is less daunting than two. There were, however, risks when Herts College of Art and Goldsmiths' College established discrete Diplomas in Art Therapy at a time when art therapy was an ad hoc practice in the NHS, and students were only eligible for discretionary as opposed to the mandatory awards for teacher training. Awards are still discretionary, yet, for instance, Goldsmiths can choose one in six applicants, with the application rate continuing to rise.

The one-year full-time, two-year part-time model is, of course, familiar. What will be the feelings of art therapists who have done the one-year training? Will they be similar to those of the 'grandparent' art therapists who, although registered members of BAAT, did not undertake an art therapy training? If we take a possible scenario of someone who in future might take a Foundation Art Therapy course (one-year part-time), go on to a two-year full-time professional training, work for two years while attending a supervision group and then return to take a two-year part-time Masters, we can see that if such a procedure became the norm, we should be talking about a professional group who might well be demanding better financial rewards than they currently enjoy. Would there be a role for such people in the health and social services and education, or would they 'price themselves out of the market'? Is there any vested interest, anywhere, in keeping art therapists at their current level? Would it suit the purposes of regional managers to hire 'health care assistants' to undertake recreational or diversional art activities with patients, rather than expensive art therapists who are possibly a subversive group in encouraging patients to take responsibility for their condition at the same time as developing a critical sense of their relationship to others: as well as, of course, introducing the nonrational into the institution by way of the art process. We have to remember that for a very long time the Department of Health was content to define art therapists as 'having a two-year post-A level qualification in art' and did not require any training in therapy whatsoever!

Meanwhile, art therapy educators are looking towards 1992 and the possibility of introducing a 'European dimension' into the training through links and exchanges with countries in the EC. The introduction by the European Community of its directive on the recognition of professional qualifications (89/48/EC) will mean that the competent body for the professions allied to medicine (the Council for Professions Supplementary to Medicine) will, in co-operation with BAAT, be required to consider applicants for art therapy posts from member states where art therapy is a regulated profession. By law, the applicant must, if necessary, be given the chance to take an aptitude test or undergo a period of adaptation in order to meet the standards of the host country. Given that it is primarily in Britain and the USA where art therapists are normally art graduates before taking professional training, and that elsewhere they may come from psychology, psychiatric nursing, medicine and so on, and have no practical art experience, there may be considerable differences in philosophy and treatment approach to work with. As yet there is no way of knowing what effect the EC directive will have on art therapy, or on any other profession. There are advantages, in terms of increased contact with other European countries, but there could also be problems of marrying highly conflicting treatment philosophies. It is a time of great change and potential, but accompanied by serious financial problems in higher education and the health and social services.

Inevitably there are conflicts and differences within any occupational group and art therapists are no exception. Sometimes these conflicts have been submerged in order to achieve a common aim, as in the field of art therapy education. It remains to be seen how agreement can now be reached between those responsible for the organization of the profession and those who would have to implement the training, given institutional constraints and new funding arrangements for polytechnics and universities. For it seems that art therapists remain, as ever, committed to the notion that training should take place in the public (polytechnics and universities), as opposed to the private sector, however unfashionable that view may be.

References

BAAT (1978) Registration and Training Sub-Committee Report and Recommendations, *Inscape* **II** (January).

Ben-David, J. and Collins, R. (1966) Social factors in the origins of a new science: the case of psychology, *American Journal of Sociology Review* **31**(4): 451–65.

Birtchnell, J. (1977) Alternative concepts in art therapy, *Inscape* **15**.

—— (1978) Catharsis, *Inscape* **III**(I).

—— (1981) Is art therapeutic?, *Inscape* **V**(I).

—— (1984) Art therapy as a form of psychotherapy, in T. Dalley, (ed.) *Art as Therapy*, London: Tavistock.

Byrne, P. (1981) Art therapy training at Birmingham Polytechnic, *Inscape* **4**(I): 2–7.

Department of Trade and Industry (1989) EC Directive on the Recognition of Professional Qualifications (89/48/EEC): Aptitude Tests and Adaptation Periods for Incoming Professionals whose Qualifications fall short. A Consultative Document, December.

Donnelly, M. (1990) Report and Recommendations of the BAAT Training and Education Committee on the Future of Art Therapy Training, BAAT.

Dyne, D. (1985) Questions of training in psychotherapy, *Free Associations* **3**: 92–145.

Evans, J. (1979) Training in art therapy at Hertfordshire College of Art, *Inscape* **3**(2).

Flavell, J., Rosson, R., Waller, D., Walters, S. and Webb, B. (1974) In pursuit of change in education and society, London: Goldsmiths' College.

Gilroy, A.J. (1989) On occasionally being able to paint, *Inscape*, Spring: 2–9.

Goodson, I. (1981) Becoming an academic subject: explanation and evolution, *British Journal of Sociology of Education* **2**(2): 163–79.

Hill, A. (1945) *Art versus illness*, London: George Allen and Unwin.

Hill, A. (1951) *Painting Out illness*, London: Williams and Northgate.

Ingleby, D. (1972) Ideology and the human sciences: some comments on the role of reification in psychology and psychiatry, in T. Pateman, (ed.) *Countercourse*, Harmondsworth: Penguin.

Kramer, E. (1958) *Art Therapy in a Children's Community*, Illinois: Thomas.

—— (1971) *Art Therapy with Children*, Elek.

Maclagan, D. (1989) The aesthetic dimension of art therapy: luxury or necessity? *Inscape*, Spring: 10–13.

Madge, C. and Weinberger, B. (1973) *Art Students Observed*, London: Faber.

Naumburg, M. (1958) Art therapy: its scope and function, in E.F. Hammer (ed.) *Clinical Applications of Projective Drawings*, Illinois: Thomas.

Naumburg, M. (1966) *Dynamically Oriented Art Therapy: Its Principles and Practices*, NY: Grune and Stratton.

Pateman, T. (ed.) (1972) *Countercourse: A Handbook of Course Criticism*, Harmondsworth: Penguin.

Petrie, M. (1946) *Art and Regeneration*, Elek.

Silman, R. (1972) Teaching the medical student to become a doctor, in T. Pateman (ed.) *Countercourse*, Harmondsworth: Penguin.

Waller, D.E. (1979) Personal reflections on art therapy training at Goldsmiths' College, *Inscape* 3(2).

—— (1987) Art therapy in adolescence: a metaphorical view of a profession in progress, in T. Dalley *et al. Images of Art Therapy*, London: Routledge.

—— (1991a) *Becoming a Profession: A History of Art Therapists 1940–82*, London: Routledge.

—— (1991b) Art Therapy Training in the United Kingdom: Current Position and Future Issues. In Conference Proc. of Our European Future, St Albans: Hertfordshire College of Art.

—— and James, K. (1984) Training in art therapy, in T. Dalley (ed.) *Art as Therapy*, London: Tavistock.

13

Research in art therapy

ANDREA GILROY

Introduction

Lately I have been interested to observe an ambivalence amongst art therapists towards research. The mistrust, not to say active dislike, of the idea of research has in the past almost amounted to a resistance (Males 1979, 1980), and although such feelings doubtless still exist, I believe they are increasingly tempered by an interest in and acknowledgement of the *need* for research. In this age of cost effectiveness of treatment it is important to do research not only to improve our practice and enhance the credibility of our profession to colleagues, critics and employers, but also to preserve and create jobs. The conviction that art therapy works is gained through personal experience and the continuing affirmation that comes from clinical practice, yet we can no longer expect this to be taken on trust.

Whilst I am puzzled by the reluctance of a number of art therapists to explore their practice in a systematic way, I also find myself in sympathy with some of the expressed feelings about it. The corner-stone of the hostility to research seems to me to be the feeling that it is always 'scientific' and therefore inherently unsympathetic to a discipline based in art and in therapy. When I began my research (in 1983) I was very much of this persuasion, my fears being based on the assumption that *all* research methods were the same – reductive, numerical, unhelpful in the extreme – and that none of them would suit my purposes. I used the traditional research methods of survey, questionnaire and interview which fitted reasonably comfortably with the issues I wanted to explore (see Gilroy 1989), but during the course of becoming a researcher I have been interested to find other research models which would have been equally appropriate to my study. Later on in this chapter I will describe some of these possibilities, and indicate what I think are the good and bad aspects of both 'old' and 'new paradigm' research models.

It seems to me that a simple lack of information and knowledge about research is a prime cause of many art therapists' mistrust in terms of what it actually is as well as how to go about it. I think it is important to differentiate between, on the one hand, the gathering of information about a particular subject that everyone does as part of their job, or because of a particular interest, or in order to write an essay for an academic course or a paper for a journal, and on the other, research. Research involves rather more than straightforward 'fact finding' and constitutes a set of skills that have to be acquired over and above those of an art therapist. I believe some of the skills of the artist and of a therapist are similar to those that one uses in research and that art therapists could be good researchers – more of which anon. Research skills are usually learnt under the auspices of a research degree, and although this need not be the route for everyone to take, resources for learning about research are rare outside academic institutions. In a few years time it may be possible for new art therapy researchers to be supervised entirely by art therapists experienced in research, but meanwhile much can be gained from sympathetic supervision from members of allied professions.

This indicates to me that part of the problem that art therapy research faces is to do with the stage the profession is at, its relative youth as a discrete discipline and infancy as a recognized profession within the National Health Service (NHS). Energy has hitherto been expended in establishing the profession, public relations work, political negotiations, the struggle for autonomy, and many art therapists have left the profession because of the inadequate financial rewards and opportunities for career progression. Those who remained have had little time and energy left for research. It is therefore interesting to note that almost all the completed and/or published material and commencing dates of ongoing art therapy research are post-1982 (see Gilroy *et al.* 1989), i.e. post PM/82/6 and the formal recognition of art therapists by the Department of Health and Social Security. The researchers are experienced art therapists, a few of whom are doing a doctorate (some now completed) and the majority of whom are involved in art therapy education, i.e. they have direct contact with or are working in places which value and actively encourage research. I can imagine that it would be very difficult indeed to do research in a hospital without a culture and working ethos that is oriented towards research as part of clinical practice. My feeling is that research in art therapy is therefore a function of considerable practical experience in the field coupled with an environment sympathetic to the acquisition of research skills.

Although art therapy is recognized in some spheres of work it is still a relative newcomer in comparison with other disciplines such as psychology, social work, art teaching and so on. Research that endeavours to demonstrate the efficacy of art therapy as a primary treatment could go some way to increasing the recognition of our practice and to our becoming 'established' staff in the NHS and the education and social services. However, I think such recognition could be a paradoxical stumbling block for art therapists as a whole group. Diane Waller has suggested that art therapy is a profession in the throes of adolescence, that it is 'creative, subversive, change-seeking, and critical-of-status quo attitudes' (Waller 1987: 212). This hardly describes a group of people who would wish to join the ranks of the truly established professions! Perhaps we prefer to remain the artistic oddity in the multi-disciplinary team who does something vaguely helpful with the patients, to retain the romantic and disreputable atmosphere of mess and craziness in the old laundry at the end of the corridor, rather than become one of the white-coated lot who regularly prove their worth through empirical science.

My aim in this chapter is to demonstrate that as a profession we are slowly beginning to take on the mantle of research although in such a way as to allow us to keep our paint-smudged clothes and to keep well away from rats. I hope to encourage those art therapists who would like to do research and give some pointers to ways in which they might begin. I do not think research in general, and art therapy research in particular, is as bad as it might at first appear.

Art therapy research – so far, so good?

In this section I will review the existing art therapy literature in terms of the discernable trends within it and influences upon it. I cannot hope to include analysis of every project but rather intend indicating specific issues that seem relevant to the future development of art therapy research.

It is interesting to compare the present state of British art therapy research with that of music therapy. I was impressed by the music therapists' Fourth Annual Research Conference which I attended in 1988. During the conference Leslie Bunt described a review he had done of the *British Journal of Music Therapy*, which had demonstrated parallel developments in music therapy writing and research in Britain and America (Bunt 1984). In the review he stated that a period of descriptive and philosophical writing is characteristic of emerging professions prior to beginning research, and suggested that the predominance of descriptive writing in the *BJMT* between 1962 and 1982 indicated music therapists' readiness to embark on research (which seems to have been borne out since by their regular research conferences). A similar analysis of *Inscape* revealed only 13 research-based papers in its 20-year history and an overall emphasis on articles which explored theoretical and philosophical concerns, in contrast to the descriptive writing of the music therapists. However, recent issues under the editorship of the *Inscape* 'Group' have seen marked changes – a dramatic increase in clinical and descriptive papers with the emphasis shifting distinctly away from the rather esoteric papers to one where practice is paramount (Gilroy 1991). Accurate description and observation forms the basis of all research, so perhaps the changes in *Inscape* indicate art therapists' preparedness to follow in the footsteps of the music therapists.

The notable absence of research in the British art therapy literature overall is slightly at odds with the information in the recently compiled Directory of Art Therapy Research (Gilroy *et al*. 1989). This revealed that quite a few completed research projects, papers, theses and so on are gathering dust in libraries and on authors' bookshelves, and that a small but significant number of art therapists are engaged in research of varying kinds. The fact that not all of this work has been published is perhaps because of fears of failure and criticism, but might its very existence, together with the changes in *Inscape*, the emergence of research issues in the BAAT Newsletter (for example, Dean 1988) and the enthusiastic response to the recent Arts Therapies Research Conference (Kersner 1991) indicate that art therapists are now at least willing and becoming able to do research?

That research has little impact on psychotherapy practice is a widely recognized phenomenon, two recent commentators being Bloch (1988) and Boston (1988).

Art therapists are reputed to be similarly uninfluenced. McNiff (1986) relates this to the research not proceeding according to the profession's 'articles of faith', Edwards (1987) to healthy scepticism of the methods used and to the irrelevance of the findings to clinicians' daily experience with their patients. I wonder if this is exacerbated by art therapists simply not knowing about the little completed work there is as, first, it is not published in the most accessible place, *Inscape*, and second, because it does not always conform to the easily recognizable stereotypes of research – the measurement of dependent and independent variables, and evaluations and correlations which involve control groups and statistical analysis.

Research has many meanings. In the physical sciences research is usually empirical, laboratory based and strives for unbiased objectivity; social scientists and psychologists often employ similar research designs to examine less tangible and observable phenomena. Research in the humanities is harder to define and tends to draw on the more qualitative methods of history and aesthetic enquiry. For some, research is only the 'hard' quantitative work of experimental science, for others every patient we work with and every painting we make constitutes a piece of research. In the final analysis what it actually *is* remains uncrystallized, so much is it a matter of one's personal point of view.

Strupp (1973) differentiates between two kinds of research in psychotherapy, the *clinical* as used by psychotherapists and psychoanalysts, and the *experimental* as used by psychologists, the methodologies reflecting the temperaments and working methods of the researcher. Both approaches have their vehement critics: the conventional psychological models for reducing therapeutic relationships to specific factors which operate in a mechanistic and predetermined way (Smail 1978), the clinical approaches for their theoretical assumptions and the therapist's emotional stake in the work (Eysenck 1952). Smail says that '. . . psychological research does not proceed in a uniformly disinterested spirit of scientific inquiry' (Smail 1978: 50). Similarly, art therapy researchers pursue their personal interests, developing styles and using methodologies that suit their practice and beliefs.

Generally speaking art therapy researchers in the UK show a preference for the 'soft' historical, sociological and philosophical approaches rather than the 'hard' methods of behavioural science (for example, Henzell 1980b, Schaverien 1987, Waller 1987). Art therapists have used source material in historical and archival research (for example, Waller 1987; see also the work of M. Edwards and D. Maclagan listed in Gilroy *et al.* 1989). Surveys are popular for the exploration of different kinds of research questions relevant to the profession: for example Holtom (1977) demonstrated that art therapists were generally unsupported in their work; Liebmann (1981, 1984) showed the range of theme-centred interactions that art therapists use with differing patient populations; McNab and Edwards (1988) found that the work of the small minority of art therapists who work privately has considerable implications for the development of the profession within state services; Teasdale (1988) surveyed the working environments of registered members of BAAT; and my research has shown how art therapists' involvement with their art fluctuates through the influence of art therapy education and clinical practice (Gilroy 1989, 1992). Similar professional issues have been explored in the United States: Fryrear and Fleshman (1981) found the arts were widely used but not by workers designated as arts therapists; Cashell and

Miner (1983) discovered worrying levels of fatigue and isolation amongst arts therapists. All of these studies address research questions which are of considerable importance to art therapy in terms of its future development as a profession, both politically and clinically.

To date there is very little clinical research in the UK. What there is tends to be case work based and either evaluative or descriptive, although the mixture of phenomenology and case-study appears to be a heady one as it is producing some fascinating theoretical formulations (for example, Schaverien 1987, 1991). Sometimes the patient is actively engaged in the research process when evaluations are made either alongside or as part of the therapeutic process (for example, Dalley 1979, 1980, Waller 1981). Alternatively the therapist/researcher conducts longitudinal research, for example running a group with specific aims and objectives in mind which is carefully documented throughout and evaluated at the end (for example, Cortazzi and Gunsberg 1972, Henley 1986 in the USA); or it may be that specific sessions are organized to generate data-based hypotheses which can be explored further in a future study (for example, Bassin *et al.* 1983, also American). Follow-up and outcome studies are very few and far between (see Nowell Hall 1987 [UK] and Kramer Borchers 1985 [USA] for two quite different approaches).

Art therapists in the UK are at pains to preserve their working practices and beliefs when engaged in clinical research and rightly do not wish their research interests to impinge on their patients needs – hence, perhaps, the emphasis on descriptive studies. But coupled with a preference for philosophical, epistemological and phenomenological research models, this has led, in my view, to the language of some British art therapy research becoming too discursive and occasionally ahistorical. This can make it difficult to recognize research for what it is, purely because the design, the methodology and the explicit theoretical context are not clearly delineated. I wonder if the unwillingness to be explicit is a reaction to the severity of experimental, 'scientific' research, and the efforts to remain true to clinical practice a determination to counter the irrelevancies of so many unhelpful research projects in art and art therapy.

But despite the fact that therapeutic processes do not lend themselves happily to deterministic methodologies there are a few empirical studies which successfully address significant research questions in art therapy practice. Free and Stone Stern (1982), for example, did a laboratory-based experimental investigation of situations which facilitate creativity and found that the use of a theme had a greater positive influence than the presence of other people, findings which have implications for art therapy practice and add another element to the debate concerning theme centred/group analytic approaches with groups. Males's (1986) and Stott's (1985) research was a comparative study between skills-based art therapy and non-directive art therapy with the mentally handicapped, using evaluations of behaviour and imagery. Although they found little difference in patient improvement between the differing approaches and a non-art-based activity, the study refuted the myth that art therapy was simply a pleasant recreation. Kramer Borchers's (1985) outcome study of short-term group art therapy with the chronically mentally ill demonstrated that there were long-term gains from the group. The study had all the benefits of 'scientific rigour' that employers and medical colleagues might expect, although sadly it does not address or even describe the processes of how it happened, simply that it did! Luzzatto's evaluative pilot study (1987) of the internal world of drug abusers related their imagery to their specific problems and disturbed object relations. In all these studies the methods were those of experimental psychology, using control groups and/or statistical analysis, so it can be done. Research like this is relevant to clinical work *if* the methodology suits the research question and *if* the questions being asked, are worth asking.

On the other side of the Atlantic art therapy research is well established. The Americans have nailed their methodological colours (of the experimental kind) firmly to the mast and, I think, are suffering accordingly. Reading through the research papers in the American art therapy journals published during the 1980s was an exasperating and depressing exercise. I was struck by the sheer number of articles, one in almost every issue, yet I had the feeling that despite the immense amount of time and energy spent on research it had been to little worthwhile effect. That research is an everyday part of American art therapy practice (in principle 'a good thing') may be due to the inclusion of basic research methodology within American art therapy education. Research is viewed as an integral part of the training of art therapists in order to assist their professional survival as they conduct and become consumers of research (Dulicai *et al*. 1989, Lusebrink 1989). In Britain research skills are seen as more appropriate to advanced training once the art therapist has gained in practical knowledge and experience. This could account for much of the somewhat naive and unhelpful research that emanates from the USA, as well as the paucity of material in the UK.

The scene in America seems to have been set by the classic study of 'abnormal drawings' by Anastasi and Foley (1944), since when the majority of research has been oriented towards diagnosis and assessment through art, drawing heavily on psychological and psychiatric research conventions (for example, Tate and Allen 1985, Sidun and Rosenthal 1987, Wood Howe *et al*. 1987, Cohen *et al*. 1988). The search is for 'graphic indicators' (such as certain symbols, figure distortion, line pressure, use of colour and so on) which document and diagnose a patient's disturbance and form part of a battery of projective tests that pin-point the existence of this, that or the other problem (for example, Neisenbaum Jones 1985, Martin Manning 1987, Silver 1988). The drawings have usually been produced in a one-off, laboratory-like situation with isolated subjects given minimal materials to complete the drawing task within a specified time; these are later 'scored' by blind raters (for example, Miljkovitch and Irvine 1982, Hagood Slegelis 1987, Peek and Sawyer 1988). This kind of research is based on an assumption that findings relating to imagery produced on request in two minutes in a laboratory situation can be transferred to the artwork of someone in a continuing therapeutic relationship with an art therapist. It is as if the artificially produced artefact automatically taps the core of the issue under discussion and can magically be 'read' by a blind rater without any other kind of communication that would, within art therapy, contribute to a far richer and more accurate understanding of the image.

The questions asked in this kind of research have no relevance to art therapy as I understand it, yet seem to relate to the kinds of tasks that our American counterparts undertake. The predominance of such work in America is an interesting phenomenon, for although it may reflect the gulf between British and American art therapy practice (Woddis 1986) it is noticeable that not all of this research is by art therapists but by psychiatrists and psychologists, and that there are occasional art therapy voices calling for a move away from the wholesale application of a quantitative model (McNiff 1986, 1987, Gantt 1986). But the fact remains that the work is published by art therapy journals and so given credence by the profession, perhaps because the diagnosis of health and illness using pictures is integral to American art therapy practice and so forms part of a campaign for greater professional recognition. However, it seems to me that they are in danger of colluding not only with simplistic pathological and schematic views of art but also with the dominant research culture of the psychiatric market-place, and in the process could be giving research a bad press within the profession of art therapy. The data and results which arise from irrelevant research questions and inappropriate design suffer from the 'terminological incrustation' that Arnheim describes (1966), is very one-sided and leads to hollow findings that have no relevance to art therapy as a primary treatment, or to the nature and function of art, therapeutic relationships or psychodynamic processes.

It is interesting to note that initial attempts at art therapy research in Britain (by psychiatrists) were along similar lines, attempting to categorize and pathologize the 'art of the insane' (for example, Cunningham Dax 1953). This kind of work was satisfactorily debunked by a multi-disciplinary team of researchers, including an art therapist (Russell-Lacy *et al.* 1979), who used an experimental design to demonstrate what many art therapists have long believed, i.e. that the art of schizophrenics does not display any particular visual characteristics sufficient to warrant differential diagnosis through art. This important study has gone largely unnoticed, perhaps because the result contradicted a view of art therapy widely held by those who would appreciate the method used, yet the method was probably distasteful to those who might support the result!

I suspect that most British art therapists will agree with Smail's point, that strict, 'scientific' objectivity is neither possible nor wholly desirable in research on human subjects who are in relationships which mutually influence one another (Smail 1978). Thus, art therapists cannot and, on this side of the Atlantic, usually do not expect mechanistic psychological determinism to be helpful in research which is about therapeutic relationships rather than about visual equivalents for various psychological states. I think art therapy has to depart from research orthodoxies which limit our approach to imagery to a single aspect or which attempt to place art therapy in a hierarchy of treatments, to research processes from other allied disciplines which maintain equal methodological rigour. It seems to me that art therapists in the UK are making moves in this direction and are beginning to ask research questions which *matter*, so cautiously I will say 'so far, so good'.

The search for sympathetic methodologies

Finding the right methodology for a research question is an issue that faces every researcher. Questions regarding the outcomes of art therapy may be explored through the tools of empirical science but these do not help us understand how the processes within a therapeutic relationship enable patients to change, the problem being compounded by the fluid and elusive processes of art. What we need are research models that will enable us to explore such questions and which we, as artists and therapists, find 'user friendly'.

Criticisms of art therapy research have focused on the use of orthodox scientific models and their inappropriateness for the study of art and therapy (M. Edwards 1981, Henzell 1978, 1980a, 1985, McNiff 1986, D. Edwards 1987). There are suggestions that art therapists design entirely new methodologies more suitable to our work (Edwards 1981, Henzell 1978, 1980a), although not all authors argue against the use of empirical science in art therapy. Males, for example, believes that art therapy must prove its efficacy through scientifically based experimental research and that rigorous examination of the quality of service to patients is an issue of considerable ethical importance (Males 1979, 1980). Whilst no one would disagree with the principle, few art therapists would accept that controlled experimental designs and the 'objective study of art products' (Males 1979), would help prove art therapy's worth:

> ... it may be that the mechanical, statistical, chemical or whatever other instrument of measurement remains clumsily unable to differentiate the finer points of an evaluative analysis, rather as a scientific investigation of a painting, piece of music or theatrical performance might yield a wealth of interesting information without actually shedding any light whatsoever upon the aesthetic merits, the intrinsic worth of the subject.
>
> (Edwards 1981: 21)

However, I do not wish to consign empirical research to the dustbin completely. Empiricism does not automatically equate with experimental design but aims at rigorous objectivity. Subjecting art therapy to such enquiry might call some of our cherished beliefs into question but neglecting to do so could lead to a preciousness about our practice. Commenting on psychotherapy and research Bloch says:

> Without the art, the therapist is reduced to a mere technician, the patient to an object for manipulation. Without the science, the therapist is subject to the current fashion or bound inflexibly to his preferred belief system.
>
> (Bloch 1988: 283)

Methodological rigour in art therapy research and attempts to bring our work into line with established research *which we respect* can be balanced against models which overdetermine the research questions and the resulting data and findings. Methods which involve measurement and statistics can be used to explore certain kinds of questions that lend themselves to that model. For example, comparisons of the effectiveness of brief individual as against brief group art therapy, evaluations of reactions to various therapeutic interventions and to different approaches in groups and so on, preferably with a synthesis of quantitative and qualitative material.

Research like this has the knotty problem of how to define a 'successful' outcome; is it the removal of a symptom, certain changes in imagery, a specified degree of patient satisfaction or the therapist's perception of improvement?

Psychotherapy outcome research faces similar problems which arise from therapist variables, global ratings applied to many individuals and so on, but useful findings nevertheless occur (for example, Stiles 1980, Piper *et al.* 1984). Art therapists continually emphasize the importance of listening to the patient's interpretations and understanding of their work, so perhaps as researchers we should pay attention to the patient's assessment of a successful outcome in art therapy.

I have been interested to read how some researchers regard attempts to conduct scientific research with and on people as being old fashioned. Peter Reason argues that there has been a basic shift in approaches to human enquiry from the 'mechanistic' to the 'holistic', through the abandonment of the fragmented and alienating scientific view to the espousal of a view that involves dialogue and knowledge arising from practical experience on the part of the researcher. It is 'non-heirarchical thinking-in-action' rather than 'hierarchical cause and effect' (Reason 1988a: 11).

For me this relates to Winnicott's ideas about truth in research. Winnicott drew a distinction between 'poetic truth' and 'scientific truth'; poetic truth reaches after a whole truth 'in a flash', offering deep satisfactions and opportunities for new creative experience; it is based in feelings and therefore unlikely to be the same for everyone. Scientific truth is harnessed to a limited objective, to predictions, experiments and results; it seeks facets rather than wholes and for agreement in small areas but 'boggles at the problem of human nature' (Winnicott 1965: 173). A distinction can therefore be drawn between the kind of knowledge that is desirable vis-à-vis therapeutic processes and that which may be accessible by empirical means. The process-oriented issues with which art therapists may wish to grapple are probably to do with poetic and holistic truths rather than the scientific and mechanistic ones which employers, and so on, might require. So are there other research traditions we could call upon, and are there such things as 'poetic methodologies'?

Case-studies were Winnicott's solution:

> Psychoanalytic research is not to be cramped in to the pattern that suits research in the physical sciences. Every analyst is doing research, but the research is not planned as such because the analyst must follow the changing needs and the maturing objectives of the person undergoing analysis. This fact cannot be warped by research needs, and so the setting for an observation can never be repeated. The best is that the analyst looks back at what has happened and relates this to theory, and modifies theory accordingly.
>
> (Winnicott 1965: 174)

He goes on to write that research is 'the collective experience of analysts' (p. 175) and that to neglect research is to be: '... systematically wasting the systematic observing that is being done by every analyst who is awake while working' (ibid.: 174). It was the *cumulative* case work of Winnicott, Klein, Freud and Jung that enabled them to construct their theories of human development through what Klein described as the 'meticulous attention' (Klein 1959) to the behaviour, feelings, actions and thoughts that occurred in a session.

While I am sure that art therapists are awake while working, I doubt that our day-to-day accumulation of case material is either sufficiently detailed or systematic to constitute research. For me it is only when the material/data is placed in an explicit theoretical context and systematically described and evaluated that it can be called research. For example, one may have a feeling that a certain symbol is used recurrently by patients with a particular diagnosis; an art therapist observing this as a phenomenon has a research idea. This could become research if he or she conducted a review of the relevant literature and implemented a prescribed period of detailed observation, description and collection of material with the particular patient population, and *perhaps* a comparison with a different patient group, all from a stated theoretical position: 'To do research one must have ideas. There is a subjective initiative of a line of inquiry. Objectivity comes later through planned work, and through comparison of observations made from various angles.' (Winnicott 1948: 158). Of course at this point one has to be careful that images are not being equated with symptoms or pathology in too simplistic a manner so as to end up with exactly the kind of reductive research described earlier, but rather that the research is truly based in continuing case work and retains the voices of the patients and the uniqueness of their inner worlds, and the importance of understanding imagery within a therapeutic relationship.

This kind of case-study-based research often involves large amounts of data and many patients with similar symptoms (who invariably disappear as soon as the project begins!), perhaps with the involvement of several therapists (for example, Malan 1976). Research which relies on laboratory situations with human subjects or on assumptions that all patients in a particular diagnostic category are somehow the same often gives a false emphasis, but descriptive case-studies involve the accumulation of material which maintains the naturalism of the sessions. The patients are included in a process which is both therapeutic and research oriented through the use of diaries and personal narrative about the images, alongside the careful reporting of the therapist. If this is beginning to sound like a lengthy and complex procedure then the reader will be getting the feel of the kind of research that may be necessary in order to avoid the reductive examination of artefacts divorced from their maker and their context.

A more manageable alternative would be single case-study research. It has been suggested that single case-studies combined with evaluations from staff and self-assessments from patients could provide an efficient means of gathering information about the processes and outcomes of art therapy whilst remaining within the parameters of clinical practice (Edwards 1987). Several art therapists have designed material for use in such evaluative projects alongside standard systems for psychiatric diagnosis such as DSM-111 or the SCL-90 (see Edwards 1987, Dean 1988). The experimentally based single case-study, with an initial period of assessment and pre- and post-art therapy measurements, leads to data which is easily comparable with other case-studies and types of therapeutic intervention, although it may not be quite so philosophically amenable to art therapy practice (see Barlow and Hersen 1978).

Single case-study research has been criticized for the use of 'deadening jargon' (Henzell 1978), its proliferation and because of the problems which arise in transferring findings from the particular individual to broader issues (Males 1980). Although it is difficult to generalize from individuals it is possible to make a broad point arising from the study of a series of idiosyncratic cases, as did Oliver Sachs in

The Man Who Mistook His Wife for a Hat (1986). Recent work on the new Gold-smiths' College MA in Art Therapy has demonstrated that published case-studies on patients with the same diagnosis (for example, depressives, phobics, alcoholics) remain in single figures, so there is much work to be done. Detailed individual cases, which are neither experimentally based nor part of a larger study, can contribute to theory *per se* (e.g. Schaverien 1991), but also to the cumulative evidence on a given issue; at a later date a researcher could conduct a meta-analysis of all the published work and generate hypotheses to be explored further.

Stories and narrative are a naturalistic way of gathering material which can also be used in survey research (see Graham 1984 for a feminist perspective on story-telling in her research on experiences of motherhood). Stories need not be solely those of the patients. We could tell our own stories, for example using the techniques of participant observation where the researcher enters, observes and records a situation being sure to remain neutral throughout (see James 1984 for an account of participant observation in hospices and of the inherent difficulties in field-work research). Such descriptive and observationally based research would suit many art therapists' beliefs and practices. Descriptive material can also be collected within an empirical framework like that of the ethologists, who use detailed, non-inferential observations (for an example of an art therapist using this model see Rees 1984). 'Action research' is another method which could be useful for art therapists to document, for example an entry into an institution and the implementation of a new art therapy service. This draws on psychoanalytic concepts of institutional dynamics; good examples are the work of Maxwell Jones (1982) on the processes of institutional change, Krim's account of change in management systems (1988) and Menzies Lyth's work on children in hospital (1982).

An extension of researcher participation in the research process has come about through 'new paradigm' research (or 'experiential, participatory learning', as it now prefers to be called). I have been impressed by some of the ideas of this model and, whilst not being wholly uncritical, I think it could be an amenable method-ology for some art therapy research projects. New paradigm research prefers holistic approaches; it implies and requires the participation of the researcher and considers the experiences of all as part of a total system which integrates theory and practice. It involves people as co-researchers so that the differences between researcher and the researched upon all but disappear as everyone co-operates in a 'collaborative enquiry'. The fundamental premise of this model is that the research process is not linear, from hypothesis through to the finite result, but cyclic; it involves repeating cycles of action and reflection, experience and think-ing. It moves from the objectivity of the researcher/outsider to the 'critical sub jectivity' of the 'new paradigm' 'initiatior' (Reason and Rowan 1981, Reason 1988a).

As with every method there are pitfalls. The process is group based with the researcher relinquishing control of the research, and the group involving itself in processes which are demanding in what can be an uncontained and boundary-less situation. Reason advises new paradigm researchers to have some involvement in personal growth work, self-knowledge being necessary both for work in a research-based dialogue which uses dynamic processes, and to enable the researcher to mediate between subjective and objective responses (Reason 1988a). It is suggested that there be sessions where interpersonal and intrapsychic issues are attended to (and I would add there is a need for the initiating researcher to have considerable skills in leading experiential groups). But it seems to me that the concept of the researcher becoming nought but an 'initiating facilitator' could lead to confusion and ambiguity if some aspects of leadership are not retained, as could the emergence of transference issues if working with patients – it may be difficult to maintain a balance between containment and egalitarianism.

This model borrows from humanistic psychology and uses group processes; it welcomes the personal process of the initiating researcher and his or her co-researchers. Because of such parallels with therapeutic processes it may, as a research method, enable us to unpack some of the processes that make art therapy so effective, and is one which can involve the participants throughout. Of course it would not be possible to work in such a way with patients who are limited because of their illness, handicap or age but the 'new paradigm' model can be used in a variety of ways, from its full form where respondents/patients design and see the process through to writing up, to the partial form with co-operative evaluation at the end (for an account of GPs researching their use of holistic medicine see Reason 1988b). Despite the problems it may be that Reason is justified in arguing that for research which involves and is about people, it is sufficient for the methodology to be 'good enough':

> In human inquiry it is better to be approximately right than precisely wrong. It is also better to initiate and conduct inquiry into important questions of human conduct with a degree of acknowledged bias and imprecision, than to bog the whole thing down in attempts to be prematurely 'correct' or 'accurate'.
>
> (Reason 1988a: 229)

The possibilities for art therapy research are endless but we have yet to discover how to conduct research which will preclude a reductive consideration of the images and include our sensitivities as artists. It is as if the very concreteness of the art object, often what makes art therapy such a dramatic, lively and engaging process, somehow causes hurdles to arise. So much research attention has been paid to art objects made by patients in a manner totally divorced from the session and the individual, that in rebelling against this we may have overemphasized the intuitive approaches in treatment which are not immediately amenable to *any* kind of research methodology. But critical attention to the subjective responses of the therapist and the patient might lead to a more sensitive understanding of the role and function of imagery than has been possible hitherto. And perhaps we could also borrow a few more models, though from rather different quarters.

Shaun McNiff (1986, 1987) has said that the absence of research traditions in the arts therapies is positively helpful as it leaves us at liberty to borrow from an extensive range of allied disciplines. He advocates attention to Arnheim's collaboration with artists to produce research which 'must smell of the studio' (Arnheim 1974). Arnheim draws on close observation of the artist at work, their comments, aims and diaries and so on, and on the artist's cultural and social environment as well as the formal and aesthetic qualities of the finished piece. Arnheim says that researchers should have a direct and continuing experience of art:

> . . . that will keep the feeling of genuine artistic experience alive in his eyes, ears and hands . . . science requires not only the mastery of stringent method but an intuitive flair for the essentials and a keen anticipation of the truth to be verified. The careful application of the standard techniques of research will not in itself give a study in the psychology of art that indispensable flavour of authenticity which emanates from Delacroix's journals, Cezanne's conversations or the writings of Van Gogh, Matisse, Henry Moore, or Paul Klee.
>
> (Arnheim 1966: 18)

This is a far cry from research in art and art therapy which is either without familiarity and intimate experience of it, or which is suspicious of attempts to analyse for fear of destroying the creative or therapeutic process.

Linda Gantt (1986) refers to researchers in the fields of linguistics, anthropology and art history, and emphasizes societal and cultural factors more than psychodynamics. She describes models for understanding images based on an 'iconographical analysis', which draw on the literary and symbolic references within the artist's cultural tradition. Iconographic studies of imagery and anthropological and linguistic approaches consider cultural and stylistic 'rules' in visual traditions. Methodologies which take account of conscious choices by the artist and direct influences from the environment and people close to him or her does not necessarily equate images, either whole or in part, with symptoms and psychopathology. A focus outside the therapeutic arena, away from pathology but alongside an intimate knowledge of the patient and their art work, could inform us about other references and allusions. For example, Crosson's (1982) study of creative blocks experienced by women artists and writers is not directly concerned with art therapy but is none the less relevant to analogous art-making processes.

Whilst we are still learning to use recognized research tools, we cannot hope to conjure up new methodologies from the thin air of ignorance and inexperience, so perhaps we should set that particularly difficult task to one side for the moment. For as I have tried to show there are many issues into which art therapists can research in a balanced and productive way borrowing from a range of existing sympathetic methodologies, perhaps with the same question being explored from varying angles using different models. The methodologies may not always be poetic, but they are 'good enough' for the time being.

Research as a creative process

Lack of attention to the creative aspects of research can lead to impoverished design with frameworks that are, as described earlier, either too rigid or too loose. Bannister describes this process as ending in a polarization between 'death by chaos' from overextended, vaguely philosophizing/psychologizing studies and 'death by boredom' from piles of studies of minute irrelevancies, so we end up with 'either the vaguely significant or the specifically irrelevant' (1981: 194). He emphasizes the importance of creativity in research – the thinking, speculating, day dreaming – and of having a personal investment in the project:

> . . . you are free to choose personally relevant issues of research, to draw on and make explicit, personal experience, to enjoy the wisdom and companionship of your 'subject'.
>
> . . . you may be as soaring and as psychotic and as specific and obsessional as you wish, so that you may explore the relationship between the two. Thus research can be both an act of the imagination and a hard-nosed testing out process.

(ibid.: 199)

Creative, imaginative, even intuitive responses to research questions, tempered by logical analysis and formulation of ideas, could lead to exciting research design and findings which are helpful to our practice.

It is worth remembering that this mixture of instinct and observation, gut reaction and clear analysis is exactly the kind of process with which art therapists work in their sessions. The exploration in therapeutic work of our subjective responses and counter-transference issues, tempered by disciplined objectivity, is paralleled in the research process. The fundamental curiosity about people and their imagery which makes us tick as art therapists surely extends into the detective work of research. And perhaps most importantly, the ability to 'not know', to suspend interpretation and judgement in art therapy or while gathering and analysing data, and then to string ideas and facts together in a creative and playful way, are skills that are essential to the therapist *and* to the researcher. Thus, therapeutic practice can have an intimate influence upon research and vice versa, rather than becoming quite separate entities, as has happened in some areas of psychotherapy and psychoanalysis (Bloch 1988, Boston 1988). Therapists who engage with clinical work and research are free to adjust both settings according to the needs of the patient/respondent/co-researcher and the therapist/researcher/co-researcher (Hoskyns 1987).

But some difficulties remain when we try to understand *exactly* why things are happening and then everything gets too specific, we begin to categorize and separate and it gets edgy; the problem lies in analysing something without destroying it (as Wordsworth said, 'we murder to dissect'). Perhaps this is another source of reluctance to engage in research, the bit that involves cutting things up and pulling things apart – an uncomfortable process.

However, I think this is where art therapists can begin to use their experiences as artists and where research becomes a creative activity. Think about the process of painting: you begin and it's OK; you continue but something is not quite right; you decide to junk some of it or all of it; you tear it up, turn it upside down, perhaps destroy it and certainly make a mess; then it begins to feel better as you pull something out of it; you capitalize on the mess and finally make something new and satisfying. Marion Milner eloquently describes the anxieties that arise in making art when faced with this conflict between fragmentation and completeness and between intellectual and intuitive approaches;

> . . . (the) ineradicable conflict . . . between, on the one hand, desire for the wholeness of experience, and on the other the necessity to analyse and break

it up into bits for the sake of communicability and the growth of further wholes. And it looked as if conflict might be increased by anxieties to do with wholes and bits. Thus it might be possible to come to overvalue the intuitive approach and shrink from the effort of logical analysis. . . . I had so often felt, when a thought was first experienced in terms of a glimpsed visual picture, that to try to turn it into words would be to lose something irreparably, that its wholeness and splendour would be forever destroyed. It seemed now that I had been right in supposing something would be lost, wrong in assuming that it would be forever, wrong in not realising that the acceptance of division, analysis, bits, acceptance of the partialness which was inevitable in logical communication, was necessary for the growth of new wholes.

(Milner 1971: 125)

This is what research is like and, as with art, one has to maintain an iconoclastic attitude. Making something new and finding out something new means being able to tolerate confusion, fragmentation and chaos which, it seems to me, artists are ideally trained to do.

I equate the first stages of the research process (reviewing the literature and forming the aims and hypotheses) to the disruptive act of tearing up bits of paper, throwing them in the air and letting them fall. Creating a research design gives the whole process a frame wherein more bits and pieces (the data comprising interviews, observations and so on and the analysis of the material) can be added to the collage as it is torn up and reconstituted again and again so the whole process becomes 'as disorderly as it could be without completely falling apart' (Reason 1988b: 125). The final stages are when the fragments are beginning to settle and form new patterns, though these too remain fluid until a coherent and satisfactory gestalt is formed. There is nothing quite like poring over other people's ideas and finding that someone else has got a similar bee in their bonnet, then to watch, listen and see the research come alive in front of you during an interview or a session, and finally to sit down and play with the new juxtapositions until the collage/jigsaw eventually comes together. Unlike artistic processes the journey of the researcher has to be well mapped so others may follow and tear things up in their turn. But in the midst of careful and accurate documentation it is important to keep hold of the seemingly unconnected ruminations and associations and not let the research picture get frozen. Of course research can also be tedious and immensely time consuming but it need not become like fossilized remains that have been subjected to carbon analysis, thereafter to be carefully stored in a museum.

Research that is intrinsically interesting and entirely relevant to clinical work and to the profession can only have a positive influence and serve to enliven and improve our work as well as increase our professional recognition. Art therapists have a lot to gain from research but it has to be *our* professional and personal interests, needs and ways of working that we follow as far as possible. It is important to remember that the whole process is reflexive. As therapists and researchers we have an influence on our patients and are influenced by them; the institutions in which art therapists work, colleagues and supervisors all have expectations which influence our individual research styles. We should bear this in mind when planning our research and beware of bending too much before the prevailing winds of psychological and medical research orthodoxy.

References

Anastasi, A. and Foley, J.P. (1944) An experimental study of the drawing behavior of adult psychotics in comparison with that of a normal control group, *Journal of Experimental Psychology* 34: 169–94.

Arnheim, R. (1966) *Towards a Psychology of Art. Collected Essays*, Berkeley and Los Angeles: University of California Press.

—— (1974) *Art and Visual Perception*, Berkeley and Los Angeles: University of California Press.

Bannister, D. (1981) Personal construct theory and research method, in P. Reason and J. Rowan (eds) *Human Inquiry. A Sourcebook of New Paradigm Research*, Chichester: John Wiley.

Barlow, D.H. and Hersen, M. (1978) *Single Case Experimental Design*, NY: Pergamon Press.

Bassin, D.I., Wolfe, K.M. and Thier, A. (1983) Children's reactions to psychiatric hospitalization: drawings and story telling as a data base, *The Arts in Psychotherapy* 10: 33–44.

Bloch, S. (1988) Research in group psychotherapy, in M. Aveline and W. Dryden (eds) *Group Therapy in Britain*, Milton Keynes: Open University Press.

Boston, M. (1988) In search of a methodology for evaluating psychoanalytic psychotherapy with children, *British Journal of Child Psychotherapy* 5(1): 15–46.

Bunt, L. (1984) Research in music therapy in Great Britain: outcome research with handicapped children, *British Journal of Music Therapy* 15(3): 2–8.

Cashell, L. and Miner, A. (1983) Role conflict and role ambiguity among creative arts therapists, *The Arts in Psychotherapy* 10: 93–8.

Cohen, B.M., Hammer, J.S. and Singer, S. (1988) The diagnostic drawing series: a systematic approach to art therapy evaluation and research, *The Arts in Psychotherapy* 15: 11–21.

Cortazzi, D. and Gunsberg, H.C. (1972) The bottom of the barrel, *Inscape* 6 (Autumn): 15–25.

Crosson, C.W. (1982) Creative block: a brief inquiry, *The Arts in Psychotherapy* 9: 259–62.

Cunningham Dax, E. (1953) *Experimental Studies in Psychiatric Art*, London: Faber and Faber.

Dalley, T. (1979) Art therapy in psychiatric treatment: an illustrated case study, *The Arts in Psychotherapy* 6: 257–65.

—— (1980) Assessing the therapeutic effects of art: an illustrated case study, *The Arts in Psychotherapy* 7: 11–17.

Dean, P. (1988) Process, structure and outcome: quality assurance and assessment, *Newsletter, British Association of Art Therapists*, December: 5–7.

Dulicai, D., Hays R. and Nolan, P. (1989) Training the creative arts therapist: identity with integration, *The Arts in Psychotherapy* 16: 11–14.

Edwards, D. (1987) Evaluation in art therapy, in D. Milne (ed.) *Evaluation in Mental Health Practice*, Beckenham: Croom Helm.

Edwards, M. (1981) Art therapy now, *Inscape* 5(1): 18–21.

Eysenck, H.J. (1952) The effects of psychotherapy: an evaluation, *Journal of Consulting Psychology* 16: 319.

Free, K. and Stone Stern, L. (1982) Conditions for creativity, *The Arts in Psychotherapy* 9: 113–19.

Fryrear, J.L. and Fleshman, B. (1981) Career information on the arts in mental health, *The Arts in Psychotherapy* 8: 219–24.

Gantt, L. (1986) Systematic investigation of art works: some research models drawn from neighbouring fields, *American Journal of Art Therapy* **24**(4): 111–18.

Gilroy, A. (1989) On occasionally being able to paint, *Inscape*, Spring: 2–9.

—— (1991) *Changes in Inscape 1969–1991*, in press.

—— (1992) Art therapists and their art. Unpublished DPhil. thesis, University of Sussex.

—— Hoskyns, S., Jenkyns, M., Lee, C. and Payne H. (1989) *Proceedings of the First Arts Therapies Research Conference*, City University, London.

Graham, H. (1984) Surveying through stories, in C. Bell and H. Roberts (eds) *Social Researching. Politics, Problems, Practice*, London: Routledge and Kegan Paul.

Greenwood, H. and Layton, G. (1987) An out patient art therapy group, *Inscape*, Summer: 12–19.

Hagood Slegelis, M. (1987) A study of Jung's mandala and its relationship to art psycho-therapy, *The Arts in Psychotherapy* **14**: 301–11.

Henley, D. (1986) Emotional handicaps in low-functioning children: art education/art therapeutic interventions, *The Arts in Psychotherapy* **13**: 35–44.

Henzell, J. (1978) Art and therapy, *Inscape* **2**(2): 3–11.

—— (1980a) Ambiguity, art and symptoms, *Inscape* **5**(1): 21–6.

—— (1980b) Image making and the mentally ill: a critical examination of the theories and models underlying its study and uses, unpublished MPhil. thesis, Birmingham Poly-technic, School of Art Education.

—— (1985) The patient and Dr Procrustes, unpublished paper presented at 'An International Review of the Arts in Therapy', Conference held at Goldsmiths' College, University of London.

Heron, J. (1981) Philosophical basis for a new paradigm, in P. Reason and J. Rowan (eds) *Human Inquiry. A Sourcebook of New Paradigm Research*, Chichester: John Wiley.

—— (1988) Validity in co-operative inquiry, in P. Reason (ed.) *Human Inquiry in Action*, London: Sage Publications.

Holtom, R. (1977) Measuring change attributable to art therapy, *Inscape* **1**(17): 3–10.

Hoskyns, S.L. (1987) Productive and counterproductive issues for therapist and researcher, Proceedings of the Third Music Therapy Research Day Conference, City University, London.

James, N. (1984) A postscript to nursing, in C. Bell and H. Roberts (eds) *Social Researching. Politics, Problems, Practice*, London: Routledge and Kegan Paul.

Kersner, M. (1991) The art of research, Conference Proceedings of the Second Art Therapies Research Conference, City University, April 1990.

Klein, M. (1959/1988) Our adult world and its roots in infancy, in M. Klein *Envy and Gratitude, 1946–1963*, London: Virago.

Kramer Borchers, K. (1985) Do gains made in group art therapy persist?, *American Journal of Art Therapy* **23**: 89–91.

Krim, R. (1988) Managing to learn: action inquiry in City Hall, in P. Reason (ed.) *Human Inquiry in Action*, London: Sage Publications.

Liebmann, M. (1981) The many purposes of art therapy, *Inscape* **5**(1): 26–8.

—— (1984) Art games and group structures, in T. Dalley (ed.) *Art as Therapy*, London: Tavistock.

Lusebrink, V.B. (1989) Education in creative arts therapies: accomplishments and chal-lenges, *The Arts in Psychotherapy* **16**(1): 5–10.

Luzzatto, P. (1987) The internal world of drug abusers. Projective pictures of self–object relationships. A pilot study, *British Journal of Projective Psychology* **32**(2): 22–33.

McNab, D. and Edwards, D. (1988) Private art therapy, *Inscape*, Summer: 14–19.

McNiff, S. (1986) Freedom of research and artistic inquiry, *The Arts in Psychotherapy* **13**: 279–84.

—— (1987) Research and scholarship in the creative arts therapies, *The Arts in Psychotherapy* **14**: 285–92.

Malan, D.H. (1976) *Toward the Validation of Dynamic Psychotherapy*, London: Plenum Press.

Males, J. (1979) Is it right to carry out scientific research into art therapy?, *Therapy* **3** May: 5.

—— (1980) Art therapy: investigations and implications, *Inscape* **4**(2): 13–15.

—— (1986) Art therapy as an approach to change in mental handicap, Ph.D. thesis, University of Surrey.

Martin Manning, T. (1987) Aggression depicted in abused children's drawings, *The Arts in Psychotherapy* **14**: 15–24.

Jones, M. (1982) *The Process of Change*, Boston: Routledge and Kegan Paul.

Menzies Lyth, I. (1982) The psychological welfare of children making long stays in hospital, Tavistock Institute of Human Relations Occasional Paper No. 3.

Miljkovitch, M. and Irvine, G.M. (1982) Comparison of drawing performances of schizophrenics, other psychiatric patients, and normal schoolchildren on a draw-a-village task, *The Arts in Psychotherapy* **9**: 203–16.

Milner, M. (1971) *On Not Being Able to Paint*, London: Heinemann.

Neisenbaum Jones, R.M. (1985) Comparative study of the kinetic family drawing and the animal kinetic family drawing in regard to self-concept assessment in children of divorced and intact families, *The Arts in Psychotherapy* **12**: 187–96.

Nowell Hall, P. (1987) Art therapy: a way of healing the split, in T. Dalley *et al. Images of Art Therapy. New developments in Theory and Practice*, London: Tavistock.

Peek, L. and Sawyer, J.P. (1988) Utilization of the Family Drawing Depression Scale with pain patients, *The Arts in Psychotherapy* **15**: 207–10.

Piper, W.E., Debbane, E.G., Bienvenue, J.P. and Garant, J. (1984) A comparative study of four forms of psychotherapy, *Journal of Counselling and Clinical Psychology* **52**(2): 268–79.

Reason, P. (ed.) (1988a) *Human Inquiry in Action*, London: Sage Publications.

—— (ed.) (1988b) Whole person medical practice, in P. Reason (ed.) *Human Inquiry in Action*, London: Sage Publications.

—— and Rowan, J. (eds) (1981) *Human Inquiry. A Sourcebook of New Paradigm Research*, Chichester: John Wiley.

Rees, M. (1984) Ethological constructs of territoriality and dominance, and their implications for the practice of art therapy with institutionalized mentally handicapped patients, Conference Proceedings of 'Art Therapy as Psychotherapy in Relation to the Mentally Handicapped', Hertfordshire College of Art and Design.

Russell-Lacy, S., Robinson, V., Benson, J. and Cranage, J. (1979) An experimental study of pictures produced by acute schizophrenics subjects, *British Journal of Psychiatry* **134**: 195–200.

Sachs, O. (1986) *The Man Who Mistook His Wife for a Hat*, London: Pan Books.

Schaverien, J. (1987) The scapegoat and the talisman: transference in art therapy, in T. Dalley *et al. Images of Art Therapy*, London: Tavistock.

—— (1991) *The Revealing Image*, London: Routledge.

Sidun, N.M. and Rosenthal, R.H. (1987) Graphic indicators of sexual abuse in draw-a-person tests of psychiatrically hospitalized adolescents, *The Arts in Psychotherapy* **14**: 25–33.

Silver, R. (1988) Screening children and adolescents for depression through draw-a-story, *American Journal of Art Therapy* **26**: 119–24.

Smail, D. (1978) *Psychotherapy. A Personal Approach*, London: J.M. Dent.

Stiles, W.B. (1980) Measurement of the impact of psychotherapy sessions, *Journal of Counselling and Clinical Psychology* **48**: 176–85.

Stott, J. (1985) An examination of methods used in art therapy with mentally handicapped adults, unpublished paper presented at 'An International Review of the Arts in Therapy' Conference, held at Goldsmiths' College, University of London.

Strupp, H. (1973) *Psychotherapy: Clinical, Research and Theoretical Issues*, NY: Jason Aronson.

Tate, E.B. and Allen, H. (1985) Colour preferences and the aged individual: implications for art therapy, *The Arts in Psychotherapy* **12**: 165–9.

Teasdale, C. (1988) *Conditions of service of art therapists*, London: MSF.

Waller, D. (1981) Art therapy and eating disorders, Proceedings of the 8th World Congress of Social Psychiatry, Zagreb.

—— (1987) Art therapy in adolescence: a metaphorical view of a profession in progress, in T. Dalley *et al. Images of Art Therapy*, London: Tavistock.

Winnicott, D.W. (1948/1975) Paediatrics and Psychiatry in D.W. Winnicott *Through Paediatrics to Psychoanalysis*, London: Hogarth Press.

—— (1965/1986) The price of disregarding psychoanalytic research, in D.W. Winnicott *Home is Where We Start From*, Harmondsworth: Penguin.

Woddis, J. (1986) Judging by appearances, *The Arts in Psychotherapy* **13**: 147–9.

Wood Howe, J., Burgess, A.W. and McCormack, A. (1987) Adolescent runaways and their drawings, *The Arts in Psychotherapy* **14**: 35–40.

Name index

Adamson, E., 17, 75-6, 81, 213
Adelman, E., 176, 178, 180
Albert-Puleo, N., 174-5, 179-80, 181, 183
Alfred (case study), 115-23
Allen, H., 234
Allen, P.B., 176, 180
Anastasi, A., 234
Ann (case study), 199-205
Arguile, Roger, 15, 36
Arnheim, R., 113, 114, 235, 240-1
Audergon, A., 194
Audergon, J.C., 194

Bannister, D., 241-2
Barlow, D.H., 238
Baron, C., 49
Bassin, D.I., 233
Bateson, G., 191
Ben (alcoholism case study), 183-6
Ben (Asperger's syndrome case study), 150-2
Ben-David, J., 219
Bentovim, A., 128
Bettelheim, Bruno, 82
Bick, E., 14
Bion, W., 14
Birren, J., 92
Birtchnell, J., 212, 217
Bloch, S., 231, 236, 242
Boston, M., 231, 242
Bowlby, J., 112-13, 114, 175
Boyadzhiev, V., 49, 51
Bridget (case study), 148
Briggs, Dennis, 54
Bunt, Leslie, 231
Burgess, C., 38
Bryne, Peter, 212, 214, 222

Cane, Florence, 6

Case, C., 15, 141, 142
Casement, Patrick, 85-6
Cashell, L., 232-3
Castricone, L., 176, 178, 180
Catala, Joaquim, 106
Champernowne, Gilbert, 54
Champernowne, Irene, 10-11, 39, 54, 81, 213, 224
Charlton, S., 76-7
Chernin, K., 155-6
Cizek, Franz, 6, 140
Cohen, B.M., 234
Cohen, D., 88
Cole, P., 49, 58-9, 60
Collins, R., 219
Corcoran, A.L., 109, 118
Cortazzi, D., 233
Crisp, A., 158
Crosson, C.W., 241
Cunningham Dax, E., 235

Dalal, F., 12
Dalley, T., 6, 15, 76, 141, 143, 233
Dana, M., 157, 165-6
Davis, Robin, 18
Dean, P., 231, 238
Donnellan, B., 181
Donnelly, M.J., 28, 78, 132, 211
Donnenberg, D., 179, 180, 181
Driscoll, Coral, 107
Dubowski, J., 110-11, 112, 117, 122, 141
Dulicai, D., 234
Dyne, D., 218, 221-2

Edwards, D., 232, 236, 238
Edwards, Michael, 12, 49, 51-2, 214, 232, 236
Ehrenzweig, Anton, 215
Eichenbaum, Louise, 160

Eissler, R.S., 94
Elliott, Lea, 214
Epting, F.G., 197, 198
Erikson, E., 92
Esser, A.M., 111
Evans, John, 214
Eysenck, H.J., 232

Flavell, J., 220
Fleshman, B., 232
Foley, J.P., 234
Foulke, W.E., 177, 179
Free, K., 233
Freud, Anna, 14
Freud, Sigmund, 10, 12, 175, 237
Freund, H., 182, 183, 186
Fryrear, J.L., 232
Fuller, P., 17

Gantt, Linda, 235, 241
Gardner, Howard, 109, 110
Gheorghieva, Z., 49, 51
Gibbs, Evelyn, 215
Gilhooley, M., 94
Gilroy, A.J., 217, 222, 225, 229-32
Goffman, E., 88
Goldberg, D., 16
Goodall, 143
Goodbread, J., 202
Goodson, I., 222
Gould, S.J., 12
Graham, H., 239
Greenwood, H., 20, 78
Gunsberg, H.C., 233
Gustafson, J.P., 20, 191
Guttman, H., 129

Hagood Slegelis, M., 234
Hales, R.E., 191
Hamer, N., 49
Hammans, S., 106
Harlan, Jane, 91
Harris, M., 14
Harrison, C., 91
Head, V.B., 173
Henley, D., 233
Henzell, John, 50, 51, 217, 232, 236, 238
Hicks, H., 132
Hill, Adrian, 10, 17, 213, 219
Hinde, R., 110
Holden, U., 94
Holtom, Robin, 81-2, 232
Hoskyns, S.L., 242
Hughes, Rose, 107-8

Ingleby, D., 215
Irvine, G.M., 234

Jacques, A., 92
James, K., 50, 212, 216, 217

James, N., 239
Jan (case study), 168-71
Jenkins, H., 132
John (case study), 150
Jones, Maxwell, 54, 55, 56-8, 60, 88, 239
Jung, C.G., 11-12, 77, 92, 237

Kandinsky, Wassily, 140
Kaufman, G.H., 173
Keller, T.W., 177, 179
Kellog, Rhodda, 108, 110
Kelly, G.A., 189, 197-8
Kennedy, Katherine, 82
Kersner, M., 231
Klein, J., 188
Klein, Melanie, 13-14, 15, 237
Knauss, W., 182, 183, 186
Korer, J., 87
Kramer, Edith, 9, 10, 11
Kramer Borchers, K., 233
Krim, R., 239
Kwiatkowska, Hanna, 128-9, 131

Laing, Joyce, 10, 54-5
Laing, R.D., 88
Lambert Brittain, W., 108-9, 110
Landgarten, H., 128
Langer, S., 112
Lawrence, M., 156, 157
Layton, G., 20, 78
Levens, M., 20, 158
Lewis, S., 78
Liberman, A., 84
Liebmann, M., 19, 30, 178-9, 180, 232
Lipsedge, M., 12
Lishman, H., 128
Littlewood, R., 12
Lowenfeld, V., 108-9, 110, 140
Lusebrink, V.B., 234
Luzzatto, P., 175, 179, 181, 191, 234
Lyddiatt, E.M., 11, 76, 81

McClelland, Sheila, 21, 30
Maclagan, David, 8-9, 18, 19, 49, 53, 61, 224, 232
McNab, D., 232
McNeilly, G., 18-20, 30
McNiff, S., 232, 235, 236, 240
Madge, C., 219-20
Mahony, N., 55
Malan, D.H., 238
Males, B., 106-7, 107
Males, J., 229, 233, 236, 238
Martin Manning, T., 234
Martindale, Brian, 94
Matthews, J., 109, 110, 140-1
Meltzer, D., 14
Menzies, I.E.P., 49
Menzies Lyth, I., 239
Midgley, M., 114

Miljkovitch, M., 234
Miller, Alice, 165
Miller, B., 31, 93
Milner, Marion, 14, 17, 39, 242-3
Mindell, Arnold, 195-200 *passim*
Miner, A., 232-3
Minuchin, S., 128
Molloy, T., 49, 52, 77-8, 87-8
Moore, R.W., 173, 177, 181, 182
Morris, Desmond, 111
Moss, L., 39
Mottram, Pauline, 82
Muller, E., 132
Murphy, J., 158
Murray Parkes, C., 91

Naumburg, Margaret, 6, 7-9, 10, 11
Neisenbaum Jones, R.M., 234
Nowell Hall, Patricia, 11, 53, 233

Orbach, Susie, 160
Osler, I., 91
Ovretveit, 46-7

Pateman, T., 218
Peek, L., 234
Petrie, Marie, 10, 212, 213
Pickford, Ralph, 10, 140
Piper, W.E., 237
Pitt, B., 94
Pomryn, B.A., 57
Prinzhorn, H., 75

Rabiger, S., 142-3
Rack, P., 12
Rapoport, R.N., 55, 57, 60, 62
Ravenette, A.T., 190, 197
Reason, Peter, 237, 239-40, 243
Rebecca (case study), 148
Rees, Mair, 111-12, 117, 122, 239
Richardson, Marion, 6, 140
Robbins, A., 175, 178, 180
Robert (case study), 148-50
Robinson, M., 54
Rosenber, H., 114
Rosenthal, R.H., 234
Ross, Kubler, 93
Rowan, J., 239
Rubin, J.A., 12
Russell-Lacy, S., 235
Ruth (case study), 85-8
Rycroft, C., 113-14
Ryle, Anthony, 191

Sachs, Oliver, 238-9
Sagar, C., 142
Sawyer, J.P., 234
Schaverien, J., 5-6, 18, 30, 49, 52-3, 159, 202, 232, 233
Schwartz, M., 49, 50
Segal, Hannah, 14

Sherr, C., 132
Sidun, N.M., 234
Silman, R., 218
Silver, R., 234
Simon, Rita, 17, 91
Skaife, S., 19
Smail, D., 232, 235
Spotnitz, H., 174
Stanton, A., 49, 50
Stephen, I.B., 54
Stevens, A., 54
Stiles, W.B., 237
Stokes, A., 17
Stone Stern, L., 233
Stott, J., 106-7, 108, 233
Strand, Sue, 20, 107
Strupp, H., 232
Swainson, C., 19, 78

Tate, E.B., 234
Teasdale, C., 28, 31, 42, 232
Terry (case study), 153
Thomson, Martina, 75, 76
Thornton, 20
Tomkins, S.S., 114
Tomlinson, R., 6
Toon, P., 181, 183
Trewin, Les, 107

Ulman, E., 7
Ursano, A.J., 191

Vasarhelyi, V., 141-2
Viola, Wilhelm, 6, 140
Virshup, B., 174-5
Virshup, E., 174-5, 177, 178, 183
Von Bertalanffy, L., 126
von Zweigbergk, Britta, 82

Wadeson, H., 128, 129-30
Wald, J., 91
Waller, Diane, 9, 11-13, 17, 20, 27, 29, 36, 39, 49, 51, 158-9, 212, 216, 217, 221, 230, 232, 233
Watkins, Mary, 77
Watzlawick, P., 191
Weinberger, B., 219-20
Weir, F., 14, 15, 30
Wendy (case study), 79-80
Whiteley, J. Stuart, 55, 57, 60
Wilks, Roger, 99-100, 101-2
Winnicott, D.W., 14, 16-17, 98, 107-8, 140, 175, 178, 183, 186, 237-8
Woddis, J., 235
Wood, Christine, 80, 217
Wood Howe, J., 234
Woodman, M., 159
Woods, R.J., 94
Worden, J.W., 91

Yalom, I.D., 20, 191

Subject index

'abnormal drawings', 234
accountability, 26, 45–7
'action representation', 110
action research, 239
'activity-based' treatment, 6
acute patients (first-admission), 31
acute states, *see* brief therapy (process-oriented
    approach)
addiction (substance abuse), 173–87, 215
adolescents, *see* children and adolescents
Advanced Diploma in Education, 213
'aesthetic gloss', 8
after-care services, 88
Age Exchange, 92
ageing population, 103
agrophobia, 183–7
alcohol/drug abuse
    case study, 183–7
    conclusion, 187
    counter-transference, 180–3
    discussion, 180
    introduction, 173
    theoretical perspectives, 173–7
    theory-practice relationship, 177–9
Alcohol Education Group, 179
Alcoholics Anonymous, 176
Alfred (case study), 115–23
'altered state', 190
Alzheimer's disease, 94, 99, 103
American Journal of Art Therapy, 7
animals (in case study), 200–1, 205
Ann (case study), 199–205
anorexia nervosa, 156, 158–9, 160
anti-psychiatry movement, 214
appraising processes, 112–13
art-making processes, 145
art as a channel, 195–6
art framework, 144–5

Art as Healing (Adamson), 75–6
art object, 7, 9–11, 107, 145, 155, 183
    intermediary preconscious messenger, 162–
        3
    means of reaching 'gut', 163–4
    as mirror, 165–6
    role, 100, 161–2
    as tool for enactment, 165
art process
    arena for transitional space, 164
    contained space, 166
    metaphorical way of perceiving, 167–8
Art Psychotherapy (Wadeson), 129–30
Art and Regeneration (Petrie), 10, 212
art students (socialization), 219–22
Art Students Observed (Madge and Weinberger),
    219–20
Art Teacher's Certificate, 221
Art Teacher's Diploma, 214, 215, 217
art therapist
    artwork and relationship, 83–5
    current definition, 4–5
    principles of professional practice, 42–3
    professional responsibilites, 44–7
    professional support, 43–4
    registered, 26, 28, 31, 33, 42
    response (to counter-transference), 180–3
    role (with children), 144–5
    therapist's process, 196–7
    transference relationship, 5–6
art therapy
    children and adolescents, 140–53
    chronic long-term patients, 73–89
    as container, 142
    elderly in statutory care, 90–103
    families, 125–38
    literature review, 158–9
    organizational context, 49–69

art therapy (*continued*)
  psychodynamic model and, 159–61
  research, 110–12
  treatment of substance abuse, 173–87
  treatment of women with eating disorders,
    155–71
Art Therapy: A Way of Healing the Split (Hall), 11
art therapy (new problems/solutions)
  child abuse, 37–9
  conclusion, 40–1
  in education, 35–7
  hospital art and, 39–40
  introduction, 25–7
  in NHS, 27–31
  principles of professional practice, 42–3
  professional responsibilites, 44–7
  professional support, 43–4
  social and community services, 32–5
  transfer to community care, 31–2, 42
art therapy (theoretical perspective), 3
  art therapist defined, 4–5
  British developments, 10–13
  child in, 13–17
  group work, 17–20
  historical perspectives, 6–7
  Naumberg and Kramer, 7–9
  in 1990s, 20–1
  transference in, 5–6
Art Therapy Advisor, 29
art therapy group, 59, 61–7
art therapy process, 143–6
Art Workshop (at Henderson), 57–61
'artist body', 195, 196
Artist in his Studio, The (Liberman), 84
Arts Therapies Research Conference, 231
artwork, relationship and, 83–5
Asperger's syndrome, 150–1
assignments, 177–9
Association of Professional Music Therapists,
    33
attachment, loss, and, 112
Attenborough Report (1985), 39
authority, 45–6, 218
autonomous functioning, 91
autonomy, 27, 47, 109, 143

Barlinnie Prison, 54–5
basic response, 112, 117
basic scribbles, 108, 110
belief systems (edges), 192–4, 196–7, 198,
    203–4, 206
Belmont Hospital, 56, 57, 60, 64–5, 67, 68–9
Belmont Workhouse for Men, 56
Ben (alcoholism case study), 183–6
Ben (Asperger's syndrome case study), 150–2
bereavement, 91–2, 93, 95, 97
Bexley Hospital, 82
Birmingham Polytechnic, 212
Birmingham School of Art Education, 214, 217
'blank access', 195

Board of Guardians, 56
bodily meaning, 155–6
boundaries, 142–4, 200, 203
Bridget (case study), 148
brief therapy, 20, 30, 34, 179, 236
brief therapy (process-oriented approach)
  art as channel, 195–6
  case study, 199–205
  conclusion, 205–6
  introduction, 189–91
  theoretical context, 191–3
  therapist's process, 196–7
  therapy process, 193–5
  working briefly, 197–9
Bristol Art Therapy Group, 20
British Association of Art Therapists (BAAT),
    4, 7, 74
  Inscape, 10, 12, 20, 107, 212, 216, 231, 232
  principles of professional practice, 26, 42–3,
    44
  problems/solutions, 25–6, 28–30, 32, 33, 38,
    40–1, 43
  professional responsibility, 26, 44–7
  training policy, 211–17, 221–3, 225–6
British Journal of Music Therapy, 231
Bulgaria study, 51
bulimia nervosa, 156–7, 160
  case study, 168–71

Cardiac Neurosis, 56
career structure, 26–7, 32, 36, 39
case loads, 43
case studies, 233, 238–9
  children and adolescents, 148–53
  chronic long-term patients, 79–80, 85–8
  elderly residents, 99–103
  family art therapy, 128–34
  Henderson Hospital, 57–69
  mentally handicapped clients, 115–23
  process-oriented approach, 199, 205
  substance abuse, 183–7
  women with eating disorders, 168–71
case work, 233
  with children/adolescents, 146–53
cerebral arteriosclerosis, 94
Certificate in Remedial Art, 214
changes, family therapy and, 126, 127
channel (process information), 193, 194–8,
    200–2, 206
chaotic processes, 196–7
Chicago School for Autistic Children, 82
child-centred approach, 6, 35, 37
child abuse, 27, 37–9, 142
child art, 140, 215
children
  in art therapy, 13–17
  drawings, 107, 108–10
  in family therapy, 125–38
children and adolescents
  art therapy process, 143–6

case work, 146–53
  introduction, 140
  theoretical context, 140–3
choice, 142, 143
chronic long-term mental patients
  approach of art therapy, 75–8
  basic principles, 79–88
  conclusion, 88–9
  introduction, 73–5
circular causality, 126
classroom art, 145–6
clay modelling, 201–2
client-centred approach, 30
client's home (work in), 83
'clinging', 175
clinical research, 232–3
clinical responsibility, 45
closed group, 107, 191
co-counselling, 168
co-ordinating (leadership role), 46
co-researchers, 239, 242
Code of Practice, 88
codes, symbols and, 145, 150
colours, 109, 116–21 *passim*, 195–6
communication, 189
  channel, 193, 194–8, 200–2, 206
  child, 148, 150–1
  emotional expression and, 112–15
  family, 126–7, 133
Community Art Therapy teams, 33
community care, 20, 26, 31–3, 42
Community as Doctor (Rapoport), 57
community services, 25, 32–5, 88
Community Services Sub-committee (of
  BAAT), 32, 33
Complex Secret of Brief Psychotherapy, The
  (Gustafson), 191
compulsive eating, 157
concept model (addiction), 176–7, 181
Conditions of Service of Registered Art Therapists
  (1989), 32, 33
confidentiality, 26, 42, 80, 168
conflict, 7, 10, 190, 219
  ideology, 49–50, 59–61, 67–8
confrontative techniques, 177, 178, 180, 181,
  186
confusion (in elderly people), 98–9
conscious, 113, 192
  control and, 166, 190
  unconscious links, 10, 11–12, 15, 17, 98
consecutive themes (family therapy), 132–3,
  134
contained space, 142, 143, 166, 169
contemporary practice (examples), 76–8
context
  family as, 126
  see also organizational context
contextual background (training), 212
continuous care register, 87–8
control, 168, 190

contained space, 142, 143, 166, 169
  lack of (addiction), 173
core course, 212, 216, 223
core problems (family), 132
Council for National Academic Awards, 217,
  222
Council for Professions Supplementary to Medicine, 5, 26, 222–3, 226
counter-transference, 6, 13, 15, 20–1, 64,
  94
  substance abuse, 174, 182, 183–7
'Countercourse', 218
couples, 129–30
Creative Therapist (at Henderson), 57, 59, 61
creativity, 11–12, 17, 52–3, 54
creativity cycle, 189, 192, 197–9, 206
cross-cultural issues, 12–13, 16, 51
cultural experience, location of, 16–17
culture/transculture, 12–13
culture of institutions, 50–1
curative transference, 174
current position, 20–1
cycle of action, 189, 192, 197–9, 205, 239

day units, 32
Daytop programme, 173
De la Pole Hospital, 82
death, 91–2, 93, 95, 97
defence-detouring, 131–2
Department of Health, 4, 27, 29, 211, 212,
  217, 218, 226
dependency
  elderly in statutory care, 90, 94–5, 100–1,
  103
  long-term patients, 74, 78
  see also alcohol/drug abuse
depression (case study), 183–7
descriptive studies, 233, 239
deterioration (senile dementia), 94
development stage (drawings reflect), 107, 108–
  10
DHSS, 4, 25, 37–8, 44, 61, 230
didactic model, 176–7, 179, 180
Diploma in Art and Design, 220
Diploma in Art Therapy, 215–18, 222, 226
directive approaches, 19–20, 106–7, 158
Directory of Art Therapy Research, 231
disease model, 176
dominance, 111
doodles (Ann's case study), 200
double-signals, 193
drawings (and development), 107, 108–10
dreams, 11, 161, 201
drug abuse, 215, 234
  see also alcohol/drug abuse
DSM-111 system, 238
dual accountability, 46–7
dynamic approach, 6, 7
dysphasia, 94
dyspraxia, 94

eating disorders (women with)
anorexia nervosa, 156
art object, 161–4, 165–6
art process, 164, 166–8
bulimia nervosa, 156–7
case study, 168–71
compulsive eating, 157
conclusion, 171
introduction, 155–6
psychodynamic model, 159–61
review of literature, 158–9
edges (belief systems), 192–4, 196–7, 198,
203–4, 206
education, 26, 35–7
Education Acts (1981, 1988), 35
Effort Syndrome, 56
ego development, 13, 15, 16, 108, 174
elderly people (in statutory care)
case studies, 99–103
conclusion, 103
death, 93
introduction, 90–1
loss, 91–2
psychogeriatric ward, 98–9
reassessment of past life, 92–3
senile dementia, 93–4
therapeutic relationship, 94–8
emotional expression, painting and, 112–15
emotions, *see* counter-transference; transference
empiricism, 236
enactment (art object as tool), 165
ethnic origin/background, 12–13
ethological techniques, 110, 111, 112
European Community, 40–1, 212, 226–7
exhibitions, 42–3
experiencing, intermediate area of, 16, 17, 107
experiential learning, 239–40
experimental research, 232
expression in childhood, 140, 141
Expressive Arts Model, 178

'facilitating environment', 107
families, art therapy with
case study, 134–8
conclusion, 138
family art therapy, 128–34
introduction, 125
theoretical context, 125–8
family art diagnosis, 131
family art evaluation, 131
family drawing, 132
family networks, 73–4, 95
family therapy, 20
fantasy, 14–15, 144, 145, 153
potential space, 16–17, 107, 140, 150
Fat is a Feminist Issue (Orbach), 160
father-daughter relationships, 168–9, 171, 199
feedback, 126–7, 194, 196, 198, 202
feelings
emotional expression, 112–15

see also counter-transference; transference
fees (training), 225–6
feminism, 155, 160, 239
fine art ideology, 217–18, 220, 221, 222, 225
finger painting, 175, 195–6
first meetings, 79–81
fixation stage, 174–5
Forgotten Millions (Cohen), 88
Fourth Annual Research Conference, 231
free association, 7–8, 96, 161
free expression, 7, 221
freedom, boundaries and, 144
Freudian analysis, 7–8, 9, 13, 14, 50, 174
friends (network), 73–4, 95
frustration (at loss of physical abilities), 95–6
full management (leadership role), 46

GCSE, 36, 37
General Systems Theory, 126–8, 132–3
generational-levelling, 131–2
genograms, 132
genuineness, 129–30
Goldsmiths' College, 147, 212, 215–17, 220,
223, 226, 239
'good enough' mothering, 16, 123
graphic indicators, 234
grief, 91–2, 95, 97
Griffiths Report (1988), 32–3, 42
group analysis, 30, 107, 182, 233
Group Analysis (journal), 20
group dynamics, 177, 178
group work, 17–20, 85, 146
closed, 107, 191
at Henderson, 59, 61–7
open, 61–2, 76, 107, 179, 191, 221
guilt (felt by carer/therapist), 94–5
'gut feeling', 163–4
Guy's Hospital, 191

Healing Arts movement, 27
health-care arts, 39
Health and Safety Act, 43
Henderson Hospital, 49–50
art and art therapy at, 57–61
history of, 55–7, 68–9
phenomena relating to context, 64–7
practice, 61–4
heroin addicts, 178
Hertfordshire College of Art, 212, 214–17,
222, 226
hidden agenda, 51
historical perspectives, 6–7
holistic approach, 141, 239
hospital arts, 39–40

iconic expression, 141
iconographical studies, 241
ideology, 215
conflict, 49–50, 59–61, 67–8
fine art, 217–19, 220, 221, 222, 225

images
    eating disorders, 161–2, 166
    family art therapy, 136–8
    group work, 19–20
    – making, 3, 5, 7–9, 12, 39
imagination, 80
immediacy, 129, 130
individuality, 96, 141
Industrial Neurosis Unit, 57, 58
industrialization, 220–1
information processing, 193–8, 200–2, 206
innovation, 219, 225
Inscape, 10, 12, 20, 107, 212, 216, 231–2
instinct theory, 185
Institute for Group Analysis, 18
institution as metaphor, 50–1
institutional context, 52–5
institutionalization, 76, 88, 105
integrative aspects of art, 10, 11, 179, 180
intermediary preconscious messenger, 162–3
intermediate area of experiencing, 16, 17, 107
internal world, 13–17
International Journal of Therapeutic Communities,
    181
interpretations, 16, 76, 145
intervention, 3, 178–9, 181, 206
    as art process, 147–8
    categories, 194–5
    directive approach, 19–20, 106–7, 158
    non-directive approach, 6, 19–20, 21, 106,
        158, 233
isolation (of addiction), 178

Jan (case study), 168–71
John (case study), 150
Jungian model, 12, 54

key worker role, 34, 224
Korner statistics, 29

Labour, Ministry of, 56, 57, 60
language
    of art, 8, 145, 148
    children's use, 140, 141, 145
    of medicine, 218
    symbolic, 140, 142, 145
    of therapy, 219, 224
    verbal psychotherapy, 8, 49, 62, 67, 98
'languaging' system, 189, 197
leader-centred group work, 19
learning difficulties, severe, *see* mental handi-
    cap (severe learning difficulties)
'leavers' at Henderson, 62, 63
Leavesden Hospital, 106, 107
legal position, general, 44–5
Leybourne Grange, 107
Leytonstone House, 105, 106
life review process, 92–3, 96
line management, 27, 29
linear causality, 126

linguistic expression, 141
Lobby Art Therapy Programme, 178
Local Government Act (1929), 56
Local Government Board, 25
location of cultural experience, 16, 17
London Centre for Psychotherapy, 18
London County Council, 56
London Institute of Education, 213
loneliness, death and, 93
long-term patients, 20
    see also chronic long-term mental patients
longitudinal research, 233
loss, 112
    bereavement, 91–2, 93, 95, 97

Man and His Symbols (Jung), 11
Man Who Mistook His Wife for a Hat, The (Sachs),
    238–9
management, 27, 29, 43
Manchester Hospital, 82
mark-making (scribbling), 106, 108–9, 141
    case study, 115–23
    emotional expression, 112–15
    pre-representational stage, 110–11
Maudsley Hospital, 56, 214
me/not-me, 191, 192–4, 196, 197
meaning/meaning system, 141, 198
medical audit, 26–7
medical model, 9, 34, 222
medical responsibilities, 45
memory loss, 93–4, 97
men
    father-daughter relationships, 168–9, 171,
        199
    patriarchical society, 155, 160
mental handicap (severe learning difficulties),
    142
    art therapy research, 110–12
    case study, 115–23
    children's drawings, 108–10
    emotional expression, 112–15
    introduction, 105–6
    severely disabled clients, 106–8
Mental Health Acts, 44, 88
mental patients, *see* chronic long-term mental
    patients
meta-communicator, 192, 194, 198, 200
metaphor (use of), 4, 9, 141, 167–8
Mill Hill Emergency Hospital, 56
Ministry of Labour, 56, 57, 60
mirror, art object as, 165–6
monitoring (leadership role), 46
mother-child interaction, 13–17
mother-daughter relationship, 158, 160–5,
    168–70, 199, 201, 203
motivation, 97, 103, 143
movement process, 200, 201
multi-disciplinary approach, 33–4, 213–14,
    222
murals, 181

NALGO, 32, 33
narcissism, 174-5, 176, 179, 181, 182
narrative (and stories), 239
National Advisory Council of Ministry of
    Labour, 57
National Association of Independent
    Maintained Special Schools, 146
National Association for Mental Health, 212
National Committee for Vocational Qualifica-
    tions, 33
National Curriculum, 35, 36
National Health Act (1946), 44
National Health Service, 8
    art therapy practice, 27-31
    Griffiths Report, 32-3, 42
    transfer of services to community, 31-2, 42
    Working for Patients, 26-7, 30, 75
National Joint Council for Local Authorities,
    25, 33, 212
National Register of Art Therapists in 1986, 26
National Schizophrenia Association, 79
negligence, tort of, 44, 45
Netherne Hospital, 75, 82
Nodder Report (1980), 44
non-directive approaches, 6, 19-21, 106, 158,
    233
non-representational art, *see* mark-making
    (scribbling)
'norms of practice', 28
Not the Same as You (Korer), 87

object relations theory, 5, 155, 175, 182
    alcohol/drug abuse, 183-7, 234
    child in art therapy, 13-17
    see also art object
objectivity, 107, 108
occupational therapy, 27-9, 212-13, 216
On Art and Therapy (Thomson), 75
OPCS studies, 103
'open door' arrangements, 30
open group, 61-2, 76, 107, 177, 191, 221
organic deterioration (brain), 94
organization of training, 212-17
organizational context
    conclusion, 67-8
    Henderson Hospital, 55-67
    history of Belmont/Henderson, 68-9
    introduction, 49-50
    theoretical considerations, 50-5
out-of-control space, 142, 143, 166, 169
outcome research, 237
Overeaters Anonymous, 168

Paddington Centre, 215
painting
    case study, 115-23
    emotional expression and, 112-15
    finger painting, 175, 195-6
paradigm research models, 229, 239-40

paradigms of intervention/treatment, 3
parental transference, 101-3
participant observation, 49, 239
past life (reassessment), 92-3
patriarchal society, 155, 160
personality disorders, 55, 215
phenomenology, 233
Phoenix House programme, 176
physiognomic properties, 113
pioneers (in art therapy), 75-6
placement patterns, 108, 110
play, 14-15, 16-17
poetic methodologies, 237
policy setting (leadership role), 46
Poor Law Schools, 56, 60
Post graduate Diploma in Art Therapy, 33
potential space, 16-17, 107, 140
POWs, 56
pre-representational stage, 110-11
preventative medicine, 10
primary processes, 192-4, 196, 200, 206
prime responsibility and primacy, 45
prisoners of war, 56
probation service, 178-9
problem-centred approach, 53-4
process-oriented approach
    art as channel, 195-6
    case study, 199-205
    conclusion, 205-6
    introduction, 189-91
    theoretical context, 191-3
    therapist's process, 196-7
    therapy process, 193-5
    working briefly, 197-9
process model, 20-1
process structure, 200-1
professional practice
    in NHS, 27-31
    principles of, 26, 42-3, 44
professional qualifications, 25, 33
    see also training
professional responsibilites, 26, 44-7
professional status, 25-6
professional support/supervision, 43-4
professional training, *see* training
projective techniques, 177-9
proprioceptive movement, 200, 202
psychiatric care (in community), 20, 26, 31-2,
    42
psychiatric hospital, 52-3
Psychoanalysis of Artistic Vision and Hearing, The
    (Ehrenzweig), 215
psychoanalytic models, 50-1, 173-5
psychodrama, 59, 61-5
psychodynamic model, 18-19, 27, 30, 37, 98,
    107, 179, 182
    art therapy and, 159-61
psychogeriatric ward, 98-103
psychological shadow, 77-8
psychopathology of everyday life, 50-1

'Psychosocial factors in primary health care', 51
psychotherapy, 4, 107
  art therapy as, 176-7
  research, 236, 237
  training, 211, 213, 215, 218, 221-4
  treatment/rehabilitation dilemma, 57, 60-1, 67
public expenditure cuts, 30

qualifications, 25, 33
  training, 211-27

racism, 12-13
readmissions, 78
reality, 16-17, 107, 140
Rebecca (case study), 148
record keeping, 42
referral system, 26, 30-1, 43
referring agent, 27
regeneration, art as, 10, 212
Regional Advisory Committee, 215-16
Registered Art Therapists, 26, 28, 31, 33, 42
rehabilitation, 10, 52, 54-5, 77-8, 212
  of addicts, 176
  movements, 17, 213, 219
  - treatment dilemma, 57, 60-1, 76
relationships
  art therapist and artwork, 83-5
  assessment, 198
  father-daughter, 168-9, 171, 199
  mother-child interaction, 13-17
  mother-daughter, 158, 160-5, 168-70, 199, 201, 203
  therapeutic (role), 94-8
  see also counter-transference; transference
reminiscence therapy, 92
representation, 109-10, 140-1
research, 41, 110-12
  creative process, 241-4
  introduction, 229-31
  methodologies, 235-41
  trends, 231-5
Research Society, 192
residential care (of elderly), 90-103
resistance (and effects), 49-50, 52, 58-9, 67-8
Robert (case study), 148-50
role hybridization, 219, 225
role play, 62, 63
roles (determining), 194, 219-22
Romanticism, 12
rooms, art therapy, 81-3
Rorschach test, 178
Ross Clinic, Aberdeen, 10
Royal College of Pschiatrists, 44
Ruth (case study), 85-8

safeness (of contained space), 142
St Albans School of Art, 212, 214
St Barnards' Hospital, 214

St Mary's School for Children with Special Needs, 146-53
Salford Project, The (Korer), 87
schizophrenia, 79, 99, 235
'scientific' research, 229, 233, 235-7
SCL-90 system, 238
Scottish Society for Arts and Psychopathology, 10
scribbling, *see* mark-making (scribbling)
'sculpting', 132
secondary processes, 192-4, 196-7, 200, 206
self-consciousness, 113, 114
self-employed art therapists, 43-4
self-esteem, 93, 96, 98, 221
self-expression, 142, 143, 225
self-hypnotism, 153
self-image, 77, 158, 159
self-mastery, 78
self-portrait, 130
senile dementia, 93-4, 96, 97, 99
sensation, 112-14
sensitivity (Ann's case study), 204-5
separation-individuation phase, 175
severe learning difficulties, *see* mental handicap (severe learning difficulties)
sexual abuse, 142, 195-6
  case study, 199-205
sexuality, 155, 170
shame (at loss of physical abilities), 95-6
sharing, 129-30
Sheffield University, 212, 217
short-term therapy, 175, 233
skills-based art therapy, 233
snake image (case study), 153
Social Rehabilitation Unit, 57
Social Science Research Council, 214
social sciences movement, 125-6
social services, 25, 32-5
social skills (loss), 94
socialization of art students, 219-22
sociotherapy, 60-1
special educational needs, 35-7
spontaneous artmaking, 7-9, 11, 131, 179-80
Spontaneous Painting and Modelling: A Practical Approach in Therapy, 11
Springfield Hospital, 81, 82
'squiggle technique', 178
'Standing Committee of Arts Therapies Professions Report', 39
statementing, 35, 36
statutory care (of elderly), 90-103
steady state (family), 127 *bis*
story-telling, 143, 145, 239
strategic family therapy, 128
'strip cartoon' assignments, 178-9
structured approach, 128, 177-80, 182-3
Studies in Psychiatric Art (Pickford), 10
studio-based art therapy, 106
sub-system, 126
subjectivity, 107, 108

substance abuse, *see* alcohol/drug abuse
supra-system, 126
Survey of Conditions of Service for Registered Art Therapists, 28, 31, 42
Sutton Emergency Unit, 56, 57
Sutton Training Centre, 56
Synanon programme, 173
symbolic expression, 15–16
symbolic language, 140, 142, 143, 145
symbolic processes, 54
'symbolic statement', 111
symbolism, 4, 11
symbolization, 110
symbols, codes and, 145, 150
synthesis (art/therapy), 217, 223–4
systemic family therapy, 128
systems theory, 126–8, 132–3
systems therapy, 20

tactile experience, 142
  clay modelling, 201–2
  finger painting, 175, 195–6
Tavistock Clinic, 214
TB patients, 10
technological development, 220–1
territoriality, 111
Terry (case study), 153
Thematic Apperception Test, 178
theme-based assignments, 177–9
theme-centred approach, 19–20, 232, 233
theme-setting, 132–3, 134
theoretical considerations (organizational context), 50–5
therapeutic community, 52, 53–4
  Henderson Hospital, 55–67
  Turning Point, 179
therapeutic relationship (role), 94–8
therapy process, 193–5
time-limited therapy, *see* brief therapy
Tort of negligence, 44, 45
touch, 100
  see also tactile experience
training, 21, 25, 32–3, 40–1, 43
  contextual background, 212
  fine art ideology, 217–19
  introduction, 214
  near future, 225–7
  organization of, 212–17
  position today, 222–5
  socialization of art students, 219–22
transculture, race and, 12–13
transference, 37, 64, 159, 224, 240
  in art therapy, 5–8, 20

brief therapy, 196, 197
child in art therapy, 13–17
elderly people, 94–5, 101
narcissistic, 174–5, 179, 181, 182
substance abuse, 174–5, 177, 181, 182
  see also counter-transference
transitional object, 16, 98–9, 107–8, 183
transitional space, 16–17, 164
treatment/rehabilitation dilemma, 57, 60–1, 67
treatment team, 34
tree images, 167
triangular interchange, 128
truth in research, 237
tuberculosis patients, 10
Turning Point, 179

unconscious, 7, 20, 113, 160, 166, 192
  conscious links, 10–12, 15, 17, 98
United Kingdom
  development, 10–13
  research, 230, 231–4, 235
United States research, 234–5
University of London, 212, 223
University of Sheffield, 212, 217

verbal psychotherapy group, 8, 49, 62, 67, 98
Vienna Secession Movement, 6

wages, 32, 33
ward social systems, 111
Warnock Report (1978), 32, 35
Wendy (case study), 79–80
Whitley Council, 25, 29, 33, 214
'withdrawal', 175
Withymead Centre, 10, 12, 54, 213, 214
women
  eating disorders, *see* eating disorders (women with)
  father-daughter relationship, 168–9, 171, 199
  mother-child interaction, 13–17
  mother-daughter relationship, 158, 160–5 *passim*, 168–70, 199, 201, 203
work ethic, 60, 67
work groups, 49, 58–64 *passim*, 67
workhouse (and work ethic), 60
working conditions, 33, 43
Working for Patients (1989), 26–7, 30, 75
workshop instructor (at Henderson), 57, 59–60, 61
World Health Organization, 51